BULWER: A PANORAMA

Part one: Edward and Rosina

1803–1836

EDWARD BULWER

Aged 28

From the portrait by Pickersgill in the National Portrait Gallery

BULWER:
A PANORAMA

· I ·

EDWARD
and
ROSINA
1803 · 1836

BY MICHAEL SADLEIR
Author of "Trollope: A Commentary"

WITH ILLUSTRATIONS

BOSTON   1931

LITTLE, BROWN,
AND COMPANY

The story of Bulwer should remain, when all is told, a thing of melancholy grandeur. But during the telling it must pass through varied phases; for its hero is pert, foolish, romantic, pathetic, cruel, generous, admirable, pretentious according as fate uses him and as he meets it unworthily or nobly.

At moments tragic, at moments ludicrous; outwardly triumphant, inwardly pitiful; this long life spent in fighting on two fronts against inherent weakness and cruel circumstance may be viewed as a morality or as a bitter farce. It is something of both and yet a great deal more than either. Rather does it offer a panorama in miniature of England and of English humanity during the changing decades of the nineteenth century; with, as its central figure, an individual who might have been one of the dominant figures of his age, had he but possessed the two or three special qualities which in England make for dominance; who might, conversely, have ended in disaster but for his stubborn gallantry of mind. For Bulwer conquered without a sense of victory, failed where he thought to have achieved; and has become a legend half-impressive, half-absurd, to a posterity which can see his faults and read the satire of his enemies, but cannot appreciate wherein lay his power over his age, or understand why, if he was the great man he must have been, he was not greater still.

Note

Grateful acknowledgment must be made of the generous assistance of the Earl of Lytton, without whose help the idea of writing any book about Bulwer would have been a vain one. I would like to express to him my grateful appreciation of the kindness which led him not merely to give free access to his family papers, but also to find time, often at very short notice, to answer questions or give an opinion on disputable points.

In footnotes throughout this book Lord Lytton's own biography of his grandfather (published in 1913) is referred to as "Lytton", while the work on the same subject by the first Earl of Lytton (published in 1883) is designated as "Owen Meredith." The full titles of these two books will be found in Appendix VII.

CONTENTS

EDWARD AND ROSINA

EDWARD AND OTHERS

ham — His character and melancholy life — His betrayal by Brougham — His influence over Bulwer — Bulwer's tribute in *King Arthur* — Rumour of Bulwer's death — A chance of minor office — Why he refused.

APPENDICES

ILLUSTRATIONS

Edward

Chapter One

General Bulwer of Heydon—The eccentricities and matrimonial troubles of Richard Warburton Lytton — Elizabeth Barbara Lytton and her upbringing — Knebworth — Elizabeth Lytton becomes Mrs. Bulwer of Heydon — Her three sons — Edward, the youngest, born on May 25, 1803

I

Bulwer was proud of his lineage. This consciousness of race was at times overconscious; at times it betrayed itself in mannerisms which unkind people took for arrogance, and either loathed or ridiculed; but it was a justifiable pride enough, and he was right in declaring it, for good or for evil, one of the most powerful influences in his life.

Once during the early sixties (he was Sir Edward Bulwer-Lytton Bart. by then and a very important person) a newspaper editor asked him for biographical data. With the required notes he wrote a characteristically self-justifying letter in which he said:

I must confess that what I have said on genealogical matters looks very like absurd ostentation. But in looking back on the formation of my own mind I felt so sensibly the effect of hereditary associations — so much of my writing has been coloured by them, whether in the tone of feeling, the love of the past or the selection of peculiar characters for analysis — that I felt any attempt at intellectual biography without touching the subject would be of necessity crude and shallow.

This was very true, and not only in the intended sense. It is indeed impossible to conceive either the man or his works without remembering that his father's family had owned their Norfolk lands since the Conquest; that his maternal ancestors, the Lyttons, had been for centuries eminent both for wealth and intellect. But even more essential to an understanding of the queer out-of-jointness which was the chief cause of Bulwer's manifold unhappiness, is the story of how, and with what success, Bulwer and Lytton came together in his parents' marriage; of the failure of the father to impose a blustering personality on the consciousness of his own time; and of the effect on her favourite child of the powerful character and imperious mind of the long-widowed mother.

II

General William Earle Bulwer, master of Heydon Hall and of Wood Dalling in Norfolk, was one of those forceful, rather naïve Englishmen, who confuse great local importance with ultimate significance. A fine soldier (he was appointed to the command of one of the four districts into which England was divided to resist a Napoleonic invasion), a good man of business and a large landowner, he came to regard himself as a person of national consequence and looked a little wistfully for suitable reward. Because it tarried (the intricate scruples of politicians were beyond his blunt and violent comprehension), he fell into puzzled rage, and, thus angrily bewildered, died. But that came later.

As a young officer he carried off a beautiful girl from boarding-school and made her his mistress. She was not of his class, and he could not so far throw off the conventions of his kind as to avow her his wife. But, with a delicacy rather unexpected in such a man at such a time, he steadily refused during her lifetime to consider regular marriage with any one else. This loyalty held good against the strongest of all temptations. Colonel Bulwer (as he was then) had the land-lust of his kind. A wide inheritance would be his when his father died, and to join properties, to round off estates, were already among his passions. Nevertheless, when a

nobleman with a large Norfolk property offered him the hand
of his daughter and the ultimate ownership of many acres
adjoining the Bulwer lands, he bluntly refused.

Some time during the early seventeen-nineties Colonel
Bulwer's love-girl was killed by a kick from a horse. This
horrid accident shook the poor man sadly; and his temper,
never of the mildest, became rapidly worse. Succeeding to
a great part of his property, he settled to its administration
with a fierce competence which lay heavily on his neighbours
and servants. The old desires for territorial aggrandisement eagerly awoke, and with their revival he realised that
he was now free to marry for land.

At this time chance threw him into the company of Mrs.
Warburton Lytton, a lady of East Anglian origin, shrewd
sense, gay manners and pleasant appearance who, although
living apart from her husband, shared with him the responsibility of their only daughter. To this daughter, who was
heiress to a considerable property, Colonel Bulwer made
his proposals which she, after a few months of resistance,
accepted.

III

The family of Lytton, if not so unchallengeably ancient
as that of Bulwer, was of considerable antiquity and of a more
persistent spiritual distinction. The Lyttons, indeed, had
a tradition of culture and intellectual quality which, thanks
to their wealth, they were able to maintain themselves and,
occasionally, to graft by marriage on to other families. Thus,
the grandfather of the girl to whom William Earle Bulwer
had suddenly proposed had been born "Warburton", but
had acquired a second name and a large fortune by marriage
with a Miss Lytton from Hertfordshire. Their son Richard
proved himself one of the leading scholars of his day; and
his remarkable mental powers were as clearly inherited from
his mother as they were by him transmitted to his daughter,
and by his daughter again to her youngest son.

Richard Warburton Lytton has been remembered mainly
for his friendship with the great Doctor Samuel Parr. Together with Sir William Jones, Doctor Bennet, Bishop of
Cloyne, and Richard Archdale, he provided a sort of permanent background of wealth, classical debate and firm friendship to the staunch, admirable but stormy life of the man
whom Macaulay called the greatest scholar of his age. But
Lytton was no unworthy member of this distinguished group;
and the most generous and impressive witness to his profound,
if erratic, scholarship is Doctor Parr himself. In one of the
letters which years later he wrote to young Edward Bulwer,
Doctor Parr spoke warmly of the boy's grandfather and made
clear how close had been their intimacy:

My acquaintance with Richard Warburton Lytton began when he
was a boy at Harrow School. It continued for more than thirty
years. His singularities were numerous; but his erudition was stu-
pendous. He visited me in Middlesex, and spent nearly three weeks
with me at Hatton. I have spent weeks and months with him at
Bath, and we were often together at Knebworth. He consulted me
frequently on subjects of the highest importance; and, together with
the late Sir William Jones, I was selected by him as guardian to your
Mother.

But with learning went a very unpractical mind. On every
occasion when prudence or management was required Richard
Warburton Lytton came to grief; and only the ownership
since the date of his majority, of extensive property in several
counties enabled him to indulge his passion for Latin, Greek
and Hebrew; for European language and literature; for
metaphysics, theology and booklore generally, and to escape
for a time, at any rate, the inevitable consequences of his fecklessness. Miscalculation began early. Indeed the very first
time he ventured to pit his own unworldliness against the
world, he was badly defeated. At the age of twenty-two,
dazzled by the shrill graces of a virgin of sixteen, he married
in haste, only to find that love tales are pleasanter to read than
to realise, and that a wife and a passion for scholarship run

poorly in harness. Wherefore the married life of the Warburton Lyttons lasted only a few years.

It began with hectic participation in the gaieties of London.
The young couple were rich; the youth well-read in the
orgiastic precedents of his beloved Romans. Portman Square,
however, was no more Baiae then than now, nor was young
Mrs. Lytton any less of a snob and a conventional (for all her
wit and practical good sense) than smartly pretty English
girls have always been. The ménage, therefore, came to grief
over a contradictory sense of what was fun and what was not.
A separation was agreed upon. Richard Warburton Lytton,
as bitter against the convenances as one of his capricious
temper could contrive to be, vanished to the country and
plunged into abstruse composition and to the gathering of a
library; his wife, in a small house in Upper Seymour Street,
continued to enjoy the insipid sweets of fashionable life.
These two were the parents of Edward Bulwer's mother.
Their married life was queerly premonitory of their grandson's own; but Edward was not quite his grandfather either in
guilelessness or financial ease. Nor had the girl he chose for
wife the resourceful self-sufficiency of Mrs. Warburton-Lytton.
Wherefore their matrimonial disagreement could not be cured
by separation, but festered into agony and spoilt two lives.

IV

The Warburton Lyttons had one daughter born in 1773, in
whom, as she grew up, were revealed the qualities of both
parents, fused by the discord of their separation into something individual, something at once astringent and admirable.
It had been agreed when the household dissolved that the
child Elizabeth Barbara should undergo an interval of schooling; but her later disposal had been left uncomfortably vague.
She became therefore something of a shuttlecock between
father and mother, exposed to the latter's tartly worded opinion of the scholar-voluptuary and then subjected to the severe
régime of the former's now deliberately Spartan country home.

For Richard Warburton Lytton had reacted with all the violence of an unpractical sage against the good things of life.
If he might not be Tiberius in London, he would be Rousseau
in the provinces; and accordingly he had settled in a little
house, standing on his own land, cramped, primitive and
piled with books. The ancestral mansion of Knebworth was
in a tenant's occupation.

Not very far away lived his, at that time, idol Thomas Day,
author of *Sandford and Merton*, and on the principles of Day he
tackled the education of his daughter. Elizabeth Barbara,
fresh from the pleasure-loving but decorous gentility of Upper
Seymour Street, found herself confronted with bleak alternations of physical endurance and severe mental effort. She
was told that the under-gardener was her brother in the sight
of nature; that bodily weakness must be subdued; that Latin
could be mastered by any child of perseverance and integrity.
Her health suffered from her father's theories of hygiene;
her head ached with the labours of learning beyond her years;
her natural longing for sympathy and affection was received
with the grave austerity of a determined disciplinarian. But
despite all the discomfort and browbeating of this period of
paternal experiment, the child was learning to appreciate her
father's quality of mind. So much so that, as she grew into
her teens and, during periodical visits to London began to live
on the fringes of her mother's social life, the vacuity and
tedium of London fashionables could only be endured beneath
a mask of rather cold aloofness. Thus it was that, by the
time she was adolescent, Elizabeth Barbara Lytton was too
much of an intellectual to do more than tolerate the gaieties
which were her mother's being, too familiar with the conveniences and courtesies of civilised life to share her father's
enthusiasm for a return to nature.

And during her teens her own material position considerably changed. Preparatory to raising money by part sale of
them, her father caused to be investigated the legal position of
the wide Hertfordshire estates which centred on Knebworth,

only to find that they were not in fact at his disposal at all, but were entailed upon his daughter. She therefore was proved an heiress of great potential wealth, and became an essential element in her father's economic survival. The extravagance of Richard Warburton Lytton was of that mysterious but disastrous kind often found in men of severely simple personal tastes but lofty intellectual interests. Whither the money went no one knew; but it went incessantly, and his lands and timber in Worcestershire and Bedfordshire had mostly gone with it, before he was brought up shortly by this discovery that Knebworth at least could not be tampered with. It would be hard to exaggerate the importance of this entail to Elizabeth Lytton. But for it Knebworth would have gone the way of all the rest, until father and daughter found themselves penniless; thanks to it the girl was secure, and on her security the spendthrift scholar was, for a while at least, compelled to lean.

It would be unfair to Richard Warburton Lytton to suggest that the desire now expressed for reconciliation with his wife arose wholly from the uncomfortable financial straits in which he suddenly found himself. In his own severe and inarticulate way he was deeply attached to his daughter; and the pathetic letter which he wrote to Mrs. Lytton in November, 1789,[1] urging that, for their child's sake, the household should be reconstructed and that the family should start afresh in his now tenantless ancestral home, is unmistakably a genuine letter, written from the heart. But material anxieties can give practical point to even genuine affection; and the father would certainly have remained a while longer absorbed in his books and theories, had not money troubles rudely disturbed his peace and shown him to himself as what in fact he was — the only member of the family with no certain means of livelihood.

But his overtures were rejected. Mrs. Lytton had some private money and, being a skilful and prudent manager,

[1] Owen Meredith. I, 29–30. *Note.* See Appendix for explanation of this reference.

contrived the sort of life she wanted without disrespect to
her bank balance.   She had no wish to involve her own neatly
organised fortune with the chaotic abstractions of her husband's home;   nor did the prospect of establishing at Knebworth House the ancient glory of the Lyttons appeal to her
as either elegant or amusing.   Wherefore, with the infuriat-
ing propriety of well-bred selfishness and in the presence of
two bleak and pompous witnesses, she curtsied her husband
out of her life.   He, poor man, sore at heart and bewildered
by his defeat at the hands of small-minded but proficient
worldlings, abandoned hope of reconciliation but clung to
one fragment of his broken plan.   He himself took up residence at Knebworth and invited his daughter to act as mistress of the house which was to be her own.

Elizabeth's first experience of Knebworth lasted for about
twelve months.   She was now sixteen years old and the realisation that this vast uncomfortable dwelling would belong
to her, the fact that she was now expected to control and order
it, roused her to a sense alike of her consequence in the world
and of her responsibility toward it.   A new self-confidence,
acting on the effects of a bizarre childhood, rapidly developed
her character.   From her mother she had inherited keen practical ability;   from her father a reasoned respect for the great
minds and achievements of the past.   Knebworth — at that
time a two-storied, quadrangular house, built in early Tudor
times, without passages and requiring six staircases to give
access to its numerous inter-connected rooms [1] — was crowded
with the portraits, possessions and memories of earlier generations;   and it is a tribute to the level intelligence and mental
dignity of the young Elizabeth that, during her short reign
over this home of crowded traditions, she acquired neither
the stupid arrogance of family pride nor the sentimental
affectations of a heroine of the Gothic Romance.   She learnt
to respect her forbears, and for their sake herself;   she learnt

[1] Bulwer's own description of the Knebworth which he knew as a child was so
romanticised as to bear little relation to fact.

to admire the ancient panelling and furniture, but at the same time to consider how best, without sweeping them away, to adapt the neglected and cheerless mansion to the needs of her own time. Finally, when a visiting dowager tried match-making on the conventional lines of smart society and her father countered the dowager by inviting to Knebworth a handsome but penniless Irishman to partner Miss Lytton on her daily rides, the young girl took efficient stock of her position. She determined that if she were someone thanks to her ancestry, she would also be someone on her own account, and that there should be on the one hand no stampeding into fashionable chic, on the other no romantic frailty for the sake of a fine pair of whiskers. And in this mood of level self-sufficiency she was unexpectedly requested to leave Knebworth for London and do her spell of duty by Mrs. Lytton in Upper Seymour Street.

V

In a struggle for their daughter's affection Richard Warbur-ton Lytton and his wife were unfairly matched. He had none of the easy graces which appeal naturally to youth; himself a solitary, he hated merry-makings and the pother of social gaiety on which young people rely for extending their knowledge of their kind; further — and perhaps most im-portant — he was at war with the polite conventions of his race and class, which conventions, framed and maintained by women for their own advantage, were instinctively respected by his daughter and upheld with strenuous conviction by his wife. Mrs. Lytton, on the other hand, though mentally her child's inferior, had the mother's natural hold on a daughter's love, and into the bargain wit, social address, leisure and fondness for clothes and pretty things. She had also the determined, if opportunist, virtue so necessary to a woman who means to keep her place in the fashionable world. Talk-ing to Elizabeth, therefore, in the language of women, and herself delighting in the pleasures and interests normal to the débutante, she soon acquired so great an influence over the girl that during the next few years of her life the young woman grew into an affection for and reliance on her mother which, though it may have been unworthy of her intellectual powers, did some credit to her heart and a great deal to her practical good sense.

The father recognised his defeat. Deeply grieved, and now finally embittered against his wife, he would not stoop to plead. With characteristic impetuosity he decided to abandon Knebworth once more, laid hands on everything in the house which could legally be turned into money, and on the proceeds removed to France, taking with him the unfinished manuscript of an immense drama in Hebrew on which he had for some while been engaged. As usual he had done the wrong thing at the wrong time. Indifferent to political happenings, he had not long settled in a new house and lost himself in the abstruse byways of his play-writing when the Revolution shattered his peace and contemplation, engulfed his property, and drove him to England again, where, more morose than ever, he contrived to create for himself a new solitude.

In the meantime Elizabeth was being suitably brought forward by a mother skilled in social manœuvre. She encountered a series of suitors and then a real love affair. That this episode came to nothing was in more than one way important to her later life. Also its history revealed with distressing clearness the hopeless impracticability of her father and the difficulty of the girl's own position between two hostile parents. The man with whom she fell in love (and it was the real love of her life) was the son of a merchant. Mrs. Lytton, with the common sense which in all her frivolity never deserted her, argued that Elizabeth had property already and should marry for happiness. Richard Lytton, on the other hand, chose this moment to strike an attitude of dynastic grandeur. He, who had never made use of his wealth and lineage save to spend the former on what the latter would not

have countenanced, who had hardly so tended his daughter
as to justify any sudden use of paternal authority, wrote a
harsh letter refusing his consent to the proposed alliance, on
the ground that the suitor was an unworthy *parti* for a Lytton.
Bulwer himself, in the fragment of autobiography which he
left behind him,[1] interprets with undeniable truth the scholar's unwise and cruel interference with his daughter's inclination. Richard Warburton Lytton was in the first place afraid
that he might have to contribute to the support of the new
household; in the second place — and rather pathetically —
he still cherished hopes of winning his daughter away from
her mother, and guessed that a son-in-law favoured by Mrs.
Lytton would remain her ally. So the girl was sacrificed to
parental jealousy; the young man received his dismissal; and
the wretched incident left behind it a father ill at ease with
his own action, a mother furious at her daughter's disappointment, and that daughter, driven miserably in upon herself, forced to seek in pride and strong-mindedness a substitute
for married love. Her later mishandling of the romance and
tragedy of Edward and Rosina may be traced directly to the
influence of this thwarted passion of her own. She had quite
unconsciously a queer inability to act more diplomatically by
her son than her father had once acted by her. Because she
had submitted to a parent's command and lost her love for
the sake of her obedience, Edward should submit also.
Which of course he did not do. And it was in keeping with
the whole twisted story of the Bulwer-Lytton family that,
whereas by defying her father Elizabeth Lytton might have
married the man she loved and so lived a fuller and more joy-
ful life, her son, who would have profited beyond compu-
tation by obeying his mother's command, chose disobedience
and got misery for reward.

Always of rather imperious mien (she was a tall girl with
the aquiline nose inherited by her favourite son, a large expres-

---

[1] Printed in Owen Meredith, Vol. I, and reprinted with corrections in Lytton,
Vol. I. See Appendix for explanation of this reference.

sive mouth and a mass of red-brown hair), Elizabeth reappeared in society after her little love story was done,
and hid her sorrow under a manner even haughtier and less
approachable than before. Nevertheless suitors of convenience offered themselves. She hardly noticed them. In the
winter of 1797 she received her formal proposal of marriage. Colonel Bulwer was her mother's friend and a man
twice her age. He had a rather attractive candour and
brusque manners. Equally candid and brusque, she replied
that she did not intend to marry at all. The incident
seemed to have made no more impression on her than its
various predecessors.

And yet, not eight months later (on June 1, 1798) she
became Mrs. William Bulwer. Altogether a queer, indifferent, rather disagreeable business, which shows into what
emotional apathy her heart had sunk and suggests that the
decision was her mother's rather than her own.

VI

Elizabeth Bulwer began her married life with few illusions. There is something pitiful in the thought of this girl,
who at the age of twenty-five had already put behind her all
expectation of romantic happiness, coming to her husband's
huge, rather blatant house in Norfolk, quietly prepared to
do her duty as a member of the ruling class. But so far as can
be judged, she wasted no sympathy upon herself. It seems
as though with the surrender of her merchant-lover her own
power for passion had temporarily died away. When it
revived, it took the form of a fierce maternal love for her
youngest son which, from its very fierceness and because it
represented a thwarted passion of another kind, served rather
to harm than to strengthen him.

Her earliest years at Heydon were occupied with child-
bearing, and with the discovery that marriage can only for a
while be conducted on the lines of polite acquaintanceship.
Inevitably it must either develop into fondness or harden into

disagreement. That the Bulwer menage went the latter road
was the man's fault, not the woman's.

The mature character of General Bulwer (his promotion
followed very shortly on his marriage) was a simple one. He
was consumed with family ambition — ambition which perforce centred on himself but aimed rather at the glorification
of his clan than of his own personality. Not only the energy
and efficiency which he had put into his profession, but his
choice of a wife also, were designed to win for himself — and
therefore for the Bulwers of Heydon — a greater social prominence. Because at the turn of the eighteenth century land
and titles were the sign manuals of greatness, William Bulwer
worked and married in order, before he died, to endow his
house forever with a vast estate and a peer's coronet.

So far his rather naïve aspiration had reasonably pros-
pered. He had attained high military rank; he had married
a girl whose acreage (though in an inferior county) would do
credit even to a Norfolk landowner; and he had already
decided on the title which in due course he would assume.
When in April, 1799, his eldest son was born, he could build
air castles still more solidly, for now the succession was
secure.

But the general's temper was not a philosophic or a kindly
one; and worries, which another man might have endured
even for so material an ambition as family aggrandisement,
wore quickly through his very limited patience. The two
principal provocations were his gout and his mother-in-law;
and the more painful the former, the more was he obsessed
by the latter. Forgetting that she had at one time been his
intimate friend, forgetting that without her help he would
never have won Elizabeth, he developed an extraordinary
jealousy of Mrs. Warburton Lytton. This jealousy, added
to the ill-temper produced by almost persistent pain, soon
made life at Heydon miserable indeed. Elizabeth became
aware of even greater loneliness than she had known before.
William, her first baby, was forthwith appropriated by the

father.   She was permitted (as Bulwer puts it) "to adminis-
ter the nursery as a delegation but not to rule it as an Empire";
and she knew that, the moment the child was breeched, he
would be put into training for his future lordship and that
she would see him no more.   When in 1801 another boy —
Henry — was born, Elizabeth's mother put in a sudden
plea to have him entrusted to her care.   Mrs. Lytton was
lonely also, and her daughter was too loving to refuse a
request so urgently made.   Also (for a certain shrewdness in
material things was inherent in Elizabeth's character) there
were expectations from Upper Seymour Street, and the second
son of a father who worshipped primogeniture would do well
to make sure of an inheritance while yet he had the chance.
But while the young mother yielded her second son because
her daughterly affection and his future prospects demanded
that she do so, she grieved over his loss, and no doubt
reconciled herself to further pregnancy in the hope that at
last she might achieve a baby of her very own.   But fate
was not ready to smile on her.   In 1802 she gave birth to a
third boy who died almost at once.   Shortly afterwards the
General's hatred of Mrs. Warburton Lytton broke suddenly
out in words so violent that the lady could never again set
foot in her daughter's house.   Elizabeth's hitherto dignified
endurance of her husband's temper now turned to anger.   Not
daring an open defiance (for General Bulwer was a dangerous
man when one of his rages seized him) she worked herself into a secret loathing of the loud-voiced, commonplace
tyrant to whom she was enslaved.   She was carrying another
child; and on that slowly forming organism she lavished
not only her own yearning for affection and companionship,
but also (as a sort of counter to her husband's influence) all
the Lyttonism inherited from her scholar-father, enriched by
her own reading, and realised some years ago during her
brief but engrossing sojourn in the home of her ancestors,
and thereafter treasured as something engrained and precious
in the stones and trees and tapestries of Knebworth.

As the time drew near for the child to be born, she went to London. There on May 25, 1803, she was delivered of her fourth son. He was christened Edward George Earle Lytton and if ever a man remained a part of his mother and, whether in obedience or revolt, subject to her influence, that man was Edward Bulwer, on whom while yet unborn was centred all that she had of love and character and idealism.

Chapter Two

General Bulwer dies — Richard Warburton Lytton gives his daughter three thousand pounds — starts the education of his youngest grandson — and dies leaving his library to the widowed Mrs. Bulwer — Edward browses among his grandfather's books — Elizabeth Barbara, having inherited Knebworth, takes the surname of Bulwer-Lytton — Edward at Knebworth — Edward at his first school at Fulham — at his second school at Sunbury — at his third school at Brighton — at his fourth school at Rottingdean — Influence of this school — Edward goes as a private pupil to a clergyman near Ealing — publishes Ismael and other Poems *— their significance — Lady Caroline Lamb — Doctor Samuel Parr — Lionel Hastings*

I

Bulwer declares that his father took an immediate dislike to him; and that the hostility — which could hardly have related to the personality of a small baby — was due to his probable inheritance of Knebworth. William would have Heydon; Henry had been adopted by his grandmother; for the third son the obvious portion was his mother's property in Hertfordshire. But it is difficult to imagine that even General Bulwer was so unreasonable as to resent the potential claims of a child for whose very existence he was responsible.

More probably he resented the immediate absorption of his wife's interest in and affection for her new baby; and the more aggressive independence which she gradually began to show, as she realised that her life for the future was bound up with the little Edward, and that the joint influence of maternal love and power to dispose of property would put her in complete control of the destinies of a being whose future she forthwith decided should be a brilliant one.

But in any event General Bulwer's aversion to his youngest son was not destined to develop, for two months after the child's fourth birthday the father died suddenly in his sleep. Of his two chief ambitions — land and peerage — the former only had been achieved, and as matters turned out disastrously. In preparation for the title on which he counted, and relying on years of profitable military appointments, General Bulwer had added recklessly to his property. This property, with all the mortgages and debts which had come with it, became his family's unwelcome heritage. As for the peerage, one cannot really regret its absence. The General had selected the somewhat unconvincing title of "Lord South Erpingham"; and even Bulwer must have come to resent an elder brother with a name perpetually suggestive of one of his own novels of fashionable life. As things were, his father's aspiration provided a surname for use in *Godolphin*, and could then be conveniently forgotten.

When General Bulwer died, his spaniel crawled under the pall and died also. The incident shall serve as epitaph for a man who left behind him more land than he could afford to own, little enough of human affection, and no permanent fame. There must, nevertheless, have been something fine and lovable in General Bulwer, and that something was revealed to his dog.

By his family he was less scrupulously mourned. Edward, his youngest and most articulate son, inserted a valedictory passage in his autobiography, written with the rhetorical artificiality to which, when he thought a gesture was expected of him, he all too readily succumbed. It would have been wiser to say nothing. There was no reason why Bulwer should feel affection for a man he hardly ever saw, and of whom he can only have heard unfavourably from his mother. Why not let matters go at that? But Bulwer never knew when to stop; and this queer lapse, alike from wisdom and from taste, may here be noted as highly characteristic of the self-consciousness and uncertainty in self-criticism, which could beset a man in other respects among the shrewdest of his age.

As for Mrs. Bulwer, she may well have regarded her husband's death as something of a release. In any event she had no time for even a display of grief. Finding herself overwhelmed with the business of a top-heavy estate and the care of three small boys, she put the property into Chancery; was appointed by the court guardian of her children with sufficient allowance for their education; and removed herself and her personal belongings to London. William was now put to school; Henry was settled definitely in his grandmother's house; and Edward remained alone with his mother. He remained with her, off and on, for another twenty years.

A glance back over the chequered history of his origins and earliest years will prepare the student of the character and actions of Edward Bulwer for something at least unusual. Grandparents and parents alike had found unhappiness in marriage, and got free, the former by separation, the latter by the hazard of one party's early death. His mother, to whom more than anyone else is due both the credit and discredit of his later life, had grown up in a distracting conflict of atmosphere between one parent and another; had then married a man unlike either of them; and had been forced to submit, as best she might, a nature already matured by hard experience to a master who was in comparison to herself a mere barbarian. Finally, Bulwer himself was denied even the comfortable discipline of family life. By the break-up at Heydon he lost touch with his brothers and became to all intents an only child — and a spoilt only child — cherished and dominated by a mother of great strength of character, proud, rich and a widow.

Is it strange that this child should have grown up ill at ease with other more normally backgrounded, normally educated men? Is it surprising that his ancestry and training should have cast him in a sort of contradictory mould, so that throughout his life he lay athwart the pattern of his age and circle, at once self-distrustful and self-confident, rightly sure of his own preëminence, but never sure how to impose it on the world? No one can judge Bulwer fairly, can admire (as they deserve to be admired) his continual victories over his own diffidence and weakness and over the cruelty of others; can understand (though not necessarily excuse) his many follies and his occasional meannesses, who does not take into full account his tangled and unhappy lineage, and bear in mind that, if he seemed to others an exception to the English rule, he was always and most tragically a misfit to himself.

II

No sooner was his daughter a widow and, temporarily at any rate, in a mood of friendless melancholy, than Richard Warburton Lytton made a sudden reappearance in the rôle of sympathetic parent. The years of retirement which followed his own flight from France had to some extent repaired his fortunes. He was now living in a house near Ramsgate, with more books than ever and a balance at his bankers. Elizabeth, for all her expectations, was short of actual cash; and the old scholar, with a fine suddenness, gave her three thousand pounds with which to buy a house in Nottingham Place. He also prepared to take a part in the education of his youngest grandson.

Thus did the little Edward gain an influential teacher but lose touch still further with other members of his family. He learnt from old Mr. Lytton and from his books more than from all the schooling and teachers that came after; but he paid a big price for his learning — that of a greater isolation. He had, in effect, become involved in the old quarrel of his grandparents. He was labelled as his grandfather's boy, while Henry belonged definitely to the other camp and William, sturdy and alone, went through his schooling on the way to Norfolk and his squirearchy.

The joint administration by Elizabeth Bulwer and her father of the body and mind of the solitary child lasted for

over three years.   The severity and intellectual discipline of
old Mr. Lytton were to some extent mitigated by the mother's
fondness; but Edward had his share of reprimand and hard
learning and at least one whipping from his grandfather,
before in December, 1810, the old gentleman died of an apo-
plectic seizure.   Then, with the tumultuous arrival of his
whole library in Nottingham Place, began what can only be
termed Richard Warburton Lytton's posthumous education
of his grandson.

Bred in the mid-eighteenth century tradition of learning
for learning's sake, the dead man left little of his personality
even on his books.   A few careful annotations, fly-leaves
bearing occasional exercises in classical versification, marginal
notes to his catalogue — these (as his grandson says) "are
all that on earth survived the dust of the great scholar."
But his teaching from beyond the grave was implicit in the
books themselves, and particularly in those bought during
the last years of his life.   As an old man Richard Warburton
Lytton had taken a taste for works of imagination and chivalry.   A being less thoroughly imbued with the love and lore
of the classics would have been earlier infected with the wild-
ness and Gothic fervour before which, as long ago as the
seventeen-sixties, the classical severities of a past age were
crumbling.   But the romantic revival, which had filled Gray's
poems with a disturbing and, as it at first seemed, a wanton
music; which in 1765 had produced the *Percy Reliques* and
throughout succeeding decades a host of new experiments and
imitations, left Richard Warburton Lytton untouched (or was
perhaps kept resentfully at bay) until the turn of the century.
Then — a little shamefacedly maybe, for one can hardly conceive him exchanging ideas on mediæval romance with
Doctor Parr — Mr. Lytton began to buy works of chivalry
and to read them.   There was a characteristic remoteness in
his preference for romances in old French and Spanish, which
he would read in the original and (doubtless) contrast sar-
castically with the trivial home products of the Radcliffe

school; but, though he would never have admitted it, the impulse and enjoyment were those which had seized upon all lettered persons of the civilised world, and Richard Warburton Lytton engrossed in *Don Quixote* and filling his shelves with books on knight-errantry, witchcraft and the ghostly legends of the past, was in fact merely another victim of the Zeitgeist, although a little behind the fair.

When the deluge of his books descended on his daughter's London house, the more abstruse among them went naturally garret-wards. Books in Greek and Latin; books in Hebrew, Arabic and Chinese; scientific treatises, works of theology, were stacked away wheresoever place could be found. But in the dining-room and on the stairs crowded the indiscretions of the old man's last romantic years, and in the midst of them the eight-year old boy was left alone to browse.

I read and wondered. All variety of dim ideas thus met and mingled in my brain. Many an atom of knowledge, chipped off from the block and stored up unconsciously in the mind, was whirled into movement in later years.

So Bulwer himself describes the twelve months of ceaseless undirected reading among his grandfather's books, which intervened between their arrival at Nottingham Place and, when the boy's mother decided to move to Knebworth, their sale *en bloc* to a bookseller. Whether he had more of benefit or of disadvantage from this period of intensive dabbling in things he could not really understand, is open to question. Certainly something of the old scholar's tendency to useless learning was handed down through the books to their childish student. The over-loading of story and essay with sheer knowledge, which was to become one of the besetting sins of Bulwer the author, arose directly from the power, acquired instinctively during these months of premature bookishness, to discover and to memorise abstruse, unnecessary facts. On the other hand, the boy came early to one of the realisations most valuable to a thinking man (if also most

uncomfortable to one who has to live with other men), —
that most ideas have been conceived and discoveries made by
persons long dead; that there is nothing particularly exciting about one's own time or one's own achievements, unless
they be regarded as a product of the past and judged in
relation to what has gone before. Undoubtedly this lesson,
learnt unconsciously in youth, had a profound influence
on the mature Bulwer. It gave to his mind a dignity and
loftiness which set it apart from most of those of his contemporaries; it brought him personal unpopularity, for no
quality in a man is more distasteful to his fellows than that
of conscious intellectual superiority; and it enabled him to
control his own mental forces to an extraordinary degree,
directing them among this channel or that, according as he
felt an impulse to win a new reputation, to examine a new
branch of specialised knowledge or to excel in some fresh
field of intellectual activity.

A certain greatness of mind, then, was the outstanding gain
to Bulwer of his experience amid his grandfather's books. Of
minor ultimate importance, but of more obvious effect, was
the influence on his method and capacity as novelist of the
contents of Richard Warburton Lytton's romances of chivalry.
He was himself well aware of this influence, which served him
later both as inspiration and as discipline. An undated letter,
printed by Owen Meredith,[1] describes from memory his eager
reading of Southey's version of *Amadis of Gaul*, and how the
adventures and fabulous triumphs of this hero impressed his
mind. Then came the *Faërie Queene*, of which the sense was
nothing, but the lovely wording carried the child on a sort
of magic carpet of rhythm and half-comprehended excitement. By these and other books as well as by hours spent
with his mother, who would recite old ballads to him and tell
him long stories of the romantic past, the boy's imagination
was so forcibly stimulated that, when he grew up and began
to write tales of adventure, he found it so easy to think reality

[1] Owen Meredith. I, 106.

into his own unreality, yielded so joyously to the intoxica-
tion of words and crowding images, that he could produce
page after page of fantastic happenings and swinging rhetoric,
himself convinced of the possibility of the former and happy
in the richness and rhythm of the latter.

It was late in 1811 that Mrs. Bulwer-Lytton (she had added
her maiden to her married name when coming into her inheritance [1]) settled her son at Knebworth. He had never been
there before, and it may seem that she was unwise in exposing
to another stimulus a child already over-romanticised. Here
were mullioned-windows and gloomy rooms hung with
tapestry; here were woods in which to see dragons and Sara-
cens and all the Gothistic troupe of bandits and gallant
youths and persecuted maidens. The books had gone, but
in their place was an ideal stage on which to play the dramas
they had taught. In all probability, however, the new stimulus would have done good, had it been given a chance to
operate. A year or two of running wild at Knebworth would
have been the best possible corrective to those months of
voluntary cramming. The boy would have worked off many
of his childish fantasies in childish make-believe, and then
have been ready for a different, less highly flavoured, but
more digestible course in the tiresome menu of an English
education. Unluckily Mrs. Bulwer-Lytton, than whom few
women were more highly principled, had not the resilience
of mind necessary to give her boy's unusual qualities the
scrupulous handling which they deserved. After leaving him
too much alone during the year in London, she abruptly
changed her tactics shortly after the arrival at Knebworth
and, not for the last time in their mutual relations, took a
firm decision and too obstinately held to it. Edward must
go to school.

---

[1] The alteration did not affect Edward, who continued to sign himself "Edward
Lytton Bulwer" until he in his turn inherited Knebworth in 1843. Then, and in
accordance with her wish, he took his mother's surname in amplification of his own,
and became "Bulwer-Lytton."

He went; and in a fortnight was home again. The effects of that brief but (in his own words) "horrible initiation into the meanness, the tyranny, the obscene talk, the sordid passions of the real world" never left him. Plunged into a badly chosen school from the sheltered gentleness of home, the poor child found himself alone in the midst of noise, filth and cruelty. He withdrew into himself; lost whatsoever regret he may have previously felt that he had no other children to play with, and acquired for the first time the inner shrinking from others of his kind which, so far from being cured by time, developed steadily and became the cause of much unhappiness, and an important clue to his later character.

Mrs. Bulwer-Lytton saw no reason to change her educational policy. The child's health was suffering at Fulham, so he should be removed. He was sent forthwith to another school at Sunbury; and when this, although it lasted longer, was as great a failure as its predecessor, to another at Brighton. But even Brighton produced neither a will to learn nor evidence of well-being. In 1814 (he was now eleven) the boy was uprooted once more, was thrust into yet another fresh society. He joined a then very fashionable school kept by Doctor Hooker at Rottingdean.

Of his three or four years with Doctor Hooker it pleased Bulwer to retain a rather highly coloured memory. He speaks of them in his Autobiography as marking "a leap" in his life; as being a period of comradeship with boys who were his equals in breeding and not too markedly his inferiors in mind; as reviving his love of literature and introducing him not only to Scott, but, more important still, to Byron. And the same years provided material for one of the most interesting of several unfinished novels, whose texts throw light, if not on what actually occurred to their author-hero, at least on the peculiar quality of his self-consciousness at the various dates of composition. The fragment of *Lionel Hastings* [1] is exceptional in that it was not a piece of boyhood

[1] Owen Meredith. I, 175, *et seq*.

writing, but a looking-back by a man of forty to one phase
of his youth. The story manifestly deals with Bulwer's own
life at Rottingdean, and although the self-portrait which he
chose to draw was in some respects coloured by the ideas
which he wished posterity to retain, there is a valuable element of truth in the picture, which has real bearing on his
later life.

For clearness' sake, the larger implications of the unfinished
tale of *Lionel Hastings* may for a moment be left aside. It is
sufficient here to estimate the value of its tribute to the benefits of Doctor Hooker's school. Rottingdean certainly gave
Bulwer his first opportunity to outdo in certain subjects boys
whom he considered worthy of rivalry. Also his health,
already benefited by Brighton, improved still further on the
Downs, where he enjoyed the chance of games with his fellows and tasted the delights of leadership. In actual scholarship it is unlikely that he made great progress. Indeed the
most obvious lesson learnt from the doctor's teaching and
example (the suggestion is Owen Meredith's,[1] and a perceptive one) was the habit of using capital letters for nouns in the
definite sense and for adjectives when used as substantives.
For Doctor Hooker himself was addicted to capitals, and the
letters which he wrote to Mrs. Bulwer-Lytton about her
son's progress abound in them. These letters urged his
removal to a Public School, where his High Spirit could
Usefully Exert itself in Competition with those older than
himself, and where (though this the Doctor does not say
outright) his impatience of control and very considerable
conceit would be tamed by the discipline of a larger public
opinion. The mother took the pedagogue's advice to the
extent of removing her now fifteen-year old boy from Rottingdean; but when she spoke of his going to Eton and even
took him to call on the headmaster, he revolted. He was
done with schooling and the petty restraints of schoolboys;
if he might not forthwith go into the world, he would have

[1] Owen Meredith. I, 120. *Note.*

a tutor. Mrs. Bulwer-Lytton rather weakly gave way. By the end of 1818, or very early in 1819, he was settled as a pupil in the home of Rev. Charles Wallington, in the then country village of Ealing.

II

During his two years at Ealing Bulwer published his first book, experienced his first (and only unspoilt) love affair, learnt to dance from Macfarren and to fence from Angelo, and made his precocious début in the salons of London Society. He was also uniformly happy with his tutor, who seems to have had just the qualities of sympathy, patience and tact necessary to win the confidence of a highly strung, over-mothered and nervously self-assertive youth.

It was mainly due to Mr. Wallington's encouragement that "Ismael, an Oriental Tale; with other Poems by Edward George Lytton Bulwer" was published on April 3, 1820. The wise old man, having listened indulgently to the versifications of his pupil, realised behind the derivative unimportance of the actual poems a genuine literary talent. He judged that nothing would help the lad so quickly, on the one hand to further and better composition, on the other to an appreciation of the poems' actual worthlessness, than the formal publication of a book. Wherefore he advised Mrs. Bulwer-Lytton to permit the printing of a little volume; and the effect of the book's publication was precisely as he had anticipated. The boy was greatly encouraged; went through a brief period of portentous self-satisfaction ("I have been very busy this last month or two," he wrote to a school friend on April 2, "preparing a volume of Poems for publication, which come out tomorrow. Your perusal and approbation will oblige me much. I have put my name to them so you may ask for Bulwer's *Ismael* "); and before very long could himself make affectionate fun of his own writing in his autobiography:

Then [*i.e.* at Ealing] did I conceive the Homeric epic of the *Battle of Waterloo*, beginning with "Awake, my Muse"; then did I perpetrate the poem of *Ismael*, beginning Byron-like, with "'Tis eve" and thronged with bulbuls and palm-trees.   In short I was a versemaker and nothing more.

Poetical value apart, however, there are elements in *Ismael* which merit notice.   The book has a lofty morality which must have given Mrs. Bulwer-Lytton great satisfaction and probably intensified her later disapproval of *Falkland*.   Certainly the boy's detestation of atheism, irregular conduct and subversiveness generally, show that thus far, at any rate, maternal opinions were unquestionably accepted.   A dedicatory poem to Sir Walter Scott, after declaring that the author of *Marmion* and *The Lady of the Lake* "first inflam'd me with a Poet's fire", proceeds with comic solemnity to deny all hope of immortality to Byron.

> who so blind can be
> E'en to prefer that wayward Bard to thee,
> Sublime in what? — in what! — Impiety!
> Yes! when Oblivion o'er *his* name at last,
> Her endless and impervious shroud shall cast,
> Britons shall mark . . .

and so forth.

Two pages later begins *Ismael*, which, as the author later admitted, is pure Byron mixed with a good deal of rather turgid water.   But to imitate is not, to poets in their 'teens, necessarily to approve;   and Byron comes in for even severer handling on the moral issue in the course of the long poem *Parnassus*, which characterises several leading poets of the day.

Biographically, interest attaches to the verses addressed "To Lady C[aroline] L[amb], who, at the Private Races given by Lord D——, set a noble example of humanity and feeling; when a poor man being much hurt, she had him conveyed to her carriage and interested herself most anxiously in his recovery." This poem records Bulwer's first encounter with the strange unhappy woman who was later to have not only a disastrous influence on himself but an equally bad effect on the girl he was to marry. The meeting here described took place in 1818, when Bulwer was fifteen and still at Doctor Hooker's school. The lady two years earlier had published her novel, *Glenarvon*.

That Lady Caroline Lamb's impulsive kindness made a deep impression on the ardent sensibility of the schoolboy is proved by the more elaborate description of the same incident in the unfinished tale already referred to. "Lionel Hastings" sees the crippled figure being lifted at her order into the carriage of "Lady Clara Manford." The foppish crowd which has hung about her barouche melts scornfully away; but Lionel leaps to her side, is invited into the carriage and drives with her and the victim of the accident to a doctor's house. "Some verses, rude indeed, but not without felicitous spirit, shaped themselves in his head as he gazed on the lady — verses in homage to the good action." Those verses, thus recalled in 1845, were the ones printed in *Ismael* in 1820.

Of the notabilities to whom copies of *Ismael* were sent the most remarkable — for his personal eminence and for the nature and significance of his kindness to the young author — was Doctor Samuel Parr, the old and learned friend of Bulwer's maternal grandfather. Doctor Parr, now in the middle sixties, was living out the evening of his combative and rather unfortunate life in his parsonage at Hatton, near Warwick. Well known for a brusque and often domineering temper, the famous scholar might well have responded to the timid compliments of a schoolboy with curt civility. That he did very much otherwise was certainly in part due to the deep affection he had felt for Richard Warburton Lytton. But not altogether. So far from being sentimentally inclined, the Doctor was notoriously inept at compliment; yet his letters to the youthful Bulwer were urbane to the point of flattery.

These letters have already been printed;[1] but for their own sake and because one of Bulwer's own contributions to the correspondence has quite lately come to light, portions of them may here be re-quoted.

Dr. Samuel Parr to Edward Bulwer.

Hatton, Feb. 9, 1821.

Dear Sir, — Permit me to offer you the tribute of my praise for the very elegant letter you have lately written to me. Now Mr. Bulwer let not the summer pass away without your coming to see me at my Parsonage. My books will delight you. And here let me express my sorrow that the library of Mr. Lytton was sold, when there was in store a grandson so able to use it.

The reply was clearly a request to be allowed to send some poems for criticism. The doctor writes:

Hatton, March 17, 1821.

Dear Mr. Bulwer, — I shall read with the greatest attention any manuscript which you may choose to lay before me. . . . I well remember the large old house at Knebworth, and the rows of stag-horns which hang up in the hall. I heard some time ago that the house had been nearly pulled down, and I hope the new edifice is capacious as well as elegant. . . .[2] Send me your MS. and believe me, dear Sir, with a just and assured sense of the intellectual powers with which you have been blessed.

Your well-wisher and obedient servant."

This time we have the answering letter, written, it should be remembered, by a boy not quite eighteen.

Edward Bulwer to Dr. Samuel Parr.

5 Upper Seymour Street
Portman Square.
Friday March 23rd, 1821.

Dear Sir, — My MS. accompanies this, and I really do feel the most grateful pleasure at the kindness with which you so immediately

---

[1] Owen Meredith. I, 155–158. "Lytton. I, 373–8. *Note.*

[2] This refers to the extensive alterations made by Mrs. Bulwer-Lytton during the 'teens.

granted my request.   And now, dear sir, permit me to make you the only return I am able.   Allow me to dedicate (should you on your perusal approve of it, and think it — as I however really fear you *will not* — worth the publishing) the enclosed MS. to *you instead of*, as I originally intended, to Lord Holland.   Do not attribute this to any cause but the right one, viz: the feelings of gratitude with which I received your flattering kindness, and my strong and earnest desire to repay it, as far as I can, by so slight a token of my great respect.

It is fortunate that I did not, as I formerly intended, make my poem the least political, so that I can now, tho' I have not the honour exactly to coincide with you in party, or rather public, opinions, inscribe it with your permission to you.

When I formerly wished to dedicate my poem to Lord Holland, it was because tho' I did not harmonize in political principles with him, I looked upon his Lordship as approaching nearer than most other Public Characters, to my Definition of the Patriot; but in changing, if you will permit me, my determination and substituting Dr. Parr for Lord Holland, should I lose by the exchange?

At the same time I candidly own, that I fear you will think them very inferior, and that your advice will be *against* the publishing of them.   When I first had the honour of applying to you about them, I was so engrossed with my attempts (as we generally are, when writing them) so pleased, that I observed not their many and great faults; but on looking over them yesterday, to give the last finish, I was suddenly struck with the poorness, not to say downright badness, of my performance, but authors, however, are not the best judges of their own works, and in submitting mine to your sincerity and refined taste it will meet with a fair and just judgment of its merits or imperfections.   But I will no longer take up your time with my egotism and will therefore conclude by signing myself,

Dear Sir,

your obliged and ob^t hum^e Servt

E. G. Lytton Bulwer.

The motto I thought of taking for "England or the Patriot" was:

Necsis qua natale solum dulcedine cunetos
Ducit, et immemores non sinitesse sui.

Ovid

but probably you whose mind is so stored with classic treasure can favour me with a better.

The correspondence closes with two further letters from Doctor Parr, expressed even more warmly than their predecessors, the second containing a few lines of truly extraordinary commendation and concluding with a two-word postscript printed in capitals, which surely had its effect in the youth's future career:

Samuel Parr to Edward Bulwer.

Hatton: April 26, 1821.

Dear Mr. Bulwer, — I dictate this from a couch to a friendly scribe. I have this morning arranged all the letters with which you have honoured me; and I assure you that the impression they have made upon my mind can do no discredit to your learning, to your taste, to your ingenuity, and, above all, to the moral character of your mind. I am proud of such a correspondent; and, if we lived nearer to each other, I should expect to be very happy indeed in such a friend.

Mr. Bulwer, I mean to preserve your letters, and, before I dictate one more sentence, I will put them together. I shall enclose them in a strong envelope, and concisely but significantly write my opinion on their value.

. . . I have read your poems very attentively. I have ventured to mark every passage I wish you to reconsider, and I rejoice that you will have full time for revisal, correction, and decoration. Really, when I think of your youth, my delight is mingled with astonishment at your intellectual powers. . . .

It is quite wonderful that such a habit of observation has been formed, and such a rich store of its fruits collected and made ready for use, at your time of life. There are many vestiges of your reading in classical authors; but you have taken a wider range than is generally taken by young men: and there is a secret charm pervading all your writing, which I trace not only to your discernment but also to your sensibility.

. . . Increase your store of poetical imagery. Write whenever you find yourself disposed to write: but collect the whole force of self-command, and let not the *limæ labor et mora* discourage you.

I am, dear Sir, truly your well-wisher, your admirer, and

Your obedient, humble Servant.

S. PARR.

P. S. — BE AMBITIOUS !

The poems referred to in this correspondence do not appear ever to have been published. Bulwer's next publication, *Delmour* (1823), contains nothing identifiable with Parr's criticisms, and the book is — oddly enough — dedicated to Lord Holland.

The problem of the particular manuscript submitted to the old scholar is, however, trivial beside the impressiveness of his courtesy to a young and very slight acquaintance. What Doctor Parr wrote he wrote in sincerity. Only one satisfactory conclusion can be drawn — namely that Bulwer at this early age was indeed a prodigy. And this is no mere extravagance, but a serious contention with direct bearing on his whole life story and its development.

Let us suppose that the influence of Mr. Wallington had given just the right kind of scope to an exceptional brain, which had had an exceptional upbringing. The sudden blossoming of a genuine intellectual precocity would at once impress so experienced a student of youth as Doctor Parr (many years earlier he had given a similar encouragement to the precocity of the young Sheridan) and provoke from him even in old age an eager response. Further, if such a blossoming took place, at once the nature and the importance of the story of *Lionel Hastings* are forthwith explained.

The first impulse of the reader of *Lionel Hastings*, who knows that the tale was composed many years after the events described, is to discount contemptuously the precocious brilliance of the youthful hero. Such a glittering prodigy must (he thinks) belong either to the unreal world of the Pelhams, the Vivian Greys and the Maltravers, or to the crude excesses of Bulwer's mature vanity. But if he waits on second thoughts and decides to assume that Bulwer in his 'teens was really a schoolboy genius, he finds himself suddenly aware of the secret of the man's entire career. *Bulwer throughout his life was an intellect betrayed by character.* Again and again a pre-eminence to which his mental powers entitle him was lost through some moral weakness or obliquity; again and again credit deserved for unselfish generosity was turned to discredit, because his miserable self-consciousness tricks him at the last moment into spoiling his own handiwork. And this same inability to balance mind and character influenced all his written work. Always more conscious of his own fine intentions than of the instabilities which thwarted them, he saw himself as an expression of brilliance and nobility, whereas in fact these qualities were often not expressed at all. The result was a picture which, though fundamentally true, was outwardly false. The truth convinced himself; the falsity impressed and infuriated others.

Hence the life-long conflict between the man's opinion of himself and his work, and that of his contemporaries. Hence, also, the significance of Doctor Parr's cordiality, shown and deserved when at the golden age of seventeen the boy's intellectual power first flashed out for others to see, and when need for character was not yet. Hence, finally, the pathos and the reality of *Lionel Hastings*, which was Bulwer's search for consolation in the memory of his unshadowed youth; and, for all its rhodomontade, a not inaccurate picture of the paragon he had at one time actually been.

Alas! not for very much longer was character to keep pace with genius. Had it done so — the whole course of Bulwer's existence might have been changed. But it lagged ever more disastrously; and perhaps the saddest part of the whole tragic muddle of his later life is that the being who most wished to help and serve him only succeeded in twisting and damaging him. That his faculties outgrew his disposition in strength and scruple; that, noticing the disparity, he sought to cloak it with ingenious pretence; that gradually he became that most unhappy of mortals — a man who dared not be sincere lest he be mocked for insincerity — was due to the mishandling by his mother of the wayward precocity she never understood. Mrs. Bulwer-Lytton, for all her own integrity and shrewdness, despite her intense love for her son and fierce desire to strengthen him, seemed fated during the vital years

from 1821 to 1830 to unseasonable action.   She was indulgent
where severity was needed, inexorable where a wiser policy
would have been to conciliate and then to guide.   Admittedly, however, her task was not an easy one — the less so,
in that before leaving Ealing the mercurial youth had passed
through the emotional crisis of an abortive love affair.

Chapter Three

An idyll at Ealing — Its enduring memory — He goes to Cambridge — Delmour — Knight's Quarterly Magazine

On the banks of the little river Brent, which in those days flowed through flowery meadows and under the branches of overhanging trees, Bulwer met a girl. She was of about his own age and of gentle birth; but her real name is not known and, seeing that she has become a legend, her anonymity (or rather her pseudonymity, for he referred to her frequently in later works and under various styles)[1] has its advantages. The short-lived but complete absorption in one another of these two adolescents marked in itself a not unusual phase of youthful ardour. The boy was handsome, imaginative, and predisposed by age and temperament to wander undismayed into the mazes of a love-dream, both irresponsible and little understood. The girl was at that entrancing stage in feminine development when, because neither give nor take was asked of her, natural gentleness and an uncritical acceptance of masculine wisdom were sufficient to her happiness and his.

But however natural to their age and kind was at the time of its occurrence this idyll of first love, it came to possess for both of them a very peculiar significance. The girl's story developed tragically. After a few weeks of innocent romance, she was abruptly taken away by her father to some other part of the country (Bulwer always maintained that no one

---

[1] Probably "M" in *Knight's Quarterly Magazine* (1824) or in *Weeds and Wildflowers* (1826); also "Ellen" in the latter volume. Certainly "Viola" in *The Tale of a Dreamer* (*Weeds and Wildflowers*), and in *To The Lost: A Life's Record* (*Poems*, 1863). Certainly also "Lily Mordaunt" in *Kenelm Chillingley*. References without mention of name or initial are frequent in other works.

knew of the lovers' meetings, but this assumes a greater discretion and power of dissimulation than are common to young
women in their teens), was married shortly afterwards against
her will, and three years later buried near Ulleswater. From
her deathbed she wrote to Bulwer that those golden days
beside the Brent were all that she had ever known of happiness; that she was now in plain truth dying for their love's
sake; and that if he would some time visit her grave, she
would feel that her last request had been granted.

In the face of this true story, it is hard to join in the conventional mockery of Bulwer's later subjection to the laments
and attitudes of Werteresque romance. No more complete
rendering of its traditional melancholy could be conceived;
and that such an incident should actually have been a part of
his own adolescent experience explains and even glorifies that
tendency to mournful rhapsody which he betrays in nearly
all his work. Nor is this all. Not only was his thwarted
idyll a very pattern of unhappy sensibility, but the love episode itself was his first venture in emotional independence, and
its sudden end his first encounter with the cruelty of fate.
Whether or no he was right in believing his mistress' father
ignorant of their daily meetings, it is certain that of his own
acquaintance no living soul was in the secret. Hitherto a
mother or a tutor had watched, protested, praised; now for
the first time the boy had tasted life alone and found, not only
that it was sweet to him, but that he and he alone could make
it sweet for another. In the new and intoxicating happiness
he revelled for a few weeks; then had it snatched away.
Such an experience would be influential on any youth; on
such a youth as Bulwer it was overwhelming.

His taste in love stories was formed thus pathetically
on lines of woe; his whole character was affected by an
adventure, which in retrospect became a memory of heaven
first glimpsed, then barred against him. His son shrewdly
attributes to this ill-fated romance Bulwer's readiness
throughout his later life to respond generously and gallantly

to appeals for his protection or support.[1] The Ealing tragedy explains his kindness and energy on behalf of all suppliants for his help; and conversely (though this more indirectly) his instinctive hostility to those who claimed to rival or to criticise him.   The kindness, to which several contemporaries bear witness, might at first sight seem at variance with the ungenial superiority which, by more numerous testimony, was his normal bearing.   But the two are really complementary one to the other.   He had that particular brand of shyness, that particular quality of nervous egoism, which makes a man ill at ease in ordinary intercourse and gets him disliked for unresponsive arrogance.   But whenever he could meet a stranger without self-consciousness, he was friendly and helpful; and such meetings were usually with persons who, being weaker or less important than himself, looked to him to strengthen them. No character is at any time more unjustly judged than this, for to minds of ordinary sturdiness the tricks which oversensitive nerves can play on their unhappy owners are incomprehensible.   Wherefore, the few who bore cordial testimony to Bulwer's warmth of heart were really more perceptive than the many who disliked him for pretentious egotism, in that they realised how much of reputed vanity is always shyness, and that a man must be judged by his treatment of the weak rather than by his bearing to equals or superiors.

The girl's removal from Ealing was done with brutal suddenness.   One day her lover waited by the river but she never came.   Other days he waited, but no sign nor word of her.   He never saw her again.

The immediate effect was crushing.   Probably the non-appearance of the contemplated volume of poems may be attributed to the despair which fell on him.   Certainly the flatness of the next two years of his life reflected loss of spirit.

Ealing had become intolerable.   Mrs. Bulwer-Lytton, with or without knowledge of the cause of her son's misery, trans-

[1] Owen Meredith. I, 165.

ferred him to another tutor at Ramsgate, who lived curiously enough in the house which had belonged to Richard Warburton Lytton. Thence in January, 1822, he went up to Cambridge.

Existence still lacked edge; and for a while at least he seems to have been content to forget his own ambitions, even to sink his too ready egoism and, conforming to University custom, to have followed the crowd. He made friends; talked a good deal; rode a good deal; read a little. Then for a time he played the fledgling "blood" in company with his brother Henry who, having inherited some of his grandmother's money, had reappeared in Cambridge with horses and carriages and ultra-fashionable clothes, which must have offset rather absurdly an outward insignificance. But gradually the indifference of desolation gave way to a more conscious melancholy. Intellectual interests began to replace the taste for conventional dissipation. He appeared at Union Debates and won some reputation as a speaker. He published a second (and rather desultory) volume of poems,[1] and became increasingly aware that he was at once ahead of and behind most of his contemporaries. The unhappy love affair, acting on a mind already precocious, had carried him beyond his real age; but solitude had not taught him the ways of life in a community, nor could he acquire the knack of easy joviality.

He began therefore to drift into an unprofitable loneliness, scribbling bad poetry, brooding on his isolation, until a fortunate friendship of the right kind brought him companionship and a new interest in life.

Early in 1823 a coterie of Cambridge men — undergraduates and young dons — persuaded Charles Knight, then a newly established London publisher, to launch a quarterly magazine to be conducted somewhat on the lines of *Blackwood's*. The moving spirits were William Mackworth Praed and Macaulay, with whom were associated William Sidney Walker, the

[1] *Delmour.* 1823.

future Shakespearean scholar; John Moultrie, afterward
Rector of Rugby in Arnold's time; Henry Malden, a classical
scholar and later a well-known schoolmaster; Matthew
Davenport Hill, already winning a name as a barrister; and
several other young men of future reputation. Bulwer became
a minor, but apparently a welcome member of this company,
and among the pseudonymous contents of *Knight's Quarterly
Magazine* are several of his contributions, both poetry and
prose. He used the name of "Edmund Bruce",[1] and was thus
introduced to readers by Praed in an editorial causerie, dated
from Trinity College on April 1, 1823, and printed at the end
of the first number:

I have a friend who writes more verses than any man under the sun.
I will engage that he shall spill more ink in an hour than a County
Member shall swallow claret, and dispose of a quire in less time
than an Alderman shall raze a haunch. Lope de Vega was nothing
to him. When he dies, he will die for want of a new rhyme; he has
loose MSS. enough to make a myriad of winding sheets and an album
thick enough for a pyre. Only listen!

There follow two love poems by the new contributor.

In the second number of the magazine appeared an article
on contemporary singers; in the third a further article in
praise of Catalani, and five poems; in the fourth and fifth
a story called *Narenor*, half-satirical, half-Gothistic, which
in its mixture of grandiloquent abstraction and sometimes
laboured humour, forebodes the philosophical tales published
a decade later in *The Student*. All the work is, of course,
immature and in its various ways characteristic of gifted but
un-self-critical youth. Extreme gloom, rhetoric, and smartness mingle one with another, and when it is realised that the
tale of *Falkland* was being sketched out at this same period,

---

[1] The identification, not only of "Edmund Bruce", but also of other pseudonyms used in this magazine, was established in *Notes and Queries* (October 1, 1881) by
Mr. G. J. Gray, cataloguer to the old established firm of Cambridge booksellers Messrs.
Bowes and Bowes. Mr. Gray originally transcribed the "key" to these pseudonyms
from a run of *Knight's Quarterly* which was in the possession of Messrs. Bowes during
the seventies of last century, and had been annotated by one of the original promoters.

the purposeless ennui of that rather flaccid work is easily understood. The youth was scribbling, as he was living, at second hand; but he was at least alive enough to want to write and that precious vitality, which now grew rapidly stronger, he owed to his lucky contact with Macaulay and Praed.[1]

[1] The intellectual atmosphere of Cambridge University in Bulwer's time has been well preserved in a curious little book called *Conversations at Cambridge* (London, Parker, 1836), attributed to C. V. LeGrice but more probably written by Robert Aris Willmott. Bulwer and "T. M." are presented in a dialogue about the spirit of the age, and further chapters concern Praed, Macaulay, Moultrie and other members of the group responsible for *Knight's Quarterly*.

Chapter Four

A long vacation in the Lakes — Lodgings with a murderer — Mortimer — A History of the British Public — Over the Border on foot to visit Robert Owen — Falls in with gipsies on his way home — Gipsy love

But the long vacation of 1824 brought a change. His spirit was reviving and his individuality began for the first time to express its self. With the new buoyancy, however, came no forgetting of the lost love. Indeed he emerged from the speechlessness of grief vowed for ever to a melancholy fidelity; and it is probable that his very arousing was due to the receipt of that deathbed letter in which the heroine of the broken love story sent him a summons to her grave.

He was at Ulleswater in early July. Kenelm Chillingley, lying all night on the grave of Lily, was a septuagenarian's picture of his own youthful despair; and that he himself actually paid this protracted tribute to the dead, Bulwer declares in his Autobiography. There is no reason to doubt either statement or memory. With *Werters Leiden* for background and Byronism for contemporary chic, a young man would have made some such gesture without hesitation or insincerity. He would have felt the consolation Bulwer felt when, rising after the night of vigil, he knew that he had discharged his debt to the dead girl and that her spirit now bade him go forward and realise those ambitions which, during their walks near Ealing, the two of them had formed for him.

The first stage on the road to achievement was from Ulleswater to Windermere. Bulwer was walking, a knapsack on his back and for reading matter, Euripides and Shakespeare.

He plunged immediately into the series of adventures which
were destined to mark this summer tour.   At Ambleside he
took a fancy to lodge with a mysterious Mr. W——, against
whom he was warned by persons at the inn and other casual
acquaintances.   It was rumoured that Mr. W—— was a
murderer.   The young man was not dismayed.   He took
the lodgings, and for a few weeks lived happily under the
roof of this ill-reputed landlord, whom he found reserved but
gentle and courteous, and touchingly grateful to the stranger
who had defied his outlawry.   It is probable that Bulwer,
who was an adept at weaving threads of experience into the
pattern of his narratives, recalled this episode of the wicked
Mr. W—— when he came to describe the suspicion in which
the solitary Eugene Aram was locally held.   That another
incident of his stay made reappearance in a later fiction is so
much more than probable as to be certain.

On a long excursion from Ambleside he was benighted at
a lonely cottage near (perhaps) Wastwater.   This time the
host was sinister indeed, and actually planned to kill his
guest, while sleeping, with a bill-hook.   The boy showed
great spirit and cowed the half-witted ruffian to blubbering
submission; but he felt the effects for a long while and,
in the opening scene of *Ernest Maltravers* where Darvil and
his accomplice make an attempt upon the life of the young
stranger, he was undoubtedly drawing on the memory of his
own nerve-racking experience.

Excursions apart, the weeks at Ambleside were spent in
close reading of his two books, in making notes for possible
written work, and in hours of walking on the fells or rowing
his landlord's boat about the lake.   He took readily to
prolonged and thoughtful solitude; and though to modern
minds the extravagant devotion of the Bulwerian hero to
hours of study and to the declamation of verbose philosophy
is tiresome and unreal, there was probably more actuality in
these portraits of rhetorical prodigies than would at first sight
seem likely.   At this early date, in the full flush of a Byronic

fashion, (and equally a decade later in the first enthusiasm of his Germanism) Bulwer was himself perfectly capable of musing for hours on a hillside, of breaking into a frenzy of solitary eloquence or of spending a whole night poring over systems of philosophy. Nor was he in this exceptional, such behaviour forming a favourite affectation of the young intellectuals of the twenties and thirties.

Here then was Bulwer, a young man just turned twenty-one, consciously coming to grips once more with the world after his interval of stricken indolence. He was intensely serious about his idealisms and his philosophy of life, reading Euripides and Shakespeare, making notes for a *History of the British Public*, solemn but eager, contemplative but physically strenuous. Those weeks at Ambleside were like a seacoast convalescence after a bad illness, so delicious their sense of returning health, so quickly felt their stimulus.

The written work produced during this period was not without importance. It comprised in the first place the brightly cynical tale of *Mortimer* which, re-cast, became the novel of *Pelham*. *Mortimer* was printed in 1835 as a sort of forepiece to *Pelham*,[1] and has a rapid if superficial deftness which is rather engaging. Strongly reminiscent of Moore's *Zeluco*,[2] it affects unscrupulous levity and was clearly in some sort a counter-experiment to *Falkland* which, drafted a year before, was already heavy with sombre sensibility. But perhaps its chief interest lies in the proof that, even at this very early age, the author of *Paul Clifford*, *Eugene Aram* and *Lucretia* was tempted to tell a story from the point of view of

---

[1] Colburn's *Standard Novelists*. Vols. 1 and 2.

[2] By Doctor John Moore. 2 Vols., 1789. This important and still readable novel undoubtedly stimulated Godwin to his rather didactic experiments in criminal psychology, although *Zeluco* is a cynical and (in his creator's intention) a satirical commentary on the villainy motif which was so popular with novelists of the late eighteenth century. Godwin, alike in *Caleb Williams* and in *Cloudesley*, treated violent crime and the remorse which attends it with the shocked relish of a doctrinaire reformer. It was left for Bulwer to pick up the thread of detached (even frivolous) sensationalism where Moore had dropped it, and to reintroduce into fiction the "gentleman rascal" who has since evolved into "Raffles" and other anti-social but good-hearted amateur criminals.

one in conflict with society — not necessarily in order to whitewash anti-social doings, but rather to indulge that contempt for conventional British timidity which he felt so strongly, yet dared not express otherwise than on paper.

In 1840 *Pelham* and *Mortimer* were re-issued, and their author, according to his invariable practice, added a preface. Here he describes the writing of *Mortimer* as performed "by a boy in years but with some experience of the world", during a time of severe illness in London. This is a typical piece of mystification. It is of course only half true; but Bulwer loved to fabricate stories about his own work, and he contrived these (often contradictory) legends with a suave solemnity which is irresistible. Perhaps he felt in his tortuous way that he was getting his own back on the critics, who always tore his prefaces to pieces; if he could set them fighting over lies and chuckle secretly, he had that much balm for wounded self-esteem.

And side by side with the frivolous and challenging *Mortimer*, he prepared an elaborate schedule for a work of political and social speculation. Elements of this work were later incorporated in one of the most remarkable of all his books, *England and the English;* but one may profitably observe the evidence of the notes now made at Windermere that, even at the age of twenty-one, he had an instinct for political and social criticism which amounted to genius. Bulwer never got the hearing he deserved for his analyses of English strengths and weaknesses. Probably his sense of the latter was too keen to be other than ignored; certainly political philosophy has always been unheeded in a country where politics can be made to pay in so far as they are unphilosophical. But it is hard to read the notes for his *History of the British Public*,[1] without realising how true are some of the reflections even today, without regretting that circumstances prevented a man with so dispassionate and clear a vision

[1] Owen Meredith. I, 261 *et seq.*

from exercising his proper influence on the political fortunes of his country.

The "Plan of the Work" begins with a distinction between the British *Public* and the British *People*. "In different ages the Public is still a class and only a class. At one time it is the Barons, at another the Clergy, at another the Middle Class; rarely the Populace." . . . "The House of Commons rarely if ever represents the People; generally a fair representative of the Public." . . . "Contrast the steady silent progress of the People with the fickle changes and noisy follies of its unworthy representative the Public." [1]

He passes to the problem of education, as one of the main necessities for Social Improvement. "Care for education consists 1st, in providing for it; 2nd, in the encouragement of all distinctions which education produces. In vain to dwell on the advantages of literature to open schools and galleries, if the community sees its men of letters starving, and its artists slighted. . . . Examine the encouragement given to art and letters by the character and habitual conduct of the Public, also by the attitude of the state which reflects the character of the Public being formed in the image of it." Remedies: Increase Pension List for Literature and Science — Gallery for Living Artists, not Dead only — for drama pay rent on one great national theatre." . . . "Open to the People as much as possible the markets of their industry. Poor laws. Abolish law of settlement. Remove unequal burdens on land. *All* property should be taxed for the poor."

Some of these youthful aspirations a maturer Bulwer later worked for and achieved. To his speeches against the system of two Monopoly Theatres, to his long fight against the Newspaper Stamp Duties were mainly due the abolition of the former and the gradual reduction and disappearance of the latter. But others were beyond his power to compass and, *mutatis mutandis*, have ever since remained beyond the

[1] This distinction between People and Public makes an interesting reappearance in *Maltravers*.

power of all disinterested reformers. An indifference to things of the mind, which the boy from Cambridge sensed in his countrymen over a century ago, is still the outstanding characteristic of British governments and their supporters. The British People are as subject as ever to the hysteria and selfishness of the Public; the ruling cliques as servile as ever to whatsoever Public has enthroned them.

From lakeland the youth walked through the Border Country; visited Robert Owen; passed on to the Highlands (having another adventure on the way — this time with a flash footpad, whom shortly afterwards he met in a thieves' kitchen in London and used, together with his surroundings, in the final chapter of *Pelham*) and having by this time spent all his money, made his way to Glasgow, where by good fortune he met his eldest brother in the street. The journey home, made possible by a loan from William Bulwer, involved the wanderer in the last and most important of his adventures. Somewhere in the Midlands he fell in with a band of gipsies. Whether the attraction of the girl who told his fortune, or his own eagerness for new experience, was the real reason for his joining the tribe, he certainly became a temporary gipsy; lived in the tents; and thereby got a deal of picturesque knowledge which he might better have employed than in the tedious pages of *The Disowned*. But perhaps truth possessed memories too sweet and secret for vivid exploitation. If *The Disowned* is dull, the autobiographical narrative of the same gipsy interlude is merely smug. It throws the onus of love-making on to Mimy and, with an irritating nobility, strikes an attitude of continence. The story is more probable and Bulwer more likeable, if we believe that he took love where he found it, kissed and rode away.

In another week he had rejoined his mother at Broadstairs.

Chapter Five

Lady Caroline Lamb again — Her character and evil influence on the young Bulwer

The final week of this eventful Long Vacation was by far the most eventful of all, for it saw the second meeting (or at any rate the second recorded meeting) between Bulwer and Lady Caroline Lamb. The acquaintanceship thus renewed developed rapidly into a hectic and unreal intimacy, which, while probably agreeable enough to the jaded emotionalism of an unbalanced woman, was to have effect both abiding and disastrous on the young man.

It may well be that between the first meeting described in *Lionel Hastings* and the more sensational acquaintanceship of the autumn of 1824, the two had been in occasional contact. Brocket Park, where the Lambs lived, is within a few miles of Knebworth, so that continuing if spasmodic acquaintanceship was likely enough. Also there is evidence that the young Bulwer was at intervals in the lady's mind. Lady Caroline seems, while he was still a boy, to have produced for him as a sort of symbolic portrait the rather foolish drawing of a child sitting alone on a rock surrounded by the sea and entitled *Seul sur la Terre*, which is reproduced in his son's biography.[1] This drawing makes a curious reappearance in Bulwer's history during the following year. Again, she herself (although three or four years after the event) declared that the Good Spirit in her novel *Ada Reis* had been drawn from Bulwer "as I then imagined you." *Ada Reis* was published in 1823, and "Phaos" the Good Spirit with "a coun-

[1] Owen Meredith. I, facing p. 358.

tenance fair and beautiful" is thus described: "His hair was light, his smile radiant, and his cheeks glowing with the first bloom of health; he had an angelic expression; perfect truth and perfect honour and purity sate upon his lips and beamed from his eyes." There seems no reason to believe this a better likeness than was the disagreeable infant on its solitary sea-girt rock; but that she should trouble in 1826 to inform Bulwer that he had inspired her imagination in 1823 suggests that he had been at least within her sphere of memory as lately as his second year at Cambridge.

Wherefore, there was on the surface nothing remarkable in an invitation for the young man to spend a week at Brocket before the first term of his fourth year began. It is possible that Lady Caroline intended nothing beyond a conventional kindness to a youthful neighbour. Possible — but, as will be seen, improbable.

Lady Caroline Lamb, haunting unhappily the fringes of the Byron legend, has often been described.[1] Small, neatly made, with close, fair curls, great dark eyes and a low drawling voice, she had an irresistible gaiety of manner, a daring wit and a reckless readiness to shock which — more especially during a time of national strain — is apt to characterise rich young women of the upper class. Married to a considerate, intelligent, personable but by now somewhat weary man, she was that baffling compound of impulsive generosity and restless egotism which, forever seeking happiness, brings only disaster on itself and others. Her chief notoriety — then as now — related to her agonised love affair with Byron, the repercussions of which are not yet stilled, so that his blame or hers and the sense or nonsense of *Glenarvon* — her *roman à plusieurs clés* — are still, and will be for long enough,

[1] Both by contemporaries and later commentators. Of the former, none drew a more convincing portrait than T. H. Lister in his first anonymous novel *Granby* (1826). Throughout this tale there appears at intervals a "Lady Harriet Duncan" with a quiet good-natured husband, and endless flow of inconsequent but charming chatter, a dozen pretty little tricks and oddities, all presented with the deftness of a skilled writer and the sureness of one who knew his model well.

argued to and fro.[1] In September, 1824, the story and its consequences were still topical. Byron had died in April; the news had reached England in May. On July 12, driving out for the first time after the fever into which the shock of the poet's death had thrown her, she had reached the gates of Brocket Park at the moment when his funeral procession was passing by. The macabre coincidence had prostrated her again. Through August she struggled back to health; and an early act of her second convalescence was the invitation which brought the young man from Knebworth to her house.

It is hard not to suspect that Bulwer was more or less deliberately fetched to Brocket to bear the brunt of the emotional reaction caused by Byron's death. May it not be that the sight of the poet's bier having brought back to Lady Caroline all the misery of her ill-fated passion, she — partly to avenge herself, partly to satisfy sexual cravings now once more aroused — sought the likeliest substitute? The theory is at least arguable.

But in any event, and even assuming that her original gesture was a mere civility, it is not possible to account for the affair of Lady Caroline Lamb and Edward Bulwer save by regarding the lady as having become, involuntarily maybe, a seducer of the meanest kind. Civility, in that tormented spirit, could turn quickly to something more purposeful. When the visitor arrived — pleasant-looking, well-dressed, well-mannered and unusually intelligent — there awoke in her the demon of her uneasy vanity, and, helpless in the toils of her own temperament, she set her snares.

By her intelligence and wit she had provoked from Byron the rare (but by women little-relished) compliment that she was the only woman who had never bored him. Yet his boredom came quickly when she pressed her intimacy; and his later remark to Medwin that "there are few Josephs in the world and many Potiphar's wives" expressed his satia-

[1] Cf. particularly Ethel Colburn Mayne's Byron. I, 215-250.

tion with delights too persistently accessible. Byron cast her off; threw her back on herself, hungry and wounded. But time, and the equivocal renown which came with time, soothed the wounds, and set her seeking for appeasement of her hunger.

That it was nine tenths a hunger for excitement and flattery and admiration, and only one tenth the emotion which men call love, could hardly have been evident to ignorant but complacent youth. And it is not too much to say that the young Bulwer came to Brocket ready dressed for sacrifice. Guilelessly self-reliant, with poetic ambitions and the Byronic pose universal among the young intelligentsia, he was half subjugated in advance, so strong was the appeal to his imagination of a woman who had loved Byron and now was kind to him, so irresistible to his inexperience his hostess' alternate melancholy and merriment. It needed little effort on the lady's part to complete her cruel conquest. In two days the boy was following her about; in a week he was carrying the lordly and ludicrous airs of a prospective lover. Outwardly tender, secretly amused, a little titillated by the thrill of his enslavement, at times deliciously incensed by the pretensions of his puppydom, Lady Caroline sent him off to Cambridge with a whispered promise of long and intimate letters. She kept her promise; but Bulwer, as a rule orderly and a preserver of documents, kept very few of her letters. They came to have painful associations.

The intimacy developed. She liked to play the cultivated female friend, and sent him four pages of criticism (and very intelligent criticism) on some of his poems. He preserved these criticisms as well as their covering letter, the last sentence of which was to prove influential and start him on that hostility to the "nature" school of poetry in which he firmly persisted:

you are like me — too fond of Lord Byron — Pray steer from the modern school back to the old one and write for and from yourself.

At other times she spoke of Byron more personally. Undoubtedly she told of the bitter pain caused to her by the appearance in 1824 of Medwin's *Journal of the Conversations of Lord Byron*, which book must almost have synchronised with the young man's actual visit to Brocket. We know that in November, 1824, Lady Caroline wrote to Medwin a long and piteous letter [1] protesting against the passage in his book referring to her liaison with Byron,[2] pleading and justifying herself. It is interesting to note that Bulwer so far succeeded in identifying himself with her distresses that he also — at a date unrecorded but, one would suppose, at about the same time — wrote to Medwin, appealing to him to suppress the bitter verses written by Byron on a fly-leaf of *Vathek*, and even asking for the omission of all mention of *Glenarvon*.

Medwin's reply contributes something to the general controversy and suggests that *Glenarvon* was financed on the lines of Harriette Wilson's *Memoirs*. The original, strangely but unmistakably, is postmarked 1825; a date as difficult to explain as is the absence of all mention of the new edition of the writer's book, published late in 1824 and omitting entirely the passage complained of.

Captain Medwin to Edward Bulwer.

Sept. 10 [1825]

I am sorry I was not in England at the time your note was written, as I think I should have felt inclined to have complied with your appeal so feelingly urged. I am sure, however, that in justice to Lord Byron's memory I should not have felt authorised in omitting the mention of *Glenarvon*. On the continent at least Lord Byron's character has suffered more from that publication than from any other cause, as it is to the circumstance of his having been made the hero of that novel more than to any intrinsic merit in the work that it has owed so much of its popularity in France and Germany, where it has been looked upon as the real history of his life. Goethe,

[1] *Letters and Journals of Lord Byron.* III, 446, also quoted, with valuable comments, in Ethel Colburn Mayne's *Byron*. I, 229 *et seq.*
[2] *Cf. Medwin's Conversations.* First quarto edition, pp. 213-215. The "New edition" is also dated 1824.

almost copying the words of the authoress, says in an essay on The
Genius and Character of Lord Byron: "when a young, bold and
highly attractive personage, he gained the favour of a Florentine
lady. The husband discovered this and murdered his wife. But
the murderer was found dead in the street on the same night under
circumstances that did not admit of attaching suspicion to anyone.
Lord Byron fled from Florence and seems to drag spectres after him
for ever." [1]

It was one day after reading this passage that Lord Byron entered
into the subject of *Glenarvon* and of the lady who shall be nameless.
The particulars of the liaison with her were never a secret and what
occurred at Lady Melbourne's was in the mouth of all the London
world. I cannot think, therefore, considering the notoriety of this
circumstance that her Ladyship has suffered much in the public
estimation lately by what has appeared.

Whether some of the misery inflicted was unmerited I will leave it
to your candour (and putting aside private friendship) to decide,
when you have read the following two anecdotes which I pledge
myself as having come from Lord Byron.

A lady whose name I am not allowed to mention told Lord Byron
that when *Glenarvon* was in the press she received a letter threatening
her with cutting a very prominent figure in the novel unless she sent
£300 as hush-money. Since his death I have made enquiries of the
lady mentioned, who not only confirmed the anecdote but added
that the sum was paid.

The second anecdote is this and one which gave occasion to the
dreadful lines written in a blank page of *Vathek* — "She offered"
says Lord Byron "young Grattan her favours if he would call me
out." With the truth of this I have nothing to do; but, if a fact,
can we wonder that he who never forgave should have called up in
judgment against her what he did.

The actual chronology, duration and intensity of Bulwer's
philandering with Lady Caroline are not easy to determine.
Between October and Christmas, 1824, it passed through stages
of rapidly intensifying fervour. In a long letter to a friend,
describing his final supplanting by the handsome Mr. Russell,[2]

---

[1] *Cf. Glenarvon* 1st edition, vol. II, pp. 83–85, 2nd edition, vol. II, pp. 81–82.
[2] Owen Meredith. I, 334–335.

Bulwer implies that Christmas day saw the beginning of the end. On January 14, 1825, he wrote to his mother a letter which certainly implies that the affair was over. Probably Mrs. Bulwer-Lytton had written to warn him that he was making himself conspicuous and had better act with caution:

When I went to Brocket first Lady Caroline, after two or three days of constant conversation, not merely upon common topics, but those more sentimental ones which knit people together in a few hours more closely than a whole age of talk upon commonplace, attracted me more than it is easy to imagine. But I did not make what is called "love" to her till I saw how acceptable it would be. In short, she appeared to feel for me even more than I felt for her. It is but justice to her to say that we had every opportunity of acting ill; though I was young and almost in love, though everything conspired to tempt her, I believe she resisted what few women would have done.

When I left her in London to go to Cambridge she wept bitterly, and there was not a day during my stay there in which I did not receive letters alternately full of passion and sentiment. All this was very flattering to me as you may suppose. I believe my love to her has as much its origin in gratified vanity as anything else. On both sides I think it had little to do with the heart but a great deal with the imagination.

But although the intimacy itself may have ended in January, it was doing social mischief as late as May. On May 24 Frederick Lamb wrote to Countess Cowper:

The stories circulated in town which have done her [Lady Caroline] most mischief had come from putting herself in the power of foolish boys; and this I convinced her by mentioning some things which had been told by Edward Montagu, Henry Montagu, young Villiers, Bulwer-Lytton and others.[1]

To what the affair itself amounted is, of course, disputable. The actual degree of love-making is a matter of unimportance;

[1] *Lady Palmerston and Her Times*, by Mabell, Countess of Airlie. London. 1922. I, 118.

but its effect on Bulwer cannot be passed over.   Miss Mayne
treats him contemptuously:

It is like some child's travesty of a great stage scene; and in the
very year of Byron's death it happened — that affair of hers with
the pseudo-Byron of our literature, the feeble, flashy imitation of the
great Romantic, known at first as Edward Bulwer-Lytton.   Nothing
in her confused and miserable destiny is more disconcerting than this
ludicrous repercussion of the past.[1]

Leaving aside the possibility that the lady provoked the
repercussion for sadistic reasons of her own — that, in fact,
the term "pseudo-Byron" is so just, that to use it at all is
almost cruelty — this ridiculing of Bulwer's part in the affair
is surely to attribute to him a too considerable initiative,
and to make insufficient allowance for the social background
of the whole episode?   Elsewhere in her Life of Byron, the
same writer speaks of Lady Caroline's "lovers" as in the main
intellectual, and compares her with Sydney Morgan, who
delighted to describe her own youthful admirers by the same
ambiguous word.   But there was this great difference between
Caroline Lamb and Sydney Morgan — that the latter was not
in youth rich, socially prominent or idle; and no mischief lies
more readily to the hand of wealthy feminine idleness than
that of toying with the vanity of younger or of poorer men.
It is not easily credible that Bulwer was ever, save in philandering, Lady Caroline's "lover"; but whether he was or not,
it was her choice that he set foot upon the road to love-making, and her fickle selfishness which shut the promised gate
against him at the end.   Further, whereas to her the youth
whom she had deliberately provoked became first a bore and
than a half-forgotten episode, he was to bear the mark upon
his life for ever.

The Bulwer of Windermere, with all his exaggerated moods
and the conceit born of good health and mental energy, was
still both natural and sincere.   But the Bulwer who, after

[1] *Byron.* I, 249.

being flattered into coxcombry and teased into desire, was
abruptly cast off when a new and handsomer admirer came
the lady's way, was a being suddenly and wryly matured.
He lived his few months of fevered vanity; made his crude
boasts; then during an angry period of mortification the very
core of him shrivelled and soured. The end of this wretched
amourette saw the end of Bulwer's instinctive confidence in
others vis-à-vis himself; and from an incident into which he
entered light-hearted and candid, he emerged, (though of
course unconscious of the change) uneasy, a little defiant and
socially distrustful of himself.

But the worst was yet to come; for, by the most evil chance
of his whole life, he chose for wife a girl who had passed
through the irresponsible and youth-despoiling hands of this
very Lady Caroline, and so took not only into his own mind
and character but into his most intimate human relationship
a poison which could never be eradicated.

Chapter Six

Sculpture, a prize poem — Bulwer leaves Cambridge and goes to Paris and Versailles — Mrs. Cunningham — "Seul sur la Terre" — An evening party at Miss Benger's — Enter Rosina Wheeler

At the end of the summer term of 1825, after reading in public a poem entitled *Sculpture*, written probably early in the year and awarded the chancellor's medal, Bulwer left Cambridge. Morbidly miserable himself, he fretted everyone with whom he came in contact; and it is likely that during his last two terms at Trinity Hall he sowed the seed of some of the unpopularity with his fellows, which was later to cause him so much agony. He was suffering the bitterest unhappiness known to clever youth — the sense of having been publicly fooled and of having acted like a fool. The excitement of Lady Caroline's frivolous patronage would have set him swaggering and posturing; he would have given offence to former friends by aggressive affectation of the well-born Lothario, at whose feet languished society beauties, behind whom stretched wide ancestral acres and all the pomp of family. And then he had been snubbed. Envy would not have been slow to spread abroad the mocking dismissal from Brocket of the one-time fancy boy; and the fellow-undergraduates of the now fallen favourite would, with all the heedless cruelty of their age, have made him conscious of his fall. Too self-conscious to admit his folly; lacking the genial humour which enables a young man, after a short period of angry shame, to join the laugh against himself, Bulwer — haughty, foppish and with that sense of grievance against the world which was never to leave him — went indignantly to France.

In Paris and Versailles he remained about eight months. His time was spent partly in the usual dissipations of a young man with money in his pocket, mainly in solitary reading. It pleased him, when describing in *Pelham* the Parisian adventures of a young gentleman of fashion, to imagine that he himself had lived hard and brilliantly as his hero. "I drained with an unsparing lip," says Pelham, in finest Bulwerese, "whatever enjoyment that enchanting metropolis could afford." Thus, in the variously appropriate language of his period, will every clever undergraduate describe his first independent stay in Paris, and there is no likelihood that Bulwer's trivial invasion of the French capital was any more lurid or impressive than that of his ten thousand counterparts. A little gambling, much alcohol and talk of literature, a girl or two — and for the rest, that pleasant sense of being somebody, which only comes from wandering among foreigners who neither know nor care that one is nobody.

The young man had a few letters of introduction, and was entertained with the surface-courtesy so beautifully practised by French families of breeding. Here was more balm for wounded vanity. With the same pitiful conceit which turned commonplace dissipation into gilded sin, he exaggerated these quite ordinary social experiences into embellishments of his own unique distinction. "I soon found admission into a circle of French society not often open to foreigners of my age. I became intimate at some of the most brilliant houses of the old noblesse domiciled in the Faubourg St. Germain, and was received with marked courtesy at the select soirées of the principal members of the Administration."

But the most interesting of his acquaintanceships was hardly grand enough for grandiloquent memory; and, although she plays a minor rôle in *Pelham* the autobiography makes no mention of Mrs. Cunningham, a sensible and charming Englishwoman, who with her husband and daughter was at this time living in Paris. Mrs. Cunningham, had circumstances permitted, might have been to Bulwer what

Sara Austen was to Disraeli, and have saved him from many of the unhappy follies of his young maturity. But her time of influence was very short; and, though she succeeded by wise sympathy and unobtrusive guidance in winning back for him the sense of proportion destroyed by the wicked levity of Lady Caroline, she was unluckily not at hand to control the next stage in his destiny.

Having succeeded in winning the confidence of the over-wrought and nervously suspicious youth, Mrs. Cunningham encouraged him to write or tell her all his thoughts and doings. He went to live at Versailles after a month or two of Paris; and if there, writing and reading and riding in the woods, he regained a great measure of serenity, the credit must be Mrs. Cunningham's, who bore with his peevish egoisms and replied with tolerant playfulness to the very juvenile outpourings of his mind. The letters which have survived of the many written to this admirable lady, are illuminating by their evidence of his slowly improving mental state. At first he is in all respects the disgruntled undergraduate — now morbid; now comically worldly; now pretentious; now, with a flash of returning high spirits, elaborately gay. Gradually he becomes fuller of plans for work, more alive to the humours of existence, less self-centred.

While staying at Versailles he printed privately a book of poems called *Weeds and Wildflowers*, which he dedicated to his friend Alexander Cockburn, afterward Lord Chief Justice. This work opens with an abbreviated version of his Cambridge Prize Poem [1] and ends with a poetical and rather moving reminiscence of the Ealing love episode, and thirty-two very world-weary maxims in the French manner. Between are several lyrics — three of them reprinted from *Delmour*, others, addressed to his mother and to miscellaneous (or ostensibly miscellaneous) young women — a poetical tale or two and a satirical description of *Almacks*, written with

[1] It had been published in full and officially in 1825.

the sprightly vagueness suitable to a fledgling fashionable, rashly offensive to Samuel Rogers, who did not forget the impertinence but also containing a passage referring to Lady Caroline Lamb, which is generously expressed and certainly generously meant. This noticeable piece of civility in a poem otherwise impudent enough has an important general significance. Bulwer rarely bore malice and never — save in the most terrible case of all — against a woman. His poetical tribute, therefore, to Lady Caroline shows that even as a very young man he could swallow his mortifications, forgive their author, and suffer them in silence.

But (and of this counter quality, also, the stay in France gives evidence), though he could conceal with dignity the secret pain and spiritual damage of social calamity, he had a curious shamelessness in taking sidelong vengeance for a slight. Diffidence took him that way. His pride strengthened him to bear an insult with apparent calm; but his nervous longing for revenge would occasionally drive him to mean and often clumsy dishonesty. The most striking example of this strange duplicity belongs to the forties and was concerned with the anonymous publication of *The New Timon*. A minor incident, but an outcome of the same obscure impulse, was the following note to Mrs. Cunningham which must have been written about the same time as the poem *Almacks:*

I have been making a drawing for you — a boy on a rock, clouds behind and nothing but the sea around. Underneath is the motto *"Je suis seul sur la terre"* and lines underneath to you.

The drawing, of course, was either the one actually made by Lady Caroline Lamb and already referred [1] to or a copy of it. In the face of humbug so extraordinary and, at first sight, so futile, one stands amazed. But the foolish little action becomes significant and pathetic, if it be regarded as a left-

[1] *Cf.* p. 49.

handed attempt by an angry boy to get even with a woman who had badly treated him.

Early in April, Bulwer prepared to return to England. The decision must have been sudden, and was probably forced on him by a summons from his mother. He had been planning a visit to Russia, and had filled a commonplace book with notes on Russian history and society which were used to some effect in *Devereux*. Also he spoke to Mrs. Cunningham of Switzerland, while in a letter of February 25 he was even vaguer:

> I shall return to Paris for five days. And then — then? I am like one of the leaves I now see before my window, whirled away by the wind, without an aim, without a use; its destination unknown, its end unregarded.

"*Seul sur la terre*" in fact. He was a young fool and young fools are all alike. But this one, with all his folly, never idled. He could affect the friendless waif; could declare solemnly: "Love is dead for me for ever. I shall probably not marry till late in life — supposing, which is very unlikely, that I ever shall be late in life." But in the intervals of such portentous melancholy he worked — reading, making his voluminous notes, writing, re-writing.

Already his dramatic poem *O'Neill* was in the press; already his novel *Falkland* had been revised and completed and must seek a publisher. With characteristic self-consciousness, and an affectation of adored masculinity entangled with weeping maidenhood, he wrote' to apprise Mrs. Cunningham of his departure:

> [probably early April]
>
> I am at this time in a state of great and unceasing anxiety. You may form an idea about this when I tell you that in England, to which I go solely by necessity, there is a person to whom I am bound by honour to sacrifice myself, and that at Paris at this moment another person is beseeching me every hour to take her with me to England. The matter is at once ludicrous and triste beyond conception.

(April 15) *from Rouen.*

The reason of my dislike to society is a painful sense of my own un-fitness for it.   One year has altered me so much in person and mind, has rendered me so little amiable or even tolerable, that I never enter a room without the idea that I am going to be still more disliked, and never leave it without the impression of being so.

As the journey proceeded he grew more natural and cheer-ful :

(April 21)

Me voici at Abbeville!   Good heavens, was there ever such ink, such pens, such paper as those produced at Abbeville by the *Tête de Bœuf.*   Mozart wrote his music on gold-edged foolscap.   Rousseau stitched his Héloïse with rose-coloured ribbon.   Lord Byron wrote his billets doux on paper of the most delicate pink.   And shall our correspondence be recorded, like that of a Tompkins or a Smith, upon this vile material?

Two days later from Boulogne :

Damn the ink! . . .   When I was stopping to dine at a little inn upon the road hither the landlady asked me if I would not like a *diner à l'Anglais.*   Of course I said yes.   And I was served with soup and potatoes, dry mutton chops and potatoes; hard beefsteaks and potatoes, tasteless chicken and potatoes; and last scene of all this strange eventful history, in came, by way of the most delicate dish of the dessert, centrally situated in the midst of cheese, apples and walnuts — potatoes again!   Who would think to find such a touch of satire in Normandy!

Two days later he was in London.   It was evening and he found his mother dressed to go out.   She had promised Miss Benger, a well-known blue-stocking, to go to one of her parties.   She begged her son to accompany her.   Rather unwillingly he agreed.   The small rooms were crowded and Mrs. Bulwer-Lytton, an impressive figure in turban and jewels, with her good-looking and dandified son at her side, stood a moment surveying the company.   Suddenly she touched his shoulder :

"Look, Edward! What a beautiful face."

Bulwer turned his head, and saw a young girl who, on the arm of an elderly man, had just entered from another door.

They were Sir John Doyle and his niece, Rosina Wheeler.

Rosina

Chapter One

The Wheelers of Ballywire — Character of Mrs. Wheeler — She leaves her husband and settles with her daughters at her uncle's house in Guernsey — Sir John Doyle, Governor of Guernsey — His lavish way of life — The Margravine of Anspach — Sir John Doyle retires to London — Fury of Mrs. Wheeler — She becomes an oracle at Caen

On the seacoast, a few miles from Limerick, lay the demesne of Ballywire. In the early eighteen-hundreds the long grey house was already in decay; and its owner, Francis Wheeler, had neither the money nor the energy to renew the leaking roof, clear the drive of weeds, or check the continual ruin of the boundary walls. Instead he lounged about his stables in shabby hunting kit; spent half the day on horseback, avoided so far as possible his wife and her sister; petted his youngest daughter Rosie, and every evening drank himself to stupor. Mrs. Wheeler was considered the reigning beauty of the countryside; but the qualities of loveliness which made her the toast of men in other houses were allied to qualities of character which drove her own man equally to alcohol, but with better cause.

As Miss Doyle she had, at the age of fifteen,[1] married Francis Wheeler, who was himself a minor. The boy got his bedfellow and the girl freedom from her mother's house, so that the immediate objects of the marriage were secured. But neither found in the other an abiding satisfaction, nor was Ballywire sufficiently in the world for the young couple to forget in society their mutual

---

[1] Lytton. I, 158. Devey, quoting Rosina's Autobiography, says sixteen.

indifference. Wherefore the man took to drink and the woman to the reading of advanced political philosophy, which she consumed by the hour but never learned rightly to digest.

When her sister came to live with them, the atmosphere of desultory tedium was stirred by frequent quarrelling. Bessie Doyle thought Mrs. Wheeler an indolent prig and Wheeler an ill-used man; the former retorted by sneering at Bessie's novel-reading and bullying her husband's favourite child; the latter himself fled from the plague of womankind and drank more than ever.

At one time and another Mrs. Wheeler produced six children,[1] of whom all but two died in infancy. The survivors were both girls, and because the younger was petted by her father and her aunt, she was teased or beaten by her mother. On the whole, therefore, life at Ballywire was uncomfortable; and there could have been neither surprise nor regret in the minds of any one concerned when in 1812 the household broke up.

At that date the Wheeler children were respectively twelve and ten years of age. Henrietta, the elder, was a self-possessed orderly little creature, who seemed equally indifferent to the turmoil of home and to her mother's favouritism; Rosina, the younger, was less balanced. She had inherited something of her father's aloof indolence and the physical beauty and reckless intelligence and the love of display of her mother — which were dominant elements in Mrs. Wheeler's nature. Rosina's remarkable likeness both in face and character to her mother seems to have increased, if it did not actually provoke, the persistent cruelty with which the child was treated by the woman who should have cared for her. Probably deep down in Mrs. Wheeler's selfish heart there was a frightened loathing of her own qualities, which led her to chastise those qualities in the helpless person of her little girl. Certainly Rosina's failings intensified under

[1] Lytton. I, 158. Devey, quoting Rosina's Autobiography, says five.

ill-treatment; so that what had been mere childish waywardness became a permanent inability to control tongue or
temper; what had been mere youthful vanity grew into a
senseless and insatiable extravagance. It is imperative that
the home atmosphere and the maternal influences of Rosina
Wheeler's childhood should at the outset of her story be recognised for the sordid and evil things they were. It may not
be possible to excuse the vulgar demoralisation of her passionate and tragic life, but it is more than possible to understand how she developed as she did, and to pity her.

The break-up at Ballywire was Mrs. Wheeler's doing.
Under the joint stimulus of her revolutionary reading, her
sister's provocative sarcasms and her husband's drunken
apathy, she became more and more violent in deed and in
complaint. Mealtimes were pandemonium. She would
start nagging at Wheeler for the down-at-heel squalor of her
home which, she would have him believe, contrasted unbear-
ably with the gentility to which she had been used and with
the splendour in which, even now, lived her uncle Sir John
Doyle, Lieutenant Governor of Guernsey. Bessie would
instantly take the husband's part; and in a moment the sisters would be raving and screaming at one another, while the
little girls looked on, scared and bewildered, and their father,
sneering in silence in his chair, drank glass after glass of
claret.

When in August, 1812, the two women, who had made his
home a hell, who fought one another day in day out, but
could no more separate than hold their tongues, announced
that they could endure Ballywire no longer and were forthwith departing to Guernsey with the children to live with
their kind rich uncle, Francis Wheeler bowed an unsteady
acknowledgment, hiccoughed, and left the room. It was
the end of Mrs. Wheeler's married life, and a release both
for her and her husband. But his indifference threw her
into another fury; Bessie joined issue and, as for the last
time they drove from the door of Ballywire, the dark interior

of the carriage was loud with the familiar noise of railing and recrimination.

The end of the Wheeler menage set a limit also to the domestic peace of the Governor of Guernsey. Sir John Doyle, who had been a soldier of considerable distinction in his time and, during the early years of his governorship, had done good service to the then important garrison post of Guernsey in road-building and defence works, had become, with luxury and the grandeur of petty sovereignty, a self-indulgent and rather frivolous old man.[1] Genially vain of his position and surroundings, easy-going to the point of folly, his constitutional inability to say "no" to anything, while it had gained for him in Guernsey a certain popularity, had also involved him in many thousands of pounds of debt. It had now done him its worst and final turn, by landing him with two nieces who were at once furies and spendthrifts.

He did not, however, recognise for some time the doom which had come upon him. Eager to impress the new arrivals and his entourage with his princely hospitality, he had prepared elaborate apartments for his nieces and a suite of nurseries for the little girls. For a short while his semi-regal life, with its dinners, receptions, picnics and visiting notabilities, went the more brilliantly for its beautiful reinforcement. Mrs. Wheeler preened herself in the midst of so congenial a splendour. Her large-scale beauty entranced the Governor's guests. She was flattered by the Duke of Brunswick; toasted by the officers of the German Legion who called at Guernsey en route for the war in Spain; and asked in (apparently) regular marriage by a French royal duke of seventy-two. All of which caused a temporary eclipse of equalitarianism, dukes, diamonds and dinner parties having captured her shallow and suburban mind.

---

[1] A summary of the military career of Sir John Doyle and a portrait will be found in *A Hundred Years of Conflict: being some Records of the Services of Six Generals of the Doyle Family, 1756–1856*, by A. Doyle. London, 1911. He died in 1834 aged 78 and a column was erected in Guernsey to his memory.

Meanwhile the children embarked on the second stage of their disastrous upbringing. Ballywire, with its fecklessness, bullying and strife, had been bad enough; Guernsey, where unsuitable neglect alternated with public flattery and wholesale petting, was worse still. A French governess, an Irish nursemaid, and a highly equivocal lady called Mrs. Johnson, who ranked as housekeeper and diverted the leisure moments of the Lieutenant Governor, were their normal companions. At any moment — and as often as not late in the evening when they should have been sleeping — they would be forced into precocious frocks and brought into the great drawing-room or the saloon, to sit on uniformed knees, to play with medals, to eat sweetmeats and, for the delight of their great-uncle's female guests to show off their recitations or, in Rosina's case, an unlucky genius for mimicry. On one occasion the children's aunt woke them up after midnight by bringing to their room the still lovely Margravine of Anspach, who, although over sixty at the time, perpetuated by every device of *maquillage* the beauty which had been her fortune. The triumphant make-up of this noble demirep was never forgotten by Rosina; and probably her own later experiments in rouge and kohl, which were to provide a comic item in the indictment framed by her future mother-in-law, were an indirect outcome of that midnight visitation.

Mrs. Wheeler, her sister and her daughters, traded for about four years on the good humour of Sir John Doyle. At the end of that period his patience was wearing thin and his local credit had almost vanished. Maybe because she had a sense that the régime of extravagant folly was near its end, Mrs. Wheeler began to treat her long-suffering uncle to a taste of her temper. At the same time she renewed her persecution of Rosina, whose ripening beauty added jealousy to the mother's old dislike. Life at Government House became rapidly unbearable; and there can be no doubt that, when the unlucky Sir John discovered that he owed twenty thousand pounds and must either make restitution or decamp, he chose resignation and quick departure, because by this means at least he would be rid of women who had only sought him out for what they could get. He calculated rightly. Apprised of his immediate retirement to London, Mrs. Wheeler gave way to one final burst of rage and sailed for France. In a few months she had become "Goddess of Reason" to a small group of embittered cranks in Caen. Her unhappy children played acolyte on either side her altar.

Chapter Two

Discomfort at Caen — Rosina, the younger daughter, quarrels with her mother and returns to Ireland — Mary Greene — Rosina finds her father vulgar — She leaves Ireland a second time — With Sir John Doyle in London

The next three years were passed by the Wheelers in a crescendo of family disagreement. At last Rosina, unable any longer to endure her mother's tantrums and by now at loggerheads with her sister also, left Caen and, after a brief stay with her great-uncle in London, returned to Ireland.

But not, of course, to Limerick. She was taken in by her mother's brother, a clergyman of small means living at Kilsallaghan, eight miles north of Dublin and, soon after her arrival, was invited to dine with a family of the name of Greene, friends and neighbours of her uncle. At this dinner Rosina met for the first time a woman destined to play an important part in the melancholy drama of her future existence.

Mary Greene, at that time in her middle thirties, had precisely the qualities which had been lacking in those responsible for the girl's upbringing. With courage, good sense and high principle went an infinite capacity for sympathy and patience; and although she herself had little but unhappiness for reward, her services to Rosina, to Bulwer, and most of all to the children of their disastrous marriage, entitle her to the deepest respect which posterity can pay. Indeed Mary Greene was to prove herself one of the selfless, self-effacing heroines of history, and one to whom in her lifetime came virtually no credit for her heroism. She suffered for her virtues to the extent of becoming permanently involved in the sordid imbroglio of a household which had no real claim on her; her sense of duty was put to cruel and continuous test; but she emerged from the tragedy, her motives unassailable, her integrity unquestioned.

One further tribute must be paid to the memory of Mary Greene. Thanks to a diary kept over a long period and later written up into a private memoir of the persons concerned, she is the only reliable authority on the domestic calamities of Bulwer and his wife. To this memoir, itself a document of absorbing interest, the narrative of the married life of Edward and Rosina as hereafter set down is continuously and vitally indebted.

The Greenes were quiet folk, and the first appearance in their modest home of the seventeen-year-old Rosina — vivid, lovely, and rather overdressed — made an immediate impression. She was slightly rouged, too easy in manners, and had the shrillness of precocity; but the instinctive adaptability of her quick intelligence kept her wit within bounds and taught her to behave with sufficient tact to flutter her unassuming hosts into an agreeable mixture of interest and alarm. During the days which followed and through the early stages of a rapidly increasing intimacy, Mary Greene studied the girl carefully. She saw that the child was beautiful, intelligent, but very crude. Chattering with random exaggeration of her great-uncle's fondness and lavish self-indulgence; of her mother's tempers and injustices; of her sister's affectations; of the love letters from a young officer which she carried in the bosom of her dress, she seemed vain, ill-natured and underbred. But at other times Mary Greene was conscious of a note of pathos under the noise of the girl's high spirits; and guessed that there was something fine and generous beneath the callowness, if only it could be reached and tested. Wherefore her heart was moved to befriend and, if possible, to humanise this lonely young creature, whose body was so fair, whose talents were so evident, but the mind and character neglected and already running dangerously wild. As a kind of moral duty, she set herself to know Rosina, to win her confidence and gradually to train her to some degree of mental and spiritual balance. The task was destined to occupy her for nearly thirty years, and then to be left incomplete.

An early incident of Rosina's second period in Ireland was a visit from her father. He had not seen his favourite child for nearly ten years, and as the interval had been spent in drink and in the raffish companionship of horsey friends he was unlikely to cut a sympathetic figure in the eyes of a sham-fashionable young person. Nor did he. Mary Greene was present when they first dined in one another's company, Francis Wheeler was ill at ease and rather deprecating, the girl openly contemptuous. Her subsequent comment on the encounter was simple: "Papa is very vulgar," she said; "did you see his worsted stockings?" A day or two later father and daughter quarrelled, and parted. They never met again and within two years he was dead.

As for the girl's relations with her mother, they were, through all those years, as bad as could be. At first, when Rosina had left Caen, Mrs. Wheeler had declared that she would never again see her daughter. The girl had chosen to run away from home and to flout the authority of one who, by the unanimous suffrage of the local intelligentsia, was the most gifted woman of the age. But the banishment was never made official, partly perhaps because its victim remained unimpressed. Indeed Rosina bore her exile with impudent equanimity. She regarded her mother as not only cruel and selfish, but also as a bore. The first two judgments were probably, and the third one certainly, correct. Evidence from other sources goes to prove that Mrs. Wheeler, obsessed with her own confused and turgid intellect, had indeed set up as a sort of revolutionary sybil. Atheism, communism of an Owenite-plus-Jacobin kind and, most

emphatic of all, militant feminism, filled her mind with
heady abstractions and her mouth with rhetoric. She
talked incessantly, and was the more quickly convinced of
her own inspired rightness because no one interrupted her.
Her household was afraid to do so; and the group of thinkers
with whom she spent her time were so accustomed all to talk
at once that they found it unnecessary. Nevertheless, and
despite its silly shallowness, Mrs. Wheeler's extremism had
a large share in disturbing the always unsteady equilibrium
of her younger daughter's mind. Naturally enough, when
first she fled from the quarrels and declamations of Caen,
Rosina reacted violently against all advanced ideas. Mary
Greene records a conversation in Ireland when the girl upheld
the sanctity of the Bible and of established institutions generally against the theories of the very Robert Owen whom
her mother so admired, whom a year or two later the young
Bulwer was to visit in Scotland. But during the very early
years of her married life, when Bulwer was himself tending
to economic and spiritual radicalism, when under the influence of Saint-Simon he was becoming a champion of female
emancipation, she came into a sympathy with Mrs. Wheeler
as violent as had been her former hostility. For a short
while Bulwer, Rosina and Rosina's mother were to revel har-
moniously in an orgy of subversiveness. But a final irony
came when, having quarrelled with her husband (who in consequence went back on his theories and became in his wife's
word a "bashaw"), the daughter hardened into a permanent
replica of her mother, becoming and remaining a feminist as
wrong-headed and as tedious as ever had been the Goddess
of Reason herself.

For the present, however, the girl was in flight from the
sound and sense of maternal propaganda, which pursued her
even to Ireland. When Francis Wheeler died, his widow
invaded her native land in search of his estate. She settled
herself and Henrietta on her unfortunate brother; played the
peevish grand lady constrained to live awhile in dowdy dis-

comfort; and summoned her younger daughter to receive forgiveness for past disobedience. But the family reunion was a failure. Most of the dead father's small property went to Henrietta, which set the three of them at loggerheads. Mrs. Wheeler's arrogant lecturing provoked Rosina to defiance. By the middle of 1825 she was back in London with her great-uncle Doyle and had made up her mind to stay there. Her mother and sister returned to France and settled in Paris.

Chapter Three

*Rosina as the post-war girl — Among the " blues " — Lady Caro-
line Lamb once more — Lessons in husband-catching — An evening
party at Miss Benger's — Enter Edward Bulwer*

Of Rosina Wheeler's life and friendships in London during
the next twelve months, some letters written to Mary Greene
are virtually the only evidence. But they are good evidence
and suggestive. They show a girl in her early twenties —
fuller of wit than of knowledge, innocently though a little
purposefully unconventional, quick to observe and to ridicule,
an amusing if an indiscreet talker. The child over-writes,
and her humour is rather common. Flirtations and gossip
of flirtations, weddings achieved and weddings *manqués*, parties, absurd old ladies, clothes, the latest novel or play —
these are her usual themes. But here and there, with a flash
of ugly bitterness, comes a reference to her mother or sister,
and one is conscious — as Mary Greene was at the very outset conscious — to what extent the girl was a solitary, living
perforce by her wits, backgroundless and pathetic.

Rosina, in the half and half world to which she had access,
was an immediate success. Her uncle let her use his carriage;
and her pin money, though precarious, kept her in gloves
and lace. Strikingly lovely, unhampered by shyness or by
chaperon and full of the surface gaiety which makes a party
go, she was precisely the kind of girl whom pseudo-Bohemian
London delighted (and still delights) if not to honour, at
least to use awhile. She was in great demand for evenings
with the "blues" and dances with the young bloods from
St. James's, who liked to go slumming among the intelli-

gentsia if pretty girls were free and easy and the hostess not too vigilant.   She was driven in the park, either by her great-uncle or by the patroness of the moment.   She met Mr. Jerdan of *The Literary Gazette* and his kindly little prote-gée Miss Landon, who made her poetical portrait and pub-lished it.[1]   The warm-hearted Miss Benger and the ludi-crous Miss Spence asked her to their parties to talk books and personalities.   And at one of these parties she caught the volatile attention of Lady Caroline Lamb.

The meeting took place late in 1825.   It seems a sort of evil joke that Lady Caroline should, within the space of a few months, first have amused herself with the young Bulwer and then taken a fancy for the girl he was to love, but of whom he had not yet even heard.   To the lady herself the pair of them were mere diversions.   There was room in her youth-greedy heart for girls and boys alike, and here, thanks to a kind provi-dence, was a girl ideally to hand.   What more agreeable than to take this fair eager thing about with her; to see her eyes light with pleasure at this small gift, that little luxury; to show her off at parties and in public places; to be admired and thanked and whispered to, while the world nodded and smiled to see the loveliness of Lady Caroline's discovery?   What, con-versely, more natural than that Rosina should succumb?

The pair became inseparable.   Miss Landon, who knew too well the difficulties of a solitary young woman's life among well-to-do dabblers in art and literature, ventured a timid warning.   But the flattery of Lady Caroline's friendship had gone to Rosina's head.   She would not listen; and the sort of life she was leading, her general excitement, her pose of cynicism, and a suggestion of knowingness none the less unpleasant for being an obvious pretence, are shown by a letter written early in 1826 to Mary Greene.

[1] In *The Golden Violet*, published 1826.   For precisely which of the several (but inter-changeable) heroines of this series of lays Rosina was model is not quite certain; but in view of her letter to Miss Greene, quoted below, she sat most probably for "Olympia" in the Italian minstrel's tale *The Rose*.   Possible alternatives are "Lolotte" or the heroine of the Irish minstrel's legend *The Haunted Lake*.

Rosina Wheeler to Mary Greene.

London. Jan. 23, 1826

Since my recovery I've been employed in exercising the only virtue within my power — good nature. You must know that Spence is writing a novel, and having laid the scene in the reign of Charles II and chosen Sedley for one of her heroes, she all of a sudden discovered herself at a non-plus as to technicalities and not bad enough by fifty percent to frame speeches and situations for the heartlessly depraved but witty and insinuating Sedley, and so requested me to do that part of the work for her. I believe the book will be out in May.[1] I entreat you not to mention this joint stock brain Company of Spence and myself, as it would make me appear very paltry.

I have by no means relinquished my intention of magazine-writing which is to the literati the same species of odd-jobbism that attending miscellaneous parties is to waiters out of a place. I see no other chance of my scraping together sufficient money to enable me to run down to Cheltenham and make you my guest at what I agree with your favourite Dr. Johnson is the most agreeable place in the world — a hotel.

I do not feel justified in sending you L. E. L.'s lines on me as they form part of the new poem which is coming out in May when you will have the gratification of seeing my portrait in full length, and so beautifully unlike as not to be able to recognise anything but the name.[2] She gets £1,000 for this her third volume. . . . And now on the score of her being too impassioned for my friend (N. B. she never was in love in her life) I would give you one little piece of advice, which is never to decide that because in writing poetry a person summons "thoughts that breathe and words that burn" that they are as a matter of course practically to illustrate what they describe. In this science (for love is very scientific nowadays as in all others your able theorists seldom reduce their system to practice. . . .

To set your mind at rest and prove to you that she is almost as prudent as yourself, I enclose you a lecture I got from her a week ago about poor dear Lady Caroline Lamb who is the most fascinating, bewildering, attractive creature I ever knew — one whom the more I know of her the more convinced I am has been "more sinned against than sinning."

[1] "Dame Rebecca Berry." Saunders and Otley. 1826.
[2] *See* footnote, p. 79.

ROSINA BULWER

From a drawing by A. E. Chalon

And now to show you what *prudent* people are, I return to L. E. L.
Three days after I received the enclosed billet which was two days
after I was out of my bed and one day after she was out of hers, she
insisted on my going to a ball with her. After much genuine *pru-*
dence and ineffectual remonstrance on my part off we drove, bearing
about us the relics of blisters and lancets as a charm against influenza
and sore throats. Never did I feel or appear more stupid in all my
life; but no doubt it passed off as maidenly propriety and had due
effect, as I made the conquest of a youth of £20,000 a year; but
should he go the length of pressing his suit you cannot suppose I
would have him for his name is Hopkinson. Oh Mary! If one
could but get £20,000 a year without a man mortgaged upon it I
should be the happiest tabby alive!

There is all of the youthful Rosina in this letter, with its
zest, its commonness, its flashy misdirected talent. She
was the post-war young person to her finger tips — restless,
hotel-loving, conceited, and full of a dangerous form of
inexperience.

Throughout the early months of 1826 the pleasure-hunt
went its reckless way, the infatuation with Lady Caroline
intensified. There can be little doubt that from this experienced but irresponsible friend, Rosina had lessons in the attributes of men. She learnt something about their weaknesses
and for the first time began seriously to estimate her own
capacities for their subjugation. Hitherto she had been out
to amuse herself; and as men were fools enough to want to
fetch and carry for a pretty girl, it was but natural to let
them. But now she realised that something more abiding
than flowers and drives and compliments could be secured by
a young woman who, having chosen her victim carefully, set
herself to capture him. She also realised that for a girl in
her position, the only certainty of future ease lay in a well-
considered marriage. By April, 1826, in fact, Lady Caroline
Lamb had convinced Rosina Wheeler that sooner or later
she would need a husband.

Near the end of that month, yielding to Miss Benger's pres-

sure and despite a bad cold in the head, she went to a party.
She wrote a long account of this party in the unfinished Autobiography which after her death passed to her literary execu-
tor Louisa Devey, and is printed in that lady's clumsy, partisan, but rather appealing vindication of her unhappy friend.
The description, written years after the event and very different in detail from Bulwer's account of the same party, is
facetious and full of ill-natured ridicule of everyone concerned.
Miss Spence and Mrs. Blaquière are pictured as repulsive fools;
Miss Landon as a gushing insignificance. Rosina herself sits
on a sofa by the fire and snuffles resignedly. There is a stir
at the door, and Miss Benger whispers to her pretty guest:
"Oh, here is that odd rich old woman Mrs. Bulwer-Lytton
and her son, her favourite son. I must introduce you."
Rosina begs to be excused. Her cold is too bad; the old
lady (whose prominent aquiline nose, large mouth and long
teeth, dull slate-coloured morning dress, diamond necklace,
string of cameos, immense topaz brooch and numerous brace-
lets are viciously described) is alarming and unattractive;
the youth with his Frenchified lingerie, long glittering hair,
jewelled studs and dangling ebony cane would, for all his
patrician air, be too overwhelming for her heavy head. But
Miss Benger insists. The introduction is made. Mrs. Bulwer-Lytton is affable and invites the young lady to her own
house on the following evening. The young man is markedly attentive. When standing in the rain without a hat,
he has at last shut the door of Sir John Doyle's carriage on the
departing beauty, she waves a languid good night and leans
back in the friendly darkness. Her head aches with cold and
fatigue; but she remembers Miss Benger's words: ". . . that
rich old woman . . . her favourite son. . . ."

Chapter Four

A young man in love — The "idle hands" of Lady Caroline — Lovers' quarrels and lovers' kisses — Mrs. Bulwer-Lytton intervenes — A broken engagement — Rosina makes up her mind — The engagement renewed

The events of the fifteen months from May, 1826, to August, 1827, offer as complete a drama of conflicting human inclinations, of folly, ingenuity, mischief-making and obstinacy, as the most hardened cynic could desire. A sardonic fate had prepared the way for trouble; it only remained for the persons concerned to cheat fate or to follow it.

There were four principal actors. The youth, the girl, the youth's mother and Lady Caroline Lamb. The first could hardly have saved himself, for he was bemused by beauty and at twenty-three desire and love are closely tangled. The second did not intend to save herself, nor would she have admitted that salvation was in question. The third, after the unlucky impulse which threw the young people into one another's company, awoke only too fully to the dangers of the situation but chose the wrong method of dealing with it. The fourth, on whom alone no responsibility rested, heaped fuel on a fire which could not burn her personally, because she liked the flames.

During May and June Bulwer was constantly in London, meeting Rosina (and usually Lady Caroline also) at this house or that, coming ever more deliciously under the influence of his new acquaintance's gaiety and charm. He was to be seen by her side at the various parties given by their mutual friends. S. C. Hall retained a memory of an evening in Miss Spence's lodgings: —

. . . Lady Caroline Lamb was accompanied by a young and singularly beautiful lady, whose form and features were then as near perfection as art, or even fancy, could conceive them. Lively, vivacious, with a ready, if not brilliant, word to say to every member of the assembly — displaying marvellous grace in all her movements, yet cast in a mould that indicated great physical strength — she received in full measure the admiration she evidently coveted, and did her utmost to obtain. . . .

It was not difficult, however, to perceive in this handsome young invader of Miss Spence's drawing-room something that gave disquieting intimations concerning the spirit that looked out from her brilliant eyes — that he who wooed her would probably be a happier man if content to regard her as we do some beautiful caged wild creature of the woods — at a safe and secure distance. . . .

By her side, and seldom absent from it during the whole of the evening, was a young man whose features, though of a some what effeminate cast, were remarkably handsome. His bearing had that aristocratic something bordering on hauteur, which clung to him during his life.[1]

Another reminiscence, published anonymously in *Bentley's Miscellany*, recalled the two young people at that very Miss Benger's under whose eye they had first met:

Beside Lady Caroline Lamb stood two fair beings, since well known to fame — then only intent on each other. The one in the dawn of his far-famed manhood, with the light hair curling on his fair high brow, his eyes sparkling with that genius which has left undying trophies of his powers. The other was a creature exquisite in figure, and comely rather than beautiful in countenance, for the features wanted elevation. She stood bending over Lady C——e, her dark hair braided back over a brow of ivory, her neck and arms much bared, for her dress was classical."[2]

Bulwer's letters written at this time betray his high spirits. Thus on May 8, he writes to Mrs. Cunningham from the *Athenaeum:*

[1] *Retrospect of a Long Life.* By S. C. Hall. I, 264.
[2] *Literary Retrospect of the Departed* by a Middle Aged Man. *Bentley's Miscellany.* XX. 1846.

People in good society find London full and gay. People in the second state say it is dull. I have been nowhere but once to —— it matters not where — and I went not from choice, but to see someone and I could not see that person for hours but ran into Schoenfield (do you spell his name so?) and he was walking up and down all curl and complacency, as fat and foolish as ever.

Again on June 9, from Knebworth.

I am a great foe to population as exemplified in poor Pigott's case; but when Irish folk do get together, by the Lord Harry, it is a good thing for the midwife. Mr. Malthus and Mr. Mills, who have great dread that some 10,000 years hence we shall eat one another for want of anything else to eat, say that the only way to prevent the evil is to educate the poor people and that in proportion to their prudence they will despise the folly of propagation. Alas, it will be a sad vogue for the young folks in the month of May when Messrs. Mills and Malthus have made the world prudent! I wonder, by the by, what Mrs. Malthus says of the system? Probably that it is all very well in theory. . . .

On June 25 comes a significant enquiry: *from Knebworth*

Pray did you ever hear in Paris of a Mrs. Wheeler? Do find out about her. Reasons in my next. I believe she is a Liberal and the widow of a Col. Wheeler — tell me all you can find out.

Meanwhile, in the intervals of seeing her, he was writing to Rosina herself, working up from "Mr. E. Lytton Bulwer presents his compliments"; through: "I am utterly at a loss how to express to Miss Wheeler the pleasure I have derived from her note"; to "My dear Rosina." By August, when he is at Margate, the letters are intimate and rather more than friendly. And at this point Lady Caroline invited the pair of them to meet one another at Brocket.

Under the spell of his new absorption Bulwer forgot the injuries which he had suffered; the state of affairs when he was last at Brocket; what had happened since. Rosina was there, and nothing else mattered. In Lady Caroline's garden, therefore, through the summer days Edward and Rosina wandered into love-making. There is much that is pitiful in this brief idyllic interlude, when the youth forgot his egoism and the girl her scheming and both slid happily along the tide of sentiment. Their mutual absorption was genuine enough. The first recorded note, written by Rosina to Edward and dated at the end of August, is full of the simple happiness of a young girl in love. "Do you remember," it begins, "that day in the shrubbery . . ." and ends with a mention of the rosebud which he gave her. Did he remember?

As for Lady Caroline she was enchanted. To stage-manage in her own home a romance between two handsome young people, both of whom — and separately — had been her slaves and ministered to her vanity, offered an almost perfect entertainment. It only needed, to be quite perfect, some vicious little dislocation at the end, so that if matters should go wrong she could take credit for the failure as well as for the success. This crowning ingenuity she duly contrived. By the end of August the two were frankly lovers, and to their own satisfaction formally engaged. Bulwer went home to Knebworth, but Lady Caroline kept Rosina at Brocket for a while longer; [1] told her a garbled version of the amourette of the previous autumn, undoubtedly sneered at Mrs. Bulwer-Lytton for having regarded her son as in the toils of an adventuress; and concluded by this seeming-solemn declaration: "Don't let Edward Bulwer hunt you down. They are a bad set."

Many years afterward, when stoking the fires of her hatred by rereading the old passionate correspondence of her courtship days, Rosina endorsed one of Bulwer's letters with these words, declaring that they were actually spoken by Lady Caroline; and although many of her retrospective memories of that distant past cannot with prudence be accepted, there seems good cause to credit this one. For such a remark, made at such a time, would have been wholly characteristic of Lady Caroline's tortuous egoism. She had that quality of perverted

[1] Until indeed almost the end of September.

curiosity about other folks' business which seems inherent in some women, and succeeds in tangling the simplest situations into a maze of mischief. Also she was desperately vain, with a vanity turned savage and reckless by Byron's contemptuous desertion. These two pretty children had each danced separately to her tune and now believed that they would dance together. So they should, for a while; but the tune would still be hers and they must know it. Wherefore she betrayed to Rosina Bulwer's quite recent infatuation for herself, implied that he was tied to his rich mother's apron strings, and left the poison to work.

It worked precisely as — if she troubled to think the matter out at all — she would have anticipated. The girl, not quite sure whether to be jealous of her lover's former passion for this older woman, but determined to show neither embarrassment nor distress in front of Lady Caroline, laughed the incident away. Nevertheless at the first opportunity she must have questioned Bulwer by letter as to the events of the previous autumn, for in reply to her "very sensible and saucy epistle" (undated but almost certainly written at the very beginning of October) he says: "You asked me about Lady Caroline. I must tell you some day my history with her. It is exquisitely comic." [1] In other words, not so proud of his past follies as to wish Rosina to think that they were in any way serious, he also sought to laugh the incident away. But Rosina, one guesses, was not satisfied. She seems to have returned to the charge (it must be remembered that her letters of this pre-marriage period do not survive and rely for reconstruction on Bulwer's voluminous correspondence), for a week or two later he makes another, rather too casual, reference to Lady Caroline, whom he had met at a party and in the presence of his supplanter Russell. There is no other mention of his tormentor until February, 1827; and by then the whole situation had changed, for Mrs. Bulwer-Lytton had begun to play her part.

[1] Devey: *Letters of the late Lord Lytton.* P. 52.

It was early in September, while Rosina was still at Brocket
but Edward dividing his time between Knebworth and London, that Mrs. Bulwer-Lytton was officially informed of her
son's romantic attachment. She took an unfavourable view
of his infatuation and expressed it frankly. Possibly she had
already and of her own initiative been making a few enquiries
about the beautiful but unknown girl in whom the boy had
from the first shown interest; certainly she cannot have
approved the two of them staying together under the careless
régime of Brocket Park. She stated her opinion with disconcerting precision, not advising or even urging, but issuing her decree. Let him win distinction for himself and he
could marry whomsoever he liked; but at present, a girl
living apart from her mother, portionless and obscure, would
not be acceptable even as a prospective daughter-in-law.

This blunt refusal even to show sympathetic interest in her
son's enthusiasm was the first of the several blunders Mrs.
Bulwer-Lytton was destined to make. However unsuitable
his choice, the young man was seriously infatuated; and if
the mother had begun by respecting his emotion, had shown
herself glad to be a confidante in the serious problem of his
mating, she would have gained for her later, more practical,
arguments a readier hearing. But pride, and the almost pos-
sessive love which she had for the boy, jarred her to an
abruptness which hurt and angered him. The link of affection was temporarily snapped and left him subservient for
money's sake alone.

Bulwer rode over to the Lambs' and confessed to Rosina
the forthrightness of his mother's opposition. They parted
fondly if a little subdued. But when she came to think the
matter over, the opportunist element in the girl's affection
(which, drugged by the love-making of the last few weeks,
had remained dormant) keenly awoke. It was one thing to
marry out of hand the good-looking favourite son of a rich
old woman, to sweep him in the first flush of passion into a
life of fashionable pleasure and have a good time ever after-

ward; it was quite another to commit oneself to a long —
maybe a very long — engagement and wait for him to untie
maternal purse strings by winning some sort of individual
distinction. Rosina considered her position. There came
into her mind the hint which Lady Caroline had given of
Edward's enslavement to parental orders. She tossed her
pretty head and told herself that she was not the girl to be
fooled by a mother's darling, however pleasant his love-making and however rich his mother. To Edward she declared
angrily that Mrs. Bulwer-Lytton had no real affection for
him or care for his happiness, but thought only of her dignity.
The words went home. He flamed out at his mother, who
remorselessly set forth the several and unanswerable objections to Miss Wheeler as a future wife. He was in despair.
Rosina, appealed to for comfort, wrote coldly and correctly.
By October 20 the engagement was at an end.

But the poison injected into Rosina's mind by Lady Caroline
was not yet worked out. Bulwer, it is clear enough, had
made up his mind that the affair was over. He wrote in so
many words to Mrs. Cunningham on October 25 that he was
about to enter a new life and take up politics, that "my fate
has been nearly altered entirely and forever, but the die has
been cast differently and I am still unchanged." But Rosina?
Was she content to see her golden opportunity go by, merely
because the gilding was perforce delayed?

The weeks which followed the breaking of the engagement
were spent in shrewd and calculating thought. She shrank
from returning to her former solitude amid the racket and
forced gaiety of endless London parties. She had imagined
herself married and secure. Was she now to confess her failure by reappearing in her old haunts as the same penniless
Miss Wheeler, whose mother lived with atheists in Paris and
whose only correspondent was an Irish lady nearly twice her
age? There was no one to advise her. Sir John Doyle could
hardly be consulted; Mary Greene was far away and had,
from an obscure uneasiness on Rosina's part, been kept only

vaguely informed of the doings of the last few months. She had to rely on herself, which meant that she must seek guidance from her own natural instincts, from the lessons of her youthful training, and from the worldly wisdom of her only worldly friend — the fatal Lady Caroline. Natural instinct impelled her to seek for social position and for luxury; the circumstances of her childhood and adolescence reinforced this impulse, taught her into the bargain that a woman must help herself first and then consider others, that other women are her most dangerous enemies; the gossip of Lady Caroline showed her that men were clay in the hands of skilful beauty.

She made up her mind that after all she would marry Edward Bulwer. It was evident that he was brilliantly clever. It was inevitable that sooner or later, and whatever her personal opposition to his marriage, his mother's estates and social eminence would pass to him. It only remained to get him back and, having got him back, to keep him.

Rosina knew her Edward well enough by now. She had heard him talk grandly of his honour; she guessed that, weak though he might be in other respects and on material issues open to maternal influence, he would be stubborn in chivalry, and proud to put into public practise the fine sentiments he so loved to speak and write. She decided, therefore, to do as other girls have done, both before and since. She decided to lead him on, and then tempt him, by non-resistance at a critical moment, to commit himself.

The little scheme proved pitifully easy. A plaintive message, indirectly sent, that she was ill and grieving, brought him all fever and repentance to her side. In the heat of reconciliation, prudence, maternal wishes, practical obstacles were all forgotten.

By the end of November, 1826, the engagement was most effectively renewed.

Chapter Five

Bulwer at work — Falkland *and* O'Neill — Glenallan — *Mrs.*
Bulwer-Lytton versus *Rosina* — *Vain opposition* — *Marriage of*
Edward and Rosina

The two of them were now very much in love. The seeming passionate surrender of this beautiful girl threw Bulwer
into an ecstasy of gratitude and pride; Rosina, in the joy of
giving joy, forgot that she had acted in part from policy and
came to love the man because he was her lover. By the
ordinary, but queerly important, fact of intercourse, the
situation had been subtly transformed. The woman had
indeed caught her man; but, having caught him, wanted him
for himself; the man, thrilled by a victory which masculine
vanity forbade him to regard as other than a tribute to his
qualities, sought to outdo his mistress' generosity and, by
devotion, tenderness and loyalty, to live up to her ideal of
him.

He plunged into his work with renewed zeal. *Falkland*
was completed, accepted by Colburn and published in March,
1827. Three months later appeared from the same house
O'Neill or The Rebel, a narrative poem in three cantos with a
very generalised Irish setting and dedicated, with flowery
compliment and under the disguise of asterisks, to Rosina.
To her influence also must be ascribed the abortive romance
Glenallan,[1] of which only a few (but perhaps sufficient) chapters were written. Bulwer's infatuation invested Ireland and
all things Irish with a charm that made knowledge unnecessary. Hence the rash venture of a novel about a country he

[1] Owen Meredith. Vol. II, 69 *et seq.*

had never seen and a novel with no *raison d'être* save a desire to present Rosina as "Ellen St. Aubyn" and himself as her hero.

But work was by no means his only preoccupation. The opposition of Mrs. Bulwer-Lytton to the projected marriage hardened in the face of the renewed engagement. Many of her arguments and appeals, together with her son's long and solemn replies, are fully presented in earlier works [1] on the subject and need here only be supplemented. The correspondence, futile though it proved, is full of pathos in that the two disputants, who should have been so near together, are so hopelessly apart. For the time their very mentalities have no mutual contact. The mother uses logic where only love could have convinced; the son replies by declaring an affection which would only have been believed had it taken the form of dutiful submission. Mrs. Bulwer-Lytton, by her injudicious abruptness of the previous autumn, had not only put her son into an impossible position but had destroyed her own power to get him out of it. She now made a bad situation worse by obstinate persistence in her original fault. She refused to compromise with her own pride, but would make no allowance for his. Further, she acted in such a way as to stimulate the very tenacity she wished to subdue. Instead of using the undeniable raffishness of Rosina's background to undermine Bulwer's belief in future prospects generally, and so to isolate and gradually to minimise the influence of his fiancée's personal attraction, she attacked directly the character and truthfulness of the girl herself. She charged Rosina with *maquillage*, and with being intimate with Lady Caroline, both of which statements were the more ineffective for being better known to Bulwer than to anyone else. His reply is rather touching, and has a naïveté not too common in his correspondence of the time:

[*probably July*]

In answer to the faults of visiting Lady Caroline Lamb and rouging, I say to the first that she was at the time very ignorant of Lady

[1] Owen Meredith. Vol. II, 137-145. Lytton. Vol. I, 190-201.

C's real character, that the same seduction of manner which imposes upon everyone else imposed upon her also, that she had no one to advise her but her uncle, who permitted it. In answer to the second, Miss Wheeler never made a *practice* of rouging, and at the same time the custom is more likely to prove diffidence than vanity, for a vain person would think herself perfect. It cannot in any way be worse in a girl than a married woman, and for the rest she has never done so since.

The mother's next move was to accuse Rosina of being two years older than she pretended. This seems so foolish as to be hardly credible; but it was taken very seriously by everyone concerned. The already projected wedding was put off to give time for investigation, and Bulwer even went to the length of promising solemnly that he would break his engagement if it were proved that the girl had deceived him as to her age.

I have, he writes in early August, at last fixed the day for my marriage — the 29th of this month, which will allow ample time for news from Ireland, and I promise you still that in the event, which I tell you frankly I think impossible, of Miss Wheeler being born in 1800 or 1801 I will not marry her.

Researches were made in Ireland which resulted in a sworn statement from a convincing source that the girl had been born on November 3, 1802.[1]

But still Mrs. Bulwer-Lytton would neither yield nor compromise. As the 29th of August approached, she became more and more injudicious in her words and threats. At last Bulwer, who had undeniably borne these months of almost brutal harassment with respect and patience, wrote a last defence of his mistress and himself. It is perhaps as sad a little letter as any written throughout the whole miserable business; for it has simplicity, courage, and at the end an assertion of his loyalty and devotion which are so obviously genuine as to underline the tragedy of their rapid dissolution.

[1] A document dated July 19, 1827, signed by J. Arthur.

When you talk of disentangling me I can assure you that I have no entanglement at all. I have no other ties but these — common humanity, common honour and common conscience to Miss Wheeler. You said she was unworthy. I gave you every opportunity to prove it; you could not. You then spoke of her age. I promised if she was 27 I would not marry her. You obtained some anonymous and utterly unproved authority; against this I have a written testimony of a person who must have known and could not have been bribed.

It is much more likely that you who know nothing of a person could be deceived in her than I who have seen her every day almost for five months and known her intimately for a year. Nor is my love to her at all of the blind sort you suppose. I see all her faults, such as they are, and I love her mind one million times more than her person.

Mrs. Bulwer-Lytton's reply to this letter has not survived, but must have amounted to an angry withdrawal from the field of argument and an intimation that her money had withdrawn also. For the remaining letter written to her by Bulwer before his actual marriage reads as follows: —

August 18, 1827.

The die is inevitably cast. . . . You will see now that on this subject there can be no further discussion. . . . I have no claim — I never advanced any — upon you. Whatever my future fate is I must support it. God bless you, my dear mother, and farewell.

On Wednesday, August 29, and directly against the wish of her future mother-in-law, Rosina Wheeler was made Mrs. Edward Bulwer.

Edward and Rosina

Chapter One

The 'twenties — Post-war society then and now — The tawdry affectations of fashionable life — William Beckford — Sir Egerton Brydges — Social climbers — General demand for a higher standard of living — Increased expenditure on pleasure — The theatres — Sex-exploitation by women — Robert Plumer Ward and his novel Tremaine — *Fashionable Novels — Theodore Hook and " Silver Fork Fiction" of the 'twenties*

I

The immediate effect of Bulwer's marriage, combined with temporary alienation from his mother and the cessation of her allowance, was to confront him, and for the first time, with the problem of making a living. The attempt to solve that problem involved him directly in the quicksand of restlessness, ostentation, propaganda, apathy, bewilderment and opportunism, which served as social terra firma to the eighteen twenties.

Hitherto, though ostensibly in the world and aware of it, he had actually lived a life of almost compulsory irresponsibility. He had had money without working for it; amusement without paying for it; opinions and ideals which he was not called upon to practise or to test. His life, indeed, had been of all kinds of life the most enviable, in that it had combined freedom with shelter and had given every opportunity for tasting without any necessity of swallowing.

Mrs. Bulwer-Lytton, though she had disapproved of some of her son's friendships, had more than tolerated his expensive affectations and his graceful samplings of fashionable society. She had counted on her personal influence and on the respect due to her as the controller of his inheritance, to restrain the young man from any serious excess or from com-

promising by unwise commitments the position and dignity
to which she intended him to attain. She had encouraged
him to play the gilded youth; to dabble in literature; to
move in those circles where he would be likely to make friends
suitable to a career of political and intellectual eminence.
And if social conditions and period psychology had been as
she estimated — as, that is to say, she remembered them from
her own younger days — her method might well have justified itself. But they were not. She had, in fact, designed
an upbringing in the aloof but fundamentally high-minded
manner of the late eighteenth century, not realising that
during the twenty years preceding 1825 the spirit of the age
had changed.

It was no longer enough for the youth of family to tour
Europe with kindly condescension; at home to pit his wits
against his kind and take his pleasures where they offered.
It was no longer easy, if the wild oats — spiritual or material — grew too rankly in his wake, for him to withdraw into
his own well-tended grounds and mature, despite himself,
into an English gentleman. Privacy and privilege could
still be enjoyed; but now they must be bought and expen-
sively maintained. The automatic seclusion of old-time
breeding had vanished.

Indeed the walls of caste, just when they were most needed
for protection, were considerably breached. All manner of
folk were now to be encountered in places where formerly
was one genus only. New ideas, new pretensions were evident and powerful. At one end of the social scale, money had
first rivalled rank and then engulfed it; from the middle
classes, speakers, writers and religious enthusiasts were forcing themselves and their ideas on public consciousness in
Parliament, at crowded meetings, in rapidly multiplying
newspapers, magazines and books; among the populace hard-
ship created discontent, and under the vigorous inspiration
of a democratic and puritan religion, that discontent began
to express itself in clamour for reform.

But although the impulse to freedom and novelty was universal, outlets were few. Radicalism produced reaction; experiment, from its very manifold excitability, wasted its energies and achieved at most the uneasy tremor of a boiling pot. In short, many of the social characteristics of the eighteen-twenties were those of a post-war period, and as such may be expected to have meaning to the so similar period which a century later has at least superficially largely reproduced them.

For indeed the parallel between now and then can be drawn with strange completeness. To a point this is as one would expect. In each case an epoch had come to an explosive end, and the force of the explosion had set the fragments warring among themselves. In each case and in every land the catastrophe weighed most heavily on those most innocent of its contriving — on quiet gentlefolk, on persons retired with a modest and often hardly earned competence, on workers who combined industry with thrift; rewarded most richly the skilful politicians, the spendthrifts and the race of middlemen.[1]

The upheaval of the late eighteenth century, though smaller in scale than the war of 1914, was so long drawn out (it lasted in effect from 1794 to the Battle of Waterloo) that, in England at any rate, it left an exhaustion and a distortion of values little less complete in proportion to the persons involved than that which followed the peace of 1918. From time to time during its weary history, phrases were used and phenomena observed which forestalled literally phrases and phenomena of a dozen years ago. A King's Speech described the country as "victorious, but paying the price of victory"; Sir Francis Burdett contended that over-taxation was causing under-consumption; another member maintained that the

---

[1] The share of British industrialism in the conduct of the war, and the burden on certain classes of the community left behind in the shape of debt and taxation, were described by Southey in 1829 in words which might have been written exactly a century later. *Sir Thomas More:* or Colloquies on the Progress of Society: 2 vols. 1829, Vol. I, pp. 158–159, 186–187.

poor were cared for and the rich triumphant, but the middle-classes left to pay for both; a third that currency inflation was essential; a fourth that it was disastrous. There were food tickets; and popular jokes about the value of a handful of Russian rouble notes. Sir Walter Scott declared in 1817 that "every avenue to employment is choked with appli-cants, for the number of disbanded officers is greatly increas-ing"; Lord Grey in 1819 expressed a view of social prospects in words which might easily have been written a century later: "My views of the state of England are more and more gloomy. Everything is tending to a complete separation between higher and lower orders of society, a state of things which can only end in the destruction of liberty or in a convulsion which may too probably produce the same result." Government gener-ally fell into discredit, so that one trained observer could remark that: "The spirits of men seem either fermenting in discontent or deadened to all feeling of interest about *any* gov-ernment."[1] Everywhere, in fact, brooded that now familiar malaise blent of economic dismay and political scepticism.

With the coming of the post-war years the parallel between then and now becomes perhaps more striking than ever. And, if suitably limited, it has a direct bearing on the individ-ual life story which is our theme. In the first place, it was post-war excitement which drove Bulwer into the toils of a typical post-war girl, and so upset the calculations of an otherwise shrewd-minded mother. In the second place, the kind of London and the kind of smart society into which the young man was plunged during the late 'twenties had a vital influence on his deportment during his early married life, on the nature of his first literary successes, and on the simul-taneous popularity and detestation which they earned for him.

"If suitably limited" — the qualification is compulsory. Young men react rather to superficial appearances than to fundamentals, and only to their immediate experience, how-

---

[1] *Memoirs of the Political and Literary Life of R. Plumer Ward*, by the Hon. Edmund Phipps, 2 vols., 1850.

ever incomplete. If, therefore, in what follows we concentrate on surface phenomena, and ignore many aspects of thought and many strata of society, it is because Bulwer's young maturity was nourished on evanescence, and his encounters with the spirit of the age were localised and partial.

With certain of the most important characteristics of the time he had no contact whatsoever. With the religious developments, for example, — the Oxford movement and the corresponding activity of evangelicals and dissenters — he was not involved either by taste or companionship. Even the radical movement, in whose agitations he was later to take a considerable part, did not at present stir his life or his enthusiasm. Indeed at the time of his marriage and for a year or two after it, the influences to which he was exposed were purely social and literary; and to those only in so far as they reflected the preoccupations of the world of fashion. To such influences therefore, if it is to be relevant, must our period-investigation be confined.

Socially the fashionable area of the London of the 'twenties (an area small but self-assertive, and to Bulwer at once a training ground and a corruption) was dominated by pretension and novelty. New wealth, new titles, new fads, new slang, new snobberies frolicked in the sunshine, while politics appeared to sleep under the curtains of the Liverpool ministry, and the restlessness of the populace, recently diverted from organised disturbance by the sensations and partisanship of the Trial of Queen Caroline, was still uncertain of itself and waiting for a lead. There was an air of crisis but, so far at any rate, no actual outbreak; and in the unreal silence which presages a storm, a hundred frivolities and make-believes danced like gnats. "Throughout Europe," in the words of one of the keenest-witted social novelists of the century, " it was holiday time for people intent on promoting the greatest happiness of the smallest number." And England, for the nonce, was part of Europe.[1]

[1] Mrs. Gore: *Cecil a Peer*, 3 vols., 1841.

There was additional cause, as the 'twenties went their
tawdry way, for the shrillness and strenuous affectation of
fashionable life. With the heedlessness of sham security
went the bad manners of a society three parts *roturière*. Prolonged war, which destroys the spirit, the wealth, and much
of the personnel of an existing aristocracy of breeding, creates
in their place a new aristocracy of money who, desiring above
all things to emulate the outward trappings of their predecessors, make much parade of culture and of elegance, and contrive all possible publicity for their efforts. Wherefore, post-
war fashion is inevitably an exaggeration of pre-war fashion;
it is more aggressive because its votaries are more competi-
tive, it is more clamorous because persons unsure of themselves and of one another are apt to shout to keep their courage up; but its pattern and aspirations are the same, because
those who follow it are without inventiveness and only wish
to imitate. And of such persons the 'twenties knew an abnormal number. Apart from the gatherers of actual war-wealth,
an earlier generation of cash-barons swarmed lustily. So
long ago as the seventeen-sixties had begun a lavish distribu-
tion of titles, and it was notorious that by 1820 the proportion of noble families, who dated their nobility from recent
years and owed it to tactful financing of some grateful government, was very large indeed. By the time that Cobbett made
his tour of England, "new men" were already occupying most
of the great houses of the one-time aristocracy; by the time
Bulwer began to play an independent part in the comedy of
London life, society was a jostle of ambitions and mutual
jealousies, of families who, enriched and ennobled during the
preceding fifty years, now found themselves spenders in a
city of stringency and were making all haste to capture the
manners as well as the haunts of the *ancien régime*.

To certain observers, with memories of an earlier period
and personal reasons for resenting what had followed it, the
complacent glitter of the post-war *ton* was too hateful to be
silently endured. Beckford, having failed himself to get a

peerage, was busy compiling his "Liber Veritatis", in which
he spilt the gall of his disappointment on those more fortunate or more unscrupulous than himself. Poor Sir Egerton
Brydges, likewise denied a title which would have brought
him happiness and no other soul a moment's harm, had withdrawn into an embittered retirement on the Continent, where
he varied his absorption in antiquarian research with note-
making for his memoirs. "The true principles of aristocracy," he wrote in 1825, "are at present grossly outraged in
England; the aristocracy of money is the worst in the world,
though perhaps the aristocracy of *false genius* is as bad." . . .
"The highest born man in Europe, if untitled, cannot be pro-
tected from the slights of the stupid and base in the presence
of a new Duke . . . and if a lawyer of yesterday bred in a
clerk's office gets, by the most odious and time-serving cor-
ruptions, a coronet on his carriage, he thinks himself changed
into imperial essence." [1]

And so, indeed, to all practical purposes he was. Everything that glittered might not be gold; but, most things,
provided they glittered sufficiently, served for currency.
Wherefore the railings of critics, equivocal or remote, did not
trouble the *arrivé;* nor were they of importance to the still
aspiring elegant, beside the happy conviction that, if he tried
hard enough, he too might join the elect. To this end he
worked; for this reward he paid — lavishly but joyfully.
And there were not lacking persons of existing eminence and
shrewd cynicism to help him — for a consideration — on
his way.

The most popular routes to social prominence lay through
sport, the fashionable "hells", scandal and literature, and the
leaders of fashion in all departments were ready, if suitably
rewarded, to guide and to befriend. Money, whether gathered from trade or from a lucky coup in the stock markets (for

[1] *Note on the Suppression of Memoirs.* 1825. The theme had already been touched
on in the same writer's *Recollections of Foreign Travel*, 1825, vol. II, pp. 199–200, and
was developed ten years later in his *Autobiography*, pp. 195–197.

stock gambling marked inevitably that period of uncertain currencies) could land an unknown by the side of Lord Chesterfield or Sir St. Vincent Colton at Crockford's; more money, applied with a little tact, could scrape an acquaintanceship. Thence might come half a dozen opportunities. The paddock at Newmarket, the cockpit in Lambeth, perhaps a book on the St. Leger, or a trotting race — all of these and other contacts would be full of possibilities.

Other climbers there were who, by sheer effrontery, contrived to force themselves into acceptance. Provided their names became known, indignity and degrading publicity were blandly endured. Many of the libellous paragraphs in *John Bull* or *The Age* were wryly welcome to their victims. It was more important for "Ball Hughes" [1] to be guyed than ignored; and "Kangaroo Cooke" [2] wasted no regret on pride or pedigree so long as modishness and money landed him at each jump on a more conspicuous ledge.

Naturally out of such insensitive folly was bred petty blackmail; and among the fake fashionables of the age were several engaged in the semi-secret industry of supplying innuendo and gossip to the scandal sheets. "Tell me — do tell me, and I'll keep it such a secret," says Lady Harriet Duncan to Trebeck in *Granby*.[3] "Did you ever put naughty things into the *John Bull?*" There were Trebecks in fact as well as in fiction,[4] and *John Bull* was edited by Theodore Hook.

---

[1] "Golden Ball" Hughes was the nickname (abbreviated as above) for a young officer in the 7th Hussars who inherited a large fortune from an Admiral uncle and, while it lasted, lived accordingly. "Ball" Hughes, his amours, his ignorance and his ostentations, were among the favourite themes of the more scandalous papers of the time. Westmacott introduced him as "Joseph" in the satirical novel *Fitzalleyne of Berkeley* (*cf.* p. 309), while equivocal anecdotes, based on his supposed efforts to talk French in Paris and elsewhere, were innumerable.

[2] Brother of General Sir George Cooke and Lady Cardigan. Notorious for his social *arrivisme*, his nickname had a certain point.

[3] By T. H. Lister, published 1826. *Cf.* p. 172.

[4] Captain Jesse in his *Life of Brummell* (2 vols., 1844) declares that "Trebeck" was intended as a portrait of the Beau. If this were indeed the case, Lister was no portraitist, a conclusion hard to accept in the face of the novelist's successful presentation of Lady Caroline Lamb.

The ladder of literature was more lightly scaled by women. Lady Dacre held gatherings of fashionable blues; perhaps she or the Countess of Morley would put her name as editor upon the aspirant's first fiction. Failing an invitation to the right "evenings", candidates for fashionable notice could approach one of the leading Annuals.[1] Temporary accommodation to an editor had been known to bring a poem or story before the eyes of aristocratic loveliness, and indeed, as time went on and the possibilities of Annuals were more clearly recognised, the editors themselves (by then usually ladies whose rank was more emphatic than their means) made profitable room for portraits of the climbing fair.[2]

Thus and thus was new wealth called upon to redress the bank balance of the old.

So far then as "high life" is concerned, when the pot boils the same scum rises, whether the century be the nineteenth or the twentieth. But the similarity goes further. Ordinary social manners, no less than class ambitions, were affected by the general upheaval and in a way only too familiar. People were no longer content with their old simplicities. The shifting of wealth, and the consequent determination of a newly enriched minority to buy luxury now they could afford it, produced a general expectation of greater comfort and more amusement. Even among persons with no individual expectation of wealth or rank, there was evident an eagerness to be little grander than before and then to seem a little grander still. In consequence expenditure on pleasure of every kind greatly increased, and the now familiar (but then unprecedented) spectacle was seen, of a financially crippled nation living more luxuriously than ever before. A passage in Maginn's anonymous novel *Whitehall*, published

[1] *The Forget-Me-Not* began in 1823, *Friendship's Offering* in 1824, *The Literary Souvenir* in 1825, *The Amulet* in 1826, *The Keepsake* in 1828.

[2] E.g. in *The Book of Beauty* (1833 onwards), *Fisher's Drawing Room Scrap Book* (1832 onwards), *Flowers of Loveliness* and the later 8vo numbers of the *Keepsake*.

in 1827, aptly describes this paradoxical aspect of the London of the day:

> London was in a strange situation at that period. It was in a manner besieged and half its population was discontented. The grievances of the subject were enormous. . . . And yet with all these corroding abominations, the face of things was gay. Everybody admitted that the nation was ruined; and yet, if you visited their palace-like theatres, they were full. The Opera was crowded; private parties were given in all quarters. Tattersall's was crammed — Crockford's crowded. In fact every place where money was to be spent displayed crowds of people, who all could testify to the melancholy fact that there was no money in the country.

A natural outcome of the general desire to live more elaborately and gaily than before was a spreading downwards of the surface manners of so-called "polite society." Everywhere was an urge to ape gentility. John Galt tells of an actress who attributed the unpopularity of a certain rôle to the fact that, although of considerable dramatic possibility, "it was from its necessary low attire, one which no lady would like to perform." [1] And in other respects the state of the theatres was significant. Monopoly patents were held by Drury Lane and Covent Garden,[2] and up to the last years of the eighteen-teens, managers and dramatists contrived to satisfy audiences and at the same time to make profitable use of their privileged position. But about 1820 the public took a taste for melodrama with magnificent staging and, simultaneously, began to follow individual star-players with their favour. Beyond a certain point, however, they resisted an increase in the price of seats. The cost of productions

---

[1] *Autobiography.* II, 238. "I was not aware till then," adds Galt, "of the importance of confining the characters of tragedy to kings and queens, princes and princesses, and men of high degree."

[2] These patents conferred the right to give dramatic entertainments pure and simple, and dated back to a time when the Government sought to restrain sedition in the playhouse by rigid control. Non-licensed theatres could only present plays if they diversified them with music or variety so as to be able to claim that they were staging burlesque or giving a miscellaneous entertainment.

doubled and trebled; the stars demanded salaries out of all proportion to their former earnings; finally the owners of the actual theatres (money-mad as everyone else) raised the rents beyond an economic figure. In consequence the monopoly-theatres saw a succession of bankruptcies, as one gambling management succeeded another and endeavoured by spending more than they were allowed to earn, to cater for the growing elaboration of public taste.[1]

Everyone, in fact, joined in the scramble for frippery; and so lustily, that to the ardours of those ten years of the reign of George IV may be credited the birth of a particular strain in British vulgarity, which achieved its latest, blossoming in the artificial refinement of the nineteen-twenties.

Inevitably women set the pace in the new carnival of self-indulgence. Themselves a form of dissipation, they were able by pricing their favours highly, to secure for themselves liberty, amusement and cash from men bemused by vanity and greed. "The Englishwomen," to quote Mrs. Gore again, "who laid aside their prudery to make a virtue of hero-hunting certainly went lengths in the excitement of the hour which it would be difficult to match in the *histoire galante* of less highly reputed countries."[2] Young women scandalised their elders by heedless daring of behaviour or dress; the popularity of the new-fangled waltz sent them dancing-mad, and encouraged movements and intimacies of an alarming impropriety; the sports girl made an appearance,[3] less adver-tised perhaps but no more alluring than that of her modern counterpart. Gold-digging — the respectable alternative to harlotry — entered upon one of its periodic bouts of shame-lessness; and although in those days masculine folly was exploited rather by the mothers than by the daughters them-

---

[1] General conditions in the theatre from 1800 to 1830 are forcibly described by Professor Allardyce Nichol in his *History of Early Nineteenth Century Drama* (2 vols. 1930). The student may be referred to this admirable work for facts and deductions necessary to fill in the interstices of the above skeleton argument.

[2] *Cecil, A Coxcomb.* 3 vols. 1841.

[3] *Cf.* Montgomery's satire, *The Age Reviewed.* 1827.

selves, the dexterity with which the feminine eighteen-twenties contrived to deplore sex appeal as morally un-English but to study it as commercially profitable, may claim admiration even from a more enlightened posterity.

All of which may suitably be summed up by quoting a contemporary pronouncement which is not only convincing (because of the mental quality of its author) as a general estimate of the post-war conditions of the eighteen-twenties, and also relevant to the particular problem of Bulwer and his development, because the book from which it is taken had a great influence on his own literary career.

In 1825 was published *Tremaine*, the first novel of Robert Plumer Ward. At one time member of Parliament and Under Secretary of State for Foreign Affairs; later a commissioner of the Admiralty; later still Clerk of the Ordnance, Ward was sixty years old when he issued this leisurely but impressive book. Here was a pre-war mind — well-read, judicious, a little disillusioned — which, having lived through the period of upheaval in an official position of confidence and security, inaugurated its retirement by semi-fictional distillation of a subtle and well-bred intelligence. Of the eighteenth century by training, of the nineteenth by experience, Plumer Ward, thanks to a rich marriage, had neither a personal grievance against the new epoch, nor interest in its conciliation. There was, therefore, a complete impartiality in his impatience at its callowness, an impatience expressed in the dedicatory preface to his novel:

If it should be asked why I have recorded the series of retired scenes, and sometimes abstruse conversations, which compose the following narrative my answer is a very simple one. In the present state of the world they may possibly do good, and cannot do harm . . . .

The wide spread of that luxury which is consequent on wealth, by extinguishing the modest style of living which once belonged to us, has undermined our independence, and left our virtue defenceless. All would be Statesmen, Philosophers or people of fashion. All, too, run to London. The woods and fields are unpeopled; the plain mansions and plain manners of our fathers, deserted and changed; every thing is swallowed up by a devouring dissipation; and the simplicities of life are only to be found in books.

There is in the world a spread of instruction, as well as of luxury; and also, I think, more zeal, more lively attention to duty in our religious instructors. Yet I question if there is, either in the higher or middle ranks, that regard for the religious or even the moral feelings and principles of one another, which would check either man or woman in the choice of friends, or in forming the nearest and dearest of connections.

Most women of whatever rank are, or would be, fine ladies; . . . Scepticism has again laid hold of us, and if there are more saints among us than formerly, there are also more infidels; most of all, perhaps, persons who never inquire. How should it be otherwise, when all-absorbing ambition, attended by a dissipation which is nothing less than frantic, consumes our youth and hardens their hearts!

If the date and provenance of these words makes them apt and impressive, their connection with the novel of *Tremaine* qualify them for a place in the record of Edward Bulwer's literary education. *Tremaine* was the chief impulse to *Vivian Grey*,[1] and *Vivian Grey* must bear a large part of the responsibility for the existence of *Pelham*. Although the young Disraeli and the young Bulwer (as befitted their youth) found in the affectations of the age cause for mockery rather than for grave and melancholy reproof, both were pupils of Plumer Ward and, winning honour for themselves, honoured their master also. Nor is this all. Bulwer, in several of his later novels, was to contract a further and a larger debt to Ward, whose men of "refinement", "independence" and "constancy"[2] and whose talent for combining criticism of contemporary manners with instructional philosophy were to exert a greater influence on the author of *Devereux* and *Paul Clifford* than he was himself inclined to admit.

[1] *Cf.* the introduction to Disraeli's *Dunciad of Today*. (Ingpen & Grant. 1929.)
[2] *Tremaine or The Man of Refinement* (1825); *De Vere or The Man of Independence* (1827); *De Clifford or The Constant Man* (1841).

Wherefore, not only may Ward's comments on his time command unusual respect, but he himself may claim a permanent place in the history of fiction. The inspiration of the two most immediately influential novelists of the thirties and forties; a deliberate traditionalist in the more thoughtful modes of an earlier generation, he stands, with his remote and cultured gravity, at the junction between the philosophic fiction of 1780 to 1810 and the school of novel-writing which dominated public taste from 1830 to 1850. That school, with more or less of elaboration or satire, dealt in actuality; and in the fact that they convinced — or at any rate satisfied — their readers, lies the best of all endorsements of the psychological sense and topical judgments of the author of *Tremaine*.

And now, in our summary parallel between the post-war epochs of the nineteenth and twentieth centuries, we come to a point where, if general similarity continues, a particular divergence begins. With the hitherto recorded manifestations of a post-war snobocracy the present day is, *mutatis mutandis*, tolerably familiar; and it is likely that sentences almost word for word the same as those just quoted from Plumer Ward have been printed in books and periodicals during the last ten years.

But whereas in 1825 such observations appeared acceptable as the preliminary to a work of fiction, in 1925 they would in such a guise have been unread. For the eighteen-twenties saw and approved the rapid supremacy of one phenomenon which for various reasons has since lost its vogue — that peculiar fictional genre of fiction known as the "fashionable novel."

It is true that the nineteen-twenties also have had their fashionable novels; and where, as in *Sonia* or *The Green Hat*, the high life has been flavoured with an acceptable dash of heroics or of daring, popular liking has not tarried. But nowadays best-sellers of the kind hardly owe success to ele-

EDWARD AND ROSINA 111

gance alone, whereas a century ago the fashionable novel triumphed by its very fashionableness. It served as a kind of Court Circular for the ambitious, as a text-book in etiquette for the parvenu, as a means to pin-money for clever society women, and as outlet for the satiric bile of well-connected *révoltés*. Beginning its vogue in the mid-eighteen-twenties it flourished until about 1840, and was equally delightful to those within the pale and those without. The latter were mere ordinary British folk, who loved to read of lords and ladies. The former in their various ways had a more personal interest in the books' continuing popularity. "Silver-fork fiction", as it came to be called, was either designed to permit outsiders to flatten their noses on the windows of the aristocracy, or was avowedly fiction *à clé*. In the former case it forestalled the sneak-guest columns of the popular papers of today; in the latter it combined opportunism with personal prejudice, now taking a private revenge, now paying a private debt of gratitude, but all the time judging its public shrewdly enough to flatter a few by flattery and many by derision. For just as the new gentry, in their desire to be thought smart, became willing victims of a scandal-mongering press, so also were they ready to serve as foolish models for novelists of manners, provided only that they might posture in titled company. They liked to be subjects of satire or of gush, and cared nothing that sour critics or grave old-fashioned readers despised them for their antics. What mattered was to be able, if not actually to read of themselves and one another, at least to lick lips over the luxury and deportment of the great; to marvel at the nonchalant splendours of life under Lord Normanby,[1] at the dissipations and rascalities of London fashionables as racily described by Theodore Hook,[2] at the daily amusements, emotions and conversation of the wife of

[1] *Matilda: A Tale of the Day.* 2 vols. 1825. *The English in Italy.* 3 vols. 1825. *Historiettes: or Tales of Continental Life.* 3 vols. 1827, as well as other works published after 1830.

[2] *Sayings and Doings.* 1st series. 3 vols. 1824. 2d series. 3 vols. 1824. 3d series. 3 vols. 1828.

a Prime Minister of England;[1] to spot originals through the three volumes of *Granby*[2] or the first two of *Vivian Grey*.[3]

The causes of the popularity of fashionable novels are nowhere better summarised than by Bulwer himself in his book *England and the English*. Surveying English social development during the twenties, he discusses among other things the prevalent reading-tastes of the upper and middle classes:

The novels of fashionable life illustrated feelings very deeply rooted, and productive of no common revolution. In proportion as the aristocracy had become social, and fashion allowed the members of the more mediocre classes a hope to outstep the boundaries of fortune, and be quasi-aristocrats themselves, people eagerly sought for representations of the manners which they aspired to imitate, and the circles to which it was not impossible to belong.

But as with emulation discontent was also mixed, as many hoped to be called and few found themselves chosen, so a satire on the follies and vices of the great gave additional piquancy to the description of their lives. There was a sort of social fagging established; the fag loathed his master, but not the system by which one day or other he himself might be permitted to fag. What the world would not have dared to gaze upon, had it been gravely exhibited by a philosopher (so revolting a picture of the aristocracy would it have seemed), they praised with avidity in the light sketches of a novelist.

Hence the three-years' run of the fashionable novels was a shrewd sign of the times; straws they were, but they shewed the up-gathering of the storm.

Few writers ever produced so great an effect on the political spirit of their generation as some of these novelists, who, without any other merit, unconsciously exposed the falsehood, the hypocrisy, the arrogant and vulgar insolence of patrician life. Read by all classes, in every town, in every village, these works, as I have before stated, could not but engender a mingled indignation and disgust at the parade of frivolity, the ridiculous disdain of truth, nature and mankind, the self-consequence and absurdity, which, falsely or

[1] In *Women as They Are or The Manners of the Day*, the first fashionable novel published anonymously by Mrs. Gore. 3 vols. 1830.
[2] See p. 50. *Note*.
[3] By Disraeli. 1827.

truly, they exhibited as a picture of aristocratic society.   The Utilitarians railed against them; but they were effecting with unspeak-
able rapidity the very purposes the Utilitarians desired.[1]

It may be observed that the detachment with which Bulwer
in 1832 could write of a fictional genre once very much his
own, indicated that he, at any rate, had by then moved on to
something else.   The fact was that fashionable fiction had
served him well for making a name among the *ton;* but when
he set out to bid for the larger popularity and sought big sales
among the general public, he abandoned satire on smart
society in favour of melodrama and richly coloured history
and found his shrewdness well rewarded.

II

The literary origins of the fashionable novel were more
authentic than is generally assumed.   Certainly the conscious refinement of the eighteen-twenties had a peculiar
quality of its own — created, indeed, that outer-suburban
standard of gentility which has since become inherent in
British culture.   Certainly, also, the vogue for luxury at
second-hand greatly stimulated the production of this particular type of novel and gave it a twist congenial to its age.
But, *per se*, the genre represented a direct development of the
popular story-telling of the preceding fifty years.

The sensibility novel of the late eighteenth century seldom
failed to emphasize the delicacy of its sentiments and the texture of its exquisite raptures by selecting for hero or for
heroine persons of gentle, if not of noble, degree.   Similarly,
the satirical novel of contemporary society written at the same
period found its favourite humour in contrasting the vulgarities of the nabob parvenu, returned from the Indies to dazzle
the metropolis with his wealth, with the polite restraint of
pedigree and breeding.   When to "sensibility" and novels
of manners succeeded, on the one hand, terror and villainy,

---

[1] *England and the English.*   Book IV, chapter II.

on the other the sentatious reforming fiction of the school
of Bage and Godwin, the aristocratic element persisted.
However humble the birth of the heroine, however obscure
the origins of the hero, it was inevitable by the end of any
Gothistic tale of the Radcliffian brood, that the lover should
throw off the veil of mystery, enter into his hereditary glories
and take his mistress with him.   The leading villains also —
on the principle that only persons of quality merit prominence even in crime — were generally titled; and if their
titles were more often foreign than English, the convention
was one of healthy nationalism, and was cheerfully reciprocated in French and German romances of the same school.

Reform fiction, concerned though it was with libertarian
propaganda against (among other things) an idle or dissolute
nobility, often pointed its moral (and at the same time profitably adorned its tale) by contrasting the wicked earl or the
cruel and brutish baronet with a hero who contrived to be a
child of nature or a philosophic prophet of the new humani-
tarianism, although himself of large fortune and admirable
origins.

The parallel class of fiction — historical romances and
"tales of early times" — were equally, but less purposefully,
concerned with noble characters.   History, as it was known
to the mediæval enthusiasts of the seventeen-nineties and
early eighteen-hundreds, was an affair of royalty and feudal
grandeurs, with the lower orders forming a generalised background of humble fidelity or venal turbulence and occasionally supplying a witch, a homely ancient or a bandit to the
speaking cast.   Not the least part of Scott's share in giving
to the nineteenth-century novel a character distinct from that
of its eighteenth-century predecessor was his popularisation
of the romance in which the principal characters, not only
might be, but often were, of lowly origin.   This innovation,
however, while it produced the Scotch school of Galt, Lockhart, Moir and Wilson, and the Irish novels of the brothers
Banim needed a little while to become generally influential;

and although by 1830 it had revolutionised costume-ro-
mance and tales of contemporary country life, novels of
metropolitan manners persisted in their elegance until, first
Bulwer and Ainsworth with their "Newgate novels", and
then Dickens with his proletarian comedy, breached the
defences of refinement and opened the way to the gradual
supremacy of the novel of middle-class life, which was the
typical entertainment of the mid-Victorian age.

The fashionable novel, therefore, as loved by the eighteen-
twenties and the eighteen-thirties, had good traditional
excuse for its aristocratic personnel. Its individuality — for
individuality it had, although of a group-type, like the plots
and style of the Gothistic favourites of the preceding generation — lay in its passivity. Heroics, adventures, even love
episodes were not essential to its completeness or its popularity. It set out to portray the ordinary lives of contemporary aristocrats; and the greater the detail in which the
gilded leisure, foreign travel, the informal talk, the houses,
rooms, carriages, clothes and aspirations of these enviable
folks were set forth, the more acceptable the "tale" to a public greedy for just such luxurious precision.

To fix the date of the first appearance of genuine silver-fork
fiction is a tempting if difficult task. The genre evolved
directly but inversely from what had gone before and, save
by somewhat arbitrary standards, the dividing line is not
easy to draw. The languors and selfishness of the *ton* had
for long been a theme for improving novelists. Maria Edgeworth betweeen 1809 and 1812 published six volumes of *Tales
of Fashionable Life*, and in 1814 four volumes of *Patronage*. In
1813, while Susan Ferrier and Miss Clavering were playing at
collaboration in the story which ultimately became *Marriage*, the latter wrote to the former:

What you have written I like very well except the speech of the
Duchess of M., which is the style of conversation of duchesses only
in novels.

I don't like those high-life conversations; they are a sort of thing by consent handed down from generation to generation in novels, but have little or no groundwork in truth.

Far from giving occasion to describe character, I know nothing more insipid or uniform than fashionable manners and conversation, and to attribute designs to them from their conduct is ninety-nine times out of a hundred quite a mistake. A true picture of the fashionable society of London would be very dull.[1]

But Miss Edgeworth and Miss Clavering (to a certain extent Jane Austen was of their party) were writers not of "fashionable novels" but of novels about fashionable people. And the two genres were not identical. The high-life romances of the tens and teens, whether flattering to the *ton*, hostile to it or merely satirical, introduce pictures of fashionable life which bore no necessary relation to fact; their authors squandered refinements, estates, titles, affectations and debaucheries as freely as ghosts, monks and banditti were squandered by Gothistic terrorists, and with the same intention of creating a desired atmosphere. But the "fashionable novel" in the orthodox sense aimed before anything else at verisimilitude. It might be dull and silly, but it must appear correct; further, although it was the convention to enlist both hero and heroine in the cause of virtue, their moral triumphs were really less important than their clothes and furniture. Uplift, in fact, became merely incidental to realism; and in the place of Austenian raillery (which never failed to contrast middle-class candour and sincerity with the false amiability of smart society) emerged the insolent gaiety of Disraeli and Bulwer, and the meticulous, witty but never censorious observation of Mrs. Gore.[2]

[1] *Memoir and Correspondence of Susan Ferrier, 1782–1854.* Edited by John A. Doyle. 1 vol. 1898.

[2] Oliver Elton in his *Survey of English Literature 1830–1880* (II, 193) declares Maria Edgeworth and Susan Ferrier to be the immediate forerunners of Mrs. Gore. But the descent, if descent it be, was by reaction rather than by evolution. Indeed the difference between the didactic simplicity-versus-artifice story-telling of the two first writers and the charming but rather cynical detachment of the third is precisely the difference here emphasised between the novel involving fashionable folk and the genuine "fashionable novel."

Further silver-fork fiction the more easily supplanted the fiction of Edgeworthiness

A definite materialism was, therefore, the quality of the fashionable novel most markedly in contrast to what had gone before; and on this fact primarily may be based the case (recently and elsewhere skilfully argued)[1] for Theodore Hook's *Sayings and Doings*,[2] as having been the first outstanding achievement of silver-fork fiction.

Hook was a professional author who lived by his wits, and was quite clever enough to forecast a coming craze for realistic descriptions of fashionable life and deliberately to exploit it; also, in the course of his rather sinister activities as editor of *John Bull*, he was able to collect plenty of material for convincing description of the seamier side of gilded dissipation. So much in the way of qualification. As for achievement, he presents in *Sayings and Doings* traditional novel plots from the preceding decades sore-conditioned as to have a special quality of crisp and veracious intimacy.

His stories buttonhole the reader. They invite him to take pot-luck with a noble family; to look in and mock the vulgarities of a parvenu; to witness an election meeting; to peep behind the scene sat a "hell" and learn the schemes of card-sharpers and pigeon-pluckers. And while these glimpses of life as it is led by the great or the wealthy are carefully presented so as to *convince*, the connecting link of narrative is conventional, almost perfunctory. Which is also quite as it should be. To Hook, therefore, may perhaps

because the latter came to be regarded, on the one hand, as dowdy and dull. "Lady Harriet Duncan" from *Granby* may first bear witness: "Do tell me your favourite novels. I hope you like nothing of Miss Edgeworth's or Miss Austen's. They are full of commonplace people that one recognises at once." On the second count we have the evidence of her friend Laman Blanchard that the poetess Letitia Landon gained a reputation for loose morality partly because she admired Maria Edgeworth's stories more than those of Mrs. Sherwood, while the Edgeworths themselves, father and daughter, had been in many quarters and for long enough shunned for irreligion is proved by their rather anxious preface to the second edition of *Practical Education* (3 vols. 1801) where they "disavow in explicit terms the design of laying down a system of Education founded upon Morality exclusive of Religion."

[1] In *Theodore Hook and His Novels*. By Myran T. Brightfield. Harvard University Press. 1928.
[2] *Cf.* p. 111. *Note.*

be ascribed, among other more embarrassing paternities, that
of the fashionable novel; and to *Sayings and Doings* the credit
of offering for the first time the precise blend of detailed realism, epigram, and structural fatuity which was for two
decades to be characteristic of the norm in silver-fork fiction.

Further consideration of the fashionable novel will come
more aptly at a later stage of this narrative, because its heyday
belonged to the thirties rather than to the twenties. But
by the autumn of 1827 — the date to which our argument
hitherto has been directed; the date of Bulwer's marriage, the
date at which the economic prospects of literature became of
urgent importance to him — the vogue had been established;
and in that vogue Bulwer, with his unerring sense of popu-
larities to come, saw the chance of a livelihood. He also saw
that his chance was a lucky one; seeing that the production
of silver-fork fiction was almost the only creative activity
for which his hitherto circumstances and inclination qualified
him.

Chapter Two

The Bulwer household characteristic of its time — Woodcot — Finding a publisher for Pelham *— Pelham published — Miss Greene visits Woodcot — Birth of Emily Bulwer — The child is nursed away from home — Mrs. Wheeler forces a re-entry into her daughter's life —* The Disowned *published — Bulwer and his mother — His extravagance — His excited vanity — He buys a house in Hertford Street —* Devereux *published — The Bulwers come to Town*

The ménage of the newly married Mr. and Mrs. Edward Bulwer was to prove sadly characteristic of its time. A surface proficiency, an appearance of delighted happiness, a show of monied comfort, covered an actuality of inexperience, conflicting selfishness and hand-to-mouth finance. Pretentious from the first, both husband and wife mistook heedlessness for courage; and although they made much play of worldly prudence, they did not really face the fact that money to spend on pleasure and friends and luxuries was not so plentiful as he had hitherto assumed or as she had expected to find it. Rosina had looked forward to a careless round of amusement, with the thrill of love-making and a pretty pretence of housewifery to give it savour and she was not yet ready to undeceive herself. Bulwer, although he certainly realised to a point that a capital of £8,000 and a wife's income of under £100 a year [1] would not of themselves suffice for the kind of life he had always led, kept his anxieties from his partner. In his heart of hearts he knew that she had married for elegance as well as for love; and, infatuated

---

[1] Miss Devey declares that Rosina had about £300 a year, but Lord Lytton, after investigation, endorses Owen Meredith's original and smaller estimate of her private income.

with her beauty and her ready wit, he lacked the moral courage to confess that he was no longer above the cares of money.

To his own relations, on the other hand, he made a parade
of sturdy endurance. Refusing an offered loan from his eldest
brother he declared that "Rosina is prepared with me to run
the risk of poverty"; to his mother (on whose speedy change
of heart he confidently relied) he spoke of "living according
to my fortune", and defended with a blend of pomposity and
acumen the rather grandiloquent announcement of his wedding which had appeared in the *Morning Post*. Even the cub-
bishness of this very cubbish epoch of his life could not
obscure his shrewd talent for gauging the follies of the day
and turning them to personal profit; wherefore the final sentence of his letter presents the fashionable twenties in two
dozen words:

With regard to the paragraph in the paper announcing my marriage at which you appear offended, I am not aware there was anything in it bombastic or unusually detailed. As a literary man not
altogether unknown in the world, it was natural to one who felt his
marriage an additional stimulus to ambition, to wish that it should
appear as little disadvantageous in a worldly point of view as possible. I shall henceforth have to get my absolute living by writing,
and the publishers look in an author of novels rather to his rank as
a gentleman than his ability as a writer.

But these wage-earning gestures were little more than gestures, and in their different way as artificial as his continued
lavishness toward Rosina. He was still playing at life; had
still to learn that it was one thing to be a young bachelor of
family with a good allowance from his mother, but quite
another to set up house, keep a wife and go out in person to
fetch all but a fraction of the financial wherewithal. Inevitably the process of learning was a painful one; and, because
of the false basis on which in this respect his married life had
started, the pain, when it came, could not be endured by husband and wife in mutual sympathy, but set them blaming one

another for faults which both had committed but neither would admit.

At the outset, however, all was sunshine and optimism. Bulwer rented a large country house — Woodcot, near Nettlebed on the borders of Oxfordshire and Berkshire — with many acres of land, gardens, stables and work for a considerable staff. There, in great affection with his wife and eager to convert the half-written *Mortimer* into the completed *Pelham*, he settled happily. In two or three months the novel was finished and its author began a series of visits to London. He had to find a publisher; he had to buy more furniture and carpets; he had to engage more and better servants. He wrote frequent letters to Rosina, full of lovers' nonsense but over-excited and betraying a restless egoism ill-calculated to console a never very patient young woman in a compulsory and unfamiliar rustic solitude. She was expecting a child and he was full of solicitude for her health; but exhortations to take care of herself were not equivalent to his presence, and their inadequacy was the more painful for the accounts given of his own zestful occupations:

"I have selected some things for the Miss Greenes . . . both the newest fashions and look as if they cost much more" (*October 24, 1827*); "I am so very uneasy about you. Do take care of yourself; never get out of bed without your slippers: do take exercise" (*October 25*); "I can't get the carpet under £12. I hope it will do for the Library and Drawing Room both." (*October 27*)

At this point she seems to have ventured a wish to see him at Nettlebed; but the business of authorship and servant-hunting is too pressing: "I long to come to you. *Pelham* must sell, whether to Colburn or elsewhere. But I am obliged to wait till Monday. You see the necessity of staying here till things are concluded. . . . I have found a cook but could not take her, not having a character. I have fixed on a very old fat man as a butler." (*December 15*) "You alarm me beyond measure. I shall lose no time in returning

to you — indeed were not the state of our servants as it is, I
would come down immediately. Pray for my sake keep up
your spirits — all will do very well and we shall yet triumph.
. . . Never mind that paltry bill of Kay's; 'tis not worth
thinking about — besides we need not pay it till we can
afford it." (*December 17*)

Home for Christmas, he was off again immediately afterward. "Poor darling love — to have got a cold and to have
had so much trouble with those nasty servants! Pray, pray
take all possible care of yourself. . . . I have written for
the character of a very prepossessing gardener and I think of
engaging a very creditable man who lived with Lord Ex-
eter. . . . I have been making active and zealous enquiries
about a seat in Parliament. Having convinced myself that the
thing is hopeless at present *even for any money*, I have been this
morning in treaty for that place at the Palace. I think it very
possible that we may come to terms. I find it is a post of
great honour and pretty sure of procuring a title. . . . I
have read *Herbert Lacy* by Mr. Lister;[1] it is what may be
termed neat, or even elegant mediocrity; but is no rival to
Pelham. *Herbert Milton*, since published with a second name
of *Almacks Revisited*, is wretched stuff, written by a man rather
clever, but very ignorant, very canting and very vulgar. . . .[2]
"I have bought the prettiest Dinner Service you ever saw —
Berlin china with our initials "L. B." and got £26 for the
Dresden dishes in exchange." (*January 2, 1828*)

"My mother's letter is rather meant to vindicate herself
from harshness than anything else. She is evidently coming
round and I have written her a very long and kind letter, likely
to facilitate our reconciliation."[3] (? *January 6*) "I am very
very sorry to hear you are so ill. I wish you would send for
medical advice. *Do*, my own poor dear Poodle. I too have

---

[1] The second "fashionable novel" by the author of *Granby*.
[2] By Charles White. 3 vols. 1828.
[3] Probably the undated letter from "Marshall Thomsons Hotel" printed in Owen
Meredith II, 174–175. It is not so patronising as the mention of it to Rosina would
suggest, and speaks with dignified loyalty of Rosina herself.

been very ill. I thought yesterday night I should have died, the pain in my heart was so acute. But I am better now — indeed quite restored. . . . I took this day the first volume of *Pelham* back to Colburn. Saw Forbes, civil and obsequious as usual, but evidently thinks very little of *Pelham*. . . . I am going tonight among the thieves and "prigs" of St. Giles. They will furnish a scene in my next novel." (*January 7*) "At last I have got you a very nice maid. . . . I have also got a cook — a French cook, a *man* cook. Now don't frown, dearest! He will be very economical and his wages are not more than a woman cook's. . . . The ministers are out — Peel is to be Prime Minister, and my place and Baronetcy go to the devil." [1] (*January 10*) "I saw Ollier [2] today; he speaks (to my great surprise) in the highest terms of *Pelham* — says nothing has come out equal to it since *Anastasius* [3] — thinks it will succeed greatly. *Nous verrons!* " (*February 2nd*) "Pray, darling, what think you of a thought that has come into my head? Sir John Milley Doyle is surely the last person your Uncle would leave his Baronetcy to; Frank is provided for. It does not seem to me he has any nearer connection than your husband and your children — if so, don't you think it would be worth writing to your mother about me? She might do what we would not — suggest it to Sir John Doyle. Think over this well," [4] (*February 18*)

Rosina's baby was due in June. On May 10 *Pelham* was published. The book appeared anonymously, and speculation as to authorship was cleverly stimulated by a publisher who had perfected this kind of publicity over *Vivian Grey*.

---

[1] Bulwer's forecast of a Peel ministry was incorrect. With the collapse of Lord Goderich's government, which had been patched together after Canning's death in August, 1827, the King unexpectedly sent for Wellington who formed a Tory administration. For the problem of the baronetcy *cf.* p. 132.

[2] Charles Ollier, author, friend of Keats, Shelley, Lamb and Leigh Hunt, and formerly an independent and enterprising publisher was at this time reader for Colburn.

[3] *Anastasius or Memoirs of a Greek.* By Thomas Hope. 3 vols. 1819.

[4] This puerile suggestion is here recorded as a good example of the excited absurdities which were liable at this period to take possession of Bulwer's mind.

An essential feature of such salesmanship was well timed
betrayal of the secret, and the author of *Pelham* was soon generally (if unofficially) identified. The appearance of Bulwer's
first full-length novel was to him an event of natural consequence. When the book began to sell, the author's excited
optimism increased. He ran to London again, all agog for
the reviews.

"I find *Pelham* taking greatly among the better classes. . . .
My mother has it and calls it 'very poor', 'vulgar', 'no plot.'
(*May 28*) "Admire the *London Weekly* saying I succeed better
in the comic than the serious! I find strangers think *Pelham*
good but my friends are disappointed." (*May 29*)

Back again at Woodcot, he helped his wife to prepare
for a visit from her old friend Miss Greene. She, good soul,
had been sent a copy of *Falkland* ("that horrid *Falkland*" she
calls it in her Recollections, "which may be clever in point
and style, but shocked us all from the bad sentiments it contained and infamous morals and written in a loose and daring
strain as if the author scarcely knew better") and now
approached with some trepidation the home of a novelist
whose mental attitude frightened and displeased her, whose
second story, though less Byronic, was much more impudent
and more cynical than his first. But Miss Greene, for all her
puritanism, could keep a fairly open mind; and the downright
and impressive simplicity with which she wrote her
judgments of host and hostess on this her first visit to the
Bulwers' home is at once reassuring and pathetic, for then,
at all events, things were going well, though maybe with a
certain over-emphasis on both sides:

I arrived at Henley Nettlebed, a small town within a few miles
of their country house, Woodcote, when Mr. Bulwer came in his
carriage for me. The first sight of him pleased me much, but I said
to myself, he is too young, for young as he was, (25 years old) he
looked still younger. He was dressed most elegantly, quite as a
man of fashion, and left all arrangements to his own man, who sat
at the back of the carriage. We had a drive of about an hour, and

I found him most conversable and agreeable, and his manners not at all those of the boy he looked, but quite those of a man of the world. He talked with great admiration and affection of his beautiful wife, and of the approaching event! and I forget exactly how he brought it about, but he certainly did let me know that she was not to nurse her child, as it might injure her health, as he feared consumption was in her family.

It was nearly dark when we drove up the pretty lawn which led to the very handsome house, which was elegantly lighted up and in the Hall, I was met by certainly the finest and handsomest woman I ever saw (except her Mother). Never shall I, or ought I to, forget her reception of me; it was most cordial and affectionate and elegant. She was most beautifully dressed and very much improved since I had seen her, both in appearance and manner. After a few moments spent upstairs with her in arranging my dress, we came down to a dinner of every rarity of the season, served in the most superior style, she taking the head most gracefully as lady and leader of everything concerning the table — even so much as to carve. Her whole object seemed to be to save her husband trouble, and attend to every thought, word and deed of his, which he received in a manner I had never seen a man receive such attention. Indeed I had never before seen a man paid such attention, but I had never before been domesticated with an English husband. But upon a more intimate acquaintance I was not surprised at her devoted attention, and thought he well deserved it, and would often see bursts of admiration, attention and affection from him which reconciled me to all she did for him, except that I feared she would spoil him for herself, as the devotion she paid could not increase (or perhaps always last) and when this happened, the consequences might be disagreeable.

One of the ways in which he showed his love and respect to her was his kind and polite affection to myself; and one of the instructions she gave me, before her confinement, was to remain with him after dinner to talk with him instead of leaving him to come upstairs to her.

Over and above the general interest of this clumsy but queerly vivid narrative, emerges one peculiarly significant fact. Bulwer, in apparent solicitude for his wife's health,

had decided already that the coming child must be wet-
nursed — and wet-nursed away from home.

The disastrous effects of this advance determination to
separate a young mother from her baby were neither surprising nor long delayed. He may or may not have had sound
reason to suspect consumption in Rosina's family, but it is
hard to believe that she would have wept and pleaded for her
child (as she certainly did) had the threat of consumption
been at all menacing. More likely that he picked on a rumour
of hereditary disease to justify his at that time unthinking
egoism. He was unwilling himself to sacrifice mobility and
independence for the good of a little child; he was very proud
of his wife's beauty and wanted it preserved so that she could
go into society with him and help him to cut a dash among
the fashionables. Wherefore, he decided that the baby
should hamper neither its mother nor father; and he held
obstinately to his decision, thus wantonly providing his wife
with the first of the many genuine grievances which she was
to accumulate against him.

On June 27, 1828, Emily Bulwer was born. Miss Greene
describes the accouchement; declares that even in labour
Rosina's only thoughts were for her husband's comfort ("In
the midst of her agony she seemed to think more of him than
of herself. I shall never forget her sending me to see that the
maid had taken care to leave a warm nightcap he was in the
habit of wearing ready for him to sleep in"); and shows
clearly that already she herself was assuming the patient
responsibility toward the offspring of this ill-fated union,
which, willy-nilly, she was to bear for years. It was Miss
Greene who cared for the invalid; Miss Greene who tried to
obtain a better wet-nurse than the one chosen by Bulwer himself; Miss Greene who woke him from an uneasy sleep on the
library sofa to tell him his daughter had come into the world
and to lead him to Rosina's bedside; Miss Greene who sat
night after night beside the complaining mother during her
slow and painful recovery. When the week-old baby was

MISS MARY GREENE
About 1845
From a drawing at Knebworth

dressed ready to be driven off to its foster-mother's house some miles away, and while upstairs the father and mother were quarrelling noisily, Miss Greene held the infant on her lap, worried over its evident ailments,[1] wept that it should be sent away. A few days after it had gone she herself succumbed to a bad fever. By the time she was better Rosina was about again, Bulwer cheerful, the house full of visitors, and the baby as much out of mind as out of sight.

Thus by the very earliest needs of their first-born child was Mary Greene implicated in the fortunes of Edward and Rosina. Thanks to her sense of duty, the implication was permanent, but it is doubtful whether services as great as hers have ever been so scurvily repaid. Emily indeed looked to Miss Greene for mothering and loved her for it. Emily's brother, who was likewise to owe to this admirable woman whatsoever of happiness brightened his childhood and adolescence, rewarded her care by growing to a manhood of graceful eminence. But the real mother, whose place Miss Greene so devotedly took, and the father, whose wayward obstinacy she was forever softening in his children's interests, became too blinded by their hatred for each other, were too fettered by pride and shame, ever to expiate their faults by honouring a woman whose life-work was a damning criticism of themselves.

But the qualities which bound Mary Greene to the service of Bulwer's children also made her indifferent to reward. She was not conscious of doing more than her simple duty, and her recompense lay in the fulfilment of her trust.

If in this devoted woman Edward and Rosina entertained a good fairy unawares, at the same time and more consciously they were very soon to harbour a bad fairy also. It is clear from Miss Greene's diary that Rosina's child-bearing gave

---

[1] "The child's mouth was all covered over inside with white blisters which I thought the Thrush. Never shall I forget sitting with the poor little child, in my lap, wrapped up in her little cloak and bonnet in her father's library, and my tears falling on her face hoping to the last he would relent. But no — she was sent off."

to the long-evaded Mrs. Wheeler an opportunity to force a
re-entry into her daughter's life.   This pedantic *déracinée* had
been successfully kept at a distance ever since the girl had left
Ireland for the last time and come to her uncle's house in London.   Rosina feared her mother as much as she disliked her;
and now that she was happily married had less desire than
ever for a reconciliation.   She dreaded — and with reason — a
possibly hostile encounter between so aggressive a Bohemian
and a being so formal and conceited as her husband.

Nevertheless — and despite Rosina's indirect obstruction
— Mrs. Wheeler came to Woodcot, if not for her daughter's
actual lying-in, at any rate very soon afterwards.   The first
visit was followed by others.   Her name begins to appear in
Bulwer's correspondence, and in such a way as to imply that
by pertinacious flattery (Miss Greene says: "I knew she
could put on manners to bewitch any person whom she
chose") she had gained not only his tolerance but his liking.
Rosina, after vain attempts to convince him of the falsity of
her mother's character, submitted to the inevitable.   By the
time they were established in London, Mrs. Wheeler was
almost an *habituée* of their home.

Bulwer was to pay heavily for the weakness which had
allowed a woman skilled in spoiling other people's lives to
find a footing in his own.   After a period of lively harmony,
her loud-voiced extremism first wearied and then disgusted
him; and because the revulsion from his mother-in-law coincided with his by that time growing alienation from his wife,
he was fated himself to drive the two once hostile women
into close and unscrupulous alliance.   It can be imagined
with what readiness Mrs. Wheeler threw the force and eloquence of a lifelong feminism into her daughter's quarrel;
how gleefully, while breath was in her body, she stoked with
the solemn cruelty of her fanaticism the fires of her daughter's
hatred.

For another three months or so, the Bulwers remained at
Woodcot, Miss Greene staying on for a part of the time and

noting with disapproval an apparent philandering between Bulwer and Miss Landon, who, with Jerdan, editor of the *Literary Gazette*, paid a visit of some days.   When a little later William, the eldest of the Bulwer brothers, came with his recently acquired wife to spend some time with Edward and Rosina, she commended the affectionate bearing of the two brothers but anticipated friction between the wives, which indeed developed, and became almost an open quarrel.[1]

In September Rosina was ordered to Weymouth for an eye-cure.   Edward established his wife by the sea in a "very pretty but small house" at the handsome rate of eight guineas a week.   In the midst of the disturbed happenings of the last ten months he had been writing rapidly (too rapidly) at the successor to *Pelham* and, after much negotiation, had struck a bargain with Colburn at the beginning of July by which the publisher was to pay £900 for the new novel and for the right to print a second edition of *Pelham*. This considerable contract swept from Bulwer's mind whatsoever misgivings as to money may hitherto have gathered there.   Everything continued easily and prosperously.   The new book was finished and despatched.   During the last half of October it was published under the title of *The Disowned*.

With the preparations for the issue of his book Bulwer resumed the habit of frequent absences in London.   He had now the additional excuse of wishing to be near his mother. From the moment of his daughter's birth he had begun to lay siege to Mrs. Bulwer-Lytton, writing her letters, trying to see her, over-wrought in conciliation as in everything else. He described Rosina's ailments with occasional exaggeration, and even elicited a letter of regret and enquiry from the still unforgiving old lady.   Progress was reported to Weymouth in frequent letters:

---

[1] In a letter to Miss Greene written about six months later, Rosina says: "When you write, never allude to my amiable brother-in-law or his petrified carrot of a wife, for I have told Edward in very plain terms that I would not brook the slightest interference from him."

"This morning my letter went to my mother, O Poodle! She left town on Saturday night! Was there ever anything more provoking! However we must make the best of things. I have written requesting to see her in the most affectionate manner, saying I will either come to Knebworth or return to Town when she does. . . . Met Charles Villiers who was mighty complimentary about *Pelham*, and says that the Duchess of Bedford and the élite of la Noblesse say that 'he is the happiest fellow possible to know the Author." (*December 23*) "Ollier says a third edition of *The Disowned* will probably soon be called for. I have seen a French review of *Pelham* in the *Revue Encyclopedique*. I have also in the letter from Jullien an offer to write in the *Revue* at about £5 or £6 a sheet. Fancy! I hope to hear from my mother tomorrow." (*December 24*) " This morning a letter came from my mother which I enclose. . . . She does not say a word about seeing me, but she evidently will." (*December 25*)

On December 27 he reports another letter from his mother, but still no arrangement for a meeting; he proposes to visit little Emily in Oxfordshire and is once again hunting for a cook. He has sent Rosina a French cloak and shawl, two dresses ("which I think ugly, but they are so much the rage that I was persuaded into having them"), a costly gold chain, four superfine handkerchiefs, some collars and cuffs and a lace veil.[1] On December 29 he admits wincing under the brusque words of *The Examiner* reviewers who have read *The Disowned* "very attentively and have not found a single thing to interest them from the first page to the last." The characters are declared "stony and forced" and the whole "a failure." The criticism remarks, however, that a man who could write *Pelham* is eminently enlightened and accomplished. "I must own," he adds, "that this has hurt me because it is evidently

---

[1] Rosina's description of these prodigal follies will be found in a letter to Miss Greene printed in Lytton I, 214–215. On page 216 is an account of further extravagant purchases (a fifteen-guinea thimble for her, a gold toilet set chased and crested for him) made respectively by husband and wife a few months later.

written in kindness, and shows the opinion of clever men well disposed to do me justice."

He was now busy writing *Devereux* and making whatsoever incidental money came his way. Colburn offered him twenty guineas a sheet for contributions to the *New Monthly Magazine*, with the cordial approval of the poet, Thomas Campbell, who was the paper's ostensible editor. This amiable but rather desultory old man was already inclined to treat him with familiarity and kindness.

A few months earlier, when Emily was born, Campbell had published a poem in his magazine in celebration of his young friend's paternity; [1] and their continued friendship was to have consequences of a practical kind. When Campbell resigned his editorial chair, Bulwer after a short interval succeeded him, an arrangement with which the poet must have been indirectly concerned.

The manœuvring for maternal forgiveness now scored a bleak but definite success:

"I received a very unhandsome letter from my mother today," he wrote on January 5, 1829, "but saying she *will* see me, if I wish."

The meeting — the first since his marriage — took place on January 7. "Everything has been much better than I expected." But a further meeting the next day was less propitious. Mrs. Bulwer-Lytton received her son "very civilly

---

[1] The following extract from this poem shows it to have been more laudatory than prophetic:

"My heart is with you, Bulwer, and pourtrays
The blessings of your first paternal days;

* * * * * * *

Joy be to thee, and her whose lot with thine,
Propitious stars saw Truth and Passion twine!
Joy be to her, who in your rising name
Feels Love's bower brightened by the beams of Fame!
I lack'd a father's claim to her — but knew
Regard for her young years so pure and true,
That, when she at the altar stood your bride,
A sire could scarce have felt more sirelike pride."

(*New Monthly*. September, 1828)

and coldly"; referring to *Pelham* she "spoke with acrimony of *my* having therein said 'old women were not human'."

The interview concluded with a tart (and one must confess a justifiable) comment from the lady on her son's expectation of an easy baronetcy of which signs had already appeared. "Just as I was going, she said, 'I heard the other day you were to be a "Sir!" Only think how absurd!' 'I believe it *is* in contemplation to make me one,' said I guardedly." Baronetcies at this date were certainly notoriously cheap; but it is evidence of the value which the young man set upon his own importance that he should have had so continuous an expectation of entitlement. As long ago as the summer of 1828, he was adding "Bart." to the pet name with which he signed his letters to Rosina. And now, even after the visit to his mother, the apparently serious ambition persisted. "People very generally know that I am to be made a Bart.," he wrote on January 13, 1829; "even strangers mention it; but it does not seem to be known in which way I get it, and I suppose therefore that it transpires thro' the offices."

From Weymouth Rosina moved to Tunbridge Wells. She had Emily with her from time to time but for the most part the child remained at Woodcot with her aunt. Bulwer was partly with his wife, partly with his brother, partly in London. He had decided when the William Bulwers' lease was up, to relinquish Woodcot altogether "and go a little into Society." He must needs therefore start looking for a house in town, an occupation very congenial to his tastes, though less so to his still uncertain resources. But at present the slightest monetary gain launched him blithely on new and quite disproportionate expenditure. In February he concluded a very favourable contract for *Devereux* and could count on £1500 in the early summer. His assiduity had at last broken down his mother's aloofness and produced in May a promise of an allowance of £300 a year. Forthwith he made up his mind to buy a house in Hertford Street for 2,400 guineas, and began attending auctions, at which he bought furnishings of various kinds. Throughout the spring insensate extravagance went its way. *Devereux* was nearly finished and the agreed payment was thrown into the pit of prodigality.

All the time he was working desperately, driving his too fluent brain to page after page of fiction. A great part of every night was occupied with earning money to spend the following day. But always expenditure exceeded income, and the debts began to pile. At the home end economics were no less crazy. That Rosina — put in charge of other people's furnished houses, often alone, untrained in domestic management, readier to play with her dogs or read the latest novels than supervise her household or learn the value of money — should have let herself slip into the same habits of feckless wastefulness was inevitable. She saw her husband spending money on costly presents and on his own indulgences; she received his letters with their talk of titles, of thousands for this house or that, of novel-sales and articles solicited. Small wonder that her natural distaste for management became a sort of pride in non-management, and that the less she knew of domestic prudence, the finer she thought herself to be.[1]

By July Bulwer and his wife were back for a final stay at Woodcot. *Devereux* appeared on the 29th, and work started immediately on *Paul Clifford*, Rosina now taking a direct share in the preparatory labours by reading the Newgate Calendar from beginning to end. In September Woodcot was given up altogether and the young couple moved to London. Because Number 36 Hertford Street was in the hands of decorators, a temporary home was made in Fulham. Here

---

[1] A letter of September 22, 1829, to Mary Greene, written after a reading of Mrs. Grant's *Letters from the Mountains*, betrays this not unusual misconception and shows how typical was Rosina of one type of post-war femininity : " It was certainly a most unparalleled piece of vanity to think of publishing such stuff . . . saying that it is quite impossible for a woman to manage her house well and do anything else. I only know I should be very sorry to give more than an hour every morning and two of a Monday to the management of the largest establishment that ever was."

(though again for a short time) little Emily joined her parents. In January, 1830, the Bulwers came into residence in Hertford Street and prepared to conquer society.

The campaign was to make a brilliant start, to achieve rapid and spectacular results. But disruption from within and from without, flank attacks from fresh and unsuspected enemies, were quickly to turn triumph to disaster. There is a sinister irony in the first appearance, almost simultaneous with Bulwer's new and splendid installation, of *Fraser's Magazine*, which periodical was with its third number (April, 1830) to begin a protracted and venomous persecution of his work and personality. That his own social début should have been thus coincident with that of the magazine most destructively hostile to his reputation seems, in the light of what was to follow, a horrid symbol of torments to come.

Chapter Three

Social activity in Hertford Street — The Bulwers as viewed by their contemporaries — Lavish entertaining — Money troubles — Mrs. Bulwer-Lytton and her daughter-in-law — Bulwer's nerves begin to wear —Dutiful patience of Rosina — More extravagance — Rosina becomes jealous of her husband's work — Partial reconciliation of Bulwer and his mother —His political beginnings — elected to Parliament as member for St. Ives

And now opened the first full-dress campaign of Bulwer's married life. The two and a half years at Woodcot, Weymouth and Tunbridge Wells, revealing though they were of his own susceptibility to period-hysteria and of the wayward mentality of the girl he had married, represented rather a preliminary skirmish than a serious assault on livelihood and reputation. As for happiness — that dominant but intangible element in any protracted companionship — neither he nor Rosina knew enough of it to realise that they knew it not, until the chance of it had passed, leaving its converse grimly recognisable.

The crowded activities of these preliminary years could not alter their impermanence. He had published three full-length novels with conspicuous success; had fathered a child; had impressed himself on a small but vivid section of society as a rising young man of intellect and energy; had haunted the corridors of patronage; had made many acquaintances, several enemies, a few friends. But in all these things had been a something of improvisation, as though he had not yet fully found his feet, was not yet quite ready to turn brilliant beginnings into steady achievement nor decided in which direction to apply his marked, but volatile talents. On one point only was his mind clear and definite — he was going to excel; and the summit he meant to reach was that of fashionable prominence, no matter how steep the slope of it; no matter what shifts and ingenuities its climbing might involve.

His wife was similarly awaiting the fulfilment of her plans. She had not as yet had the chance to experiment with the kind of life she most wanted and to which she was most suited. Trained to the sham-smart standards of a rather raffish London life, she had neither the temper nor mentality for country houses and provincial towns. Her wit, acceptable to the free and easy parties where it had grown and flourished, was too keen and too personal for circles less astringent; her need for excitement and flattery was starved, once it came to depend on the intermittent attentions of an over-worked and self-centred husband; finally, whatsoever of potential mother-instincts may have lain dormant in her undisciplined and selfish soul were stunned, almost as soon as they had been awakened, by the cruel removal of her baby within a few days of its painful birth.

So she also had rather tided over than lived the opening years of her wifehood, hoping for something better, biding her time until she could give rein to her ambition and make a bid for the real object of her marriage. She meant first of all to impose herself as one of the smart intelligentsia of London; that achieved, she meant, with her beauty and her skill in hospitality, to hasten her husband's climb to fame, wealth and (why not?) to nobility; last of all, she was determined to prove once more that native Irish wit and loveliness could, when allied to English money and to English breeding, mount the social ladder to its highest rungs.

Thus agog with the ambitions and random impatience natural to their kind, Edward and Rosina came gleefully to the assault on London. In their enthusiasm money cares were forgotten, the occasional disagreements and sadnesses of recent months vanished in a renewal of mutual adoration.

Physical desire had originally bound them together and could still give them times of ecstasy; this new excitement brought them into an intimacy of plans and expectations which heightened the illusion of happiness. Indeed, so far as love was possible between them, it now united them more completely than ever before.

Wherefore, when from Number 36 Hertford Street they launched their attack on social prominence and literary fame, few suspected how insecure was in fact their base, how overwhelming the odds against which each of them had individually to fight. Outsiders marked the success achieved, and were impressed by the determination, vigour and mental dexterity of the campaigners. So much the more may posterity marvel who, possessed of inside information, knows the awful cost of that considerable victory. Until late in 1833, when the pair of them returned from their ill-fated tour in Italy, the Edward Bulwers were among the most talked of (and consequently the most admired and best hated) figures of the London social scene. Who should know that, behind the screen of gaiety and adulation and luxury, nerves were being torn to shreds, a love story drowned in bitterness and the happiness of a father, a mother and (in time) of two little children also permanently wrecked?

Needless to say, the earliest to suspect the truth was Mary Greene. But even she, judging from Rosina's letters and her first visit to Hertford Street, was tempted to believe that for the moment all was going well:

Here [*i.e.* in Hertford Street] began a new Era, and Rosina launched into the very position she wished for and seemed by nature fitted for — namely at the head of a nice establishment of servants and a good house in a fashionable part of London. Here both she and he worked on with an energy and perseverance worthy of the best cause, and succeeded in making a very good appearance and bringing forth his literary talents to the best advantage. She made the most zealous and efficient exertions with his literary friends with whom she had much interest; added to this they gave some dinners which she knew well how to guide, and all went on to the best of their wishes. All this I heard as it was passing by letters from her.[1]

Other observers, judging perforce by outward appearances only, flattered the young couple or made amused comment on their languid arrogance or costly way of life. Miss Landon introduced them both into her novel *Romance and Reality*.[2] The syntax is a little indeterminate; the compliments are ludicrously over-pitched, as were all the ingratiations of this luckless and transient Sappho; but with due allowance for their author's saccharine servility, and remembering that Bulwer had been one of the several daylight lovers which she incautiously allowed herself, we may take the description of "Emily Arundel's" sight of them as fairly representative of the opinion held of Edward and Rosina among sympathetic blues.

Lady Morgan, whose natural acidity was increased by the fact that her own Irishism could call Rosina's bluff, was as critical as L. E. L. was fulsome:

> Last night at Mr. Perry's, son of the editor of the *Morning Chronicle*. The manner of all the men cold and languid; reserve, shyness and morgue make up the character and manners of English society.
> Mrs. Bulwer, handsome, insolent and unamiable, to judge by her style and manners; she and all the demi-esprits looked daggers at me; not one of them have called on me and in society they get out of my way.[3]

Evidently Rosina did not disguise her contempt for her fellow-countrymen even in her own home. The following paragraph from the reminiscences of S. C. Hall refers probably to 1832:

> During his editorship of the *New Monthly*, Bulwer gave a dinner-party to O'Connell and several Irish members. I was not present; but the next day I saw Mrs. Bulwer directing some arrangements

---

[1] Some of these letters are printed in Lytton, I, 253 *et seq.*
[2] 3 vols. November, 1831. *Cf.* Appendix II.
[3] Lady Morgan's *Memoirs*. 2 vols. 1862. II, p. 365.

in the dining-room, which she told me she was *fumigating* in order to get rid of the brogue.[1]

Her ostentatious scorn of her husband's working friends must often have embarrassed him. There is a letter written by him to the editor of *The Times* in January, 1832, of which the last paragraph reads:

So much for business. You dine with us as usual on Sunday, if you are not sent for by Brougham, and bring as many of your stenographers with you as may chance to be disengaged; but hint to them, do pray! not to call for cigars and pipes in the evening; or, if they must have them, tell them they ought to learn to consume their own smoke — the last time they came Mrs. Bulwer complained, with truth, that they made the furniture smell abominably.

But Rosina's affectations and bad manners, though they may well have made her husband's daily life more difficult, did not check his rather showy hospitality.

Entertaining at 36 Hertford Street was lavish and continuous. Tom Moore, in his diary for April 1, 1832, records: "Mrs. Lytton Bulwer's assembly", where he met "such a collection as is seldom brought together", including Byron's half-sister Augusta Leigh, Lord Mulgrave (afterward Lord Normanby), Godwin, an Indian prince and young Disraeli.

As for Disraeli, he was something of an habitué of Hertford Street. After dining there one night early in 1832, he wrote to his sister:

Our host, whatever may be his situation, was more sumptuous and fantastic than ever. Mrs. Bulwer was a blaze of jewels and looked like Juno; only instead of a peacock she had a dog in her lap called Fairy. . . . We drank champagne out of a saucer of ground glass mounted on a pedestal of cut glass.[2]

[1] Samuel Carter Hall. *Retrospect of a Long Life.* I, p. 265 (*Note*).
[2] *Lord Beaconsfield: Correspondence with his Sister.* 1886. pp. 3–4. An adaptation of this, combined with the earlier, not dissimilar dinner-party recorded by Monypenny (I, 124–125), provides the first chapter of the second volume of Disraeli's last novel *Endymion* (3 vols. 1880). "Hon. Bertie Tremaine", Benthamite and exquisite, is Bulwer; his brother Augustus is Bulwer's brother Henry, and the scene represents the author's rather flamboyant memory of an evening of half a century earlier.

Throughout the spring he continues to report *réunions* and *soirées* at Hertford Street, where he meets all the elegant intellectuals of the day from Lord Normanby to the "snub-nosed, Brompton Sappho", L. E. L.   Early in 1833, after visiting Bath with Bulwer, he dines again, has the good fortune to meet his host's mother-in-law, and pictures not only that repellent sybil but the whole already unstable ménage in a few brilliant sentences:

I dined with Bulwer *en famille* on Sunday "to meet some truffles" — very agreeable company.   His mother-in-law, Mrs. Wheeler, was there; not so pleasant, something between Jeremy Bentham and Meg Merrilies, very clever but awfully revolutionary.   She poured forth all her systems upon my novitiate ear and while she advocated the rights of woman, Bulwer abused system mongers and the sex, and Rosina played with her dog.[1]

Hertford Street, at any rate, was no abode of lofty and austere simplicity.   How was it done!   How was a certain income of five hundred pounds, plus an uncertain allowance of three hundred more, so supplemented as to support life on this luxurious scale?   The problem was Bulwer's, and he faced it with an almost savage industry.   From this period of his life he emerges with almost every discredit possible to a man of education.   He was selfish, flamboyant, unscrupulous, a mass of conflicting insincerities.   *But he worked* — worked unflaggingly, efficiently and (as even those who do not fancy his novels must admit) to remarkable effect.   During these three tearing, raging years of social climbing, domestic squabbling, political wire-pulling, parliamentary work, editing and pamphleteering, he produced three more novels, a long satirical poem and, most impressive of all, that remarkable piece of constructive research — *England and the English*. A noteworthy achievement for any man; for a man distraught with private worries of the most acute kind — little short of a miracle.

[1] *Lord Beaconsfield: Correspondence with his Sister.*   1886.   p. 15.

They were worries indeed — and no easier to bear because
his own weaknesses provoked and magnified them.   Earliest
in date, and gradually poisoning his whole private life, was
the question of money.   Quite soon after his establishment
in Hertford Street, his mother was persuaded to pay a visit to
Rosina.   It was manifestly absurd for the two ladies to live
in London, to risk meeting at this house or that, and yet to
maintain a pretence of non-acquaintance.   Mrs. Bulwer-
Lytton yielded to Edward's plea,[1] and called on her daughter-
in-law; but, for some causes unknown, she took offence at
her reception.

Was it too much to expect, she demanded of her son when
next she saw him, that Rosina should behave civilly to the
older lady who was "maintaining her"?   The unlucky phrase
caught Edward on the raw.   He flared into anger and threw
back his mother's allowance at her feet.   Probably when his
anger cooled, he felt a new indignation that she should have
stooped to pick it up.   So was it, however; and he faced his
debts and his ambitions three hundred pounds the poorer for
a flash of temper.

To fight a financial battle on two fronts — not only against
creditors and the wearisome pressure of daily expense, but
also against a proud old lady, who permitted a clash between
her own pride and that of her son to close her heart — would
have been struggle enough for a husband and wife in close and
affectionate alliance.   It became doubly severe, when between
the two developed first differences, then disagreements, and
at last discord.

And yet it cannot be denied that the gradual breakdown of
his married happiness was initially Bulwer's fault.   It has
been said that he and his wife began their new era as thoroughly in love as circumstances and training enabled them to
be.   But of Bulwer, more than this cannot truthfully be said.
He was too introspective by temperament ever wholly to forget himself, even in passion.

[1] His letter is printed in Lytton, I, 232–238.

To Rosina, on the other hand, more generous credit must be given. Certainly it was not easy for her — from whom in youth the love of others had been denied — now to love anyone but herself; but, as Miss Greene bears witness, she did for a time genuinely merge her own personality in her husband's. At Hertford Street even more plainly than at Woodcot, and solely out of love for Bulwer and in his interests she deliberately and courageously strove to subdue her own desire for amusement and to keep her temper under frequent provocation. Unfortunately by patience and submission, she merely increased the evil which she sought to cure.

I began to see, writes Miss Greene, that from her extreme yielding to his whims and caprice, he had become so irritable and exigent, that her whole time was employed in trying to anticipate his wishes. She never lost her temper and when he made her unhappy, strove to conceal her sorrow from him and everybody. I must in justice to her say I then only saw her in the right and him wrong.

And Rosina showed — at first at any rate — a similar conscientiousness in the handling of their very precarious resources. On taking charge of her London house she seems to have checked in herself that tendency to useless spending which, under her husband's foolish influence, had begun to show itself in Tunbridge Wells. She was no manager because she had never been taught to manage; but to the best of her naïve ability she strove to keep the cost of life within some sort of bounds. It was a difficult task. Bulwer was more than unappreciative of her efforts; he was recalcitrant. His furnishing mania, which had already filled the house with pictures and statues, continued in costly spasms. Rosina writes to Miss Greene:

He has been to Oxmanton's sale and bought a bronze Apollo as large as life, two Louis Quatorze clocks and other things which we *did not want;* and as you know "them's the matters that provoke me!"

He it was who instigated the lavish parties, the out-of-season foods and ostentatious wines, which were not only to his taste but also an integral part of his system of self-advancement. Yet he would turn on her now and again, upbraid her for the weekly bills, withhold in peevish complaining the money for the housekeeping. However, she held bravely on, until, as previously and for the same reason, she was compelled temporarily to relinquish her control. Early in 1831, the coming of another child sent her from London to the country. The extravagance of master and servants was now left unchecked. That was bad enough. But more serious still was it that the inevitable separation of husband and wife began again its harmful work. By now he was literally unable to spare the time to visit her; so that she, kept outside the thrusting social life she loved, thrown back on her own inadequate company and subject to the nervousness and abnormalities of pregnancy, began once more to brood over her loneliness. This time the brooding took a new and sinister direction. Previously she had complained half-humorously of her husband's many (and indeed often frivolous) engagements. Now she began to bear him a real grudge for what had become not only overwhelming but necessary occupations. So long as both of them were foolish, she could be wiser than he, keep her head more level, and help him with the toil which made their folly possible. But when she became perforce prudent and quiet, a longing to be back in Vanity Fair soured her against its tyranny, and she began to pity herself for having married a man too poor to keep his family in fashionable style without labour so ceaseless that he was less of a husband to her than an occasional visitor. Thus, and for the first time, took root in Rosina's mind a sense that she had a rival in Bulwer's work.

Involved with this jealous resentment against her husband's bread-winning is a sullen suspicion of the influence which in her absence might be exercised on him by his family and particularly by his mother. When she was at his side, she could keep the old lady at bay; by her own tact and attractions she could prevent his slipping back into a milieu where criticism of herself, if not spoken, was always implied. But the knowledge that she herself could sway his sympathies taught her that others could do the same; and it was one of the thousand dilemmas which helped to complicate an already complex situation that whereas, while she was with him, she encouraged Bulwer to conciliate his mother, in her absence she dreaded their greater friendliness.

Chance made of politics a theme peculiarly liable to throw mother and son together, whose joint interest in the subject had begun in a curious way. At a by-election in 1830 Edward's brother Henry had been one of the candidates for Hertford. The seat was eventually won by the warm-hearted radical-aristocrat Tom Duncombe (who became something of a friend of Edward Bulwer's, because they shared not only many of their political opinions but also the scurrilous hostility of the Tory jackals Maginn and Westmacott [1]), but before the date of polling Henry Bulwer rather mysteriously withdrew his candidature and remained in Brussels, where he held a diplomatic post. Rumours spread, and at the complimentary dinner to Duncombe after the poll, an important fashionable of the day — Lord Glengall [2] — was sufficiently injudicious to voice local gossip and declare openly that Henry Bulwer, to his own monetary advantage, had been bought by Lord Salisbury and so let his party down. "It is unfortunately a very common thing," so runs the report of his speech in the *Herts Mercury*, "for a candidate to buy, give

---

[1] For detailed discussion of these men *cf.* pp. 222 *et seq.* and pp. 307 *et seq.*

[2] Richard Butler ("Dick Butler"), first Earl of Glengall, had been an intimate of George IV and a recognised though minor member of the buckish Court circle during the twenties. A better known and far cleverer member of the same set, Lord Alvanley, discussing in 1830 the prospects of a revolution in England and the means by which he and others would earn a livelihood under a new democratic régime, said: "I know what I shall do. I shall open a disorderly house and make Glengall my head waiter"; which gives the measure of that nobleman as accurately as may be. Lord Glengall wrote a play *The Follies of Fashion* to which Lord Alvanley contributed a prologue. This play was produced with éclat in December, 1829, and published in 1830.

or perhaps sell *votes* at an election, but it is really something
new to buy or sell a *candidate*."

The affair developed into a scandal of considerable magni-
tude, and there may well have been contributory causes which
led people to declare that Henry Bulwer would not be able to
show his face in the county for a long time to come. Whatever the details, the affair was so much on her doorstep as to
embarrass Mrs. Bulwer-Lytton considerably, and letters survive to prove that in her agitation over the gossip and ill-
feeling in the neighbourhood, she sought the advice of her
youngest son. He wrote to encourage and comfort her and,
loth to miss any chance of doing her a welcome service, took
the matter up directly with Glengall himself, insisting on a
public apology, and eventually securing one.[1]

Now the indirect significance of this incident is greater
than its actual importance. In the first place Bulwer's action
shows the instinctive, almost unreasoning, family loyalty
so characteristic of his racial pride. A very short time previously, and over this very Hertford election, he had felt
great personal bitterness toward Henry. He wrote his mind
to Mrs. Cunningham, declaring that he had intended to stand
for Hertford himself, had entrusted Henry with introductions
to help prepare the way for his own candidature, only to find
himself ousted by his brother and the introductions used in
his own despite. Yet of this grievance no trace was allowed
to appear, when need arose to champion a Bulwer against the
random gossip of Glengall.

In the second place, the counsel taken between Edward and
his mother over the living-down of Henry's indiscretion had
the effect of involving Mrs. Bulwer-Lytton with the future
political plans and theories of her youngest son, even while
she remained aloof from his domestic life. If they had not
come together in family solidarity over the Hertford scandal,
they might well have remained as much apart over politics

---

[1] The correspondence and details are given in *The Life & Correspondence of T. S. Duncombe*. 2 vols. 1868. Vol. I, pp. 139–142.

as over other matters; for Mrs. Bulwer-Lytton was as Tory as Edward was Radical. But once in alliance, they remained in alliance; both of them glad to turn the flank of their own pride, both eager for cordiality on some subject hitherto un-prejudiced, and for the sake of that cordiality agreeing to disagree.

There was, therefore, good ground for Rosina's suspicion that on political matters Mrs. Bulwer-Lytton was more in Edward's confidence than was she herself, and that suspicion grew quickly to a certainty when personal participation in politics, which had for a long while tempted him, came sud-denly within his reach.

The rising disaffection, which broke out during the spring and summer of 1830 in widespread rioting, brought down the Wellington ministry in November and served as a thunderous and prolonged overture to the Reform Bill of 1832. Its par-ticular effect on Bulwer and the closer contacts which it brought him with William Godwin, Doctor John Bowing, the Benthamites and other prominent persons of advanced views are so adequately set forth in his grandson's biography,[1] that they may here be passed over. Two elements in the situation, however, merit notice, the one as evidence of the gradual change in Bulwer's position from courtier to courted; the other for its bearing on that renewed intimacy between him and his mother which was causing Rosina such concern. It should first be observed that the opportunity to stand for Parliament was not secured by intrigue or effort of his own. His continued, though intermittent, relationship with the Mills and their group; his contributions to the *Westminster Review;* and the radical sentiments which were incidentally expressed in his early novels, had so impressed his personality on the minds of reformist leaders that all through the summer of 1830 (while Henry was misconducting his affairs at Hert-

---

[1] Lytton. I, 390–413. This admirable chapter summarises the state of the country and the general tendency of reformist theory up to the date of Bulwer's election for St. Ives.

ford) invitations and suggestions to contest this constituency or that poured in upon him. Secondly, it is remarkable how closely he kept in touch with his mother while considering these invitations and considering which to accept. Prior to the General Election he declined St. Albans in deference to her wishes (she disliked the thought of a reform candidate who was also her son fighting an election so close to the gates of Knebworth); a little later he asked for a loan (which was readily granted but in fact not needed) to pay the expenses of his final choice — a contest at St. Ives in Huntingdon-shire; when on April 30 he was elected, his first action was to write, not to Rosina but to his mother, announcing his success and using his first frank; finally, not a week after his election as a whole-hearted and indeed extreme supporter of Reform, his mother wrote to consult him as to how publicly she should herself come forward as an opponent of the policy to which he was pledged. Only a very rapid revival of their mutual confidence could have produced so paradoxical a situation as this; and the matter-of-fact opportunism of Bulwer's reply proves that, in politics at any rate, they two would always understand one another.

I see great reason, he wrote on May 4, 1831, why for your own sake you should not even quietly and coldly oppose the reform. The public are so unanimous and so violent on the measure, right or wrong, that I do not hesitate to say that persons who oppose the Reform will be marked out in case of any disturbance. It is as well therefore to be safe and neuter, especially when no earthly advantage is to be gained by going against the tide.

Chapter Four

Birth of Edward Robert Bulwer — Rosina returns to social life —
First threat of trouble

Bulwer's son, Edward Robert, was born in Hertford Street
on November 8, 1831. The father was more than usually
occupied. The Reform Bill had a month previously been
rejected by the House of Lords and the country was in a worse
turmoil than ever; Bulwer himself had lately succeeded
Thomas Campbell as editor of the *New Monthly Magazine*,
and the first number issued under his guidance appeared on
November 1; he was writing *The Siamese Twins* and *Eugene
Aram*; his social acquaintance was rapidly increasing and with
it the calls upon his time. But the trouble between him and
Rosina, which once again was provoked by the problem of the
baby's nursing, was on this occasion not his responsibility.
Probably Miss Greene had spoken her mind to him about the
exile of Emily; certainly for a moment his self-centred, rather
inhuman nature softened toward his wife and son, and he
determined this time to avoid all clumsy interference, to let
the mother have her baby for her very own.

But thus prepared to respect and encourage Rosina's wish
to nurse her child, he was brought up in abrupt disappointment by her refusal to do anything of the kind. She had
been out of the world for long enough, and was not going to
waste further weeks over an occupation which a lady of fashion could not but regard as at best tedious, at worst indelicate.
Wherefore, with slight variation, the mishandling of Emily
was repeated. The new baby, instead of being sent away,
was lodged on the top floor; but for all the part he played in

the next six months of his mother's life, he might have been
miles away or even non-existent.

The spring of 1832 seems to mark a definite stage in the
squalid tragedy of the Bulwers' married life. Hitherto the
faults — many and inexcusable — had been emphatically on
the man's side rather than on the woman's. With all the
advantages of education, intellect and breeding, he had yet
been so consumed with vanity, so absorbed in his own prospects and importance, that he seemed to have no thought or
consideration for anyone else, to have accepted every service
as his due, blamed every misadventure on to his wife. She,
on the other hand, had at least *tried;* and inasmuch as her
efforts to be helpful and dutiful involved the unlearning of
every lesson of her youthful training; the controlling of the
fierce temper inherited from her mother; the curbing of the
selfish love of pleasure which was all she had of natural instinct — her struggle had its fineness and she herself a sort of
heroism.

Now, however, the scale had touched the beam and hung
there a while, before beginning its slow movement the other
way. For the next three or four years both parties, and at
various times, were equally guilty of unreasonable pretensions, of obstinacy, of wrong-headedness, of anger ill-con-
trolled; both can claim credit for occasional self-forgetful
impulses, for patience, for moments of nobility. Thereafter,
when the ruin was complete, sympathy — with reservations,
perhaps, but still sympathy — must attach more and more to
Bulwer, as dismay grows greater at Rosina's unmanageable
violence and at the rancour with which she could pursue
the man she once really loved.

Chapter Five

Neglected condition of the children — Vulgarity of Rosina — Mary Greene decides to protect Emily from her mother — Bulwer and Rosina decide on a foreign tour — His disagreeable philandering with Mrs. Stanhope — Rome and Naples — Rosina and a Neapolitan prince — Bulwer's jealous fury — Return to London

But already at the beginning of 1832, although to the world at large the household seemed threatened by nothing worse than the consequences of an ill-judged extravagance, signs of a more serious catastrophe were, to one pair of eyes at least, implicit in the grievous condition of the children.

The attitude of Bulwer and Rosina toward these helpless unfortunates cannot by any sophistry be defended. But it can to some extent be understood, if one realises to what extent both of them were infected by the rather vulgar flippancy toward child-bearing, parental responsibility and propagation generally which in true post-war fashion was regarded as chic by the bright young people of the eighteen-twenties. This flippancy was something quite different from the bawdy candour of the eighteenth century; it was at once timid and over-emphasised, the self-conscious humour of persons who, fearful of evangelical dowdiness but full of aristocratic pretension, sought to appear both emancipated and genteel.

About two months before Emily was born, Bulwer showed his freedom from prejudice by a humorous letter to Mrs. Cunningham about his wife's figure and his own approaching paternity. He promised to limit his activities to one baby only and declared "nothing to be so ludicrously uninteresting as an author with a large family, at least of legitimates."

During the spring of 1829, while she was at Tunbridge Wells, Rosina wrote to Miss Greene about the "noted fame of this place for *faisant l'enfant*, where every second woman you see looks as if she was going to have twins", adding "we are likely to have an increase in our family — Terror for the third time within the last eight months is going to pup." On May 20, 1831, while suffering at Broadstairs from the preliminary discomforts of her second pregnancy, she wrote in the course of a long and gossipy letter:

I am glad to hear dear Mary Anne has recovered her bloom. I do hope she won't lose it again by having another little horror. When I asked Gracie if she were in that blessed state her answer was "Oh now, you don't suppose I'd be in that way" and all I could say was that more unlikely things had happened. . . . I suffer martyrdom from sickness but you will be glad to hear I drink your health every Monday morning in castor oil.

Again on September 5, 1831:

Terror has just *accouchée* of another litter of puppies — which makes in all 115 "Heavenly gifts" that she has had since you saw her.

Intermingled with remarks of this kind (those quoted are typical) were over-pitched praises of the little Emily. Rosina could so order her maternal conscience as to see the child at moments convenient to herself, gush over her pretty ways, and forthwith, having packed her off again, forget all about her. Of the first three and a half years of this little girl's life, not more than twelve months — and they inconsecutive — were spent with her parents. After her weaning, she was lodged with this kind-hearted friend or that; at the age of two and a half she was actually put to some form of infant boarding school. Shortly before her fourth birthday (early in 1833) she was brought to Hertford Street for a little while, because Mary Greene was to pay her first visit to Rosina's London home and wanted to see the child. Almost at once

the visitor's instinctive fondness for young children was jarred
to anxious activity:

Upon the whole I did not like how things went on, as I did not
see any appearance of what I could call family sociability. He
always breakfasted alone in his library, and she and I in her dressing room, and he never saw the children, though Emily had been
brought home from her school.

I did make a point of seeing her and getting acquainted with her if
possible — I say "if possible", for her mother evidently did not
choose her to come downstairs, neither did she wish me to see how
things were going on in the nursery.   I had never before seen a child
like her — a child so thoroughly neglected and uncared for and all
her feeling and even intellect seemed crushed.   She did not appear
to care for anyone nor did anyone seem to care for her, and now
when she was nearly four years old, she seemed to have the greatest
difficulty in expressing her ideas, which seemed confused from never
seeming to have been talked to.

Whenever her mother spoke of her, it was always railing against
her for her ugliness, pride, want of talent and affection; and every
servant in the house seemed to make a point of coming to tell some
false or disagreeable tale of her, which her mother always listened
to and encouraged.   As to her father, he was so much occupied and
so little at home that, so far from seeing her, he seemed to forget her
existence, except when, from civility to me, he would mention her
when I began the subject.

At the time of my first visit to London the boy was about
15 months old.   He had drawn a better card than his sister in the
shape of a nurse, as she was really fond of him and took as much care
of him as if he had been her own child.   His affections were not
crushed and he was not yet old enough to have his temper or disposition spoiled by injudicious treatment.

Miss Greene's visit had not lasted very long when it was
suddenly and unpleasantly interrupted by a fierce and foolish
quarrel between her host and hostess — the first quarrel of a
kind to become increasingly frequent and one leading from a
childish disagreement over some strawberries to oaths and
tears and several days of intolerable embarrassment.   The

EMILY BULWER

From a drawing by D. Maclise, R.A., at Knebworth

visitor, unhappy but grimly conscientious, forced a reconciliation but immediately afterward left the house. Nevertheless, when in about three months Rosina begged her to return,
she did so, her longing to do something for the children
overcoming her growing dislike of the superficial glitter and
fundamental falsity of the Hertford Street ménage. Forthwith she resumed her efforts to make life tolerable for Emily:

The turning of night into day and never hearing the subject of
religion mentioned (and indeed not seeing much of the effects of it)
began to sting my conscience. I declined going out with Rosina
as often as she wished me, and when at home alone, used to steal up
to the nursery to see about the boy. After a little, upon my asking
it, Emily was brought home again, for me to try if she was so ter-
ribly unfeeling as her mother told me she was. Upon seeing more
of her, I saw that her entire disposition had been neglected and mis-
understood, and as my friends were now come to Hounslow I begged
I might take her down there with me and see what treating her quite
differently from what she had been treated at school would do. Her
mother consented.

I fear I shall not be able to give an idea of the state of this child's
mind, intellect, affections and disposition. From the total neglect
of the cultivation of any of them, they seemed as if they were dead,
and she gave us the idea of a child of a savage, who had been at the
age of nearly five, brought into civilised society. The only feeling
which seemed alive in her was fear, and horror of the school and
people she had been amongst. At first she seemed insensible to all
our efforts to please or bring forth anything, but by degrees she
began to enjoy the society of my friend's little girl "Bennie", of two
and a half years old. . . .

The first visit she paid with me to Hounslow lasted about a month,
and I had the comfort of seeing her heart and mind open to me. I
recollect the first symptom of return I ever received from her was
when I went to kiss her in her bed when asleep, as I did every night
before I went to bed myself. One night she awoke, threw her little
arms round my neck and returned my kiss.

By now secure of the affection of the child, Miss Greene
returned for a third time to Hertford Street and tackled the

more difficult aloofness of the parents.   On Rosina she made
little abiding impression:

Emily's mother would not bear her in her sight, and kept making
faces at her and railing at her all the time she was in the room.   For
this I often spoke very seriously to her and said it was both cruel
and wicked, particularly as she petted her dog so much and really
seemed fonder of it than either of her children.   They both seemed
to think it their duty to give way to the dog, and even the baby boy
used to look frightened if, whenever he touched it, it barked, as if
to make a complaint to its mistress.

This conduct in Rosina was the very fault from which she had
suffered with her own mother, and showed itself in the same manner — not in trying to amend what she saw wrong in her children,
but in railing at them to other people, neglecting them and keeping
them out of her sight. . . .   She did not like me the less for the
interest I took in the children, and was never angry with me when
I almost scolded her about them.

With the father Mary Greene was more successful:

I set my heart upon trying to remove some of the dread Emily
had for both her parents, but particularly her father.   If she heard
her father's voice upon the stairs she would run into the first room
she found open and hide herself behind the door until he passed on.
She always called him "Mr. Bulwer" as she heard the servants do.
From what I had seen in him, I felt there was good feeling if it could
be got at.   I therefore watched my opportunity and forced the little
girl to follow him one day into his dressing room with a little book
in her hand that she had been learning to read in from me.   He
received her most kindly and said to me at dinner how much she was
improved and how glad he was to see her.   I was glad to hear him
say this and sorry to observe that it did not seem to give as much
pleasure to Rosina as it did to myself.   Whilst we remained in town
. . . I always found her father pleased and ready to talk with me
about her.

At this point Miss Greene's recollections, in so far as they
concern her rescue of poor Emily, diverge from the story of
Emily's parents.   In September, 1833, Bulwer and Rosina

decided to winter in Switzerland and Italy. Their inclination harmonised for once with the devoted spinster's mission
on behalf of the neglected child. Emily went with Mary
Greene to Hounslow; her father and mother set out on the
journey which was to carry a stage further the disintegration
of their married life.

As to the origins of this journey, Miss Greene is a witness
of importance. Undeniably the grinding work of the last
three years had brought Bulwer to a point when he must either
break down or break away. Undeniably also the moment
was favourable for an interval of travel. His editorship of
the *New Monthly* had come to an end after a duration of barely
two years so that he was free of periodical slavery; *Godolphin*,
published in strict anonymity as a result of the bitter persecution of a section of the press, had considerably failed, and he
needed material and mental stimulus for fiction of a different
kind. But there were domestic as well as mental reasons for
a change of scene. To money troubles, to uneasy ambitions
and to the various other distractions of an increasingly distracted household, was now added a wife's jealousy of another
woman.

Rosina's resentment of her husband's work and her nervous
dislike of his renewed alliance with his mother had been
jealousy of a sort — but only jealousy for her own importance,
fear for her own influence over his way of life. The trouble
which now developed over the ostentatious philandering
between Bulwer and a Mrs. Stanhope was of a much more
serious and cankering kind. Miss Greene, who noticed the
half-playful beginnings of the flirtation and remonstrated with
Rosina for her careless encouragement of behaviour no less
ill-mannered for being meant in fun, describes the increasing
fervour of the affair and declares that the Bulwers' friends
became seriously concerned. She also makes no concealment
of the fact that both Bulwer and the lady acted inexcusably
toward Rosina, humiliating her in public and causing much
unnecessary scandal. Nevertheless, Rosina, who had never

herself shown a sign of coquetry since her marriage, bore her unhappiness with great patience, and only grasped at the proposal that they go abroad for several months as a likely solution of her distresses. And so, indeed, it might have been, had not Bulwer, in one of those moments of perverse cruelty to which he was occasionally and inexplicably liable, chosen at the very outset of the tour to wreck its prospects by an act of well-nigh incredible provocation. Without saying anything to Rosina, he arranged for his precious Mrs. Stanhope to meet them both on board the Channel Packet; proposed a party of three to Paris; and in that city forced his wife to go everywhere *à trois* and subjected her to such mortifications as in his insolent frivolity he might devise.

This queer and distasteful incident merits record for two reasons. In the first place, it went a long way to destroy Rosina's hitherto staunch affection for her husband and consequently to incline her to an indiscretion of her own in Naples, which brought a furious quarrel on her head and contributed a brief but bitter chapter to the tale of tragedy. In the second place, it illustrates the kind of inconsistency in Bulwer's character which makes him the despair of would-be analysts. Generally speaking, he paid what many must regard as an extravagant homage to appearances; in some respects he took more pains to conciliate the world than any man of such individual eminence would normally consider necessary; nevertheless he could flaunt this pointless and (in all probability) quite academic amourette with a rather raffish lady in the very teeth of the society with which he wished to stand well and in such a way as to cause real misery to his wife.

With this wholly unnecessary shadow on their mutual contentment, the Bulwers travelled by easy stages to Naples. He was working hard at *Rienzi* while she — who hated sightseeing and had no interest beyond those of picnics, balls and dissipations of the mob-fashionable kind — wrote bored, but in their slapstick way amusing, letters about the bad cooking, bad smells and bad inns to which her so delicate

sensibilities were exposed.   Florence was less attractive than
Cheltenham; Rome "the most barbarous and dismal place
I ever saw"; but Naples, with a luxurious hotel, a lending
library where Bulwer's very name set the old woman in charge
a-fluttering, and the snobbish bustling social life of a snobbish
bustling English colony was heaven at last.   Here for a little
while all went well.   Bulwer, in a fever of creation over his
latest idea, spent days at Pompeii, in museums, in libraries;
his wife found first distraction, then absorption, in the gallant
attentions of a Neapolitan prince.   The affair was a counterpart to that of Mrs. Stanhope — equally blatant, equally
silly, equally meaningless.   But Bulwer, when he realised
what was happening and that the heedless crowd of elegants
were smiling at his complaisance, flew into a passion, ill-
treated his wife with the violence of a lunatic and insisted
on an immediate return to England.   Early in 1834 they were
in Hertford Street again, facing the twenty-seven months of
life in common, which now remained to them.

Edward and Others

Chapter One

I

A domestic (and admittedly an unattractive) portrait of Bulwer as he was during the first half dozen years of his marriage is only half a likeness without its more public counterpart. The two together (even though they do not at all times represent the real man, so quick to assume protective colourings was his disastrous self-consciousness) do at least blend into the man he seemed; and their very differences were to this extent interdependent — that whereas treatment at the hands of outsiders was partly responsible for making him what he was at home, circumstances at home had much to do with the impression which he made on outsiders.

The Bulwer of social and literary reputation can be rather sharply distinguished from the preoccupied, inconsiderate and unbalanced Bulwer of Woodcot and Hertford Street. This is because he was temperamentally the kind of man whose public and private lives fall into separate compartments. That a natural shyness, intensified by a solitary upbringing, drove him to erect between himself and the world a façade of manner quite different from the soul behind it, has already been seen. If that had been all, there would have been nothing actually abnormal in what befell; for many men, who are at once justifiably ambitious and confident in their own capacities but sensitive to the point of timidity in the face of mockery or criticism of others, try by some pretence of being other than they are to still their tremors. But that in Bulwer's case was not all. In the first place his "outside" manner so greatly belied his natural self that, when he began to feel at ease with a new acquaintance and, dropping the assumed character, became unself-conscious, the change startled and set the stranger wondering which, if either, were sincere.[1] In the second place the "outside" manner itself failed of its purpose. It was intended to forestall criticism or to deflect it; in cases of extreme need it was expected by a sudden assumption of lofty displeasure to crush it. But it did none of these things. The frightened soul behind the long contemptuous face peeped out of the eyes and revealed the haughtiness for mere bravado. In consequence strangers were either discouraged or provoked, and their dreaded animosity, so far from being placated, was often actually increased. Some resented what they regarded as pretentiousness; others (often for reasons of their own) insisted that this artificiality was all of Bulwer, and the nearest to sincerity that he could attain.

Which last criticism was the more damaging because there were times when, for all its ill nature, it was almost true. Bulwer at recurrent moments of his life was a deliberate and impenetrable sham; but there was a reason for such desperate make-believe more cogent and more pitiable than either shyness or ill-chosen affectation. Most men of his kind, who wear a mask in public, wear it the more easily for throwing it off in private life. Sometimes indeed they make their household suffer for their troubles abroad; but seldom are they so unfortunate as to lack some unselfish and sympathetic heart on whom without reserve they can at worst work off their spleen, at best look for consolation and encourage-

[1] *Cf.* Samuel Carter Hall's *Retrospect of a Long Life* (I, 269), where is recorded the impression that Bulwer was never in earnest but acted from calculation rather than from impulse.

ment. Bulwer had no such loving, patient ally. His wife, although during these early years she was very fond of him, had not the personality or the imagination to understand his powers and share his disappointments. She liked him best and partnered him most adequately when he was gay and amusing and eager for company and display; wherefore her favourite remedy for his periods of despondency (a remedy she regularly applied until, frightened by the household's prodigality, she made her brief but soon interrupted stand for economy) was to stimulate him to some new dissipation or extravagance. This, while it lasted, certainly drove his troubles from his head but, when it was over, they returned in double force. His mother was equally unsuited to share either his enthusiasms or his despairs. Her rather rigid principles, combined with much pride of purse and family, made it impossible for her to judge her son's actions except by her own standards of dignity and propriety. If he fell below those standards, she was displeased and showed displeasure in the way most natural to her by cutting off supplies; if he rose to those standards (or even excelled them), she assessed his achievement by the amount of favour shown to it by the aristocratic world, and praised him less for what he had done than for its success.

So it was that Bulwer in his private life had no real refuge from the world, no one to whom he could turn with a certainty of receiving, if not applause, at least a sympathetic understanding. In consequence, when he came home or went to see his mother, he merely exchanged one mask for another; and so continued until his nerves became so taut that they could bear the strain no longer. Then he broke out against Rosina. But the breach with his wife, though it relieved the pain, did not remove it. Nothing could remove it altogether. To the end of his life, he was a tortured soul beneath a mask of weary dignity; and although in these early days the mask was foppishly conceited rather than dignified, the soul was already in torment. Both moods can be accounted for — the first by the huge and rapid success which his books achieved with the general public; the second by the obstinate bitterness with which in certain quarters he was critically assailed.

II

The unfinished novel of *Lionel Hastings* (to which more than one reference has been made) begins with a letter written by "Dr. Wortham of Puzzledean" to Lady Anne Hastings, mother of the schoolboy hero. In this letter the pedagogue characterises his pupil for the mother's benefit:

> You ask me my frank opinion as to his intellectual capacities and moral qualities. His abilities are incontestable. He has great quickness, a very retentive memory, and, when he pleases, a more determined application than all the other boys in the school put together. The quality most pronounced in him is energy. He has an astonishing vitality, a superabundance of life. . . .
>
> But I should want candour, my dear Madam, if I did not add that there is another side to the medal. Your son is not an amiable boy. He seems to have little or no tenderness in his nature. He forms no friendships with his schoolfellows, which I think a bad sign both of temper and disposition. He is inordinately ambitious, has much too high an opinion of himself; and, in a word, does not seem to me likely (unless a great change is effected in him) to be popular in domestic life, nor yet to stoop to that subordination or manifest that respect for others, which I have always heard to be necessary to the conduct of any young man who would rise in public life. Still, with such vigour of character he can scarcely fail to become, one day, conspicuous either for good or ill.

Remembering that "Lionel Hastings" was Bulwer himself, and that this fragment was a retrospective portrait of his own youth, drawn about thirty years after the event with full knowledge of what had transpired during the interval, one is impressed by the capacity for self-criticism which made possible so realistic and accurate a reading of the writer's own character. For alike of the triumphs and disasters of his public life the chief causes are here set down — and with a directness which shows that on the subject of his own personality at any rate Bulwer had few illusions.

"Energy and determined application"; "inordinate ambition"; "vigour of character" — here indeed are the positive qualities of the young man, who within a few years and in the teeth of violent opposition, succeeded in forcing his way to the very front rank of the writers of his day.

"Not an amiable boy"; "little or no tenderness in his nature"; "not likely to be popular" — here, conversely, are the negative qualities which that same young man undoubtedly possessed, so that his battle with the world was doubly arduous in that he had to fight not only against others but also against himself.

Bulwer's estimate of his own character was, then, impeccable so far as it went. But it can be extended on the positive side and qualified on the negative side in such a way as to prepare us more completely for the actual happenings of these first literary years.

To energy and ambition must be added a quality which Bulwer possessed to an exceptional degree, which stood him in good stead all his life, which perhaps he could not have been expected to recognise for himself. That quality was the power to gauge a coming popularity. As will be seen, he was eminently an *intelligent* writer. He always knew what sort of a book he was writing and why; and with few exceptions the books, when they came, proved to be precisely those for which the public was waiting.

To under-statement of his capacities was added over-statement of one fault at least. The heartlessness with which he charged himself was not perceptible in his treatment of unknown authors whose work he admired, nor in the unadvertised generosity with which he always responded to appeals to his charity on authors' behalf. That he should have taken no account of this ready kindliness in writing of himself was deliberate, and in its queer way of a piece with his peculiar and rather admirable self-consciousness. He was determined to impress himself on his time in his own way and in his own guise; to gain credit by charity was to pander to a mob sentimentality which he despised. Therefore no one should know of his charity; and if the world were so crass as to judge him for a selfish *arriviste*, let it so judge. Thus with a sort of defiant pride he chose to conceal what the herd could most easily applaud.

III

It is very important, when approaching the début of Bulwer as a novelist and publicist, to remember his early connection with the Benthamite group which, under the leadership of the two Mills and Doctor Bowning, had started the *Westminster Review* in 1824. Bentham's political and ethical theories, applied to the conditions of the time, naturally produced among their admirers a state of mind which to the Conservatives of the day seemed dangerously Radical. "The greatest happiness of the greatest number" (the slogan of what came to be known as "Utilitarian" philosophy), was in itself a war cry for the many as against the few. Treatises on Penal and Parliamentary Reform gave practical direction to a general liberal tendency, and by the time the *Westminster Review* came into being its promoters were avowedly working for changes in constitution and society which may well have appeared revolutionary to supporters of established things.

Although during the middle twenties Bulwer was too young and obscure to take a direct part in the propagandist activities of the *Westminster Review* writers, he was sufficiently known to be of their party for the crime to be brought up against him by their opponents as soon as he himself appeared as an author and became a target for criticism. In those days, not only was opinion swayed to a degree difficult to imagine by the few outstanding monthly and quarterly magazines, but political partisanship was so strong that it pervaded every branch of journalistic comment. Social behaviour, literary work, even the qualities of poetry and painting, were liable to be appraised on lines of political likes or dislikes, and quite apart from their intrinsic virtues or vices. In consequence book reviews of the twenties — and the personalities which perpetually went with them — were in most cases dictated by the party predilections of the critics vis-à-vis the authors; and an author could as little hope for justice in a paper of political views different from his own as he would expect hostility from critics to whose colour he belonged. The situation was further complicated — that is to say unbiased criticism of literature was still further hindered — by the establishment during the teens of purely literary magazines belonging to important publishers. The interests of a political party were here substituted (or maybe reinforced) by the interests of a commercial publisher; and care was taken that the best reviews were given to those books whose sale would be to the profit of the paper's owner.

To the venal mercies of party critics, therefore, Bulwer, like every other new writer, was doomed to be delivered; and because, despite anonymous authorship, his identity was very soon discovered and he was known to be involved with the Reform agitation and its attendant doctrines, he became at once and automatically a victim of Tory assault. Further, because his publisher was the notorious Colburn, whose dramatic rise to prominence and pioneer methods of advertisement had set all rivals raging, his books became odious to other publishers, whose minions were commanded to damage them in any way possible.

To this point his reception by the critics was only what was to be expected. But a personal *méchanceté* (due probably to inexperience and the heady vanity of youth) gave it a peculiar turn, and he succeeded, while provoking an almost hysterical hostility from his opponents, also in alienating — or at any rate embarrassing — his friends. Despite his genuine radicalism (and it is certain that he was sincerely a reformer alike on practical and humanitarian grounds) he assumed the pose of a young man of exaggerated fashion. He lived showily and extravagantly; he carried himself with hauteur, talked a deal of breeding and family, and sneered openly at Grub street hacks and persons who pretended to write of the *ton* but could not themselves claim to be gentlemen. Such behaviour sat oddly on a professed democrat; and while it gave his enemies admirable material for satire and denunciation, it also annoyed many persons of his own party, who set great store by appearances and were not convinced that the outward affectations of a brilliant young man could be wholly detached from his inner convictions.

Exposed, therefore, to the hostility of political opponents and of the supporters of rival publishers, to the suspicious jealousy of many who might have been his friends; to the angry contempt of his social equals who feared or disliked his opinions — his public career could hardly have been a tranquil one, however conciliatory he had tried to be and however little, in getting his share of public favour, he had trodden on the toes of his competitors. He was not at all conciliatory; and his success was swift and tremendous and utterly a flouting of the critical pundits of the day. As a result he was more belaboured and belibelled than almost any author of his eminence has ever been; and the history of his writing life has a peculiar dramatic quality of its own, arising from the persistent, unscrupulous brutality of his critics and the strange alternations of contempt, sorrowful dignity, bitter counterattack, and almost hysterical appeals for justice or for consolation which composed his policy of self-defence.

Chapter Two

Falkland — Pelham — *Its readability, wit and underlying thought-fulness* — *Carlyle on* Pelham — *Bulwer and the Carlyles* — *J. G. Lockhart and* Pelham — *Character of Lockhart* — *Bulwer* versus *Lockhart* — *Bulwer as controversialist* — *Thomas Campbell* — *Isaac Disraeli*

I

Neither trouble nor triumph came at the very outset. *Falkland*, a single-volume tale published anonymously in March, 1827, attracted virtually no attention among critics or public, but shocked those of the author's intimates who read it. Miss Greene's opinion has already been quoted; Mrs. Bulwer-Lytton, while "unable to express her astonishment at the really wonderful power of her son's imagination", and comparing his "exquisite delineation of character to a beautiful portrait by one of our old masters", deplored the two final pages for their lack of the spirit of Christianity, and implied that, if she had seen the manuscript before it was printed, the morality of the whole would have been vastly improved. Lady Blessington, on the other hand, who read the book during the Paris revolution of 1830, was so enthralled that she hardly heard the bullets "striking against the walls of my dwelling"; but Lady Blessington made this statement some while after the event and was always a person of kindly reminiscence. The only printed contemporary comment of interest is a footnote in Robert Montgomery's already cited satire, *The Age Reviewed* (1827). Speaking of novel-reading and its evil influence the poet says:

Since writing the above a novel called *Falkland* has made its appearance. This work is a complete illustration of all that I have said on the baneful effect of indiscriminate novel-reading. Put *Falkland* into the hands of any young person of common mind, and he will not fail to be intoxicated with the charms of adultery. There is a most romantic scene in it — a naughty married lady and gentleman commit a terrible *faux pas* under a tree. We are told, too, that just at the awful moment the thunders rolled, the rain drops pattered and then we have . . . .

Mr. Montgomery was easily thrilled. The scene referred to (pp. 213–214 of the first edition) is admirable Bulwerese, but very temperate depravity. Similarly, the final pages which horrified Mrs. Bulwer-Lytton with their heathenism merely venture a doubt in the dying hero's mind as to whether he is certain of a future life — a doubt which Bulwer himself certainly felt and expressed in one of his more serious love letters to Rosina, written in 1826.[1] But, however slight the provocation, *Falkland* not only impressed its few readers as a work of loose and infidel tendency, but later took its place in the general indictment of Bulwer, drawn up and repeated *ad nauseam* by his enemies, as an immoral writer. An open letter to him signed "Robin Roughead" and published in *Fraser's Magazine* (December, 1831) contains the following:

For works in the sentimental line, pilfer the indecency from Faublas, the reflections from Rochefoucauld and the incidents from Harriet Wilson — and you have a *Falkland* off hand.

It is characteristic that Bulwer himself should quickly have accepted the unpopularity of *Falkland* and wasted no pains over its defence. In 1829 that rather trivial æsthete, Alaric A. Watts, who edited the *Literary Souvenir*, and in those days set up as an arbiter of taste, seems to have referred to *Falkland* with moral disapprobation. At any rate Bulwer wrote to him on July 5 from the Athenaeum:

[1] *Cf. Letters of the late Lord Lytton to his wife*, p. 45.

I cannot feel sore at any one for expressing disapprobation of the tendency of a work so generally attacked as *Falkland*. . . . An author is often the worst judge of the moral spirit of his own works. It may easily be permitted to a very young man to make a little mistake on this score; and all that I ask of my friends is this — to believe that the author did not mean to write an immoral book.[1]

Less than a year later, in the Dedicatory Epistle to *Paul Clifford* (April, 1830) he wrote:

When I speak of my *fourth* novel, I omit *Falkland* from the number, an early and crude attempt which I have never hitherto owned — beyond my own small circle of friends — and which I should not now speak of were it not generally known to be mine.

Finally, in a preface specially written for the 1835 edition of *Pelham*, he disposed once and for all (to his own satisfaction) of the luckless book:

The effect which the composition of *Falkland* produced upon my mind was exactly similar to that which (if I may reverently quote so illustrious an example) Goethe informs us the writing of Werther produced upon his own. I had rid my bosom of the perilous stuff; I had confessed my sins and was absolved. I could return to real life and its wholesome objects.

This condescending relegation of *Falkland* to the limbo of well-meant but forgotten things suited Bulwer's convenience when in the full tide of his mid-thirties' popularity. But actually he as much under-rated the book's "oneness" with his general development as its outraged critics exaggerated its moral failings. *Falkland*, like most first novels by clever young men, is in many ways a silly little book; but at least its silliness is Bulwer's silliness and not any one else's. Indeed it is much more completely its author in embryo than is usually the fledgling fiction of an afterward famous novelist. Its epistolary form, its strong element of sensi-

[1] *Alaric Watts: A Narrative of His Life by his son.* 2 vols. Bentley. 1884. II, 39-40.

bility, and the emphasis laid on the worthlessness of worldly things in comparison with natural simplicities, are crude but unmistakable signs that his abiding interest in the novel-writing and philosophy of the late eighteenth century had already taken hold of him. Also, though as time went on the direct influence of Rousseau was tempered in his mind by other more serene philosophies, the mark left on *Falkland* by his half-reluctant absorption in the *Confessions* is a recognisable mark which re-appears in several of the later books. Finally, during the writing of *Falkland* (it was begun at Cambridge in 1824 and re-cast at Versailles in 1826) he made gradual but enthusiastic acquaintance with the works of Richardson, Fielding and Smollett, with *Caleb Williams* and *St. Leon;* and with the novels of Ann Radcliffe. All of these had a share in his first book, but the last named an especially important one. *Falkland* shows the prentice attempts at Gothistic use of landscape, at the employment of lurid natural effects to heighten emotional or dramatic situations, of one who was never to lose a fondness for the terror motif in fiction.

Wherefore, although posterity may not read *Falkland* with great pleasure, the book cannot be brushed aside as a mere youthful indiscretion. It should rather be prized for evidence as good as any we possess that a purposeful and consistent mind lay behind the long, varied, but fundamentally controlled list of Bulwer's fictions, and was definitely, if fumblingly, active from the very first moment of his novel-writing life.

II

Between the appearance of *Falkland* and the publication of his first three-volume novel on May 10, 1828, Bulwer was too busy getting married and settling into his house in Oxfordshire to have time for contacts with the outside world. A few letters, mostly to Mrs. Cunningham, mix praises of Rosina with references to current literature. Gossip attributes *Vivian Grey* to Edward Gibbon Wakefield [1] and Bulwer's comment is tritely malicious: "When a man has committed bad actions all his life it is certainly just possible that his retirement may be very well calculated for writing bad books." (April 8, 1828.) He greatly over-rates the poetry of L. E. L., and expresses the opinions of the novels *Herbert Lacy* and *Almacks Revisited*, which have already been quoted.[2] In the main, however, his extra-domestic energy was given to the launching of *Pelham or the Adventures of a Gentleman*. In this connection — and as evidence of Colburn's personal genius for spotting best sellers — an interesting story is told. Shoberl, Colburn's chief reader, declared the manuscript worthless; Ollier, next consulted, was cool enough but thought there was something in the book and recommended Colburn to glance at it himself; the publisher turned the pages rapidly, called his advisers to his room and told them *Pelham* would be the book of the year.

Which indeed it was; though not immediately. For some weeks after publication it hung fire. It was strictly anonymous, contained neither preface nor dedication, and carried no mention whatsoever of *Falkland*, even among the advertisements at the end of the second volume. It started, therefore, as completely from scratch as had *Vivian Grey*, and somewhat on the plan adopted for *Vivian Grey* was success ultimately achieved. Colburn knew his business so well that once *Pelham* had (in Bulwer's phrase) "begun to take", it took thoroughly. The story was reprinted and parodied [3]; the name of the hero became not only an alternative one for his creator but an accepted nickname for a fast

---

[1] This remarkable person, who in 1816 had eloped with a ward in Chancery and had recently gone to gaol for an alleged attempt to abduct yet another heiress, was to become one of the outstanding figures in British Colonial history. Of his share in Lord Durham's administration of Canada and subsequent Report mention is made on pp. 342–346. Of the various books devoted to his life and personality the most convenient for general reference is *The Amazing Career of Edward Gibbons Wakefield* by Harrap (London, 1928).

[2] *Cf.* p. 122.

[3] *E.g. Pelham: Second Series*, published in *The Age* October 11 and October 18, 1829.

young man upon town,[1] and henceforward the fashionable colour for evening coats was black instead of plum or blue.[2]

Pelham is one of the easiest of Bulwer's novels for the nineteen-thirties to read with immediate enjoyment. A leading critic has recently declared it "as witty as a Disraeli novel";[3] and in some respects the wit is more modern because more nonchalant, and the satire more easily relished because the phenomena satirised are more obviously with us. Of course, to some extent the book dates. It has an element of the rather cheap smartness characteristic of fledgling genius at any time, and particularly apt to cloy even a short while after the event. There are a few interpolations and mannerisms conventional to the fiction of the day, and to us unfamiliar or *fade*. Here is a persistence of Gothic romance — notably in the agreeable melancholy of two lovers separated by mystery; in the night ramble of Pelham and his friends through London; in the vivid description of the murder of Tyrell and the midnight ride from Newmarket through rain and darkness. Finally, the fashionable world of the eighteen-twenties, being less subservient to the insolent gaiety of very young people than their better disciplined descendants, welcomed the novel with a horrified delight of which the secret has been lost. But, after making due allowance for the derivativeness and shrillness inevitable to the author's age, *Pelham*, alike in characterisation and incidental comment, is a shrewd and amusing book. The hero is neither a Werter not a clean-limbed mother's boy; he goes through a crowded social life laughing at everything and everybody, and making as much fun of

---

[1] An example of the latter use occurs in No. 2 of *The Devil in London* (one of the numerous satirical and often scurrilous sheets which lived their brief lives between 1830 and 1836). Under date March 7, 1832, is reported as fashionable intelligence the fact that "Henry Pelham, Robert Peel, John Scott and an 'Earnest'" had been arrested in a raid on a brothel in Charles Street. Of the use of the name as a somewhat offensive substitute for Bulwer's own may be noted Lord Alvanley's bon mot — that "Mr. Pelham's electioneering adventures were in any event not the 'Adventures of a Gentleman.'"

[2] *Cf.* Lytton. I, 348.

[3] Desmond MacCarthy in the *New Statesman*, December 1, 1928.

Pelham discovers the body of Sir John Tyrrell.

CONTEMPORARY ILLUSTRATION
FROM *PELHAM*

himself as of any one else. It contains plenty of period furnishing in the houses, clothes and snobberies of the crowded characters. There are portraits of the Salisburys at Hatfield; of Lord Mount Edgecumbe; and of course of Theodore Hook, who appears in nearly every social novel of the time. There are views on Shelley's poetry and Hope's novel *Anastasius* and the painting of Paul Veronese. There are deliberate exaggerations of certain fopperies made famous by Beau Brummell, the latter's two glove-makers becoming Pelham's three; while the languid enquiry where to change horses when dining anywhere outside the immediate area of fashionable London was a mere transcription of one of Brummell's traditional jokes. There are fragments of the jargon known as "flask" and other memories of Bulwer's encounter with the thief during his Long Vacation tour of four years before. The whole is peppered with epigrams and sly malicious jokes, which shows signs not only that critical young men found much the same material for criticism then as now, but that this particular critical young man was considerably in advance of his time in his envisaging of established institutions. He has views, for example, about the "Public School System":

"I was in the head class when I left Eton. As I was reckoned an uncommonly well-educated boy, it may not be ungratifying to admirers of the present system of education to recall what I then knew. I could make twenty Latin verses in half an hour; I could construe without an English translation all the easy Latin authors, and many of the difficult ones with it; I could *read* Greek fluently and even translate it through the medium of a Latin version at the bottom of the page. I was thought exceedingly clever, for I had only been eight years acquiring all this fund of information which I had entirely forgotten before I was five and twenty. As I was never taught a syllable of English during this period; as when I once attempted to read Pope's poems out of school hours I was laughed at and called a sap; as, whatever schoolmasters may think to the contrary, one learns nothing now-adays by inspiration — so of everything which relates to English literature, English laws and English history (with the exception of the story of Queen Elizabeth and Lord Essex) . . . I was at the age of eighteen, when I left Eton, in the profoundest ignorance."

He has a talent for types and topicalities:

"Lord Vincent was one of those persons who have been 'promising young men' all their lives; who go down into the country for six weeks every session to cram an impromptu reply; and who always have a work in the press which is never to be published." . . .

"Nothing, my dear sir, is like a liaison with a woman of celebrity. In marriage a man lowers a woman to his own rank; in an *affaire de cœur* he raises himself to hers."

Finally, his easy mastery of readable English may be shown by two pieces of rapid writing, of a kind very unusual at the time. The first is virtually the novel's opening:

Vulgar people know nothing of the necessaries required in good society and the credit they give is as short as their pedigree. Six years after my birth there was an execution in our house. My mother was just setting off on a visit to the Duchess of D——; she declared it was impossible to go without her diamonds. The chief of the bailiffs declared it was impossible to trust them out of his sight. The matter was compromised — the bailiff went with my mother and was introduced as my tutor. . . . At the end of the week the diamonds went to the jewellers and Lady Frances wore paste.

The second occurs halfway through the third volume and begins a chapter:

What with the anxiety and uncertainty of my political prospects, the continued dissipation in which I lived and above all, the unpropitious state of my *belle passion*, my health gave way; my appetite forsook me — my sleep failed me — a wrinkle settled itself under my left eye and my mother declared I should have no chance with an heiress. All these circumstances together were not without their weight.   So I set out one morning to Hampton Court (with a volume of Bishop Berkeley and a bottle of wrinkle water) for the benefit of the country air.

In addition to its gaiety and dash, *Pelham* has qualities of a more serious kind.   Beneath the glitter is the metal of solid thought and serious conviction; and undoubtedly part of the hostility which, simultaneously with the applause, was provoked by the novel was due to an uneasy feeling in the minds of Tory critics that here was no mere gifted trifler but a young man who, for all his affected foppery, meant business and business of a subversive kind.   About the middle of the second volume is a political discussion between Pelham and the foolish Vincent:

Pelham (says Vincent) I have something of importance on my mind which I wish to discuss with you; but let me entreat you to lay aside your natural levity.

My lord (replies Pelham, flippant as ever) there is in your words a depth and solemnity which pierce me through one of N's best stuffed coats, even to the very heart.   Let me ring for my poodle and some *eau de Cologne* and I will hear you as you desire.

Vincent proceeds to preach political discretion; warns his friend against houses tainted with democracy; and finally offers him a place in a new ministry to be formed by a new and super-selfish party led by himself and "Lords Lincoln and Lesborough."   But Pelham rejects the overture with scorn:

I would sooner feed my poodle on paunch and liver instead of cream and fricassee than be an instrument in the hands of men like Lincoln and Lesborough; who talk much, who perform nothing; who join ignorance of every principle of legislation to indifference for every benefit to the people — who level upwards and trample downwards. . . .

It did not require much penetration for the opponents of reform to read between the lines of this (and similar) pseudo-mocking scenes, and to understand that an enemy had appeared, a young man with the manners and freedom of the aristocracy but with the ideals — or at any rate with the opportunism to voice the ideals — of an already restless populace. Their alarm was doubtless intensified by the very favourable review of the novel which appeared in the radical *Examiner*, a paper little inclined to the praise of modish fiction and obviously in this case conscious of a friend behind the Pelhamism.[1] The Tory journalists, therefore, marked down their prey for dangerous; and, as soon as his identity was clear, began a counter-propaganda which, once started, quickly developed the bitterness of angry fear.

In their rather disingenuous campaign they were helped by the solemnly censorious, some of whom so far forgot their own principles as to let a momentary irritation with Bulwer's frivolity drive them into unnatural alliance with reaction. Of those well-meaning but slow-witted persons skilful use was made by Tory ingenuity, and of the strange bedfellows brought together in hostility to Bulwer few were stranger than Thomas Carlyle and the Tory bravos of *Fraser's Magazine*. In Chapter X of Book II of *Sartor Resartus* ("The Dandiacal Body") Carlyle, somewhat owlishly, takes every remark of "Henry Pelham's" as literally and seriously meant, and indulges in ponderous sarcasm at the expense of what never existed at all.

[1] "In the order of Novels of Fashionable Life we never expected to see a production of the talent and utility of *Pelham*, which immeasurably excels all other performances of the same genus. It is written by a man who can be both witty and wise, a just and well-instructed thinker, a shrewd and exact observer, carrying with his lightest observation a substratum of sound philosophy. His book presents a section of society, exhibiting at a glance things from the surface to the core; and the great benefit we hope from it is, that by its piquant exposures it will lead persons to reflect who would resist any more laboured and direct assaults of reason. We have no hesitation in affirming that of all the novel-writers of the present day, the author of *Pelham* is the best moralist — perhaps we ought to say the only moralist, in the scientific sense of the word."

The Examiner, founded by Leigh Hunt in 1808, passed into other hands in 1825. The review of *Pelham* was probably written by Albany Fonblanque, who became principal contributor to the paper in 1826 and editor in 1830. In later years Bulwer's connection with the *Examiner* became a close one through his friendship with John Forster, but at this early date he was unacquainted with its personnel and the publication of such a review as the one quoted in a paper both advanced and serious, could not fail to attract attention by its unexpectedness.

Among the new sects of England one of the most notable is that of the Dandies. . . . They have their Temples, whereof the chief, as the Jewish Temple did, stands in their Metropolis and is named Almacks, a word of uncertain etymology. Nor are sacred books wanting to the sect; these they call Fashionable Novels. Of such sacred books I, not without expense, procured myself some samples and in hope of true insight and with the zeal which beseems an Inquirer into Clothes, set to interpret and study them. But wholly to no purpose . . . that tough faculty of reading for which the world will not refuse me credit, was here for the first time foiled and set at nought. In vain that I summoned my whole energies and did my very utmost; at the end of some short space I was uniformly seized with not so much what I can call a drumming in my ears as a kind of infinite insufferable Jews-harping and scrannel-piping there; to which the frightfullest species of magnetic sleep soon supervened.

The narrator goes on to tell how he stumbled by chance on some stray sheets from a magazine containing "a dissertation on fashionable novels", which directed itself "not without asperity against some to me unknown individual named Pelham who seems to be a mystagogue and leading teacher and preacher to the sect." [1]

Further on in *Sartor Resartus* is a quotation from what Carlyle calls the preface to *Devereux* (but is really the preface to *The Disowned*), which preface one would have thought almost too obviously satirical. But the critic's gravity is undisturbed, and the possibility of a novelist making fun of himself wholly unenvisaged.

This attack, written in 1830 but not published until the August, 1834, number of *Fraser's Magazine*, may be deplored as part of the prejudice against Bulwer to which both Carlyle and his wife for too long succumbed. Without giving a

---

[1] The "dissertation" referred to is either the article on Fashionable Novels generally, or the fierce attack on Bulwer's novels in particular, published in the April and June numbers of *Fraser's Magazine* for 1830. Both articles have been attributed to Carlyle himself. (*Cf.* Mr. I. W. Dyer's Carlyle Bibliography, published in Portland, Maine, in 1928, and a letter from Mr. F. A. S. Barrett in the *Times Literary Supplement*, January 20, 1929.)

possible understanding a chance (and the two men, when at
last they contrived to overlook each other's mannerisms,
found that they had much in common), Carlyle built up
between himself and one of the few contemporaries who at
this early date frankly recognised his intellectual distinction,
a barrier of brusque contempt which it needed all his victim's
courage to remove. "A poor fribble" was one of his comments on Bulwer, while Mrs. Carlyle called him a "lanthorn-
jawed quack." To the editor of the *Edinburgh*, Carlyle wrote
urging that "the Pelham and Devereux manufacture (of
fashionable novels) ought to be extinguished"; and when he
failed to get a commission as extinguisher, found a more complacent opening in *Fraser's*. When from time to time Bulwer
made overtures of reconciliation, they were obstinately rejected. When John Stuart Mill urged on Carlyle the importance of reading *England and the English*, the latter rather
grudgingly agreed to do so, remarking that "Bulwer is an
honest kind of creature though none of the strongest", and
declaring a little later, after reading the book: "The astonishing thing is the contrast of the man and his enterprise."
Gradually, however, matters improved, and by 1840 the
two were comparatively intimate; but the balance of obliga-
tion remained to Bulwer's credit, for as long ago as January, 1832, Carlyle owed to him the idea of writing about
Frederick the Great.[1]

It does not seem that Bulwer ever felt a grudge against this
boorish but distinguished antagonist. With all his over-
sensitive vanity he had a real respect for intellect and could
forgive a man for wounding him, provided the man himself
were in his own right a person of achievement. With lesser
assailants, however — and particularly with those who made
personal use of party spite or sheltered behind a position of
power or critical anonymity — he did not so easily make
peace. Of this class was John Gibson Lockhart, son-in-law
of Sir Walter Scott, at one time co-editor with "Christopher

---

[1] D. A. Wilson. *Carlyle to the French Revolution*, p. 268.

North" of *Blackwood's Magazine* and since 1825 editor of the
Tory *Quarterly Review*.

Lockhart took the field early against *Pelham* and its author.
His hostility seems to have been quite spontaneous. It was
perhaps provoked in part by Bulwer's association with the
Westminster Review, which had from the beginning been anti-
Scotch and pugnaciously critical of *Blackwood's Magazine*,
but it had no direct stimulus from the actual controllers of
Maga, whose first reference to Bulwer was in the instalment
of *Noctes Ambrosianae* for March, 1829, and perfectly reasonable
in tone. All the stranger therefore its sudden waspishness.
Sir Walter, a great enough man to view kindly all intelligent
efforts by new writers, wrote to Lockhart in the autumn of
1828:

Pray who writes *Pelham?* I found it very interesting; the light
is easy and gentleman-like, the dark very grand and sombrous.
There are great improbabilities, but what can a poor devil do?
There is, I am sorry to say, a slang tone of immorality which is
immoral.

To which Lockhart replied:

Pelham is writ by a Mr. Bulwer, a Norfolk squire and a horrid
puppy. I have not read the book from disliking the author; but
shall do so since you approve it.[1]

There must have been other beside party reasons for Lockhart's avowedly personal dislike for a man whom, so far as
is known, he had not met, who was himself so far unsuspicious
of possible enmity.[2]

What those further reasons were can only be deduced from
our knowledge of the man's character — a character which
even his official biographer cannot always extenuate. Harold
Nicolson has called him a "sexless Antinöus"; but he was
rather an Antinöus whose sex impulses were soured by van-

[1] *Life and Letters of J. G. Lockhart.* By Andrew Lang. 2 vols. London. 1897.
II, 37.
[2] *Cf.* Lytton. I, 212.

ity into jealous malignity. It is probable that his persistent hostility to Bulwer had its origin in the instinctive enmity of a handsome *littérateur* for a dangerous rival. In Edinburgh, and even in London, before Bulwer's emergence, Lockhart had been the beau of the literary world. On the one hand mere fashionables however handsome, on the other intellectuals less good-looking than himself, could not trouble his serenity nor challenge his self-esteem. But when a man appeared whose physical and mental distinction threatened to outdo his own, he turned, almost despite himself, to plans for ruining his possible competitor. As will be seen, these plans did not fully mature; but if Bulwer had not proved something of a Tartar himself, the preliminary campaign of sneers and covert insolence might well have culminated in an "extinguishing" article in the *Quarterly* on the lines of that administered to Harriet Martineau.[1] Bulwer, however, was more of a match for an editorial bully than was a deaf blue-stocking, and Lockhart was to learn a quick lesson, if not in decent manners, at least in discretion.

Gradually, and from the gossip of acquaintances, Bulwer came to realise the identity of his new adversary. At first counter-action was difficult because, being in the weak position of any named individual who has become a target for anonymous sharp-shooting, he had to wait on an opportunity for self-defence. As a sort of prelude to hostilities he introduced a series of sarcastic references to Scots in general and to Scotch critics in particular into the dedicatory letter prefixed to *Paul Clifford*, combined with an odd compliment to "the impassioned boldness" of *Adam Blair*, following these up with the generalised insult to Scotland which was the character of MacGrawler. But his first real chance of aggression came when he assumed the editorship of the *New Monthly Magazine* in the late autumn of 1831. He himself scorned to use editorial anonymity, avowing quite openly in the second issue for which he was responsible the personality of the man in

---

[1] *Quarterly Review.* April, 1833, and Harriet Martineau's *Autobiography.* Vol. I.

charge. This done, and therefore to all intents over his own signature, he began in February, 1832, his campaign against the *Quarterly*. In a leader he replied to an article in Lockhart's paper on "The Progress of Misgovernment." The criticism was general, directed against the *Quarterly* and its political policy, and indeed merely countered a conventional party assault on the Grey administration by an equally conventional defence of ministers (and incidentally of Reform). In his April number he tried a different tack and charged a *Quarterly* reviewer with falsifying history in a paper on the Revolutions of 1640 and 1830.[1] Still, however, the squabble was a party squabble and on a party theme. But his coattrailing had its effect. Lockhart was tempted, and in his December number introduced into a review of Morier's *Zohrab the Hostage* a few paragraphs of rather offensive criticism of Bulwer's novels and particularly of *Devereux* and *Paul Clifford*. The words were not in themselves insolent; but the tone of lofty admonition and the suggestion that Bulwer was a clumsy fabricator of outworn modes were calculated to infuriate their victim. At once the battle became a duel between two antipathetic and angry men, and in the January number of *The New Monthly* Bulwer went for his adversary in earnest.

Macready in the Garrick Club on New Year's Day 1833, read "Bulwer's violent letter in reply to the impertinences of Lockhart" and wrote in his diary: "How much precious tranquillity of heart and mind is lost by the inability of man to let these feeble injuries and perishable insults die of themselves." [2]

The sentiment is an admirable one, but has come to be applied a little unfairly to all Bulwer's counter-offensives against his many critics. The conventional view that he was over-ready to take public offence and would have been wiser to bear all attacks in silence, hardly appreciates — or

[1] *The Wilful Misstatements of the Quarterly Review.*
[2] *Diaries of William Charles Macready.* Ed. William Toynbee. 2 vols. 1912. I, p. 1.

so it would appear — the extreme provocation which was continually given; the rather remarkable forbearance which up to a point he often showed, or (this is important) his own exceptional talent for controversial writing. It is not easy for a man who knows that he can out-pamphleteer his enemies to restrain himself from paying insults in something better than their own coin; nor to decide whether, in a contest of wits involving his personal *amour propre*, there is not more satisfaction in hitting back and preparing to be hit again, than in hoping by patient humility to secure future peace.

A fair-minded and careful survey of Bulwer's literary polemics, while showing that he often imagined a greater hostility than was really there and more frequently chose the wrong than the right moment for his counter-attacks, hardly supports the theory that he was over-ready in retaliation. Not only did he really suffer more disingenuous and ignoble persecution than any writer of his time, but toward nearly every group of tormentors he acted at first with forbearance and (if, later on, reconciliation were possible) at last with magnanimity. Certainly when he did break out, he broke out with much effect, being (as has been said) a controversialist of unusual power; but if a balance be struck between him and the various individual and corporate antagonists with whom at one time or another he came into collision, endurance and avoidance of personalities will be found to have been greater on his side, provocation and impertinence on theirs.[1]

The "Letter to the Editor of the *Quarterly Review*"[2] which although it pained poor Macready, is an agreeable exercise in contumely. The *Quarterly*, which had specialised for years in hostile criticism of the most offensive kind, was given a

---

[1] This does not of course apply to the one or two outbreaks of crusading anger to which he yielded. His attack on Westmacott (see pp. 306, 307) was only indirectly provoked, and was made partly for the general advantage of the community and partly out of loyalty to a friend.

[2] *New Monthly*, January, 1833. Reprinted in an unauthorised collection of the Critical and Miscellaneous Writings of Sir E. Lytton Bulwer. Philadelphia. 1841.

taste of its own physic, and though those concerned liked it little enough, they had no reasonable ground for complaint. That Lockhart deeply resented the well-merited mockery of his syntax; the contemptuous reference to his rise to eminence on the broad back of his father-in-law; the exposure of the log-rolling uses to which in the interests of its publisher-proprietor, the *Quarterly*, as much as any of its competitors, was ingeniously and hypocritically put may be taken for certain, especially if (as is argued below)[1] a later anonymous attack on Bulwer in *Fraser's Magazine* may be attributed to him. But although he came to be generally regarded as one of Bulwer's enemies, he was characteristically careful to avoid further public depreciation of so dangerous an opponent and the *Quarterly* itself during the next few years left Bulwer severely alone.

The enmity between the two men was never wholly removed. Lang prints an undated invitation to dinner sent by Bulwer with characteristic conciliation, to "dear Mr. Lockhart", and suggesting forgiveness for "an act of petulance in my youth." This was probably written in the early 'forties. The same biographer records (still without date) an actual meeting at Sir Robert Murchison's and a "coldness" on Bulwer's part. The only other chronicled contact between the two was at a dinner in 1853 where Lockhart had Bulwer on one side of him and Forster on the other. Assuming, therefore, that the two men were mutually distasteful to each other, one may set it definitely to Bulwer's credit that when in 1838 the last volume of the *Life of Scott* appeared and he, at that moment editor of the *Monthly Chronicle*, had a fine opportunity for disconcerting his opponent by jarring criticism at the moment of his chief bid for fame, he held his hand. Out of respect for Scott, and because he recognised the merit of a first-rate biography, he wrote with restraint and fairness, only permitting himself in memory of the part this single sentence:

[1] *Cf.* pp. 259–260.

Regarded as a composition this biography is not exempt from these blemishes of style and construction which injure most of the writings by the same author; and are the more remarkable from Mr. Lockhart's reputed scholarship and station in critical literature.[1]

But while *Pelham*, and even more the success of *Pelham*, first roused against Bulwer the unremitting critical hostility from which he was to suffer, the book and its popularity brought him new friends and a great and profitable reputation.

An intimacy with Thomas Campbell arose naturally enough. Colburn would obviously desire to bring together his latest best-seller and his eminent, if irregular, editor. He did so, and the introduction was very successful. Campbell found in the excitable youth just the type of vivid, quickly satirical and daringly outspoken protégé with whom he liked to spend convivial hours. Bulwer was still young enough to relish the rather squalid Bohemianism of the old poet and retained an amusing memory of evenings with Campbell which, years afterward, he retailed in a letter to a friend:

I wish I could repeat Campbell's conversation, though I regret to say that the wittiest part of it was somewhat profane. He suggested the idea of Le Bon Dieu coming to London to sell the copyright of the Bible and going the round of the publishers. He hit off Longman wonderfully. Longman observed to his "Lordship"

---

[1] Lockhart's quality as critic and stylist has provoked commentators to various opinions. Disraeli in a letter to Lady Blessington spoke scornfully of the man's confused and commonplace style ; but Disraeli had reason to be spiteful, remembering the haughty reception given him by Lockhart when he first visited Scotland to disclose Murray's plans for *The Representative* newspaper. Professor Saintsbury has defended Lockhart warmly against his detractors, praising him with characteristic felicity of phrase for his " faculty of writing like a gentleman without writing like a mere gentleman." Nevertheless, and despite a general inclination to follow Professor Saintsbury wheresoever he may lead, I confess to an inability to respect Lockhart either as a writer or as a man. It is not possible to study in detail his literary and personal activities as a contributor to *Blackwood's* and to *Fraser's* magazines and as editor of *The Quarterly* without coming in his general regard to the conclusions brilliantly and trenchantly expressed by Mr. Donald Carswell on pp. 209-261 of his book, *Sir Walter* (London, 1930), also Mrs. Jameson's *Diary of an Ennuyée* (London, 1826) on pp. 74-76 of which this very copy is, curiously enough, described and quotations given from Byron's marginal notes.

that the copyright was of late years deteriorated in value, hazardous to publish, but might still do for a school book; he would be very happy to print it at his Lordship's expense on commission.

Then Le Bon Dieu goes to Colburn. Colburn does not dispute the general merit of the work but doubts whether it will take with the fashionable world. He suggests a few alterations of high life — the manger and the fisherman are decidedly low — and a few piquant anecdotes about the court of King Herod.

Another idea full of humour he started, which though not profane was a little obscene. He supposed that men and women changed their sexes and imagined himself and other clever men to be women. Finally, he decided that he himself should have been a great whore. The peculiarity of his talk that night was riotous drollery and fun, yet such as only a man of a poet's rich imagination could invent.

Very different, more measured and even more flattering, was the kindness shown to the young novelist by Isaac Disraeli. To the sweet-natured serenity of this very remarkable old man, Bulwer owed much quiet and thoughtful teaching. He had long before this date become one of Disraeli's unknown admirers after reading the enlarged edition of *An Essay on the Literary Character* (first issued in 1795), which appeared in 1818 under the title *The Literary Character illustrated by the History of Men of Genius*. The fact (it is stated in the preface to the book) that a sight of Byron's annotated copy of the original issue had impelled Isaac Disraeli to undertake an enlarged and re-written edition,[1] doubtless recommended the work in the first instance to the youth whose undergraduate days were passed under an intense Byronic stimulus; but there was so much in Disraeli's argument to appeal to Bulwer's individual mentality that his enthusiasm outlasted his Byronism and became a part of his own literary training. The influence of this book (and, though in less degree, of others by the same author) on his own habit of thought is continuously evident. The Fourth Book of *England and the English* (1833) — "View

---

[1] *Cf. Byron's Letters and Journals* (Ed. Prothero). IV, 274; also Monypenny's *Life of Disraeli.* I, 14, *Note.*

of the Intellectual Spirit of the Time'' — is inscribed to Isaac
Disraeli.   More than one of the essays published in *The Student* (1835) is quick with Disraelian philosophy, which may
also be traced in other essays printed in the *New Monthly* and
in the pages of *Caxtoniana* (1863).

It may be imagined that any opportunity of personal introduction to an author whom he already deeply venerated
would have been eagerly taken; and such an opportunity
arose in 1830 from his own friendship with the younger Disraeli.   It is certain that although this friendship was intimate
and prolonged, Bulwer never had the same spiritual unanim-
ity with the son as during their brief acquaintance and from
the very first, he felt with the father.   Isaac Disraeli reciprocated his disciple's affection.   His letter in praise of *The Last
Days of Pompeii* has been printed elsewhere [1] and will later be
referred to.   When he died in 1848, his son wrote to Bulwer
in reply to a letter of condolence:

"You were frequently the subject of his conversation for
he greatly regarded you and had a profound appreciation of
your mind and achievements."   (March 5, 1848)

One is reminded a little of the perceptive tolerance of Doctor Parr, who likewise recognised an exceptional mind behind
the conceit of a brilliant youth.   Both Parr and Isaac
Disraeli were products of the eighteenth and not of the nineteenth century, and their liking for Bulwer, combined with
the strong eighteenth-century colouring which as time went
on showed itself in his mind and work, suggests, as part
explanation of his unhappiness, that he was born out of his
time.

Certainly his contemporaries seemed to find his personality
not only irritating but baffling.   One of the accusations most
commonly brought against him was that he invariably made
himself — or what he had the pretension to regard as himself — the hero of his own novels.   Because this was only a

[1] Lytton I, 443-444.

half truth, he had not much difficulty in rebutting the charge and making it seem ridiculous. For example in the preface to *Paul Clifford* he says:

The year before *Pelham* appeared, I published *Falkland;* in which the hero was essentially of the gloomy romantic cloudlike order. The matter of fact gentry who say "We" and call themselves critics declared that *Falkland* was evidently a personation of the author; next year came "Pelham" — the moral antipodes of *Falkland* and the same gentry said exactly the same thing of "Pelham." Will they condescend to reconcile this contradiction? . . . I have never even drawn two heroes alike, but made each — Falkland, Pelham, Mordaunt and Devereux essentially different.

Nevertheless, if the critics had been a little wiser in their violence and waited until, from a series of Bulwer heroes, they could have disentangled a certain consistency of portraiture, they would have had something of a case. For, different though these heroes are, they one and all have qualities or lay claim to aspirations which consciously or unconsciously were those of their creator.

It is generally accepted that "Pelham" himself was modelled on Bulwer's friend Frederick Villiers [1] (they were at Cambridge together and went abroad in company in 1825), and so in superficial respects he may have been. But knowingly or not, Bulwer endowed his hero with several of his own characteristics; and did the same to the heroes of his later novels also. It is pathetically probable that during the brief happiness of his first years of marriage he was himself nearly as care-free and impudent as the irrepressible Pelham who jarred "Messrs. the Great Unwashed" (the phrase is Bulwer's own) to sour and humourless indignation. Had the engaging dandy been forced to undergo the stress of harassing private misery, of increasing labour, and of that self-centred

[1] *Cf.* Owen Meredith I, 363, and Lytton I, 124-125. Villiers was the natural son of a Mr. Meynell and a Miss Hunloke. He later took the name of Meynell and was given a sinecure by Lord Chief Justice Cockburn who had been of the same set in Cambridge and is dedicatee of Bulwer's *Weeds and Wildflowers* and of *Paul Clifford.*

brooding to which an ambitious, brilliant, but unpopular man is liable to be driven, he would have evolved into Maltravers; for the journey from Pelham to Maltravers, past the milestones of Mordaunt, Devereux and Godolphin, represents — with the idealisation and exaggeration natural to his rococo genius — the spiritual journey travelled by Bulwer himself between 1828 and 1836.

Chapter Three

*The Disowned — First appearance and example of "Bulwerese"
— His love of fine-sounding names — His own names — Failings
and qualities of* The Disowned *—* The Westminster Review *on*
Pelham *and* The Disowned *— Greville — Promise unfulfilled*

When the *Examiner*, reviewing Bulwer's third novel,
guessed that he "had written *Pelham* for his own pleasure,
but *The Disowned* for his bookseller", it spoke shrewdly.
Few young authors in need of money and reputation can resist
the temptation to hurry the "follow" to a big success, and
The Disowned, which appeared within seven months of its
predecessor, is unmistakably a book artificially conceived and
carelessly written.

Nevertheless it is significant to the author's future development, and not least in this very quality of insufficient self-criticism and pruning.   There is hardly a novel of Bulwer's after
Pelham which would not have been vastly improved by a final
and drastic revision.   It was not so much that he wrote too
fast as that he intoxicated himself with his own fluency; and
having been driven quite early in life to the state of nervous
overwork which impels a man to begin a new book the
moment he has finished the old one, he had neither time nor
inclination to review his over-night rhetoric with a cool
morning judgment, and to reduce scenes, descriptions, and
even sentences to the proportions suitable to their real content.
The Disowned occupies four volumes of (in all) 1350 pages;
and it could have been reduced to two thirds of that amount
without anything but advantage to its author's subsequent
reputation and to the pleasure of later generations of readers.

But unluckily for Bulwer as a novelist of permanent readability, its contemporary success was very great — greater even than that of *Pelham*, so that some at any rate of its faults grew into the consciousness of its writer as elements of popularity too valuable to be ignored.   In *The Disowned* for the first time appears that tendency to elaborate, not only simple phrases, but also simple constructions, which took so firm a hold on Bulwer that many of his otherwise more admirable works must for long enough remain a toil — if not an actual irritation — to read.   This tendency drives him now to what Doctor Fowler calls "genteelism", now to "pedantic humour", now to poeticism, often to Wardour Street.   Indeed, taken in bulk and at his worst, he is so rich a mine of the faults and many of the actual phrases common to the baser journalism of today that "Bulwerese" might with advantage have had a general article in *Modern English Usage*, so expressive and so valuable would be a cautionary list of his excesses.   The symptoms appear on the very first page of the introduction to *The Disowned*, where a washstand and its jug and basin become "appurtenances of lavation."

They became gradually more serious as the next three or four novels followed one another.   Very few examples will suffice:

As soon as the Promethean Spark had been communicated to the lady's tube — *i.e.* as soon as Mrs. Lobkins had lighted her pipe.
[*Paul Clifford*]

. . . hallooed after him and bade that dark-coloured gentleman who keeps the *fire office* below go along with him. — *i.e.* told him to go to the devil.
[*Paul Clifford*]

The stream was of no ignoble repute among the gentle craft of the Angle.
[*Eugene Aram*]

Admittants of the celestial beam. — *i.e.* windows.
[*Eugene Aram*]

. . . a certain green spot, in which, despite of its rural attractions, few persons are willing to fix a permanent habitation. — *i.e.* a graveyard.
[*Eugene Aram*]

By the middle thirties the unhappy mannerism had changed
its dress, becoming more grandiloquent or antique in mode
and less facetious. But the alteration was one of form and
not of kind, and its lure to the uncertain writer became the
stronger for its variousness.

This is not the only Bulwerism which dates from *The Disowned*. Another characteristic indulgence — and one which
was a direct result of the influence of the period on his mind
— is the surrender to fine-sounding names for his characters.

The taste for noble-sounding names was very prevalent
among the reading public of the socially pretentious twenties.
In part it was an inheritance from the Gothic Romantic
period, whose writers were not only in reaction from the vulgarity of the Tom Joneses, the Shandys, the Pickles and the
Randoms, but — being concerned mainly with a romanticised past when characters suitable for a novel were necessarily of high degree — ransacked history and chronicles for
surnames suggestive of ornate refinement. When with the
coming of the fashionable novel distant periods and countries were exchanged for London and Cheltenham and the
Shires, the mode for patrician naming persisted and even
increased. It now expressed the aristocratic aspirations of a
post-war society, which vainly but stubbornly cherished a
pretence of returning to pre-war conditions. This pretence
involved (among other things) an ostentatious admiration for
pedigree; and what better evidence of pedigree than an honoured, or at any rate a long-prominent, name? In consequence, the typical novels of the time began to gild the lily
of pre-revolutionary chic, and bring back the surnames of an
old nobility with the additional touch of splendour acceptable to the new. And not only were characters given these
splendid names, but where possible the books themselves.
Almost at random a list of fashionable novels thus elegantly entitled can be set down. In one year had appeared
Vivian Grey and *Hyde Nugent;* after *Granby* came *Arlington;*
after *Tremaine*, *De Vere* and *De Clifford;* imminent were *Russell*

or the Reign of Fashion [by T. S. Surr], 1830; *Fitzgeorge* [by John Sterling], 1832; *Trevelyan* [by Lady Lydia Scott], 1833; *Dacre* [by Mrs. Lister], 1834, and Ainsworth's *Crichton*, 1837.[1]

Now Bulwer (who had shown himself inclined to aristocratical nomenclature by a schoolboy fragment called *Rupert de Lindsay* and his Byronic *Falkland*) ostensibly succumbed to this name-snobbery when he called his first novel *Pelham*. But in fact he was making the same fun of his title as of his characters. In *The Disowned*, however — perhaps because his publisher told him that, while the *ton* would tolerate one satire on themselves, their patience must not be unduly tried — he assayed a serious experiment in lofty and luscious proper names. His hero is "Algernon Mordaunt", his heroine "Isabel St. Leger"; "Clarence Linden" (who becomes "Clinton L'Estrange") and "Lady Flora Ardenne" support the leading pair with exquisite refinement. Below and about these gold-tipped beings crowd the arrogant peers and pliable politicians necessary to scenes of fashionable life, while members of the absurd middle classes, nabobs, bankers, provide the conventional furnishings proper to a social novel.

It is worth while to dwell thus particularly on what may seem one of Bulwer's less important literary mannerisms because it reflects a susceptibility to resonance in real names and particularly in his own. Fortune had endowed him, both on his father's and mother's side, with surnames of an undeniably patrician and rhythmic kind, and the harmony of these names in juxtaposition gave him an exquisite pleasure, which persons without his sensuous feeling for nobility of language could not understand. That he should have been E. L. Bulwer, and then Sir Edward Lytton-Bulwer ("what a pretty name it is!" wrote Caroline Norton to Mary Shelley

---

[1] The trick of pretentious entitlement for fashionable novels did not escape the notice of contemporary satire. In *Blackwood's* "Nox Ambrosiana" for May, 1828, Colburn's advance publicity is parodied, and the "splendid romances of *de Gammon* and *Fitzfiddle*" and the "celebrated author of *De Bore*" are suitably puffed.

in 1838) and then Sir Edward George Earle Lytton Bulwer-
Lytton, and finally all that, once more with the crowning embellishment of yet another Lytton and a coronet, seemed to
many at the time (as it has seemed to many since) a mere
snobbish self-importance. Certainly it had its element of
pride. Certainly also it was a form of self-assertion, but
fundamentally his obvious pleasure in his changing name
expressed something more secret and precious than either of
these. In writing he loved to orchestrate in words, to
roll his periods and crash his abstract nouns and epithets;
with the same delight he would set the music of his own
names sighing in his mind and hug himself at the thought
that they at least were his, and no jealous or cruel enemies
could make them otherwise. When, therefore, he discovered
that by christening his imaginary characters with tuneful distinction he could give himself a little secret thrill every time
he wrote their names, he seized on the new sensation and
cherished it. He came to think that loftiness of character
and dignity of thought almost demanded a nobility of name
to complete their perfection, and his novels from *The Disowned*
onwards are in consequence rich in names harmonious or
of high degree, and as often as not carry one such name as
title. Thus we have *Devereux*, and the unfinished *Greville;
Godolphin* and *Maltravers; Zanoni, Lucretia, Kenelm Chillingley;*
while of incidental characters a long list could be compiled
of designations chosen because their music or lusciousness
appealed to their inventor's private taste.

The *Disowned*, then, claims attention by its very faults, and
as marking the mergence of some of the less satisfactory qualities of Bulwer as a novelist. Its lack of self-criticism; its
genteelism; its pretentious nomenclature — all are important, because all became a part of his tawdry but impressive
genius. To them might be added signs of other mannerisms,
which first showed themselves in *The Disowned*, which also,
though less aggressively, grew into permanence. There is,

for example, his tendency when apostrophising in the second person the reader, the Muse, or some other extraneous immensity, to treat with fine indifference consistency in using the singular or the plural.[1] There is also the habit (shared with Marryat and others, and reflecting a rather uncritical admiration not only for the novelists of the eighteenth century but also for Sir Walter Scott) of introducing characters with a persistent and would-be humorous trick of speech. Although in one of his later essays [2] Bulwer himself criticised this "trick of farce" as a cheap purchase of laughter which "Shakespeare and Cervantes would have disdained", he never learnt wholly to resist it. Two of the characters in *The Disowned* — "Mr. Bossulton" who uses long words and "Mr. Trollolop" (sic!) who talks farcical metaphysics — lead a procession which was to lengthen steadily as book after book appeared, enrolling such tiresome comics as "Sir William" from *Devereux*, as "Squire Brandon" from *Paul Clifford*, as "Corporal Bunting" from *Eugene Aram*, right down to persons from the crowded pages of the "Caxton" series.

But in justice alike to Bulwer and his second full-length novel, it must be shown that the latter has its lights as well as its shadows. The novel opens with an extravagantly amusing preface introducing "Henry Pelham" and promising just such another gaily impudent satire on coxcombry as *Pelham* itself. Unfortunately this frivolous note (which deceived poor Carlyle as thoroughly as did *Pelham*), deepens, once the story starts, to a romanticised and rather dismal rendering of Bulwer's own sojourn with the gipsies. Only now and again does the story achieve pace or verve. The Duke of Haverfield's letter to Clarence Linden is as good

---

[1] Thus on one page of *The Disowned*: ". . . since we (*you*, dear Reader, and ourself) last saw him"; and two pages later: "What it was, we cannot as yet, my dear Reader, reveal to *thee*."

[2] "On Art in Fiction", first published in two parts as "The Critic" in the *Monthly Chronicle*, 1838, and collected with other *Pamphlets and Sketches* in a volume of the Knebworth Edition, Routledge, 1875.

as anything in *Pelham;* [1] but as it only occupies six of the thirteen hundred pages, tends to be overlooked.

The description of the character and origins of Mordaunt, the hero, are certainly those which the author liked to regard as his own; and as Mordaunt's mysterious story slowly and tediously evolves, one realises that [although the story of *The Disowned* is actually staged in the late eighteenth century] Bulwer was already trying in a fumbling way to express that belief in aristocratic tradition, quickened by enlightened liberalism, which all his life (and whether he wore the party colours of Liberals or Tories) was his guiding principle in political and social philosophy. With an ingenuity which cannot be denied, he contrives, by prophetic description of the century to come, to contrast the ideas and mental fashions of his own present day with those of the period of his novel. In the process his wide knowledge of history — and of the history of taste even more than of the more obvious history of incident — is clearly shown. An imperfect technique, and still more an unselective attitude toward words, interpolations and character, cheats this knowledge of its full effect; but it is unmistakably there. Wherefore *The Disowned* — declamatory, over-picturesque, at once priggish and spiritually uncertain of itself though it be — has qualities which mark an essential stage in the evolution of the mature Bulwer, and help us to foresee the road he was to travel.

It has been stated that in a commercial sense *The Disowned* was very successful. But in proportion as it delighted the ordinary readers of fashionable fiction, it disappointed those more serious critics who were prepared to

---

[1] After giving his friend a selection of high society gossip, the Duke reports the loss of a favourite ballerina:

"La pauvre petite Méronville! What an Ariadne! Just as I was thinking to play Bacchus to your Theseus, up steps an old gentleman from Yorkshire who hears it is fashionable to marry *les bonas robas*, proposes honourable matrimony and deprives me and the world of La Méronville. Verily we shall have quite a new race in the next generation — I expect all the babes will skip into the world with a *pas de Zephir* singing in sweet trebles: 'Little dancing loves we are —
Who the deuce is our papa?' "

chaperon its author through the follies of his nonage; who, if their favour could only have been retained, might have made him, not only a popular favourite, but also a novelist of scrupulous quality. The *Examiner* did not hesitate to criticise as bluntly as it had formerly praised; and that Bulwer took serious note of the reprimand is shown in the letter to Rosina already quoted.[1] The *Westminster Review*, which had not noticed *Pelham*, treated the two books together and, though more restrained than the *Examiner* in their criticism, made clear their disappointment with the hasty conventionality of the second.[2] Their article, Fashionable Society—Pelham and The Disowned, appeared in January, 1829, and contained certain general speculations on the social characteristics of the twenties, which so interestingly illustrate the post-war qualities summarised earlier in this book.

The reception of *The Disowned* put Bulwer in a position of perplexity. He was too intelligent not to know that the *Examiner* and the *Westminster* were right, and that the flattering fashionables, who were buying and praising his second book, were wrong. He realised (and in later comment on his own early work admitted the fact) that *The Disowned* was undigested, scamped and perfunctory. Ideally he wished to write a *real* novel for his third venture, not merely another best-seller. On the other hand, he needed money badly; and Colburn, delighted to have curbed so triumphantly the satirical propensities of his new author, lost no opportunity of urging the material advantage of a further concession to conventional taste.

At first the young man's high spirit inclined him to ignore the book-seller and obey the impulse of his own literary integrity. He started a new satirical novel of modern life called *Greville*,[3] directly in the *Pelham* tradition but more impudently critical of English manners and amusements. So far as can be judged from the eight chapters which were all that came to

---

[1] *Cf.* p. 130.   [2] *Cf.* Appendix III.
[3] The fragment is printed in Owen Meredith II, 335, *et seq.*

pass, *Greville* would have been good entertainment. The story
opens with a description of Hyde Park:

There are one or two peculiarities in this Park which are not
unworthy of philosophical speculation. The English women, being
proverbially the modestest ladies in the world, have erected in honour of Arthur Duke of Wellington, proverbially the modestest man
so far as ladies are concerned, an enormous statue, entirely naked.[1]

The deer in this Park generally die of eating leather and oranges,
and you would think by their colour and consistency that the trees
died of the same complaint.

There follows a conversational exposure of the snobberies
of the Row, and in due course the characters arrive at Mrs.
Holroyd's ball:

The hostess was a woman of the world and in the world she had
three daughters and eight friends. In the old classical times a man
generally asked his friend to marry his daughter; in the present
times it is the women who ask it. There is some difference in the
result. In the former age the friend generally accepted the offer,
in the present he generally refuses.

From the ball to a gambling hell, thence to next morning,
thence to a little love-making — so the book proceeds and
would undoubtedly have continued to proceed, had its author
been strong-minded or rich enough to carry it through. Unfortunately he was neither; and instead of three volumes of
Greville, with much period satire of great interest and occasional witticisms fifty years ahead of Wilde in date and not
so very far behind him in dexterity,[2] the world was given
Devereux, which appeared in July, 1829, and for which the
twenty-six-year-old Bulwer received fifteen hundred pounds.

[1] The jokes about the Achilles Statue were innumerable and many of them amusing
enough. A good specimen of contemporary comment will be found in Bernal
Osborne's poem "The Chaunt of Achilles."

[2] Here are two examples which occur within a few pages of the unfinished *Greville:*
"A charming place the Athenaeum. The people are so informed; it is a pity they do
not know each other. And so very entertaining; it is a pity they never converse."
"It has been said that marriages are made in heaven. Very possibly, but heaven
imports the raw material from earth. The workmanship may be admirable, but the
stuff might be better."

Chapter Four

Devereux — *Introduction of real people* — *Fascination of Boling-broke for Bulwer*

In a Dedicatory Epistle dated December 12, 1835, and added to the popular edition of *Devereux* published in 1836, Bulwer said that the book "was written in, perhaps, the happiest period of my literary life, when success began to brighten upon my labours and it seemed to me a fine thing to make a name. . . ." "*The Disowned* and *Devereux* were both written in retirement, and in the midst of metaphysical studies and investigations varied and miscellaneous enough, if not very deeply conned . . . and the effect of these studies is somewhat prejudicially visible in both romances. The workman was not sufficiently master of his art to forbear the vanity of parading the wheels of the mechanism and was too fond of calling attention to the minute and tedious operations by which the movements were to be performed and the result obtained." ". . . I remember that *Devereux* pleased me better than *Pelham* or *The Disowned* because the execution more exactly corresponded with the design. . . . In *Devereux* I wished to portray a man flourishing in the last century, with the train of mind and sentiment peculiar to the present."

Elsewhere, a little ruefully, he admitted that his own liking for *Devereux* was not shared by the public, the book proving "the least generally popular of all my writings."

Posterity, therefore, has double cause to regret that Colburn's advice (for once a fault) should have destroyed *Greville* to make room for *Devereux*. Bad enough to exchange humour for pedantry; worse still, seeing that the pedantry did not even achieve the material success and the wider popularity which were its only justifications.

For (to look first on the black side) *Devereux* perpetuates two of the failings first observed in *The Disowned* — the turgidity and the rhetorical digressions; self-consciously substitutes pursuit of the Real (with a capital letter) for the pursuit of the Picturesque; and lays a new burden on the reader in the form of accurate but excessive information derived from painstaking historical research.

On the other hand, and although much of the labour was imperfectly digested, the book has this great advantage over its predecessor — that it is impressively the result of close and careful work. A lot of hard reading must have gone to the various representations of real people; to the descriptions of Versailles and its court functions; to the long and interesting account of Petersburg in the time of Peter the Great. The pity is that labour so conscientious should have had result so ponderous. In this particular novel Bulwer failed to impress himself on the public as a writer of historical romance. Doubtless he took the lesson to heart. He never set himself to any new genre in literary work without, before he was done, so mastering it as to make it his servant; and it was not long before he conquered — and triumphantly — the difficulties of the costume-novel. Wherefore, though the historical-romantic element in *Devereux* be more or less of a failure, it was to prove a prelude to success and, as such, may be respected.

The story of *Devereux* is staged in the early eighteenth century, beginning while Anne was queen and continuing into the régime of the first Hanoverian. A prominent feature of the book is the circumstantial introduction, as characters in the novel, of actual historical personages. Colley Cibber; Addison; Steele; Fielding; Swift; Pope; Richard Cromwell; Marlborough; Anthony Hamilton; Voltaire as a young man, and — most important of all — Bolingbroke, play carefully studied parts in the drama, with continual

footnote comments designed to show how correct is every
detail. Bulwer had experimented slightly with this nov-
elisation of famous persons in *The Disowned*, introducing
Dr. Johnson, Boswell and Goldsmith, but using them frankly
as incidental music. In *Devereux*, they are part of the
actual entertainment; while the care lavished on Bolingbroke and the evident importance attributed to his appearances make him, if not the hero of the novel, at least its
dominant personality.

Bolingbroke had, from the first serious moment of historical study, exercised a strange fascination over Bulwer.
Obscurely the young man likened himself to the brilliant,
erratic, unfortunate philosopher-statesman who, after nego-
tiating the Treaty of Utrecht, turned Jacobite and was
impeached; was then dismissed by the old Pretender; returning to England, joined hands with Walpole; next quarrelled
with Walpole also, and finally withdrew to cultured retirement in France, where he wrote his *Patriot King* and his *Letters on the Study and Use of History*. The defeat of this lofty,
aspiring but essentially aristocratic mind at the hands of
lesser and more commonplace men than himself appealed to
Bulwer's romantic love of nobility in degradation. He was
going through a phase of contempt for England as a land of
stupid but arrogant barbarians; and this example of a fine
intellect broken on the wheel of stolid English jealousy was
fuel to his imaginative fire. Thus carried away by a romantic
obsession, he did not realise, until it was too late, that once
again he had given offence to his friends. Just as with *The
Disowned* he had turned the *Examiner's* favour into curt dislike, so with *Devereux* he annoyed the hitherto complacent
Westminster. For Bolingbroke was a Tory; and his *Patriot
King* a tract on what came to be called Tory Democracy.
Whether because they had an uneasy feeling that the example
of Bolingbroke might well bear practical fruit in nineteenth-
century England, or because Liberals have always resented
attempts by enlightened Tories to bid for popular favour over

the heads of parties of the left; the Millites were chilled by *Devereux* and hostile to it.   Scrupulous and upright though they were, they could not prevent their dislike of Bulwer's public idolisation of Bolingbroke from coming out in their review.[1] Is it fanciful to suggest that the reading of that review first set Bulwer's mind toward the idea of Disraelian conservatism; first modified his Saint Simonian enthusiasm for governance in the public interest by intellect, into a be-lief in joint governance, for the people's benefit and with the people's consent, by birth and intellect combined?   If this suggestion be held reasonable, then *Devereux* for all its failure was doubly significant of its author's prospects, carrying within the covers of its unpopular three volumes both his future supremacy as writer of historical romance and his politi-cal conversion from the Radical to the Conservative party.

[1] *Cf. Westminster Review*, October, 1829.

Chapter Five

Paul Clifford — *Charges of plagiarism* — *Entertainment quality of*
Paul Clifford — *Topical satire* — *Key to the characters* — "*Mac-grawler*" — *Unhappy results of this insult to the Scotch* — *Need-less provocation of* The Athenæum — *Admirers of* Paul Clifford —
Harriette Wilson — *Her letters to Bulwer*

In a daily paper of March 13, 1829, appeared the following paragraph:

At Chelmsford Assizes, Leigh Domville Halstead was charged with stealing a mare, the property of E. B. Bulwer-Lytton, a widow, on Dec. 16th. Evidence having been given the jury returned a verdict of guilty, and *his lordship directed that the sentence of death should be recorded against the accused.*

The coincidence is curious, seeing that almost at the moment of the defendant's conviction the plaintiff's son was starting work on the preliminaries to *Paul Clifford.*

The impulse to this novel was twofold. On the one hand William Godwin, whose enlightened political philosophy and actual achievements in fiction were among Bulwer's youthful enthusiasms, suggested to his young admirer an adaptation to present conditions of the idea behind *The Beggar's Opera.* In the guise of a highwayman novel the chief personalities of the day were to be tellingly satirised, the ruling powers masquerading as gentlemen of the road (with all the fine sentiments and much-paraded code of honour characteristic of this aristocracy of crime) while the British Public played their usual part of credulous and exploited dupes. But simultaneously with this idea (and blending with it) there developed in Bulwer's own mind a desire to expose the

cruel — and in his view futile — harshness of the existing
Penal Laws. In consequence *Paul Clifford*, as originally
planned, was to be a propagandist novel in favour of the
reform of the Criminal Code, diversified by an excursion into
satire à clé and one observes, with the *Schadenfreude* permissible to posterity, that the author's considerable research
into the recent annals of crime and the brutal frequency of
capital punishment began at the moment when a man
was being sentenced to death for stealing one of Mrs.
Bulwer-Lytton's mares.

But books do not always end as they begin; while this particular book was in the writing, the author's love of story-
telling got the better both of his satirical and reformist intentions. Wherefore, although the satire is there and the
penal barbarities also, *Paul Clifford* in its final form is primarily an exciting story of highwaymen, social and political
intriguers and long-thwarted lovers, with a sensational birth
secret after the best Gothistic pattern to provide a dénoue-
ment of a gratifying and emotional kind.[1]

The theme and readability of *Paul Clifford* were, from the
beginning, four fifths of its popularity and nine tenths of its
influence.[2] It undoubtedly suggested first *Rookwood* and then
Jack Sheppard to Ainsworth, and started the series of so-called

[1] An accusation against Bulwer of having copied this element in his story from
Mrs. Inchbald's novel *Nature and Art* (1796) was first made by *Fraser's Magazine:*
"Paul is made prisoner, tried by Sir William Brandon now a judge, is found guilty
but strongly recommended to mercy — and is transported. Now comes the gist of the
whole story — Paul Clifford is the son of Sir William Brandon. . . . This, say his
maudlin critics, is Mr. Bulwer's own invention. . . . But it is no such thing. It is
as old as Joseph amongst his brethren or the Electra of Sophocles on meeting with
Orestes — or the main incident in *Nature and Art* of Mrs. Inchbald — or the *Lara* or the
Corsair of Byron." (*Fraser's.* I, 529–530. June, 1830)
An instructed critic of the present day has now repeated the charge, and the similarity of this one incident is sufficient to justify its mention. In *Nature and Art* a judge
passes sentence on a street-walker who is guilty of theft, only to find that she is a
girl whom he seduced many years ago and left to bear her son and his in poverty
and disgrace.
[2] Even *Fraser's Magazine* admitted (May, 1836) that *Paul Clifford* and *Eugene
Aram* would probably retain their popularity because of the perennial attraction to
novel-readers of criminals, corsairs and bold bad men generally.

"Newgate Novels", which although moralists declared they would destroy the civic virtues of the young, became nevertheless the mainstay of *Lloyd's Atlas*, *Reynolds Miscellany* and other treasures of fierce fiction, and finally evolved into the Hogarth House shockers and other boys' "bloods" of the eighties and nineties.

The entertainment quality of *Paul Clifford* is undeniable, and is due in large degree to the gusto and enjoyment with which it was evidently written. Bulwer's ordinary life, it will be remembered, was still running smoothly. Certainly, between the courting of his mother's favour and the pressure of unceasing novel-writing, he was not without his agitations; but in comparison with the worries and torments which followed the move into Hertford Street in January, 1830, those final months of 1829 were months of halcyon calm. And this calm is reflected in the care-free surface of the novel. *Paul Clifford* is the last of Bulwer's stories to possess a genuine lightheartedness. Despite its serious purpose, it is a youthful and high-spirited book, which from its very liveliness has pathos, seeing how soon fate was to crush that element from its author's mind, substitute a strained solemnity for challenging impudence, and a forced sardonic wit for heedless playful humour.

Of the more specialist elements in the novel, that of contemporary political satire is nowadays of rather academic interest. But at the time it attracted much attention, luring critics of strong party views to heated debate among themselves. To the publishers, concerned with publicity value, this feature of the book loomed larger than any other. To Bulwer's Tory critics it was grave provocation and undoubtedly encouraged them to exaggerate their virtuous indignation at the novel's moral, which emotion they calculated would prove more readily acceptable to the public than party hostility.

"The main design of *Paul Clifford*," says one of Colburn and Bentley's advance paragraphs, "we understand to be a gen-

eral satire upon the hypocrisy of society and the various methods of rising in the world. Sometimes this design is embodied in a covert shape, sometimes openly, sometimes in masks,
sometimes in portraits."

Another paragraph reads: "The persons alluded to under
the most extravagant disguises, but in the spirit of the utmost
good humour, are understood to be the King, Lord Eldon,
Scarlett, Sir Francis Burdett, the Duke of Wellington, Mr.
Huskisson and Lord Ellenborough."

And a third: "The leading members of the cabinet and the
lords paramount of the drawing-rooms, headed by no less a
person than the —— himself will be astonished to see the
garb in which, with but little disguise, the author has
arranged them."

The intelligent anticipation of these puffs preliminary was
on the whole accurate enough. Rosina, in a letter to Miss
Greene of May 26, 1830, set out the key to the characters as
follows:

"Gentleman George"	The King (George IV)
"Fighting Attie"	The Duke of Wellington
"Old Bags"	Lord Eldon
"Long Ned"	Lord Ellenborough
"Scarlet Jem"	Sir James Scarlett
"Bachelor Bill"	The Duke of Devonshire
"Harry Finish"	Lord Henry de Ros
"The sallow Gentleman"	Mr. Huskisson
"Allfair"	Lord Alvanley
"Augustus Tomlinson"	The Whigs at large
"Peter MacGrawler"	The Scotch nation at large
"Mobbing Francis"	Sir Francis Burdett.

(Paul, Brandon, Lucy Brandon, Lord Mauleverer and Mrs.
Lobkins were imaginary.)

Lockhart, in the *Quarterly* article already mentioned, made
a great show of loyal wrath at the caricature of the king;

but as a matter of fact neither "Gentleman George" nor any of his fellow rogues cut a disagreeable figure. Granted the piratical objects of their existence and the humbug with which by general consent they cloak their depredations, they are good comrades and good company, ready to stand by one another with the honour proper to a band of thieves, and treating life in the daredevil spirit of men who pit their wits against the world and take defeat as cheerfully as victory.

It is, however, easy to understand that contemporary readers who felt strongly on political questions should, after making the easy translation necessary, have found the principles and cynicism of Bulwer's caricatures galling and offensive. And there can be no doubt, after reading some of the criticisms of the novel in papers belonging to the two opposing parties, that Colburn and Bentley were right in thinking their best chance of a good sale lay in setting party men at loggerheads.

For they succeeded, not only in embroiling disputatious readers, but also in selling the book. *Paul Clifford* was a triumph in a purely material sense;[1] and as a novel it can also be warmly commended. In addition to its high spirits it has a deftness and economy of words which seldom mark its author's work, and although admittedly the first volume goes better than its followers (this is nearly always the case even with Bulwer's best stories) there are certain elements in the tale which, whenever their turn for emphasis arrives, brighten the whole novel and keep it briskly moving. The book is further distinguished by one or two cases of genuine characterisation. James Brandon, the suave ambitious lawyer, whose unrevealed paternity of the hero Paul provided material for the charge of plagiarism above recorded, is a living personality, seen in the round, consistent and individual; Lord Mauleverer, the sly but courteous voluptuary, [though an easier type to portray for one with Bulwer's sense of the dramatic value of luxurious and cynical indolence in conflict

---

[1] "A larger first impression was printed than of any modern novel, and yet all sold on the day of publication." (*Age*. May 23, 1830)

with upright sincerity or innocence or young enthusiasm]
is also skilfully drawn; finally Lucy Brandon is undoubtedly
one of his most successful heroines, which is not perhaps
very high praise (for he was no portraitist of young womanhood) but sufficiently high to denote that she definitely stands
out from the crowd of her rather dispiriting sisters.

But if his political satire is good-humoured, his mood
buoyant, his technique and characterisation above the average, he made one bad mistake in *Paul Clifford* which cost him
a deal more worry than it was worth.

The loathsome MacGrawler, who appears as a key-charac-
ter in Rosina's list, is no individual portrait, nor even in the
same sense as the other group-impersonations, a portrait at
all. He represents partly Bulwer's dislike of his own Scotch
critics, partly also the instinctive resentment felt by a clever
Englishman at the more skilful *arrivisme* of his northern neighbours. MacGrawler represented as a dishonest
penny-a-liner, who from writing venal and spiteful criticisms
for a paper called the *Asinæum*, sinks by drink to picking
pockets and at the end betrays to justice the generous-minded
highwaymen who alone had befriended him — is a pastiche
so ludicrously overdrawn as to be meaningless to neutral
minds, but a heaven-sent cause for anger to those who might
be seeking offence. His introduction, therefore, into *Paul
Clifford* influenced no one in the sense which his creator
intended, but gave an extra sting to the lash which Bulwer's
enemies had waiting for him. Also, although more equable
Scots treated MacGrawler with the amused contempt he
deserved, they could not help remembering against Bulwer
that he had devised this silly and rather wanton insult to their
nation, and the memory served to clog channels of good will
which otherwise might have lain cleanly open. Macvey
Napier, for example, since 1829 editor of the *Edinburgh Review*
and a man with whom from 1830 onward Bulwer had considerable journalistic connection, wrote good-humouredly
enough on September 7, 1830:

As I am uncertain whether you have been returned [*i.e.* to Parliament] I do not know whether we of the Land of Cakes are to have our northern obliquities held up to reprobation by a new vigilant censor, or only to be scourged as heretofore through the medium of Messrs. Colburn and Bentley. . . . I cannot guess what effect the following communication may have upon your view regarding the said land and its sons . . . but I have got something like a promise of a favourable article on certain publications of yours by a *Scotchman*, and two tenders purporting unfavourable criticism by *Englishmen*. Now, as I would wish to keep well with you lest I should come in for a share of the anti-Scotch scourge one day or another, I would be glad to be informed whether an unfavourable article by an Englishman is more worthy of acceptance than any of Scotch manufacture, however favourable.

This letter (which, oddly enough, crossed one from him to Napier, dealing with the very problem of the *Edinburgh's* attitude toward his work) [1] put Bulwer in a quandary. How he replied to it, or if he replied at all, is not known. But the mischance of his having broached the question of criticism in the *Edinburgh* just as the editor was weighing its pros and cons had the absurd but understandable effect of suspending it altogether. Neither Scotch compliment nor English fault-finding was printed, the first review of Bulwer's work being delayed until six months later, when a kindly but unfavourable notice of his *Siamese Twins* concluded with this rather lame apologetic:

We had hoped to be able before now to notice Mr. Bulwer's novels, which, though chargeable with some considerable blemishes and mis-applications of talent, are yet in many respects vastly superior to most others of their class. But the reviewer has had no time, since their first appearance, to read them again and in a critical spirit.

This was poor comfort to Bulwer, who longed above all things for considered criticism in the *Edinburgh*, but was not to get it for another two years and then only as an isolated incident. He could never understand why the *Edinburgh* was so sparing of comment on his work, but the reason may surely be divined. Owen Meredith records the curious contrast between Napier's continual praise to his face of Bulwer's work, and the excuses for not giving them adequate notice in his review which always accompanied those praises. From another source comes the significant fact that Hazlitt, after reading *Paul Clifford*, was so enthusiastic that he made several attempts to persuade the *Edinburgh* to let him write an essay on Bulwer's novels, but was always told that Bulwer "as a liberal was an interdicted subject" [1] which of course (bearing in mind the origins of the *Edinburgh* and its policy) was nonsense. It seems that the paper's evasive failure to speak warmly of one of its most valued contributors may, partly at any rate, be explained by imagining that a vague but definite (and, it must be confessed, a comprehensible) distaste for the whole MacGrawler foolishness lingered in the minds of literary Scots.

One further embarrassment Bulwer was to suffer from his ill-advised grotesquerie. The obvious suggestiveness of the name "Asinæum" cannot have escaped him; indeed, when the *Athenæum* reviewed his book with comprehensible disfavour, he was shown to have incorporated in one of Mac-Grawler's reviews actual passages from the *Athenæum* review of *Devereux*. But the *Athenæum* was ostensibly free from Scotch influence and had into the bargain, up to the time of *Paul Clifford*, been at least civil in its criticism of him. Now he had forfeited their good will by a sheer freak of temper; a mistake he soon had cause to regret. A long letter, signed "A Literary Man", appeared in the *Athenæum* January 26, 1833, which forcibly attacked his *New Monthly* assault on Lockhart and bore several indications of sympathy with, if not stimulus from, the editorial clique of *Fraser's Magazine;* this was followed on July 27 by a review of *England and the English*, in which (quite by the way) he was read a lesson

[1] P. G. Patmore's *My Friends and Acquaintances*. London, 1854. III, 155.

on "the somewhat gratuitous and provoking folly" of "scattering insinuations against the independence of other journals." Of course he yielded to his usual impulse and made a bad business worse by arguing about it; and as long afterward as 1837 we find him still writing expostulatory letters to Dilke, debating with pained civility this criticism or that neglect of his work.

MacGrawler, then, was a *gaffe*. But he was the only one. For the rest the book received much gratifying praise. Godwin, not surprisingly in view of his semi-responsibility for its existence, wrote enthusiastic approval; Ebenezer Elliott, the Corn Law Rhymer, was equally complimentary;[1] but perhaps the most piquant compliment which this novel earned for its author was a spontaneous tribute from the famous Harriette Wilson, the greatest demimondaine of her day, whose Memoirs had appeared in 1825. Although three of Harriette Wilson's letters to Bulwer are given almost *in extenso* in his grandson's biography, they are documents of such astonishing human quality and contain such excellent criticism of his first four novels and of himself, that two of them are here in great part reprinted, and a third added. Their contrast to the stilted correspondence of contemporary respectability gives melancholy proof of the dispiriting effect of virtue (at that time, at any rate) on the companionability of the British fair; while the priggishness of the endorsement which, years afterward, he noted on the letters themselves, shows the extent to which Bulwer, for all his railing in *Greville* against the dull complacency of his countrymen, was himself subject to the tyranny of convention.

"These letters," he writes, "were written to me when I first came up to town after my marriage and in my second year of authorship. *Of course I never acceded to her wish to know me.*"

The discretion of the rising young author was, perhaps, inevitable. He was at once a child of his age and depended for livelihood on its favour. But it is frankly disappointing to find

---

[1] Their letters are printed in Lytton, I, 364–365.

sanctimony many years after the event, and permissible to regret the novel which he might have written, could he have accepted Harriette Wilson's suggestion to season his own talent with some of her amorous experience and racy irresponsibility.

The problem of the date of the letters requires a word of comment. Lord Lytton suggests that the two here re-quoted date from 1831; but it seems likely that they belong, possibly to 1830, more probably to 1829. The statement that Harriette Wilson was born in 1789 (D. N. B.) is now regarded as inaccurate. In her preface to her novel *Clara Gazul* which was published in 1830, she states definitely that she was born on February 2d, 1786 (the date February 22, 1788, given in her letter to Bulwer as printed by Lord Lytton is a fault in transcription), and Mr. Eveleigh Nash in his Foreword to his edition of her Memoirs [1] gives additional evidence in support of this date. Taking as fairly accurate (and there seems no reason to do otherwise) her information to Bulwer that she was forty-three years old at the time she wrote to him, we may date her second letter in October, 1829, and her first one just over six weeks earlier. The beginning of August, 1829, is a date at which a fashionable if frivolous novel-reader might have been expected to be one third through *Devereux*, that novel having appeared in the libraries late in July. A further argument for 1829 as the correct date of the first two letters is implicit in the suggestion in the second letter that Bulwer look over proofs of "my unfinished new book." This must be *Clara Gazul* which, as stated above, was published in 1830.

The third letter (now first printed) was written in November, 1832, as the reference to *Eugene Aram* shows.

Harriette Wilson to Edward Bulwer

[probably early August, 1829]

Sir,

Though I have disliked reading all my life unless it be Shakespear's plays, yet I got to the end of *Pelham*. It was not a book to my

---

[1] *Cf.* Eveleigh Nash. 2 vols. 1909.

taste either, for I thought the writer was a cold hearted man, and his light chit-chat was pedantic, smelling of the *Lamp* — not so good as my own. But then it was a sensible book, the fancies brilliant, the thought deep, the language very expressive. In short I got to the end of it. *The Disowned* I liked better still, and felt *very much* obliged to you for writing one of the few books I *can* come to the end of, with all my desire for amusement. But that imbecile [Mordaunt] who allow'd his wife to be starved like a helpless blockhead, *his* want of French philosophy made me *sick*. Do you consider that man virtuous or sensible whose *little* soul makes him ashamed of doing his duty in that state of life into which it may please God to call him? He had arms and legs, health and intelligence — why did not he clean his wife's room and white-wash the walls, earn her by his daily work a mutton chop, and then fry it for her à la Maintenon? There's no such thing as starving in England for an intelligent man who will *turn his hand to anything* rather than endure to see the beloved of his soul die of hunger. No, that man ought to have been sent to the tread mill.

Now for *Devereux*, I have nearly finished the first vol. and am so charmed with it, that I have laid it aside to tell you how proud I should be if you felt disposed to honor me with your acquaintance. I merely *suggest* this to you because life is too short and too miserable for us to afford prudently to risk the loss of a possible pleasure for want of asking for it, and it is just *possible* that we might derive pleasure from being acquainted — not very probable, however, because I am not a bit agreeable except to those who are predisposed to like me, and who appear to feel and understand all that is original or eccentric or amusing or likeable in my character at once. I am very shy, and when people do not flatter and encourage me by making me feel sure of their predisposition to like me, I am not a bit *amiable* because I am *genée*. I am *not*, and never was, a general favourite; but nobody likes me a *little* or forgets me when they have once liked, understood and been liked by me. I am very ignorant and can't spell, but there is this advantage in not reading, you are all of you copies and I am the thing itself. You are sure if I say anything to strike or please you that it came out of my own little head.

What do you think about it? Perhaps you would like my society better than I should like yours. . . . I am *not* ugly, as they de-

scribe me in the papers; but on the contrary rather handsome, particularly by candle-light when I am amused — although I was born
at ten minutes before eight o'clock, the 22 February 1786 and christened at St. George's Church — I love to be particular.

The beginning of *Devereux* is quite perfect in my humble opinion.
I would not change a *line*, and I believe firmly that Walter Scott
could not improve *one line* or thought up to page 266. You always
fall off in love scenes, perhaps because your heart is dry and you want
the romance, the thrill, the *body* of the thing to mix up with your
visions; therefore, you don't excite desire for *your heroines*, no man
wants their sweet favours. Matilde (of Malechade) is *pure enough*
for *your high flown notions*, yet she is drawn *the woman* and she excites
passion. No matter, the fault (as I said to the Duke of Beaufort)
"is not in your heart but in your *want of heart.*"

I never heard your person described, but can *fancy* you a little
fright just like Ld. Dudley and Ward. No matter, I am sick of
beauty, and the only small caprice I have encouraged for some time
past is for a little fat, snub-nosed old gentleman of *high degree*, high
in place too, whom I never beheld but once and that was 12 years
ago. He was then at least five and forty, but his public character
has *tête-montée* me, and me *only* perhaps. You would be surprised
that his Lordship should make any woman's dream of love, and yet
I am *always* dreaming of the dear little fat old gentleman. I have
told him in more charming letters than this that I adore him, and
he only answers thus:

"My dear Madam — Yours of the date of . . . came to hand on
the 30th of . . . and I return you my sincere thanks for the many
obliging expressions it contains, etc."

Cut me, Mr. Pelham, if you will, but give me no cut and dried
"*dates of.*" Oh!! to think that ever tender enthusiastic elderly
gentlewoman should be doom'd to love a little *fat man*, who in return
gives her nothing but "Yours Madam of the date of. . . ."!!! However, I shall take a voyage to . . . where he resides and make an
attack on him, unless you make me like you better. At present I
have not a distant *presentiment* that it would be possible; I am only
in love with your *last* work as far as I have read it, and have pleasure
in expressing to the author my perfect glowing admiration of every
line up to page 266. I have not begun the 2d vol. yet, as I only got
the work yesterday.

I am not my own mistress, but if *en tout bien et tout honneur* you were
to write me word that you would not object to favor me with a visit
some day — or will you take a walk with me some evening? I am
much pleasanter to *begin with* when I am walking, because if it is
dark I thus get rid of the shyness or nervousness which is constitutional with me and renders me a bore to strangers until I am encouraged delightfully by a certain inward conviction that they like me
enough to be indulgent.

Yours truly, and with high
respect for your superior talents,
HENRIETTE ROCHFORT
Author of *The Memoirs of H. Wilson.*

October 1st, deux heures après minuit
[1829]

Though my sister gave me your letter before dinner (in answer to
mine of "the six weeks ago instant") I had no opportunity of reading it till this moment. I am sleepy and my fire is out, and yet, the
matter having hold of my thoughts, I should not rest till I had
expressed to you my regret that *you like me*, since you refuse to shake
hands with me. *On sait à peu près ce qu'on veut*, I had therefore phil-
osophically made up my mind to endure your silent contempt, but
since you are benevolently inclined towards me, it is really rather
hard upon me this — *dead cut*. From your style of writing I did not
expect to find you a very agreeable companion for a post-chaise, etc.,
nor did I desire that we should meet under the impression that it
was at all incumbent on us to be more agreeable than our neighbours.
The very thought and fever of such a wish would only serve to red-
den our noses and damp our spirits. I conceived, as a sensible man,
you might perhaps be amused with the novelty of a woman who is
always true to nature, no matter how bizarre may be her thoughts,
creed, or wishes. However, if you won't make friends with me
you *won't*, and I must stick to my "Yours of the 15th came safe to
hand on the, etc."

Apropos! I have got another letter by this week's bag in which
. . . In sober seriousness, I must observe that you are quite justified in declining my acquaintance since it is your humour — I can
only say with the Archbishop in *Gil Blas:* "*Je vous souhaite toute
sorte de prospérité avec un peu plus de goût.*"

If, however, you believe I wished you to neglect *others* for so *insig-nificant* an individual as myself, you have done me injustice. Believing you married, I only desired the honor of your acquaintance under the impression that love or desire for me *now* was entirely out of the chapter of possibilities, and that no wife would pay me the compliment to object to her occasionally enjoying the benefit of a little chat with her husband. I should have been proud and obliged if hereafter you would have been at the trouble of looking over my unfinished new Work — the only thing I have ever written at all to my own satisfaction with regard to the romance, the language and the spirit of it. But why should I have presumed to expect so much condescension from you? The work must take its chance; I'll publish it with all its blunders of ignorance, because I like it myself, and expect others may do so too, since everybody tells me I had never had any vanity. True I am the most *unread* and truly *ignorant* woman in His Majesty's dominions, but then heart and feeling will come at the right expressions by intuition. The memoirs were written in a sort of shorthand, the first vol. in six days. I wanted to look over all that dirty paper, but Stockdale called on me every morning and tucked my foolscap MS. *à mésure* under his arm, so that when I saw it in print I was really agreeably astonished and puzzled to guess why it was not worse still. What I am now writing (a sort of female *Gil Blas* not *quite* so *loose* as Faublas) gives me much more trouble. It appears that we grow humble and difficult to be pleased as our eyes open on the glare of our own vast and melancholy deficiencies. No matter, you *won't*, and nobody else shall, meddle with my novel. I will tell you what would make a perfect novel — you write it all but the love scenes and send them for me to draw.

The papers *forced* me to allude to my *person* and voice, since who would like the few they admire to be impressed with the false idea of their hideousness and their *coarse voice?* — knowing that my voice is *very good* and that no time can quite spoil a fine face, though it may not be a pretty one. I told you the exact truth, namely that I am forty-three, very *journalière*, often *joliment abattu*, *grâce à Dieu*, particularly when I can't sleep, which happens four nights out of six, handsome (for those who like the Siddonian expression) occasionally when I have slept, never *very ugly* in the face, and as pretty as ever in person, which, by the bye, does not appear under the disguise of my costume which is as loose as my morals — to use the newspaper's expression, while in fact I am a true, faithful wife leading about as innocent a life as a hermit can well do. . . .

You say you are six foot broad. I should from my ear (not my grammar) say "six feet"; which word is right? I know from your writing that you are thin and bilious and severe, I should say dry, not graceful; but one wants variety, I should like your shrewd wisdom for a change; harsh it might sound to a lady's ear, after the gentle, voluptuous, graceful, luxurious Argyles or Ponsonbys, but the rude scenes of age and harshness *must come* and is to *nous autres* who have been loved and doted on, the *tax upon beauty*. The contrast of neglect must be borne, and borne by me like a man, for Lord Ponsonby used to say of me that my advantage over other *sweet fair ones* was that besides my pretty bosom and effeminate qualities, softness of temper etc., I really was "an *excellent fellow*" (*bon camarade*). So to preserve the impression in my favour, now I'm growing old I must be a *better fellow* than ever, in which character I forgive your cut and wish you every success, every possible happiness that can be obtained in a world *fait exprès pour nous enrager*.

Adieu,

Harry.

The next letter helps to explain why Bulwer, who obviously relished the correspondence sufficiently to play his part in it, was so shy of personal contact. It seems possible that he dreaded being laughed at as much as he feared being compromised; and was reluctant to make an acquaintance which would not only appear equivocal but might expose him to more shrewd comments on his pedantry. For shrewd they are, and the perception with which the lady contrived in this case to read her man makes it easy to understand her professional success.

69 Vauxhall Bridge Road, Pimlico
November [1832]
Lively!!
Pastoral.

I'm desperately ill and the mind wears out with body, but I fear you will be so very unhappy if you don't hear from me now and then before I die. Your other novels would have pleased me if I had not

read *Devereux*, and I should have remained in love with your talents
unto the end if you had written only *Devereux*. Don't you yourself
prefer *Devereux* to all your other novels. *Eugene!* says the boarding
school miss. *Pelham!* exclaims Beau Brummel, all the Cheltenham
liverish water-drinkers and all the Bath ladies — although it is but
a bad edition of H. Wilson's memoirs after all. *The Disowned!* cry
the sentimental ladies who would rather die of want than suffer
their hero or yours to put his shoulder to the wheel and soil his
hands. As to *Paul Clifford* it is the next best to *Devereux*, only I wish
the man of the world had been drawn with a more moderate share
of bum-fiddle. He ought to have been thin; decidedly there was
your mistake; dry as a bone he ought to have been. There is *nothing* in his character to sympathise with a large bum-fiddle — *nothing*.
Such a rotundity of symmetry surely did not belong to a man of the
world. You must have been thinking of Poncho. *He*, being a
clown, wanted a bum-fiddle and a half but your stupid man of the
world ought to have been as dry as a bone and as stiff as a poker.
Of course you stole your gentleman George from Gentleman John
of Smollett's (I think *Peregrine Pickle*)! "A Frenchman never forgives a blow!" (in *Pelham*) verbatim from the same author. If your
heart was not as dry as chalk one might make anything delightful
out of the author of *Devereux*. You make a sensible speech now and
then to be sure about Reform or the Players, but what is more dry
than even a fine fat partridge for one's dinner without gravy of any
kind and sauce piquante.

Don't be such a *pedant*. Condescend to exert your playfulness
and humour if you have any in order that we may digest your dry
solids. Be agreeable as well as wise and musty. Goodbye.

Harry.

It may be observed in conclusion that the lady had in the
meantime taken her own small revenge on the very correct
young man, who liked her to flatter him by letter but would
not meet her face to face. In March or April, 1831, Bulwer
wrote to Jerdan:

Harriet (sic) W——n has been pleased to send me a volume of
"Lies", containing a letter to you wherein some expressions of mine
applying *not* to her present work, which I have not seen, but to her

Confessions, are introduced in a very garbled and transposed manner. Verbum sap.

Evidently his incautious praise of the famous "Memoirs" had been transformed by skilful misquotation into advance publicity of the very *Clara Gazul* whose proofs he had refused to read.

Chapter Six

Fraser's Magazine — *William Maginn* — *His character and career* — *Relationship with Westmacott and Lockhart* — *Causes of the Fraserian vendetta against Bulwer* — *Thackeray* — *His genius, hypocrisy and snobbery* — *Thackeray* versus *Bulwer* — *The Fraserians open their campaign* — The Age *joins in* — *Survey of the Fraserian persecution of Bulwer*

I

Fraser's Magazine for Town and Country, the first number of which appeared in February, 1830, was a higher-powered *Blackwood's*. Very similar in plan and format to the famous *Maga*, it intensified the principal characteristics of that Edinburgh journal. Consequently, while it was certainly more brilliant, it was also considerably more scurrilous. That *Fraser's* should have modelled itself so closely on *Maga* was largely due to the identity of its promoter. Although the paper was named after one Hugh Fraser; although its finance and management were in the hands of James Fraser, unrelated to his namesake and an enterprising newcomer to London bookselling; the editorial control and inspiration came from Doctor William Maginn, who had been, after Lockhart, the principal coadjutor of John Wilson ("Christopher North") during the early and provocative period of the career of *Blackwood's Magazine*. Maginn brought to his new venture the taste for highly aggressive criticism, the extreme and often unscrupulous Toryism, the liking and talent for satirical conversational symposia, which had given to *Blackwood's* its peculiar character. And these tendencies, given scope in a London publication and freed from the natural preoccupation with Scottish men and matters which characterised its Edinburgh prototype, soon developed a degree of controversial daring which John Wilson — cautious for all his asperity — would never have countenanced. In consequence *Fraser's*, during the first eight scintillating years of its existence, roused more excited enthusiasm; contained more brilliant, but irresponsible and often caddish writing, provoked more angry retaliation, than any other magazine of the nineteenth century.

II

The history and personality of William Maginn have tempted several commentators;[1] but owing partly to the elusive and erratic nature of his genius, which makes him a pungent marginal note to the lives of many other men but leaves his own career a puzzle in anonymous or pseudonymous pastiche; partly to an actual absence of coherent evidence of many of his activities — no wholly satisfactory presentation of a figure at once fascinating and repulsive has yet been achieved. Nor can he in this book receive his proper due. But he represented so important a phase in the career of Edward Bulwer that the facts of his life, so far as they are known, may with advantage be summarised.

Born in Cork in 1793, Maginn passed with precocious brilliance through Trinity College, Dublin, and returned from college to join the staff of his father's boys' school. He was only twenty when his father's death left him in charge of the school, and his extraordinary capacities, combined with a vivid and attractive personality, soon gave to both the school and its headmaster a nationwide reputation. In 1816, at the age of twenty-three, Maginn obtained from Dublin a degree of Doctor of Laws, and shortly afterward began to send contributions of various kinds to British as well as Irish periodicals. His amazing versatility was barely exaggerated by his friend Edward Kenealy in the first of two Letters from *Barney*

[1] *Cf.* Bibliography in Appendix IV.

WILLIAM MAGINN

From a drawing by Samuel Skillin

Brallaghan to Oliver Yorke, published after Maginn's death in *Fraser's Magazine*, republished in book form under the title *Brallaghan or the Deipnosophists* (1845), and purporting to give an account of the meetings at Austin's Tavern in Cork of the highly convivial "Deipnosophist Club", of which Maginn was president. In this letter Maginn is described as "Theologian, Historian, Poet, Metaphysician, Mathematician, Philosopher, Phrenologist, Stenographist, Fencer, Boxer, Orator, Dramatist, Reviewer, Sonneteer, Joker, Punster, Doctor of Laws, Hoaxer, Political Economist, Newspaper Editor, Wit, Duellist, Pedestrian, Linguist, Arithmetician, ODoherty, Pamphleteer, Translator, Epigrammatist, Antiquarian, Scholar, Conversationalist, Novelist and true Tory to the backbone. In fact a man so various that he seems to be not one, but all mankind's epitome."

Maginn's talent for parody, and for provocative writing of the kind which combines much classical allusion with telling and uncomfortable topicality, attracted the attention of the editor of *Blackwood's* to his contributions, which from time to time, and pseudonymously, reached Edinburgh from Ireland. Wilson accepted ever more of these contributions until one day Maginn, whose identity had hitherto been wholly unknown, walked into *Blackwood's* office in Edinburgh and introduced himself. Thenceforward (and although for a while longer he continued to manage his school in Cork) he was regarded as a member of Wilson's editorial committee; and hardly a number of the paper appeared without one or more contributions from his pen. The famous *Noctes Ambrosianæ* were invented by Maginn (the first was published in March, 1822, and the series ran until February, 1835) and large portions of them regularly written by him. His favourite (though not his sole) pseudonym, "Morgan O'Doherty", became widely known; and by 1823 he was offered sufficient journalistic work in London to decide him to dispose of his school and leave Ireland altogether.

For nearly two years he lived as a free lance, writing effortless and matchless miscellanea, spending his time between scribbling and drink.   In 1825 Doctor George Croly offered to recommend him for the editorship of the *Leeds Intelligencer*, in which post he would have succeeded Alaric Watts.   The ferocity with which *Fraser's* was later to attack Watts gives the suggestion an ironical interest.   But the appointment did not mature, and Maginn stayed on in London.

The two-sidedness of his extraordinary character now clearly showed itself in his journalistic affiliations.   On the one hand, he wrote ceaselessly for *Blackwood's* and *The Literary Gazette;* the *Quarterly*, from October, 1825, edited by his friend Lockhart, took articles from him; he was so intimate with Barnes, editor of the *Times*, that young Disraeli, writing to Lockhart about Maginn's enthusiasm for the new projected paper *The Representative*, described his interview as being "most important, because really it is becoming acquainted with the private opinion of Barnes."   Further, at Lockhart's instigation, Maginn was engaged at five hundred pounds a year as Paris correspondent of that ill-fated *Representative*,[1] had his debts paid to enable him to leave England, and for some months at least drew his salary.   Finally, he was at one time actually chosen by Murray and his clique to write the official life of Byron.

On the other hand, and almost simultaneously with these reputable and important activities, Maginn condescended to gutter journalism of the basest kind.   He had, even before 1825, become an occasional contributor to *John Bull*, and a consequent friendship with Theodore Hook brought him into touch with the more unscrupulous directors of Tory propaganda.   From this connection developed the most discreditable activity of his whole career.   For when in 1827 or 1828 Charles Molloy Westmacott bought *The Age* in order to turn it to his private and sinister purposes, it seems almost certain that Maginn joined him and, by virtually acting as

[1] *Cf. Letters of Sir Walter Scott*, II, 407-409, for Disraeli's letter announcing the engagement.

co-editor, prostituted his great talents to the blackguardism of a blackmailer.

During 1827 Maginn[1] published that very amusing satirical novel, *Whitehall or the Days of George IV*, from which a quotation has earlier been made. This strictly anonymous book — with its caricature (typically *méchant*, coming as it did from a professional Tory scribe) of the Duke of Wellington in the toils of Harriette Wilson; its attacks by name on Campbell, Cobbett and Horace Smith; its friendly mockery of Coleridge and Isaac Disraeli; its footnotes, pompously referring to fake authorities; its fantastic blend of actuality and wild improbability — was almost certainly the inspiration of Disraeli's *Popanilla* and, had its author possessed the application necessary to win a lasting literary reputation, would nowadays be a classic of nineteenth-century satire. But "the Doctor" (as he was called) was, for all his brilliance, doomed to evanescence. His name in very truth was writ in spirits and water.

Perhaps the essential tragedy of Maginn's life is that his best quality served him worst. The basis of his genius was an instinctive and, at need, unflinching respect for intellect wheresoever he might find it. This respect, which would at any moment transcend the waywardness and frailty of his normal character, gave to his mind a fineness beyond that of his collaborators and companions and, at the same time, rendered him an unreliable tool of faction. Had he been more completely a blackguard, he would not have provoked the jealousy of his colleagues and would have impressed his masters as a more skilful sycophant. Then both friends and masters might have combined to prevent the squalid misery of his final years. As it was, whereas alone of the whole group of Tory sharpshooters of the thirties Maginn never lost

---

[1] In later years Maginn was not above independent excursions into journalism of the most dishonourable kind. He is alleged himself to have boasted that he wrote simultaneously in two papers of different political colouring accounts of the Norton-Melbourne case in 1836, one of which vilified Mrs. Norton as a debauched and profligate adventuress, while the other declared her purity with exaggerated moral fervour.

his mental integrity, his collapse in every other respect was the most miserable. Theodore Hook, although he died wretchedly enough, had even at the end support and reputation far greater than Maginn's; but then Hook would barter any principle on earth for a good dinner, and respected his own mental powers as little as those of any other men. Others of the same circle profited in proportion to their venality. The malignant and cowardly Lockhart suffered no retribution save the melancholy of a loneliness partly caused by the terrible series of domestic misfortunes which one by one befell him and, at the last, moved even Miss Martineau to sympathy, but mainly brought upon himself; Westmacott, having made a small fortune out of blackmail, sneaked away to France to enjoy it as he most desired; the smaller fry came in due course to their appointed frying pans. But Maginn, deserted (until too late [1]) by the party whom he had brilliantly if unscrupulously supported, and never having sought to cover his risks by truckling to authority or to lay off by careful anonymity, died in his forty-ninth year, of consumption contracted in prison, leaving a family unprovided for and debts unpaid. [2]

In 1828 Maginn doubled his part as co-director of The Age with the job of assistant editor of The Standard, a new and ultra-Tory evening paper. But even this twofold work was insufficient for his active and ambitious brain. By the autumn of 1829 he was in full conspiracy for the launching of Fraser's Magazine; and it was as editor of Fraser's that he made his tempestuous entry into the life of Edward Bulwer.

The importance to a history of Bulwer's mental development of the savage persecution to which he was subjected

[1] Peel procured him a grant of a hundred pounds exactly ten days before he died on August 27, 1842.
[2] James Hannay states that Thackeray sent Maginn £500 during the worst days of his poverty; but strangely enough, this generous benefactor is not mentioned in any of the memorial notices which I have read. If it indeed were made, Thackeray paid handsomely for the right to caricature his former editor in one of his novels.

by *Fraser's* is very great; and although by no means all of the
scurrilities there published were actually written by Maginn,
they were originally countenanced by him and formed part
of his editorial responsibility. It is, therefore, relevant to
speculate on the causes of the ready hostility shown by this extraordinary Irishman toward Bulwer. Naturally party politics provided at once an excuse and a considerable impulse.
The beginning of 1830 saw the pro- and anti-reformers
definitely lined up in bitter enmity; and Bulwer, who had
openly avowed his belief in the popular party and knew the
controversial methods of his day, must have been prepared
for a certain malignancy. But the Fraserian vendetta had a
definitely personal quality which cannot wholly be accounted
for by political disagreement. There were other causes at
work, impelling Maginn to special vindictiveness. The first
of these causes was, as has been already suggested, the long-
standing friendship of Maginn and Lockhart. Everything
tended to draw these two men together in alliance against
Bulwer — party hostility; the rivalry between Murrayites
and Colburnites; jealous resentment of a London fashionable
who combined literary reputation with metropolitan airs
and elegance, naturally distasteful to the minds of Scotch and
Irish immigrants.

Maginn's intimacy with Westmacott may also have had
something to do with his anti-Bulwerism. As will be seen,
the editor of *The Age* had grievously damaged a lady with
whom Bulwer was to become very intimate; also, during the
period of Maginn's own collaboration with Westmacott's
paper, occasional sneers at Bulwer himself and his work had
betrayed the editors' hostile bias.

But there was a further possible reason for Maginn's dislike
of Bulwer — a reason more individual to the Irishman and,
if it be accepted as probable, one more cogent than any other.
Put briefly, this theory assumes that the trouble centred
around the person of that very mysterious young woman poet
Letitia Landon, whose early friendship for and rather fulsome

praise of Bulwer and his wife have already been recorded.[1]
The argument in summary amounts to this:

There can be no doubt that Miss Landon sometimes acted
with such indiscretion as to give openings to unkind gossip
of a type more common then than now; and of all the semi-
scandals which at various times attached to her the most
circumstantial was that which accused her of an actual
intrigue with Maginn.   So far as concerns L. E. L. the gossip
was probably exaggerated.   But Maginn was a different
matter.   His readiness to criticise the morals of others
was (conventionally enough) allied to a personal fallibility
which even his friends could not deny.   Lockhart's poetical
epitaph admits that "drink and the girls" were the doctor's
failings;[2] and we may be sure that no good opportunity of
forcing an equivocal relationship on Miss Landon would have
been neglected by him.   Opportunity there was and to spare;
one may assume that it was exploited; but the exploitation
was probably unsuccessful.   In short, the sequence of events
was precisely as later described by L. E. L. herself to Lady
Blessington — namely, that whereas she was never Maginn's
mistress, he had indeed sought to capture and subdue her,
using on the one hand promises of much favourable criticism
in the various papers with which he was connected, on the
other threats of critical destruction, as weapons in his attack.

Now a relationship such as this between the Irish journalist and a girl who was also very friendly with Edward
Bulwer could have embroiled the pair of otherwise quite
unconnected men in either of two ways.   On the one hand,
it is just conceivable that Maginn came to attribute his own
rejection by Miss Landon to her preference for the rising young
novelist — that, in fact, he was directly jealous of Bulwer
as a successful rival.   On the other hand, it is more likely
that there was never any serious flirtation between Bulwer

[1] Rather than interrupt the narrative with a necessarily prolonged examination of
available evidence, I have attempted a reconstruction of the *affaire* Bulwer-Landon-
Maginn in Appendix V at the end of this book.
[2] *Cf.* Appendix IV.

and L. E. L., but only a rather foolish readiness to exchange literary compliments; that he and his wife were told in confidence by Miss Landon of her persecution by Maginn, deliberately encouraged her in resistance, and in this way cheated the importunate lover of his prey. In either event, rage would have embittered the doctor against Bulwer and provided motive sufficient for future revenge.

For a vendetta against his supplanter Maginn would have had, therefore, not only good camouflage and eager allies, but good personal reason also. In any event, with the spiteful Lockhart at his side, and Westmacott ready to reinforce any scurrility in the blessed name of Tory propaganda, the editor of *Fraser's* lost no time in ruthless indulgence of his spleen. There was naturally no difficulty in enlisting the younger Fraserians in the campaign. Clever young men, given editorial authority for insult, do not trouble their heads about the rights or wrongs of a matter, but hasten to enjoy their license while it lasts. Then, as time goes on, they grow so accustomed to regard certain individuals as enemies, that a hostility, originally merely assumed to please an editor, becomes part of their own habit of mind and through their influence spreads further. This is precisely what occurred in the case of Bulwer; and because among the thoughtless young men, who in the back room of Fraser's Regent Street office were early infected with Maginn's taste for reckless lampooning was William Makepeace Thackeray, Bulwer-baiting, which began as a sort of automatic joke, developed (thanks to the later distinction of this particular practitioner) into the accepted sport of a small but vociferous group of intellectuals.

III

Of Thackeray's share in the persecution of Bulwer, only the very opening stages can be excused on the score of youthful heedlessness. He persisted in the game far too long to excuse himself on the ground of inexperience. Not only did he continue his Fraserian insults long after the days of Maginn were over; he was also directly responsible for inciting against a man who had never injured him the second-rate scribblers who took their cue from Douglas Jerrold; and he put the finishing touch to his own discredit by the flunkeyism of a thirteenth-hour apology.

It is difficult, after careful study of his journalistic activities, to escape the conclusion that Thackeray frequently showed himself what Edmund Yates, in the famous essay which split the Garrick Club, declared him to be — both a hypocrite and a snob. Toward his family and a few close friends he would always act with charm, sincerity and tenderness; but the geniality with which he affected to treat the world at large was false. A definite moral inconsistency is shown in his novel reviews and even more blatantly in his art criticism, where flippancy and prudery are oddly blended. Scenes likely to be considered daring by novel-readers of the time are relished with worldly nonchalance, but coyly disapproved. In criticisms of contemporary painting nudes are sniggered over, but declared an offence to the purity of British womanhood. Thackeray's social conscience was no less adaptable than his æsthetic one. While he was a penniless gentleman he bitterly guyed his own class for the delight of their inferiors; when he became prominent and was himself courted by the *ton*, he turned on his earlier friends and sneered at their commonness. For the sake of his splendid literary talents, most commentators have slurred over the sycophancy, cruelty and treachery by which at different times he betrayed the quality of his egotism. Yet "St. Barbe" in Disraeli's "Endymion", with his tuft-hunting malice and jealousy, was not quite the caricature he has generally been assumed to be. Yates' references to forced bonhomie and to the cold self-sufficiency which lay behind an affectation of good nature had more justification than is always allowed; while Sergeant Ballantyne's personal reminiscences of a man very egotistical, greedy of flattery and sensitive to criticism to a ridiculous extent is as convincing as it is downright."

It must be confessed that, in his dealings with other men of letters, Thackeray gave cause for such severity. To Albert Smith he behaved with sheer malignity. While Hook was alive he flattered and used him; when Hook was dead he rent him in *Pendennis*. Even Maginn, to whom he owed not only a start in journalism but a good part of his own mental equipment, was shown up for a mere mercenary bravo in the same novel. As for his treatment of Bulwer, it offers an almost classic example of the completeness with which a change of material circumstance can effect a critical conversion. Until well on in the forties Thackeray lost no opportunity of cruel caricature of Bulwer's person and literary style. The series of insolencies almost culminated in a challenge to a duel. But when it became evident that Bulwer, for all his isolation from his kind, had a firmer hold on the public than almost any other writer; when Thackeray realised that a cordial welcome from Lady Blessington was in part dependent on civility to one of her greatest friends; when jealousy of Dickens opened his eyes to the possibility of Bulwer's joining that dangerous rival's party — there was a rapid change of tune. We have first of all a simpering letter of self-justification to the mistress of Gore House:

I wish to eggsplain what I meant last night with regard to a certain antipathy to a certain great author. I have no sort of personal dislike (not that it matters much whether I have or not) to Sir E. L. B. L., on the contrary the only time I met him, at the immortal Ainsworth's years ago, I thought him very pleasant and I know from his conduct to my dear little Blanchard that he can be a most generous and delicate-minded friend. But there are sentiments in his writings which always anger me, big words which make me furious, and a premeditated fine writing against which I can't help rebelling.

Then, and with increasing urgency, apologies for past indiscretions reach Bulwer himself through this intermediary or that. On one occasion Thackeray remarks to a British

Museum researcher whom he knows to be working for Bulwer also: "None of us have held our own so well as Bulwer," and the remark is duly repeated. He next tries direct appeal and about 1858 himself writes to his victim, retracting past insults and proposing a meeting for reconciliation, which meeting even magnanimity could not envisage.

Finally, just as the *Cornhill* is making its appearance, a friend of Bulwer's writes from Paris the following revealing note:

> I saw Thackeray at Folkestone who spoke of you a great deal. He told me how he would have given worlds had some of his writings burnt the paper. He said he would have given much to have seen you and expressed his contrition. He regretted very much that you had given Dickens your new novel — no money and no trouble would he have spared to have obtained it for his magazine, had he thought that Blackwood would not have had it. I tell you all this because I feel certain he meant me to repeat it to you. He was very lavish of his praise; his admiration was boundless and so was his regret to have given vent to youthful jealousy, etc.

The animosity of Thackeray toward Bulwer is, quite apart from the decency or otherwise of its exploitation, of considerable psychological interest. The two men were in many ways so alike that a very slight dislocation of their similarity could make the one more odious to the other than if he had been of a wholly different type. Both were of gentle breeding and old family; both had an egotism over-sensitive to the point of hysteria; both found the writing of fine sentiments compatible with the practice of mean ones; both had affectations peculiar to themselves; both were men of exceptional mental quality. But there was something in the adjustment of these qualities to Bulwer's personality which infuriated Thackeray and his irritation was probably the greater for not being reciprocated. He was jealous of Bulwer; but Bulwer was not jealous of him — and this very lack of jealousy became an extra cause of offence.

Thackeray, as has been said, was a snob who worked an ostentatious anti-snobbery to death. Bulwer, on the other hand, was not in the proper sense a snob at all, but only what jealous persons call a snob. He was rightly convinced of the superiority, to those of most of his writing generation, of his own manners and mind; and if it was a mistake to make his conviction obvious, the failure was one of opportunism, not of courtesy. But the effect of such unashamed superiority on an opponent of Thackeray's calibre was inevitable. Bulwer could not be patronised; therefore he had to be insulted. And the method of insult adopted was that of the street Arab's long nose, with this additional vulgarity that the street Arab was not a genuine street Arab at all, but a well-brought-up boy who thought it clever to appear ill-bred.

IV

The Fraserian persecution of Bulwer began in the magazine's third number (April, 1830) and continued almost without relaxation until February, 1833. Thereafter it became more desultory, and in time almost ceased, until it was revived again by Thackeray in the early forties.

It is essential that an attempt be made to give some idea of the abusive pertinacity with which *Fraser's* pursued their campaign of anti-Bulwerism. The effect on the victim of the magazine's persistent malice was so continuously and increasingly important, that, unless it be realised, we can hardly appreciate the deplorable state of angry mistrust toward critics generally to which he was finally and permanently reduced.

Maginn gauged his man with cruel skill. By opening hostilities with careful, if rather patronising civility, he counted on luring his victim to over-hasty retort. The second stage could then be a little more astringent and would likely produce a further counter cry, on the strength of which criticism could sharpen into impertinence, and impertinence be coarsened into insult. And so indeed matters fell out.

April, 1830, saw the publication of the article on "Fashionable Novels" to which, in connection with Carlyle, reference has already been made. This article is as a whole well-reasoned and sensible. Credit is given to *Pelham* for its gay readability; fault is deservedly found with the turgidity of *The Disowned* and the display of unnecessary knowledge in *Devereux*. In short, although between the lines may be read hints of what was to come — the charges of plagiarism, cheap histrionics and frenetic egoism — the essay must have seemed to the ordinary reader legitimate if rather unfavourable criticism. It had nevertheless the expected effect of producing an answer. In his preface to *Paul Clifford* Bulwer, without mentioning *Fraser's* by name, replied to "some inimical and rather personal but clever observations in a new periodical work." It was a good reply; but unluckily he permitted himself to end with a reference to his critics as "the great unwashed", a joke which, however justifiable, was not easily forgiven. And Maginn, who asked for nothing better than the unforgivable, leapt at the chance of repartee.

His June number led off with a twenty-five page article on "Mr. Edward Lytton Bulwer's Novels" which virtually repeated what had been said two months earlier, but with enough extra animus and additional detail to make the very repetition a promise of continued hostility.[1]

Nor was it long before promise became performance. Two months later, in a satirical symposium (Maginn loved to write this kind of conglomerate satire), were presented all the literary notabilities of the day as competitors for the editorship of *Fraser's Magazine*. After Croly, Campbell, Coleridge, Cunningham, Hazlitt and several others have urged their qualifications, Bulwer appears "mounting a ladder with a half-pay military air, nodding with an air of nonchalance to two or three well-rigged dandies near the Columnus Ægyp-

---

[1] This article, like its predecessor, has been, as stated above, attributed to Carlyle. The attribution which depends on parallel quotation from known work by Carlyle and from this essay, may be generally justifiable; but I confess to a consciousness of the style of Maginn and of the venom of Lockhart in many of its more insulting passages. Possibly editorial embellishment was given to a manuscript originally written by the author of *Sartor Resartus*.

tiacus, waving, with a solemn and imperious air, a branch of cyprus in imitation of the orators of old." His speech, proposing himself for editor, shows him as money-greedy, pedantic in phraseology, and vain to the point of lunacy. The pretence of civility has been finally dropped.

There followed six months (until the end of 1830) during which Bulwer was given a rest. The Fraserians were busy hunting Montgomery and Alaric Watts on the one hand, the *New Monthly*, with its editor and publisher, on the other.

The Age, however, during this interval of Fraserian silence, started a campaign of their own against Bulwer, which from its great similarity to that in *Fraser's* and the coincidence of its chronology can hardly have had a spontaneous origin. In January, 1831, *The Age* led off with a simultaneous attack on Bulwer's *Siamese Twins* and on Westmacott's old enemy Jerdan for praising the poem in *The Literary Gazette*. "The critic's weak point is a dinner, and that Mr. Bulwer knows. Before the publication of whatever he is about to spawn, he feeds the lion of the *Literary Gazette* and then writes his own review." The article goes on to accuse Bulwer of cadging notice in the *Quarterly* by praising Lockhart's *Life of Burns*, and concludes: "We know that Lockhart despises Bulwer's novels and intends to quarter them at the first opportunity."

In February, 1831, *Fraser's* resumed operations and in a review of the "Novels of the Season" carried their anti-Bulwerism a stage further. Bulwer is now a "Silver Fork Polisher", a leader of the "Footman School of Novelists" (Thackeray, among other debts to Maginn, left unacknowledged the origin of Yellow-plush); he cannot rhyme; his wit is strained and at once jealously offensive and sycophantic; as for his satire it is here "paltry drivel", there "molasses." May, 1831, sees an article which was to cause trouble later. An anonymous Fraserian describes Bulwer's private library in Hertford Street. "The living spirit of Pelham seemed to pervade the apartment," with its "carved oak table, massive yet with exquisite and minute decorations"; its "bookshelves of carved oak, each division wreathed with a pattern of ormolu and containing works no doubt of value within and of prodigious finery without"; its "bronze busts of the first quality"; its "Sèvres wafer bowl, curiously wrought inkstand and carved paper-cutter." The description (probably accurate enough, for Bulwer had a flamboyant taste and, as has been seen, often spent needed money on elaborate trifling) concludes with a trite reflection as to the improbability of genius surviving in a "hotbed of luxury" and with these words: "Decoration and display are the propensities of vulgar minds, equally obnoxious to real refinement and allied to that grossest of all worldly spirits, ostentation."

After the usual two-monthly interval the game began again. The May number of the *New Monthly* had contained a fulsome article on Bulwer as a man and a novelist written, in fact, by L. E. L. *Fraser's* for July, 1831, pretended to believe that for this article Bulwer himself was responsible. So cruelly exploited was the false premise on which the Fraserian attack was based that for the first time since the original reference in the preface to *Paul Clifford*, Bulwer was tempted to show sign of temper. Hitherto he had rather bested his tormentors by a contemptuous geniality in indirect riposte; now, however, he contemplated (or was at any rate urged to contemplate) reciprocity.

"Hall," he writes to Rosina on July 1, "the editor of the N[ew] M[onthly],[1] has been here with a copy of Fraser's Magazine for this month, which he said ought to be immediately taken notice of. It is a paper called 'The Autobiography of Edward Lytton Bulwer', attributing, and in a very plausible and solemn manner, the authorship of Miss Landon's article to me. I need not add that it is virulent and abusive to excess."

Actually, however, he made no move for five months. In the meantime, through the over-zeal of Alaric Watts, he

[1] S. C. Hall "carried on" as the *New Monthly* editor after Campbell's resignation and before the appointment of Bulwer himself. (*Cf.* pp. 263, 266.)

became embroiled with *Fraser's* over the library article of the preceding May. Watts published in his *Literary Souvenir* which, although dated 1832 was published during the autumn of 1831, a five-hundred-line satirical fragment by himself, entitled "The Conversazione." The poem itself is a deliberate attack on the Scotch-Irish Grub Street gang — Lockhart, Cunningham Hogg, Crofton Crocker, Maginn and their disciples — whose venality, alcoholism and scurrilous crudity are depicted with greater verve than one would have expected from so ladylike a source. Among other things Watts declared that poor Andrew Picken — a hard-working Scotch novelist whose books had not at the time the success they deserved [1] — had won entry into Bulwer's house on the plea of asking for a contribution to a composite work entitled The Club Book;[2] and, while there, had observed sufficient of the library furnishings to write them up into an article for Fraser's. Picken, who was quite possibly innocent of so mean an action, wrote to Bulwer to ask for a contradiction; he received a reply (dated November 2d) civil enough, so far as he himself was concerned, but carefully insolent toward *Fraser's Magazine.* The correspondence came into the hands of Maginn, with the result that the December number of *Fraser's* contained an open letter to Bulwer, and an appendix dealing with the Picken episode — the whole reaching a climax of offensive vulgarity which makes painful reading even a century later, and at the time must have been quite intolerable.[3]

Unluckily for Bulwer he had already decided to print a public comment on *Fraser's* (mentioning the magazine by name) in the very number of *The New Monthly* which coincided with this, his enemies' most scurrilous attack. Con-

---

[1] *The Dominie's Legacy* (3 vols., 1830) is the best known and in many ways the most individual, but there is much good stuff also in *The Black Watch* (3 vols., 1834).

[2] *The Club Book* appeared in 3 volumes in 1831. The contributors included Galt, G. P. R. James, Moir and the Ettrick Shepherd.

[3] One passage from this letter (the first of a series of "Epistles to the Literati") has already been quoted in connection with *Paul Clifford.*

sequently, by saying his say before the open letter appeared, he actually shot his bolt a month too soon and virtually debarred himself from countering an insolence far cruder and more obvious than the rather trivial one which he had elected to notice.

The challenge which thus inopportunely drew his answering fire had occurred in a description of "Oliver Yorke's Levee", published in *Fraser's* for November. One by one the notabilities approach Regina's editorial throne and make their characteristic obeisance. Bulwer, with Samuel Carter Hall as train-bearer and Colburn and Bentley as "Siamese-Twin" pages, simpers and languidly addresses Oliver Yorke:

I am the very first novelist of the present day and indeed of any day. . . . I am the first philosopher. . . . I am the handsomest man in England. . . . Should any further information be required respecting my merit and advantages, I refer you to my prefaces and dedications and to my autobiography which appeared in *The New Monthly*.

The "royal Oliver" replies discourteously:

I wish your magazine all the success it deserves. *You have long edited it anonymously and miserably.* As to your beauty, I beg to differ with you. You have a good hungry look which for a trading politician is appropriate enough. Your works I have never read. I heard your speech in parliament and have to condole with you thereon. Duly appreciating the honour you have done me by coming here, I beg of you never to repeat it.

It would not have been difficult for Bulwer to ridicule this taunting phantasy in the same vein. Instead he most unwisely fastened on the sentence above italicised, and proceeded to a pompous and forcibly feeble denial of its truth, quite unworthy of his powers.

As might have been expected, the Fraserians chuckled to have lured their victim into such ineffective but complete betrayal of his sufferings. With renewed zest, and without even one number's respite, they carried on the persecution.

The very first item in their issue for January, 1832, was a pretended letter from a contributor deriding in advance Bulwer's already advertised novel of *Eugene Aram* and announcing his intention of novelising The Newgate Calendar in one hundred and twenty-five volumes of which the first three would celebrate the exploits of Bishop and Williams under the title, *The Burker of Barbican*. "Oliver Yorke" approves this letter and appends an amusing jingle "written by a friend of ours", and dealing with the same theme of the forthcoming novel *Eugene Aram :*

E. A. and E. B.

A Christmas Carol, to the Tune of "God save you, merry Gentlemen!"

"Impius ante *Aram*, atque auri cæcus amore."

E. Aram was a pedagogue
   So sullen and so sad;
E. Bulwer was a gentleman
   Wot plied as Colburn's Cad:
And the deeds of both, I grieve to say,
   Were werry, werry bad.

E. Aram he whipped little boys
   With malice and with ire;
E. Bulwer wrote Whig articles,
   As Beelzebub did inspire
And both of them they did these things
   All for the sake of hire.

E. Aram killed a man one day,
   Out of a devilish whim;
E. Bulwer did almost the same —
   A deed well nigh as grim:
For Aram he murder'd Daniel Clarke,
   And Bulwer he murder'd *him*.

E. Aram's crime it was impell'd
That cash he might purloin;
E. Bulwer did his wickedness
For love of Colburn's coin:
Alas! that money should debauch
Two geniuses so fine!

E. Aram he was sent to jail,
And hanged upon a tree;
E. Bulwer is in parliament,
A shabby-genteel M. P.;
But if he writes such murdering books,
What must his ending be?
Why, that in *Fraser's Magazine*
His gibbet we shall see.

February, 1832, intensified hostilities. The issue contained no fewer than three attacks on Bulwer, of which one, though insolent, was semi-serious and the other two frankly derisory. To the first, the review of *Eugene Aram*, more or less promised in January, we will revert in due course. Of the obvious incivilities one was a resuscitation (irrelevant enough to its context and dragged in for its own pert sake) of the description of his private library which had already caused trouble and to spare; but the second was banter more sustained and of better quality. Maginn, seizing an opportunity for one of his favourite symposia, described an imaginary public dinner given in honour of the Ettrick Shepherd. As usual, all manner of contemporary notabilities were dragged into the arena and there butchered to make a Fraserian holiday; as usual Bulwer was among the earliest victims:

The whole array of the literary tribe was headed and led by Mr. Thomas Campbell and Mr. Edward Liston Bulwer[1] according to the precedent of the first crusading army under the command of Walter

[1] It may be observed that *Fraser's* had by now regularly adopted this nickname which, as the real name of a popular comedian of the day, was of course used to imply that all Bulwer's words and actions were mere play-acting.

the Pennyless, who chose as their guides to the Holy Land a goose and a goat.

The crowd surge into the Freemason's Tavern and find their places for dinner.   Toward the end of the banquet, General Sir John Malcolm (Indian administrator and writer on the politics and history of the East) is made to propose the joint healths of Bulwer and Eugene Aram.   In reply, Bulwer says:

"I reverence your title, Sir John.   I love a lord; and it is my delight to be a tuft-hunter."

After which he sings a song — and a song so typical of the ingenious torture to which the Fraserians had now the habit of subjecting him that one may overlook the fact that the verbal ingenuity which gives it point was copied literally from a poem published in *John Bull* eleven years earlier [1] and pay it the compliment of quotation:

LISTON BULWER'S SONG

Though Fraser may call me ass,
    I heed not the pitiful sneerer;
He freely opinions may pass —
    Their value depends on the hearer.
An ass! yet how strange that the word,
    Thus used in malevolent blindness,
I, blessed with adorers, have heard
    In tones of affectionate kindness.

There's Colburn avows I'm an ass-
    ortment of all that is clever;
Ask Hall — he affirms such an ass-
    istant he never saw, never!
Cries Bentley, 'My vigs, vot an ass-
    emblage of talents for puffing!'
Thus all are agreed I'm an ass —
    A fig for Regina's rebuffing!

[1] "Whig-Ass-urance" (*John Bull*).   December 17, 1820, and February 18, 1821.

Let Landon declare I'm an ass-
  onant to love and to beauty;
Cries Mrs. B. 'O what an ass-
  ociate in conjugal duty!'
There's Jerdan exclaims I'm an ass-
  ayer of poesy's pinions;
And I, too, affirm I'm an ass-
  enter to all their opinions.

The Parliament knows I'm an ass-
  ailer of all that is Tory;
The Thunderer vows I'm an ass-
  erter of Radical glory.
Though hitherto I've been an ass-
  uager of rancorous speeches,
Yet still they will find me an ass-
  aulter when liberty teaches.

I own to myself I'm an ass-
  iduous lover and praiser;
But make me of rhino the ass-
  essor, and that is my way, sir.
Poor Colburn! — But see, I'm an assassin of self by confession!
Dear traders! how quickly I ass-
  imilate to the *profession*.

And now for five months "Regina", for one reason or
another, left Bulwer alone.   Indeed, apart from a brief raid
on the self-esteem of Alaric Watts, guerilla warfare generally
was almost wholly suspended.   Possibly protests against
the magazine's protracted malice were becoming more numerous than the publisher liked.   Certainly there is evidence of
complaint from disinterested sources against the rather wearisome sprightliness of Fraserian raillery.   But once again the
columns of *The Age* showed a significant liveliness during their
contemporary's holiday.   On February 19, 1832, was printed

an unseemly anecdote about Bulwer and his female admirers; on April 1 a violent little article praises Lockhart and the *Quarterly* and is offensive to the *New Monthly* and its editor; on June 17 Bulwer is attacked for his "stupid and ignorant speech on the Stamp Duty for newspapers"; on August 5 both he and his brother Henry are amusingly guyed for recent speeches in the House.

Chapter Seven

Eugene Aram — *Its popularity* — *The constituent elements badly mixed* — *Contemporary and modern criticisms of* Eugene Aram

Bulwer's impulse toward literary exploitation of the famous story of *Eugene Aram* may, as he himself declared,[1] have come from the discovery that at one time the real Aram had acted as tutor to members of the Bulwer family at Heydon in Norfolk. It may also, as one is inclined to suspect, have been encouraged by the success of Thomas Hood's poem *The Dream of Eugene Aram*, which was first published in *The Gem* for 1829, issued separately with illustrations by Harvey in 1831, and widely acclaimed. But it is certain that his decision to undertake, first a dramatic, then a fictional rendering of Aram's tragic tale, was a direct by-product of that study of the *Newgate Calendar* which preceded the writing of *Paul Clifford*.

With his strong sense of melodrama, Bulwer was naturally quick to respond to the narrative possibilities of criminal history. His first essay in the genre had won him a wide, if somewhat equivocal reputation; and that he should forthwith pass on from a novel of highway robbery to one of murder was more or less inevitable. Such progression being, as it were, pre-ordained, he could hardly have found a theme so congenial as the story of Aram's long-undiscovered murder of Daniel Clarke, a theme recently and triumphantly revived by a popular poet, and one which of itself appealed equally to his feeling for the macabre and to his delight in hereditary association. ¦

The actual facts of Aram's history had of course for long enough been easily available. Not only were they included

[1] *Cf.* the preface to the uniform edition of 1840.

in a continuation of Hume's history, but a pamphlet, giving an account of the trial and the text of Aram's defence, had been published in the very year of his execution (1759) and continually reprinted. Also, because the story offered ideal material to the several publishers of sensational chapbooks and Terrific Registers which flourished during the first quarter of the nineteenth century, it had, in various forms and variously garbled, been universally disseminated.

Bulwer's first idea was to use the incidents of the case as basis for a stage tragedy; but he changed his mind and re-cast his material in the form of a novel, which appeared in three volumes in January, 1832. Eighteen months afterward, in the last number of *The New Monthly* to appear under his editorship (August, 1833), he printed, as a sort of curiosity, an act and a half of his tragedy, stating in so many words that it would in all probability never be completed.[1] He also added the fragment to the "Standard Novel" edition of *Eugene Aram*, published late in 1833, and retained it in the uniform edition of 1840, characteristically maintaining all the time his favourite pose of nonchalant apology for a piece of writing which, in fact, was being scrupulously preserved.

The novel *Eugene Aram* took Europe by storm and became one of the most abidingly popular of all Bulwer's works. Indeed it is probably today among the three or four of his fictions which are still more than occasionally read, being kept alive by the continued interest in the true tale of Aram and his trial.

To the modern reader the novel's qualities are likely to be obscured by its more obvious defects. Written as a "follow" to *Paul Clifford* and, so far as the author was concerned, at a time of desperate pressure, *Eugene Aram* has characteristics which were acceptable enough to period taste or arose inevi-

---

[1] Lord Lytton infers (I, 387) from a letter written by Rosina during 1832, that the play *was* at one time finished and even produced. But she probably wrote in such a way as to confuse Bulwer's unfinished tragedy with one of the several adapted melodramas (*cf.* Allardyce Nicoll: *History of XIX Century Drama*, vol. II) from Bulwer's novel and produced during the spring of 1832.

tably from contemporary circumstance, but are irritating to a less flamboyant posterity. Undeniably, Bulwer's perpetual tendency to overwrite declares itself in exaggerated form throughout the book, and for this exaggeration there was reason and to spare. Excited with the flattery which followed *Paul Clifford* and with a natural ambition this time to go one better, he was tempted to out-Bulwer Bulwer; tormented by grinding work of every kind and by the nagging malice of his enemies, he sought self-assertion in an overstraining of his natural magniloquence.

He can hardly be blamed for a certain lack of serenity by anyone who considers the sort of life he was leading during 1831. Member of Parliament since May, he shared in the excitements and exhaustions of the first abortive passage of the Reform Bill through the House of Commons and lived the hectic life of a radical member in a Tory society at a time when the country was aflame with riotous disorder and those in sympathy with Reform were regarded by the other side as blackguards and traitors. At the same time, the success of *Paul Clifford* had established him as perhaps the leader of the young novelists of the day, had exposed him to the dangerous flattery of publishers, and by November had placed him in the editorial chair of the *New Monthly Magazine;* while the jealous hostility provoked by his sudden rise to notoriety so jarred his already fretted nerves as to render him at times almost crazy with wounded vanity and a sense of his helplessness at the hands of his enemies.

Is it surprising that the hysterical self-consciousness produced by a too-sensitive egoism, by money troubles, and by work at once excessive and miscellaneous, should have expressed itself in *Eugene Aram* in an intensification of all his normal stylistic faults?

First comes a high-flown dedication to Sir Walter Scott, in the course of which Bulwer describes himself as ''one who to that bright and undying flame, which now streams from the grey hills of Scotland, has turned from his first childhood with a deep and interesting devotion." Yet it was the same man who, writing to Rosina in 1827, described Scott as "the Arch Quack of tale-writing to whom I pray night and morning that I may see justice done before I die." Then follows a Preface, addressed to the reader in the second person singular, and a sorry specimen of the affected self-advertisement with which, and to his own undoing, he continually fed the malice of his enemies. When the tale itself gets under way, the contrast between the author's genuine talent for story-telling and his refusal to be content just to tell a story becomes almost grievous. Examples of genteelisms from *Eugene Aram* have already been given; but there are interruptions longer, and no less superfluous, in the form of rhetorical digressions, rhapsodies, pruderies, learned interpolations of historical fact, and other obstacles to reading pleasure, which almost make one cry with vexation, so wilfully does the novelist seem to do injustice to his own powers and to the possibilities of his theme.

And the book is not only an obvious product of over-wrought nerves; it also bears every mark of work too hastily done and of ideas insufficiently thought out. One hesitates to accuse Bulwer of deliberate insincerity in his moments of rapturous admiration for blushing virginity and for manly candour. More probably he did not trouble (or had not the time) properly to fuse his sense of a dramatic plot with his desire to gratify his public. Consequently, to please himself, he drew his portrait of Aram (a skilful if rather laboured portrait of a high-minded scholar, who years before had been driven by misery to a deed of violence wholly alien to his nature); set it against a background of wild country such as he loved to paint; devised a number of more or less comic figures to surround and set off the remorseful dignity of the central figure; added a conventional hero and heroine, and then — but only then — framed and glazed the whole composition with the gilded ornament and gleaming surface of facile rhetoric and refined sentiment.

In consequence *Eugene Aram* is full of contradictions — not contradictions of fact but of quality; and it throws a queer light on the literary predilections of the early thirties that among the many faults charged against the book, the fault of inconcoction was passed over, while those persons who admired its good qualities complained (if they complained at all) of defects quite other than that most noticeable to a reader of today.   So far as the chief critics and the author's personal acquaintances were concerned, the book was received with a fairly balanced chorus of praise and blame.   *The Court Journal* and *The Literary Gazette* were of course favourable.   Of other more significant expressions of approval one or two may be chosen for special notice.   Plumer Ward congratulated Bulwer on "the most powerful of your writings"; Horace Smith wrote from Brighton on January 12, 1832: "Really and truly everyone who has read the book and whose opinion I think worth asking or listening to assures me that it is by far the best thing you have done"; Pierce Egan was so moved that he called on Bulwer and solemnly presented him with a most disagreeable relic of the infamous Thurtell, declaring that the author of *Eugene Aram* alone among literary men was worthy to possess such a memento of an important murderer; Charles Ollier's letter is particularly interesting, because it refers to a rather startling outbreak of the deliberate desire to shock, which later took firmer hold on Bulwer but in this early hyper-genteel period was but rarely indulged.

"I am delighted," wrote Ollier on November 18, 1831 (as the publisher's reader he had early access to the text of the book), "with the 2nd and 3rd volumes, especially with the landscape painting which is fuller of interest, truth and sweetness and genuine English character than anything I am acquainted with.   But what will the reader say to the corporal's disquisition touching fie-fies? [1]   This would have

---

[1] Corporal Buntings, asked his opinion of the ladies, replies:
Ladies — augh! — of all them 'ere creturs I respects the kept ladies most. . . .
Gad, how well they knows the world. one quite envies the she-rogues: they beats

done very well in Fielding's time, but we are all now 'san-
guinary moral', as the Irishman would say, and it is not correct to suppose in public that there is any such thing in the
world as a fie-fie.''

Finally may be quoted the opinion of John Forster, given
in one of the first of the many hundreds of letters he was
destined to write to Bulwer, and expressing a criticism passed
by several people at the time and still maintained by more
than one student of the present day:

John Forster to Edward Bulwer

Jan. 4, 1832.

I have read *Eugene Aram* with very great and greedy pleasure.
You have worked his character out with great force and with a
severe simplicity that is admirable.   There is no lurching from it to
the right or left, nor episodising.   But, forgive the impertinence, I
could have wished that you had adhered more strictly to the small
information we have of Eugene Aram, because I think the cause
which he himself is reported to have assigned for the murder —
namely that of jealousy of Clarke with his wife — is more likely
to have urged him to the deed than mere gain.[1]   I confess you have
put the last motive in a singularly novel way and managed to make
even it respectable.   Perhaps, too, the story is more effective by it;
but one likes to have as little romance as possible mixed up with a
story simple in itself, and standing out fearfully in one's contemplation of strange realities.

This letter of Forster's, though it relates only to one detail
in Bulwer's adaptation of the true story of Eugene Aram,
raises the whole problem of his wisdom in choosing for fiction
so well-known a narrative, and, having chosen it, in departing at all from recorded fact.   The *Edinburgh*, which gave
the novel a lengthy and very respectful review in April, 1832,
took the same line as Forster but with a difference.   Arguing

the wives hollow. . . . Oh, they be clever creturs; and they'll do what they likes
with Old Nick when they gets there, for 'tis the old gentlemen they cozens the best.

[1] A review in *The Literary Guardian* (January 7, 1832) suggests the very same
improvement and, together with much compliment, contains several other shrewd
criticisms.

that every reader would already have a preconceived picture of Eugene Aram in his mind, the critic objected to the presentation of the man not as a cold-blooded villain but as a scholar of refinement, capable of self-forgetful love, honourable and deservedly an object of pity in the terrible dilemma brought upon him by the sudden recrudescence of an ugly past. The writer declared this unorthodox interpretation of Aram's character to be not only a check to readers' appreciation but also contrary to nature. No man (he maintained) who had in fact done so dreadful a deed would be capable, even years afterward, of the nobility and gentleness of the Aram of Bulwer's novel. Ebenezer Elliott, who wrote to Bulwer after reading a fragment of the tragedy in the *New Monthly* (he had not, apparently, read the previously published novel at all), made a suggestion curiously opposite to the *Edinburgh's* and yet prompted by much the same feeling. In his unfinished play Bulwer had made Aram precisely the unfeeling, ruthless creature which the *Edinburgh* demanded; but Elliott cries out against this waste of dramatic opportunity. "After having in the agonies and too real madness of hunger become a murderer, let him then display his unavailing tenderness, his high intellectuality, and spectator and reader alike will be heartbroken. But make it ideal, not historical, and give your hero any name but that of Eugene Aram." Half of this advice Bulwer had forestalled; the Aram of the novel is just the Aram whom Elliott wished to see in the play. But he was nevertheless Aram.

And now, a century after the event, regret that the novelist saw fit to alter fact is still alive. One well-known critic [1] considers that, by re-writing Aram's speech for his defence and altering the procedure of the trial, Bulwer deliberately destroyed an effectiveness which, if he had held more closely to what really happened, might have become part of his novel and transfigured it. Another authority [2] includes

[1] E. E. Kellett, in a letter to the present writer.
[2] R. Ellis Roberts in *Everyman*. October 31, 1929.

EUGENE ARAM AND MADELINE

From a drawing by "Phiz"

Eugene Aram in the category of "bad thrillers", because
the author "uneasily aware that his criminal was a sordid
rogue, deliberately sentimentalized him."

But inasmuch as these modern judgments resemble their
predecessors in testing Bulwer's novel by standards purely
literary, they partake of the same irrelevance. Although no
one will deny that as a work of art *Eugene Aram* would have
benefited by forestalling most of the criticisms quoted, these
criticisms in their various ways do Bulwer injustice by doing
him more than justice. They ignore one element in his
novel-writing which was seldom wholly absent and in these
early years predominant — the opportunist element of giving
the public what it wanted.

His skill in pre-judging popular taste has already been mentioned; but it may here with advantage be touched upon once
more, because *Eugene Aram* offers a good example of his unerring prescience, not only in choice of subject, but also in the
manner of its presentation. He deliberately retained the
familiar names of Aram and some of his companions, *just
because they were familiar*. He knew that the large uncritical public responded more readily to a theme about which
they knew already, than to novelty, however ingenious.
But he knew, also, that even a subject so well-known as the
case of Eugene Aram must be presented in such a way as to
soothe the susceptibilities of the time, and that it would not
please the mass of novel-readers to find an eighteenth-century tale told in the forthright manner of its own *démodé* day.
Further, he guessed that, although time was now ripe to make
the central figure of a tale an actual criminal (Paul Clifford,
for all his brigandage, was more of a gallant than a wrong-
doer), he must so present his criminal as to appeal to readers'
sympathies. Logic in characterisation, accuracy in legal
procedure, retention of historical fact — all these were unimportant beside the imperative need to conciliate the taste of
the great public of the day in emotional and narrative pre-
sentment of a plot.

Admirably was that need fulfilled. The immediate and enduring enthusiasm shown by the uncritical public in England and Europe for the novel proved how shrewdly the author had assessed his problem, how successfully he had embellished the mid-eighteenth century to the liking of the eighteen-thirties.

And seeing how badly he needed money at this time, few people would nowadays be inclined to blame him for deliberately tickling the groundlings, if only, when the crisis had passed, he had reverted to a restraint more worthy of his talents.   Unfortunately (as in other respects had already happened after the public welcome to *The Disowned*) opportunism grew with success into a second nature.   Not only, while he was actually writing *Eugene Aram*, did Bulwer begin to believe in his own rendering of the murderer's character (indeed, later on, he became so convinced that the man had been in fact innocent of the crime that he altered the novel's ending [1]), but when in due course he came to the writing of other novels, it was the harder for him to resist a general overstraining of style and composition because in this case such overstraining had triumphantly succeeded.

Simultaneously with approbation and friendly criticism appeared in certain quarters attacks of the most virulent kind. These had no effect on the book's popularity; indeed they probably stimulated it.   But to Bulwer himself they were agony.   He was so constituted that the pain of two hostile notices could drive out all memory of twenty friendly ones, and he never learnt to console himself for the insults of the few by dwelling in silent contentment on the admiration of the many.

The assaults on *Eugene Aram* were particularly painful, because the most unmerciful of all was true enough to be unanswerable.   The Fraserian review of his novel — "A Good Tale Badly Told" (February, 1832) — was brilliantly written

[1] *Cf.* the edition of 1851.

and no less brilliantly offensive. "The Pelham version of
Eugene Aram's extraordinary history . . . is a good story
overlaid with tinselled frippery, spun out into tedious
dialogue and vapid declamation, and as unpleasant to a sound
taste in writing as is a glass of curaçao diluted in a pint of
water to an unvitiated palate." Very good and quite indis-
putable. If only Maginn (it was surely the doctor himself
who wrote this notice) had stopped there or thereabouts, his
review of *Eugene Aram* might hold the suffrages of readers of
any age down to the present day. But unfortunately it does
not. Unable, in the first place, to refrain from personal
abuse, the critic over-labours the ancient and foolish jibe at
Bulwer's liking for low company, attributes the choice of the
theme to the novelist's inability to invent, accuses him of
plagiarising *Faust* and *The Pirate* and finally — a little illogi-
cally — rails at him for elaborating or altering in the slightest particular the account of the trial published in pamphlet
form seventy years before. In the second place the writer
criticises Bulwer on moral grounds. It was bad enough to
present a murderer as the central figure of a novel; to make
him an appealing character, with whose predicament the
reader must sympathise, was worse; to base on so unsavoury a foundation "an ostensible labour to be didactic,
philosophical and practically moral" and to fill three volumes with "objectional sentiments", "habitual tampering
with sacred subjects", and a "constant hankering after pro-
fanity and blasphemy" was worst of all.

About ninety per cent. of this, coming from the editorial
clique of *Fraser's Magazine*, was sheer cant. But it harmonised with the prejudices of the time and found an echo in
other quarters where Bulwer-persecution was not a staple
trade. *The Athenæum* "hoped soon to see Mr. Bulwer laying
the rich garlands of his fancy on a more hallowed shrine than
a gibbet"; Ruskin's private school headmaster, in a book
designed to guide the pious in their reading, warned them
especially against Byron, Bulwer and Scott as writers of Bad

Books, glowed with outraged virtue. *The Age*, in the course
of a satirical description of an imaginary meeting at the
Garrick Club, summoned to pay respect to the memory of
Scott, makes Bulwer advance into the middle of the room,
"adjust his whiskers which were carrotty" and deliver a
poetical speech ending:

> The Public, who believe that I
> Come here to mourn that Scott should die, —
> Too trustful Public! Heaven spare 'em
> To puff and pay for *Eugene Aram*.

Minor journals (members of that swarm of ephemeral publications which appeared between 1830 and 1834) took the
Fraserian cue, so far as they shared that magazine's ulterior
convictions, and fell back on the conventional quips against
dandyism and self-advertisement, if considerations more serious were beyond their scope.

The Cab cut the novel to pieces on March 3, 1832: "It is the
murder of a murderer . . . an attempt to convert a swindler
and an assassin into the sentimental love-making, speech-
making hero of a sickly romance.   Why does not Mr. Bulwer
immortalize Mr. Burke? "   *The Literary Censor* (March 17,
1832) printed an amusing dialogue in verse between Bulwer
and Tom Moore in the course of which Moore asks:

> What writes my Bulwer now! What precious tale
> About some harden'd inmate of a jail!
> What thief?   What murd'rer occupies your brain,
> By which applause and pence you hope to gain?

and followed it up with: "Indispensable Ingredients for the
Composition of a Novel" which, from line 13, reads:

> Or, like Ned Bulwer, you may write a book
> About a villain of romantic look;
> Some murd'rer who for paltry lucre kills,
> Then moralizes on this life's sad ills;
> Woos some pure lady with his bloodstained hand,
> And rants away in tragic raptures grand.

The Thief (April 21, 1832) tells the story of a would-be fashionable farmer who christened the two best pigs of a new farrow "Eugene Aram" and "Pelham", and finally "once more anatomized the former for the benefit of the public."

So, while on the one hand sales mounted steadily, on the other there spread through the dusty gutters of the press little rivulets of insolence and mockery; and by the time these showed signs of running dry, *Fraser's* was ready with replenishment.

Chapter Eight

Thackeray's Elizabeth Brownrigge — *Maginn's pen-portrait of* Bulwer — *Lockhart's anonymous insolence*

The first instalment of Thackeray's *Elizabeth Brownrigge*, a tale inscribed to the "Author of *Eugene Aram*", was published in *Fraser's* for August, 1832. In the dedicatory letter "a young man who has for a length of time applied himself to the cultivation of literature" tells how the reading of *Eugene Aram* convinced him that the way to popularity lay no longer through an attempt "to interest the feelings of the reader in favour of virtue and to increase his detestation of vice" but rather through so mixing vice and virtue "as to render it impossible that any preference should be given to either or that the one, indeed, should be at all distinguishable from the other." The letter proceeds, with much ironical adulation, to salute Bulwer as "the father of a new *lusus naturæ* school"; a novelist who, wishing to introduce an adulterer into his story, makes him a country curate; who chooses his romantic hero from the pages of *The Newgate Calendar*, who even endows a cat with the main attributes of a dog. In obedience to the doctrine of improbability thus laid down, the youthful author of *Elizabeth Brownrigge* has decided to present the loathsome murderess of two helpless little girls as a beautiful young gentlewoman of wealth and culture; her crime as worthy, if not the admiration, at least the sympathies of the reader, and her lap-dog Muggletonian as, in disposition and habits, a cat. All of which he so ingeniously does that *Elizabeth Brownrigge* is still an amusing (if over-protracted) pastiche, provided it be read while *Eugene*

Aram is fresh in the memory.   This condition is not an unreasonable one.   It is unfair to any parody written for topical
consumption to judge it apart from its model, and particularly
unfair to one which follows its original as closely as *Elizabeth
Brownrigge* follows the pattern of Bulwer's tale.

This same August number of *Fraser's* contained also an
important anti-Bulwerism written by the editor himself.
For over two years one of the most popular features of the
magazine had been the "Gallery of Literary Characters" —
a series of pen portraits of prominent persons of the day, all
but a few written by Maginn himself and illustrated with
likenesses by Maclise.   As Number 27 of this Gallery Maginn
now introduced Bulwer; and his character study of the man
whom he had unremittingly derided has not only the satirical
brilliance, the verbal felicity, the occasionally tasteless humour, and the recklessness of statement which one would
expect, but also a justice in ultimate comment and a frank
recognition of even an enemy's potentiality characteristic of
that fundamental intellectual honesty with which "the doctor" has already been credited.

The brief essay begins with several of Maginn's favourite
jibes about lineage, whiskers and bad poetry.   Next comes a
reference to L. E. L. which supports the theory that the poetess
played an important, if involuntary, part in provoking the
Irishman's original hostility to Bulwer.   "L. E. L.", he
writes, "in her *Romance and Reality* has so completely depic-
tured Bulwer (we shall not say *con amore*, lest that purely technical phrase should be construed literally) that it would be
useless etc. etc."   At the very end of his pen portrait, however, the doctor sheds his irresponsible scandal-mongering
and does his subject a word of justice.   "If he would give
up his affectations — and surely he is now old enough to do
so — if he would forswear the use of such words as 'liberal
principles', 'enlarged ideas', 'progress of mind', 'behind
the age' and other nonsense of that kind . . . there is the
making of something well worth praising in Bulwer, and

when we see it nobody will be happier to proclaim it than ourselves."

Which last would probably have been proved true enough had Maginn survived as *Fraser's* editor for another ten years. But, by the time that Bulwer had passed through the fire of private misfortune and, scarred but impressive, had started his lonely pilgrimage through the forties, Maginn had disappeared; and his magazine was in other hands — hands better tended, maybe, than those of the pot-house doctor, but meaner and more treacherous.

This Literary Portrait was not quite the last attention to be paid by Maginn to Bulwer; but henceforward mockery and denigration became less the official policy of *Fraser's* and more the speciality of individual contributors. The completion of *Elizabeth Brownrigge* was Thackeray's contribution to the September number; and Thackeray's again was an article on the Annuals, published in December and containing a rather wanton little snarl at the reviewer's bugbear.[1]

But neither of these contributions had the peculiar significance of an item published in February, 1833, and hidden away as part of a miscellaneous editorial commentary. The eighth instalment of Bulwer's topical fantasy *Asmodeus at Large*, published in the *New Monthly* for the previous December, had contained some remarks unfriendly to the proposal for perpetuating Abbotsford in the possession of the Scott family as a memorial to the fame of Sir Walter; and these remarks, angrily quoted in the February *Fraser's*, were made the excuse for a particularly coarse attack on the *New*

[1] Referring to a page in *The Amulet* on which the editor (S. C. Hall) announced that "the first sheet had been reserved for my friend Mr. Bulwer whose promised contribution had unfortunately at the last minute to be postponed till next year", the reviewer breaks into apostrophe: "Hear this, ye readers of annual pocket books! Bulwer — ay, Bulwer ipsissimus — postpones his aid till next year! He must have the *first* sheet, else he would not write. Put by the pence, therefore, into your pockets that you may have money ready to purchase whatever the gentleman in his condescension shall be pleased to give you."

Monthly's editor. The point ostensibly at issue was obscurely and confusingly put, and there was little pretence of argument. In the place of discussion of the Abbotsford scheme, such phrases as "mean blackguardism", "a byword of scorn as an incarnation of everything that is shabby", "paltry spite", and "beastly impertinence" were scattered plentifully over two pages of abuse.

Neither Maginn nor Thackeray was capable of such clumsy controversialism. Both could write, and both knew well that to lash one's victim is more painful than to bludgeon him. One's first impulse is to conclude that these crudely insulting pages were written by some minor Fraserian, to whose venom a brief license had been given. But further investigation leaves little doubt that they represent Lockhart's attempt to revenge himself on an enemy whom he dared not meet face to face. Consider the evidence. Immediately following on the *Asmodeus* comments on the Scott Memorial scheme had followed a direct (and merited) criticism of Lockhart's unctuous share in the editing of Murray's seventeen-volume edition of Byron's Works.[1] This one instalment of *Asmodeus*, therefore, had contained two features personally distasteful to Lockhart, who had material interest in the final decision as to the Scott Memorial and prided himself not a little on his comprehensive editing of Byron's poetical remains. Nor is this all. The Fraserian tirade against the *New Monthly's* criticism of the Abbotsford Committee ends with the following quite irrelevant paragraph:

The author of the epistle to the editor of the *Quarterly* in the last number of the *New Monthly* [2] is a poor *valet de plume* and nothing better. That letter we had an intention of dissecting; but there is no use of cracking a cockroach on such an anvil as ours. In criti-

---

[1] This edition was originally announced as to be edited by Moore and completed in fourteen volumes; but the plan was altered and a later prospectus made clear that the annotations were by various named authorities. Lockhart's responsibility for the gathering of unpublished poems and the editing of the volumes containing them was generally recognised.

[2] January, 1833. *Cf.* p. 183.

cism absurd, in feeling base, in conception creeping and degraded, it is beneath our notice."

Unanswerable challenges are often declared beneath the notice of the man challenged; Lockhart had in an earlier quarrel shown himself a reluctant duellist, and in the present case no public answer was ever given, either by the editor of the *Quarterly* in person or by anyone on his behalf, to the very plain questions which Bulwer, over his own name, had put to him. The conclusion is surely obvious. It is a fair presumption that Lockhart, who took his revenges more readily by devious ways than by face to face, thought by anonymous vituperation in another magazine to square accounts with one who publicly and unmistakably had knocked him down.

Chapter Nine

The New Monthly Magazine — *Early history* — *Henry Colburn* — *Campbell as editor* — *Bulwer becomes editor* — *Policy of the paper revolutionised* — *New contributors* — *Bulwer and Leigh Hunt* — *Lady Blessington's* Journal of Conversations with Lord Byron — *The editor's own contributions* — *His energy and industry* — *Bulwer and Tennyson* — *Bulwer and Mrs. Gore*

What may be termed the first phase of the Tory-cum-Grub Street persecution of Bulwer was now more or less at an end. The moment is therefore opportune for filling the remaining gap in the narrative of Bulwer's life up to the summer of 1833 and examining the concrete achievement and the effects on his mind and friendships of his period of editorship of the *New Monthly Magazine*.

The *New Monthly* was founded by Henry Colburn in 1814 as a Conservative rival to Sir Richard Phillips' *Monthly Magazine*, of which the Radical principles were regarded with dismay by those in official circles and by private persons with something to lose. Until 1820 the new paper pursued the rather unconvincing career of a political journal whose policy was mainly a negation of that propounded by someone else. Whatsoever Phillips' paper advocated, the *New Monthly* opposed; and whensoever ministers were attacked by the *Monthly* they were by the *New Monthly* forthwith defended.

In 1820, however, a change in the general situation of the country and, even more importantly, in the ambitions of the *New Monthly's* proprietor, led to its transformation from a political magazine with a garnishing of belles lettres to a review predominantly literary. That the immediate danger

of a Jacobin revolution in England had passed was now evident to the most timid of conservatives; consequently, in proportion as subversive propaganda in the *Monthly* or elsewhere
ceased to alarm the upholders of established things, official
anxiety for a continuance of the *New Monthly* on its old lines
weakened and died.   Simultaneously Colburn himself determined to extend his book-publishing operations and, from the
hitherto loosely affiliated departments of his rather miscellaneous business (he had a periodical department, a lending
library, a series of agencies for French publishing houses and
a small book business of his own) to develop a general publishing house on ambitious lines.   For this purpose a full-
dress literary magazine was essential; and he had to decide
whether to develop his existing literary journal, *The Literary
Gazette*, and let the *New Monthly* die, or to convert the *New
Monthly* into a journal of belles lettres on an impressive scale
and leave *The Literary Gazette* to take its chance.   That he
chose the latter course was typical of his commercial shrewdness.   Alone of London publishers, Colburn at this moment
realised the economic trend of the new decade.   He guessed
that the country was likely for some years to frolic in a fools'
paradise of post-war prosperity; that books and magazines,
provided they were pretentious enough to be classed among
the luxuries which persons of means were eager to enjoy,
could claim their share of the benefits of a spendthrift epoch.
Consequently he made his plans on what may be suitably described as a large-paper scale.   His books should be fashionable books and his magazine a fashionable magazine.   *The
Literary Gazette* was very well in its way.   It had done good
service during the teens, and William Jerdan, its editor, was
Colburn's friend.   But *The Literary Gazette* had always been
more a record of publications than a cultural ornament for a
drawing-room table,[1] and when a good offer for a part inter-

---

[1] It specialised in short reviews of new publications and is even today of the greatest value as a calendar of appearances.   Although its original literary contents —
poems, stories, essays and the like — were not without significance, its format and
main utility were rather practical than decorative.

est in the paper was received from the firm of Longman (whose list was more serious than Colburn's and appealed rather to the library than to the boudoir) its proprietor sold a half share in it — and turned his attention to the embellishment of the *New Monthly*.[1]

His first act was to engage the popular poet Thomas Campbell as editor, with Cyrus Redding as a most necessary assistant; and this hard-working but slightly acidulated journalist afterward published amusing details[2] of the incompetence of the poet-editor in his new post and the unappreciated efficiency of his second in command.

But for all his negligence of the more technical duties of an editor, Campbell kept loyal to his magazine a good band of contributors. Talfourd, who had begun writing dramatic criticism before the journal was refurbished in 1820, continued to provide a theatrical chronicle. Horace Smith, always prolific, wrote regularly, and having become a Colburnite on periodical terms, remained one as a three-volume costume-novelist. By the same process the Banim brothers were attached as novelists to the proprietor of the *New Monthly*.

How the astute publisher brought Campbell and the young Bulwer together, and the kindness shown by the elderly poet to the clever youth have already been described. In 1830 Campbell resigned his editorship and went over to the *Metropolitan;* Redding was succeeded by Samuel Carter Hall. For a few months the *New Monthly* ran with its own momentum and without an official editor. The post was then offered to Bulwer, and in November, 1831, he issued his first number.

It has generally been assumed that Bulwer, in an editorial capacity, was more of a failure than a success. Prejudice, hostile and friendly, has declared on the one hand that he was

---

[1] Colburn's name appeared on the *Literary Gazette* for the last time on November 20, 1819. The first number of the New Series of *The New Monthly* was published in January, 1821.

[2] In his *Literary Reminiscences of Thomas Campbell* (2 vols. 1860) and in his *Fifty Years Recollections* (3 vols. 1858).

too much of an egoist; on the other, that his genius was too aspiring to achieve the stubborn self-effacement necessary to an editor who knows what he wants and means to make other people provide it for him. Undeniably his period of office saw a heavy fall in the paper's circulation. But a careful examination of the *New Monthly* as it was during his reign suggests that if the content of the magazine were indeed to blame for its loss of popularity, it was only because the quality was changed from the nondescript to the determinate too suddenly to suit the taste of the public.[1] In such a case Bulwer's only editorial shortcoming was a too rapid intelligence; and one may hazard in all seriousness that, had he not been so much in advance of his time, he might have come to rank among the great editors of the nineteenth century. He was hard-working, a brilliant improviser, and a man of retentive memory; almost immediately he transformed what had been a pleasant, but quite fortuitous assemblage of articles by various hands on various themes into an organised and forcible expression of his own convictions and his own personality; by the end of his short two years of management the *New Monthly* had a driving power and individuality which it showed neither before nor afterward.

But such volcanic improvement was too fierce for the paper's public. Bulwer was in a hurry for the millennium, and had not the patience to take his readers with him. Overflowing with enthusiasm for reform, with interest in social developments, with views on philosophy, literature and the passing

---

[1] The following comment from one of the ephemeral periodicals of the day, published just after Bulwer's retirement from his editorial duties, expresses what was probably a shrewd opinion of the bad effect on the paper of a too sudden swing-over from indolence to energy.

"Under Campbell's dynasty, or to speak more correctly, towards the conclusion of his reign, this talented periodical betrayed symptoms of exhaustion and decay. When Bulwer ascended the throne his restless spirit roused its slumbering powers and the *New Monthly* acquired the haughty stride of the political partisan in lieu of the mincing gait of a 'waiting gentlewoman.' But insipidity and turmoil are alike unsuited to the purpose of literature. Under the present commonwealth the *juste milieu* is likely to be attained betwixt platitude on the one hand and fiery zeal on the other." (*The Rover.* No. 1, September 14, 1833.)

show, he tried to rush the slow-minded British off their feet, only to find (as others of his kind have always found) that he had hurtled past them into unprofitable space and they remained exactly where they were before. He reintroduced politics (and provocative politics into the bargain) to a paper from which for ten years they had been more or less banished; he preached a great extension of education, benefits for the rural and industrial poor, the need for recognition of talent rather than wealth, the merits of foreign nations and the shortcomings of his own. In fact, he not only invited his subscribers to a greater intellectual concentration than they were inclined to achieve; but by the opinions which he thrust upon them he discomposed the old-fashioned and the frivolous alike.

When to the effects of unwanted editorial stimulus were added those of managerial disorganisation, a fall in the circulation of *The New Monthly* became inevitable. This disorganisation was serious, arising from no less a cause than a complete breach between Colburn and his partner Bentley. The two parted company in September, 1832, that is to say less than a year after Bulwer became editor. Colburn was bought out of book-publishing and retired temporarily to Windsor; but he retained the ownership of his magazine and its by-products, which were published for the absent proprietor by his former partner. Now a magazine handled by a man who was not only unfriendly to its actual owner but himself more of a book-publisher than a manipulator of periodical publicity, was not the same thing as one directly controlled by an ever present and ambitious proprietor. It is only reasonable to assume that less urgent interest was shown in the *New Monthly* under the new régime than under the old. Certainly the "proprietor's" farewell compliments to the ex-editor, which preface the issue for September, 1833, show a nervous determination to abandon controversial writing and get back to "safety first." Wherefore it is likely that Bulwer, when in the summer of 1833 he found his manifold activ-

ities too much even for his energy, was readily released, on
the one hand, because the absent Colburn was anxious in his
paper's interest for peace at any price, and on the other, the
present Bentley, having secured to himself the publishing of
at least the next three books, actually preferred to set a star
author free from all literary duties save those of novel-writing.

II

An "Address to the Public" headed the first number of the
New Monthly to appear under Bulwer's auspices, and forthwith it became obvious that a strong element of political discussion would be maintained "in order to bring before the
Public whatever seems to us to require reform or to need protection." The tone of that discussion was made equally
obvious by the article following, which debated the best way
to gain, at the second opportunity, the support of the House of
Lords for the Reform Bill. This article is a little menacing.
"Tremble — yes, Lords and Commons, high and low, rich
and poor, one with another — let us tremble lest a large
mass of men [with hatred not so much to property in bor-
oughs as to property in general] easily led and easily inflamed,
obtain a head, an organisation, a developed purpose." Small
wonder if a public accustomed to the somnolent detachment
of Campbell and the non-committal impersonality of S. C.
Hall, stirred uneasily at this sudden rumour of disturbance.
Nor were their alarms lessened by a passage later on in the
same number where the "Co-editors" discuss their future
policy and their contemporaries. *The Westminster Review* is
applauded for its steady support of a coherent reformist
policy; *Blackwood's* is attacked for "Claverhouse suggestions,
flippant with murther", for thwarting the Bill and its ideals.
The Edinburgh receives credit for an exposure of Croker's edition of Boswell ("such an ostentation of slipslop; such a
pomposity of twaddle" — the essay was Macaulay's), but
its remoteness from actuality is energetically deplored.
"Consider the character of the period, the stormy events, the

fiery and intent excitement that colour existent affairs, and
then read the list of subjects in the *Edinburgh Review*. About
twenty pages out of two hundred and seventy-five treat of
present times!"

It was therefore evident from the beginning that the *New
Monthly* under its new management would be radical, topical
and equally critical of Toryism, whether in politics or literature. And so it proved. Bulwer, who had at the very outset thus unanimously declared his policy, never changed it;
and in this at least he showed himself a real editor — a man
whose own views were strongly held and with all their faults
coherent, a man who knew how to impress those views on the
paper under his command.

And a further justice must be done to him. Despite the persistent outcry of his enemies against his self-advertisement and
unscrupulous vanity, there is no single item in any one of the
numbers of the *New Monthly* published under his control which
puffs himself or his works. He does not even admit reviews
of his own books from another hand; only when the mystification over *Godolphin* is at its height does he help to increase
that mystification by a paragraph of anonymous sophistry.

On the other hand, he is generous in appreciation of work
which pleases him and goes out of his way to help authors
who have fallen on evil days or are in need of publicity and
commendation. The novels of Lord Normanby have nowhere else been so fairly appraised as here (and they merit
more than the oblivion into which they have today fallen);
Mrs. Gore is applauded for precisely her good qualities,
implored to control that careless virtuosity which over-
writing introduced into too many of her otherwise witty and
perceptive novels; Banim, who had been plagiarised by
Pückler-Muskau and for various reasons was in some poverty
early in 1833, is defended against literary thieves and urged
on the charity of lovers of literature, with a warm-hearted
appreciation as generous as it is critically sound; John Martin, the apocalyptic painter and engraver, is enthusiastically

praised; poems are published by Elliott the Corn Law Rhymer; Hazlitt (who died in 1830) is sturdily defended; Abraham Hayward is for the first time lured from legal specialism into general journalism; and most creditable of all, opportunities for writing and badly needed support are given (and given continuously) to Leigh Hunt.

Mr. Edmund Blunden, in his recent biography of Leigh Hunt,[1] pays tribute to the sustained kindness shown by Bulwer alike to Leigh himself and to his son Thornton; and his narrative of Leigh's hazardous young manhood and of the suffering which, for the sake of their opinions, he and his brother John underwent, helps us to understand how it was that a man more than twenty years Leigh's junior was nevertheless eager, as soon as he was in a position to do so, to give much needed help. There can be little doubt that Bulwer's sympathies were first engaged, not only on behalf of the brothers Hunt but in favour of Hazlitt also, by the Mills or by members of their circle. James Mill had visited Leigh in prison; the *Westminster* had spoken up for the victims of official persecution; and the names of these and other martyrs for a radical cause had become a part of Bulwer's youthful enthusiasm for democracy and reform. He was therefore, once he found himself able to do so effectively, desirous of making some gesture in favour of men whose ideas and personalities he had for long admired; and the receipt from John Forster, late in 1831, of a preliminary appeal on behalf of Leigh Hunt's projected edition of his Poetical Works served to kindle impulse into action. The *New Monthly* for December contained an advance note of *Sir Ralph Esher*, which note Forster read and, thus encouraged, pressed Hunt's claim a second time:

(*Forster to Bulwer*)

Jan. 4, 1832.

Dear Sir,

I send you another prospectus regarding Leigh Hunt. Southey objected to the last and I have altered it therefore at his suggestion

[1] London, 1930.

in order that we may bring Hunt's claims still more strictly into the sacred territory of the world of letters, which ought ever to be considered and respected as neutral ground. Wordsworth sent his illustrious name in a very admirable way and Rogers has behaved in the right poetical spirit. Lord Holland gives us his countenance also. . . . Would you speak to Macaulay, or Shiel or Praed, or any other of your literary friends? A few House of Commons men of letters will be of infinite service. A line from you on this point I should esteem a great favour.

I say all this in consequence of the very kind interest you have expressed in the matter. The notice in the last *New Monthly* was excellent and well-timed.

In reply Bulwer asked Forster to review *Sir Ralph Esher* for his March number. He added: "The book *entre nous* wants story — is very clever, very agreeable but requires judicious treatment." When the review appeared, Bulwer appended over his own initials a paragraph recommending to the sympathy of his readers the proposal to publish Hunt's works by subscription. Men of both parties who had already given their support (several had been persuaded by Bulwer himself) were named, and the paragraph continued:

As *our* work chiefly comes under the notice of men attached to the more liberal politics, we will not scruple to remind them that one of the firmest, staunchest, most enduring friends to liberty, one true to her cause in poverty and prison, has been that man who now appeals — not to charity, but to justice. Let us who hail the coming victory of Reform, remember those who were staunch when the world was lukewarm and to whose silent, patient, unbought exertions we owe that advance in public opinion which we now celebrate.

Final evidence of his own personal exertions on behalf of this publishing project was the vote of fifty pounds by the Committee of the Literary Fund in aid of the subscription edition. "This vote," Bulwer wrote to Forster, "must be kept a profound secret."

In other directions also the *New Monthly* did its best for Leigh Hunt. During the early twenties he had occasionally contributed to the paper, but for some while nothing of his had been published there. In May, 1832, were printed, not only a poem by him, but Number 89 of *The Indicator* with a promise (unluckily not fulfilled — although Bulwer asked for another "Indicator" in a letter dated June 1) of a continuation of the papers through the present medium. Another poem appeared in the June number; the *Poetical Works* received a laudatory review in March, 1833; and meantime an intermittent correspondence went on between Bulwer and Leigh Hunt himself, which shows the former, although by chance in a position of greater authority, careful to treat the latter with the respect due to his seniority and hard experience.

On March 9, after reading the review of his novel and the sentence "the style is not free from many great and wilful blemishes", Leigh Hunt wrote to Bulwer (whom he may well have thought to have written the review) a letter of civil protest. Bulwer replied, and the reply provoked a further letter from Hunt of which a paragraph may be quoted:

Thank you for your candour respecting the remarks in *The New Monthly*. I have more than abundant reason to be satisfied with what you and others have said of me, but I have a grievous quarrel with the word "wilful." All sorts of charges of defects, errors and even absurdities are to be admitted on the score that others may know more of us than ourselves, but wilfulness implies conscious error or a propensity to set up the will for its own sake, and this I must disclaim. . . . I believe my half-tropical temperament may often have led a certain vivacity in my style to be taken for affectation. Perhaps most so when I have most thoughtlessly given way to it.

In the same letter, referring (apparently) to a contribution of his own about which he had received no news of acceptance or rejection and for the return of which he was anxious, Hunt says:

Your appeal to my editorial experience respecting the non-return of articles enables me to give the best excuse in my power for what I said on that point — namely that Mr. Hazlitt, Mr. Lamb and others of certain standing in literature always had carte blanche from me to write what they pleased on that understanding. But it is perhaps a better excuse, that I should have said nothing about it had not ill-health and the most unceasing necessity rendered the chance of a return more than usually a matter of anxiety in my own case. But it is of great importance to me to know to what extent I may write, as well as on the matter of subjects, and I should be glad to have the pleasure of seeing you.

An invitation to dine in Hertford Street caused poor Hunt acute embarrassment. He writes with charming confusion to explain that, whereas he would brave the shame of his inability to take soup or fish or to drink wine, he has no evening clothes nor time to get them, unless the dinner be postponed for a week. One can only hope that Bulwer told him not to dress. The friendship continued, and in August (1833), in the last letter from Hunt preserved among the Knebworth papers, is a moving expression of gratitude for all that has been done for Hunt by Bulwer's "noble pen."

The story of Leigh Hunt's share in the career of Bulwer's *New Monthly* has been told rather fully, not only because it illustrates the sustained generosity with which Bulwer, when he determined to help one less fortunate than himself, contrived to do so, but also as evidence of the standard of quality which the editor desired his paper to maintain. Evidence of steady helpfulness toward obscure or unfortunate individuals shows itself throughout Bulwer's life, and examples will be given as intermittently they arise. For the moment the other aspect of his editorial activity calls for notice; and a summary of the more important features of the paper, as it was while under his control, will show his conception of suitable periodical material and indicate the new friends which, by one means or another, he acquired during his term of office.

In July, 1832, was published the first instalment of the Countess of Blessington's *Journal of Conversations with Lord Byron*. The long and intimate friendship of Bulwer with Lady Blessington was so important to both of them, and the parties to it were, in their different ways, so prominent and influential in the London of the thirties and forties, that it has seemed better to treat as an independent theme and in a separate volume a story which of itself virtually constitutes the story of a literary and social epoch. At the present juncture it is sufficient to note that Bulwer, who first met Lady Blessington late in 1831, had by midsummer of 1832 progressed so rapidly in acquaintance with her as to secure for his magazine the undeniable "scoop" of her Byronian journal. The instalments ran intermittently until December, 1833, appeared in book form in 1834, and were even more successful as a volume than they had been as items in a magazine.

No other serial feature on the scale of Lady Blessington's *Journal* and from an outside contributor was published while Bulwer edited the *New Monthly*. But several shorter items were notable. Disraeli's *Ixion in Heaven* appeared in two instalments in December, 1832, and February, 1833; there were signed contributions in prose and verse by John Galt, Mrs. Gore, Mrs. Hemans and Isaac Disraeli; there were anonymous miscellanea, the authorship of which can only partially be established; but the predominant contents of the paper (predominant in importance and not far from predominant in amount) were written by the editor himself.

In one of the appendices to this book a schedule is given of those items, published in the twenty-two numbers of Bulwer's *New Monthly*, whose authorship can with practical certainty be ascribed to him. That this schedule is quite complete cannot be guaranteed; but it is already sufficiently impressive as a record of the work of one man, who was at the same time a member of parliament, a popular novelist and an active social figure. His dogged assiduity greatly impressed his assistant editor. "His industry was wonderful," wrote S. C. Hall[1]; "I have known him write an article for the *New Monthly* overnight which I well knew he had not touched before late in the evening, but which was ready in the morning when I called for it."

An early letter from Bulwer to Hall on *New Monthly* business may be quoted, as showing the breathless but unambiguous instructions which he was accustomed to give, and the rapid changes of his own whereabouts:

Bulwer to S. C. Hall.

Brighton, November 16, 1831.

My dear Sir,

I shall be in town on Friday or Saturday. Will you call on me Sunday evening at 8 o'clock? The proofs not having been sent down you cannot have them till then. Give yourself no further trouble about the cholera unless new and great alarm spreads on the subject. And for the rest you need not care about a day or two's delay. We are only *too much* crowded with matter. And I can give you as much copy as you like on Sunday. I am very sorry that we can't have Mr. Macfarlane's article, but we are quite full for the Jan. number as well as next. I am quite prepared with all the matter for that month. Will you call on Colburn or write and reiterate the necessity of getting a *good portrait* of Talleyrand for Jan. and setting about it directly?

I am reviewing the German Prince's book for this No. —— large letters; I shall make, I hope, a good thing of it. I have plenty of Tales, one very striking and terrible about the Resurrection men (anonymous) but slovenly written; yet from *the subject* it may do. But at all events let me see Mrs. Hall's as soon as it is finished. Mr. Macfarlane *might* give us a good article about Greece. But who the devil would read it? I wouldn't. No, not if Achilles himself wrote on that subject! I mean the Achilles in Hyde Park. . . .

So Mr. F. W. N. Bayley has been impertinent again! the Ninny! He'd better not —— Be on your guard in talking to these fellows. We ought to be secret as the Inquisition.

Yours

E. L. B.

"If convenient to call Saturday give me a line in Hertford."

[1] *Memories of a Long Life.* I, 270.

But more impressive even than the determination and dash which produced this flow of periodical writing is the high average level of its quality. Allowance having been made for the exuberance which, because it came more easily to him than economy of words, disfigures nearly all his work, the clear-headedness and cogency of much of his *New Monthly* writing are remarkable. The series of "Conversations with an Ambitious Student in Ill Health" (which were later included in *The Student* under the title "The New Phaedo") contain much thoughtful, if sometimes over-loaded reasoning. His leaders, and those items of the "Politician" series which may definitely be attributed to him are forcible and unhesitating in their pursuit of ideas clearly realised and strongly held. *Asmodeus at Large* is as a whole less satisfactory. Bulwer was not a satirist (despite the fact that he persisted in so regarding himself) and although the conversations of Asmodeus and the Devil are often valuable as illustrating the quarrels or foibles of the day, the series is not easy reading for anyone indifferent to the topicalities with which it deals.[1] In literary criticism Bulwer shows himself well-informed (if occasionally influenced by friendships and enmities), staunch to his own opinions and in particular obstinately convinced of the bad effect on contemporary poetry of the deliberate simplicities of the Wordsworthians. This hatred of tinkling lyricism, with its complementary anxiety to see poetry revert to the dignified sonorities of the eighteenth century, took ever firmer hold on him; and when, years later, he was writing or revising for re-issue that ewe-lamb of all his works, *King Arthur*, he could hardly write a letter without breaking out into angry denigration of this or that expression of the poetical method which to him was merely unmanly twaddle.

[1] The idea of a satirical commentary on the passing show in the form of dialogues between Asmodeus and the Devil was not an original one. In 1808 Charles Sedley, a rather scurrilous novelist, had published a three-volume pastiche on contemporary manners called *Asmodeus or The Devil in London*. But it was probably due to the popularity of Bulwer's *New Monthly* commentaries that the title as a whole came into its own again. On February 29, 1832, appeared the first number of a cheap satirical paper

In this connection in January, 1833, may be noted his review (it is surely his) of Tennyson's poems. "The Faults of Recent Poets" he calls it, and it is impossible not to detect the germ of that irritation with Tennysonian gentility which was later to break out so disastrously in *The New Timon*, when one reads the following:

It is not philosophy to utter in grand words the rhapsodies of insanity, nor a grace to babble forth in nursery rhymes the prattle of childhood. . . . We appeal to all impartial readers — not drunk with Wordsworthian pap — whether there be any just cause or reason beside the rhyme why the following two specimens of Mr. Tennyson's genius should be called *poetry*.

[Follow "O Darling Room" and the feeble epigram on "Christopher North"]

The notice continues:

Among the many sins of later poets is a want of all manliness in love. They languish and drawl and roll the eyes and faint; drivel without tenderness and gloat without being voluptuous. From this sin Mr. Tennyson is of course not free, but at times there are lines and thoughts which show that he could be really amorous if only he knew how to set about it. . . . It is time for a Poet once more to arise from the puerilities, the conceits, the effeminacies that cling around the school and the time.

It is no far cry from this to "schoolgirl Alfred", and Bulwer's poetical principles may at least claim the quality of constancy.

Happier (though more trivial) than the outcome of his duel with Tennyson was an exchange of shots between him and Mrs. Gore. A review of *The Fair of Mayfair*, published in June, 1832, but not written by Bulwer himself, pointed out that the word *embêtée*, used to describe herself by the heroine of one of the several stories published under this title was (as at that time it may have been) a word no decent French

called *The Devil in London*, which on April 21, 1832, altered its title to *Asmodeus or The Devil in London*.

woman could even hear without embarrassment. This simultaneous criticism of her French and her refinement provoked the authoress of the novel to indignant remonstrance. Writing personally to the editor on July 4, 1832, she began by rather lamely defending her use of the unhappy word, and went on to describe the criticism as deliberately ill-natured. The letter proceeds with characteristic sprightliness:

(Mrs. Gore to Bulwer)

I don't believe a word you say about impartiality in reviewing because the thing is impossible. With the best and purest intentions no one can help being biassed by personal predilections. Witness your partiality to Miss Landon's and Lord Mulgrave's novels in preference to *Arlington*.[1] . . . I will not attempt a defence of fashionable novels. I leave it to *Grandison, Clarissa, Belinda, Ennui, The Absentee, Vivian Grey*, etc., to plead their cause, and intrench myself in the obstinacy of a woman's opinion that every picture of passing manners, if accurate, is valuable from the drawing-room to the alehouse and that every writer does best who paints the scene more immediately before him. I could not have written *Eugene Aram*. Why attempt it? I *could* write the *Divorcée*[2] and if you were not a doctrinaire you would admit that it has far more truth, tenderness and power and passion. I am not sure that if you were not very hardened against fashionable novels, it might not draw an iron tear or two down your cheek.

I shall send to your house in town a volume of poems of mine now out of print to show you how very badly I *can* write when I venture off my ormolu railroad.

I think I shall write another fashionable novel in order that you may abuse it and I may show how indifferent I am to criticism, when satisfied it does not arise from a spirit personally hostile.

---

[1] This was a shrewd hit. Bulwer's review of *Romance and Reality* (December, 1831) had been obvious back-scratching, and his later notice of T. H. Lister's *Arlington* (June, 1832) as obviously soured by his hostility to the Murrayites and to the Tory strain in fashionable novel-writing. The charge of favouritism toward Mulgrave (Lord Normanby) was only superficially justified. There is reason to believe that although Bulwer met Normanby at Lady Blessington's, he never liked him as well as his novels, and these merit his praise far more than poor Miss Landon's sugared word-spinning.

[2] A story published in Vol. III of *The Fair of Mayfair*.

Mrs. Gore was to write several more fashionable novels, and she and Bulwer to become friendly correspondents. He found her first letter the easier to answer, not having himself written the paragraph which provoked it; and having found an opportunity shortly afterward of reviewing her fairly and favourably,[1] a literary acquaintance developed which bore at any rate the appearance of serenity. After her death, Bulwer endorsed the small bundle of her letters with one of his usual portrait-paragraphs. This one is very characteristic of his retentive memory for slight disagreements, his persistent suspicion of literary enmity, and his gift for appraising the essential quality of other folks' work and describing it in a few judicious words:

It would seem from the later letters that I appeased her resentment (over a review in the *New Monthly* which she disliked), though I doubt if she did not secretly seek to injure me through the channel of certain scurrilous periodicals. She was a remarkably clever woman, and her novels have a merit that has never been sufficiently appreciated. She preceded Thackeray, and as she knew good society infinitely better than he did, her satire makes his like caricature.

[1] June, 1833. "Modern Novelists and Recent Novels."

Chapter Ten

Godolphin — *Its importance in the tale of Bulwer's work — The group* Greville, Godolphin, Maltravers, Alice — *Reasons for the anonymity of* Godolphin — *" The mantle of Ann Radcliffe " — The characters in* Godolphin — *Bulwer's worldly wisdom —* England and the English — *Its sustained actuality — English manners — Money-worship — " Die-hard " stupidity — The economics of literature — Byron as a mouthpiece of his time — "Fashionable novels " —* Mrs. Gore *again — The theatre — Painting — William Etty and John Martin — Parallel between Martin and Bulwer — Bulwer, the practical idealist — Between two stools — " Supplementary Illustrations of Character " — The portrait of " Sneak " — Charles Molloy Westmacott, his career and character — Westmacott and* The Age — *Westmacott and Maginn — Westmacott and Lady Blessington — Westmacott's reply to Bulwer — The end of Westmacott*

I

Bulwer's talent for vivid and, at times, prophetic generalisation was not confined to judgments on literature. Indeed it found still more striking expression in his comments on society and politics, several of which were made into articles contributed to the *New Monthly*, and others added when those articles — refashioned for publication in book form — reappeared as part of the two volumes of *England and the English*.

Within about three months of one another were published, during the summer of 1833, the novel *Godolphin* and Bulwer's commentary on his country and his fellow-countrymen. The manner of publication, the content, and the reception of these two books were unusually typical of their author's mind, of his attitude toward two genres of literature, and of the ironical fate which, having made him an Englishman, had nevertheless endowed him with the kind of genius least acceptable to English taste.

Bulwer, for all the over-consciousness of his own literary development which always distinguished him, ignored the significance of *Godolphin* and *England and the English* to the tale of his work as a whole. When, midway in his writing life, he looked back at his development in novel-writing, he declared that *Paul Clifford* "closed an era in the writer's self-education"; that he could see "the paths which led across the boundary of invention from *Paul Clifford* to *Eugene Aram;* and, that last work done, where the first gleams from a fairer fancy rose upon my way and rested on those ideal images which I sought with a feeble hand to transfer to *The Pilgrims of the Rhine* and *The Last Days of Pompeii.*"[1] Using the privilege of posterity to reject the self-estimations of the past, we are entitled to look elsewhere for the real emphases. Without depreciating them as works of entertainment or instruction, we may declare those novels which he saluted as milestones on his way to be mere uprights in a paling, and discover our milestones where he chose to see but wayside shrubs.

Between *Eugene Aram* and *Paul Clifford* was no boundary of importance. The former was the inevitable projection of the latter and both were novels written for popularity and shrewdly gauging it. *The Pilgrims of the Rhine* was fondant-fiction at its worst, devised for silly girls at Christmas time and of no more ultimate importance than the romanticised engravings round which it was written. As for the historical novels from *Pompeii* to *Harold*, their qualities are not those of literature, nor is their spirit that of the author himself. These phenomena are, however, to be found in precisely the books which from his retrospective survey of himself were noticeably omitted. Bulwer could be half a dozen kinds of novelist; and in each rôle, thanks to his eloquence and dex-

[1] Preface to the 1848 edition of *Paul Clifford*.

terity, he achieved a certain impressive ingenuity. But there was one kind of novelist which he really longed to be, which — though structure and ornament were as *voulus* as those of a building in late baroque — he admirably was; and in *Godolphin* (to which *Pelham* and the unfinished *Greville* were preliminary), in *Maltravers* and in *Alice* (which were perfected *Godolphins*), and to some extent in *Night and Morning*, *Lucretia* and *What Will He Do With It?* he was that kind of novelist triumphantly and without shame.

Similarly, as a writer of non-fiction, he could strike attitudes to please his public or to disarm his enemies; but in *England and the English*, and in occasional essays, pamphlets or speeches, he allowed his convictions and his sense of reality to overcome his consciousness of an audience.

Godolphin, then, and the study of English character, published so nearly simultaneously during 1833, are remarkable in that each in its way is a sincere expression of the author's actual mind. And with Bulwer that is distinction indeed. It cannot be too often repeated that the great obstacle to any appraisement of him as a writer is the manifold variety of his disguises. He is for ever pretending — and not only to the world but to himself also. Further, he was that difficult blend of creative artist and student of literature, who almost inevitably develops a literary — side by side with a human — personality, and inclines to elaborate the former into as many sub-personalities as knowledge or fancy may suggest.

In consequence, it is hardly ever possible to say of one of his novels: "This represents the spirit of the man who wrote it", because the man was overlaid by the writer before ever the story was begun. Nor is this all. Criticism is often hard put to it even to judge the thickness of the overlay which, once it became endemic, varied only in intensity. *Pelham* certainly is a work of almost natural, non-literary self-expression. Bulwer, when he wrote it, was young, gay and full of optimism. To a smiling world he turned a cheerful if impudent face, and only the affectation of clever youth adorned an otherwise spontaneous tale. But with success came self-consciousness, and in *The Disowned* were observable the first signs of sham solemnity and a tendency to august humbug. Undigested reading and a sense of his own dignity loaded the book almost to the water-line of readability. The young man had begun to think himself a philosopher. *Devereux* introduced a fresh overlay. He was now not only a talented specimen of English youth and a budding moralist; he was also a historian. In *Paul Clifford* and *Eugene Aram*, to layers of philosophy and period-knowledge were added those of sociology and melodrama. When the historical romances came to be written, the same ingredients were given different emphasis; history became archaeology; generalised philosophy was enriched with classical allusion; and the personality of the novelist himself sank wholly out of sight. Later on came spiritualism; then deft concessions to the bourgeois realism of mid-Victorian taste; last of all — a pathetic throwback to the rhapsody of youth — came *Kenelm Chillingly*, a novel which tried to recapture what once had been real, which achieved in consequence an ultra-unreality.

But between the successful experiments in sensation-mongering and the first excursion into archaeology came *Godolphin*, and after *Godolphin* — at a brief interval — *Maltravers* and *Alice;* and these books, because they represent the maturity of the author of *Pelham*, because they are created according to the taste of the author himself, and not in obedience to mode or popular demand, must ultimately stand for Bulwer's novel-writing achievement.

II

Godolphin, on its first appearance in late April, 1833, was carefully anonymous. A short preface concluded with the following sentence:

Should any of the idlers who have leisure to waste on trifles attempt to pry into so unimportant a secret as the name of the individual whose humble task it has been from a Memoir to construct a Romance, their ingenuity will be exercised in vain; that secret he trusts and believes that he shall carry to the grave which (amidst a sea of infirmities and care) smiles upon him, near and welcome — the Haven of Repose.

In the June number of the *New Monthly* Bulwer himself, in an unsigned article on "Modern Novelists and Recent Novels", sought to confuse the issue still more by theorising as to the novel's origin:

We have left ourselves but a few words to say of a new work just out, which, to much that is original, seems to add nothing that is professional. *Godolphin* is the work to all appearance of an idle but cultivated person of genius; the sex of the writer does not seem to us to be easily gathered from the nature of the work; now certain passages betray a writhing consciousness of the position of women (a consciousness that no man could experience) and seem to indicate a female pen; and now some deep strong masculine burst of passion declares the author to be of the harder sex. The style of the work is an evident imitation of that of a certain author whose novels have become popular beyond their merit; but this is only a style of words and aphorisms — the style of mind is essentially different.

In a footnote to the article he observes that, inasmuch as there is astrology alike in *Godolphin* and in Mrs. Norton's story *Oonagh Lynch*, it is possible that this lady had a hand in the writing of the other book also.

In the autumn of 1833 a final touch was given to the elaboration of his masquerade by a preface specially written for the novel's second (and still anonymous) edition:

The composition, or the compilation, of this work has been attributed to various persons, some of note sufficient to make me fancy that it has a merit of which I was at first not properly aware. It is not for me to contradict such flattering reports. Let me content myself with laughing in my sleeve at the mistakes that have occurred in affiliating a foundling which can make but one step from the cradle to the grave. The real writer of *Godolphin* is yet, and ever will be, unrevealed.

Some, indeed, say that this book is a trifle of Mr. Disraeli's; others, that it is either an imitation of Mr. Bulwer, or a bantling he has good reason to disown. I have heard it attributed to Colonel Caradoc, and to Mrs. Norton — to the Turkish Ambassador, and to the joint labours of Mr. —— who is living, and Lady Caroline L—— who is no more. I suspect that none of these conjectures is right; but I am so much pleased with them all, that I will not venture decidedly to contradict one of them. This much will I say, that as no woman would have written some parts of the book, so no man could have written the whole.

Adieu, reader; wouldst thou see me unmasked — thou must come behind the scenes of the world; and when the lamps are out, and the curtain dropped, thou shalt know me for what I am. But there is only one authority who can admit you behind those scenes — and his name is — Death!

Why should Bulwer have taken these repeated precautions to conceal an identity which he was, for all his asseverations, later to avow? Partly, no doubt, to indulge that childish taste for mystification which he never wholly lost, which was on later occasions to tempt him to some of the clumsiest and most useless lies of his career. Partly, perhaps, from a curiosity to test the attention paid by novel-readers to a book's matter, apart altogether from the name on its title page. Trollope had this same curiosity when he issued *Linda Tressel* and *Nina Balatka* without his signature, and both he and Bulwer were quickly shown that anonymity meant loss of sales. *Godolphin*, like *Linda* and *Nina*, sold poorly in comparison with his other books. Even when authorship was admitted, the novel never made up in popularity for the ground originally lost.

But there was yet a stronger reason for *Godolphin's* anonymity — a reason of which Bulwer was certainly conscious but would hotly have denied. *Fraser's*, with the cruel perceptiveness of a clever enemy, detected this motive and pounced upon it. "Bulwer is obliged to sneak into the market in a mask," wrote the editor in his June number, "and to suppress his name in the hope that its absence may contribute to the sale of *Godolphin*. This is an alteration with a vengeance for which the reading public ought to be infinitely obliged to us." Here, twisted to suit the offensive purpose of the magazine, is undoubtedly much of truth. Bulwer had passed through a time of such gruelling criticism that he was literally afraid to face the music with another novel of contemporary fashionable life.

To the reader of today it seems strange that the mere anonymity of so characteristic a book should have deceived any one. Yet *Fraser's* were almost alone in detecting the true authorship, and their shrewdness (perhaps because it was combined with an arrogant claim to have been responsible for frightening Bulwer into secrecy) made no impression on other critics. For months all manner of conjecture went the rounds of society. The *Literary Gazette* [1] did not mention Bulwer nor speculate in any way as to the identity of the author. The review, however, was definitely unfavourable and this, coming from Jerdan's paper, is evidence enough that Bulwer was not suspected of any connection with the book.

The *Spectator* was more definite and in so many words gave the author precedence over Bulwer as a social satirist:

Of late novelists the writer of *Godolphin* more especially weighs upon the springs of society as they exist now; after him comes Bulwer with his genius for satire. One of the finest things ever written is Lucilla's letter to Godolphin. Mrs. Opie never reached it; Mrs. Inchbald only approaches it in her *Simple Story*.

Frankly fantastic was the theory, reported by the Lady herself, that Harriet Martineau had written the novel. Writing to Bulwer more than ten years later, Miss Martineau said:

Feb. 8, 1844.

About *Godolphin* I think I ought to answer you with plain truth. *Godolphin* came out during my first winter in London and everybody

[1] May 11, 1833.

told me I wrote it.   I chose to continue able to say that I had never seen it.   I never did see it till about four years since.   I didn't read it fairly, for I was vexed that anyone should think it could have been written by a woman.   I was also sorry for the exposure in it of poor Lord Dudley's case and for some words about Rogers.   Under these impressions I like it the least of any of your books that I have read.

Presumably the secret leaked out within a twelvemonth, for there is evidence that Bulwer contemplated a reissue over his own name in the very year following publication.   But actually authorship was not publicly acknowledged until 1840, when the novel appeared in Saunders and Otley's five-shilling uniform edition, somewhat shortened and with a dedication to D'Orsay.   Then there broke over the unfortunate author's head the storm of criticism which seven years before he had so elaborately evaded.   "Reading *Godolphin*," noted Macready in his diary for July 4, 1840, "Bulwer, the author, is of course vilified by the press."   Doubtless the realisation of their own stupidity exacerbated the comments of his enemies.   And all the time *Fraser's* had spoken, but none had ears to hear.

The novel itself almost defies analysis.   A compendium of all the ornamental quirks, social prejudices, shrewdnesses and idealisms of an author more than normally ornate, prejudiced, shrewd and idealistic, its massed ingenuities somehow achieve a strange decorative unity of their own. Whether that unity be pleasing to the taste of the present day or whether it be intolerable it cannot alter the fact that it *is* a unity, and that in this novel and its spiritual successors Bulwer achieved for good or ill his individuality.   The effect on a modern reader of *Godolphin*, *Maltravers* and *Alice* cannot be prejudged.   Those to whom the baroque in art and architecture have appeal;   those already in reaction against the severity of taste which has driven patterned papers from our walls, gilt console tables from our rooms, gothic ruins and occasional temples from our gardens, heavy proscenium

curtains from the foreground of our pictures, painted vistas
or tumultuous goddesses from our domes and vaulting — will
perhaps, if they can surrender themselves to the rhetorical
excesses of Bulwer's style and the rich trappings of his scenes
and characters, come to feel a sensuous if irrational pleasure
in the variety, abundance and gilding of these extraordinary
books.   Others, to whom the lure of simplicity is still strong,
will suspect narratives so loaded with miscellaneous embellishment to be mere scaffoldings for carrying unselective
ornament, and will turn contemptuously away.

The period of *Godolphin* is virtually the period of its writing;
Bulwer the romantic novelist used period precisely as the
late baroque architect used the basic structure of the church
or palace on which he was at work.   It was necessary
to have some core of building on which to pile ornament;
and the story-teller likewise needed a skeleton of reality for
the better display of his intricate and prodigal imagination;
but neither architect nor novelist felt bound to respect the
form and implication of his central mass to any greater degree
than seemed to him convenient.   Consequently, while in
novels of the *Godolphin* class scenes of metropolitan fashion,
political incidents and discussions, details of clothes, carriages and furnishings belong recognisably to the thirties, the
overriding effect of the plot and characters is fantastic and
deliberately unreal.

It is in his fondness and talent for romanticising a pretended
actuality that Bulwer's spiritual descent from certain of the
novelists of the eighteenth century really shows itself.   But
these were not the novelists to whose parentage he openly
laid claim.   He liked to think himself a successor to Fielding and Smollett.   Critical essays, occasional passages in the
early books, the whole of the Caxton series, were undisguised assertions, not only of a justifiable admiration for
these great writers but also of a mistaken belief in his power
to repeat their methods.   In this regard Bulwer mistook
mere imitation for re-creation.   Certainly he could contrive

skilfully to reproduce the manner of the eighteenth-century realists and to adapt their matter to a later age; but he never succeeded in bringing their spirit once more to life, because that spirit was not in him. The eighteenth century inspiration of the genuine Bulwerian novel was twofold; and its first and more important element derived from Gothic romance, — that dominant strain in the popular fiction of the late eighteenth and early nineteenth centuries, which blended the trappings of past ages or the unfamiliar scenes and manners of foreign lands with a respect for the modish sentiment and refinement of contemporary England and a deliberate exploitation of the weird and terrible. The writer of Gothic romance might choose to stage a tale in the thirteenth century, in the Apennines, or among the gloomy ravines of the Harz Mountains; but he only respected the limitations of his period or clime just so far as was convenient to the effective telling of his ghostly or sensational but always elegant story. And of all Gothic novelists none brought to greater perfection the fusion of historical or geographical detail with genteel emotion and wildly thrilling incident than the arch-priestess of the whole Gothic romantic school — the most influential woman novelist there has ever been — Ann Radcliffe.

The imitators of Ann Radcliffe were innumerable. Hardly a novelist or poet of the first three decades of the nineteenth century but to some extent looked at nature through her eyes, showed her shuddering delight in precipice and storm and forest-gloom. But in only one writer did her spirit really live again. Bulwer, from the moment when he first made public appearance as a novelist showed himself the true inheritor of the mantle of this famous writer of romance. He caused that once sombre garment to be sprigged with gold and lined with satin; he refashioned its cut to the taste of an exquisite of the thirties; but he so wore it that, for all the change in its style and texture, it hung with the same tremendous folds and made on all who beheld it a similar impression of wild magnificence. So completely indeed does the spirit

of Radcliffian romance live again in those of Bulwer's novels
which really express their writer's self, that he must not be
regarded as a mere follower of the "great enchantress".
Rather was he her ordained successor on the throne of a
kingdom still lurid and romantic, but now into the bargain
modernised and metropolitan.[1]

The second eighteenth century influence which went to the
moulding of Bulwer's fiction, though subsidiary to Radclif-
fianism, cannot be ignored.   The reformist and philosophical
novels of Bage, Holcroft and, above all, of Godwin had
had a large share in his early literary training.   Wherefore,
although he never came to regard the novel as primarily a
vehicle for philosophical or political propaganda, he was
from the beginning disposed to blend opinion with narrative;
and with the perfection of his own part-decorative, part-
instructional style in story-telling, he contrived easily
and naturally to alternate argument with incident, was
ready — when landscape or architecture palled — to vary
his background with discussion of political or social happening.

Godolphin admirably illustrates this joint preoccupation
with romance and actuality.   In its principal characters and
in the unashamed mixture of realism and improbability which
makes up its various and sensational incident, is Gothic
romance of the purest quality.   Young Godolphin, the hero
and the immediate precursor of Ernest Maltravers, is a typical
prodigy in the Bulwerian manner, to whom before the age of
twenty life has little fresh to offer and at the age of twenty-
six nothing whatsoever.   This remarkable young man "had
early learned to despise the common emotions of men."
When barely sixteen, he rejects the discipline of school and

---

[1] There could be no better proof of Bulwer's Gothicism than the fact that he was
regarded by actual contemporaries as a master of romantic terror-fiction.   His name as
dedicatee on the fly-leaf of the famous *Romancist and Novelists Library* (which contains
many tales of terror but not a single fashionable novel), published in 1839-1840,
implies that to those best able to judge he appeared the saviour of the Gothic
romance.

leaves England for a self-imposed exile, with an allowance of some hundreds a year and a conviction that he is "alone in the universe — the lord of his own fate." Shortly after his departure his father dies, and Godolphin becomes a sort of aristocratic waif, with suspected but so far inaccessible wealth, the entry to all the most exclusive houses, and for actual property the ruins of Godolphin Priory, which stood "all embrowned and mossed with age, mirrored in the waveless and silent tide of a wide and glassy lake."

So far, apart from the idealised tinge of his own personality which Bulwer gave to every one of his heroes, this youth might be the central figure of any one of a dozen Gothic romances. But here the resemblance ends, and Bulwer the social commentator takes the place of Bulwer the Radcliffian. Godolphin's Gothistic prototypes would have remained mere romantic puppets — with a store of fine sentiments, with whatsoever resources of melancholy, courage or eloquence were required by the events of the plot, but with no individuality of their own. Godolphin himself (because he is the creation of a man whose brain could hardly control its own fertility, whose conception of the novel allowed him to use it to talk philosophy, sociology or politics as well as to tell a story) is prodigal of theories and dissertations on manners, philosophy and love. There is in fact a definite intellectual personality to Godolphin, built up on the foundation of his precocious wisdom and world-weariness, and set against the melancholy splendours of his ruined heritage. This personality is the personality of his creator. He is the vehicle for the expression of Bulwer's views of men and manners; his letter-writing and the incidental reflections which he provokes are continuously revealing of Bulwer's shrewdness and rather bitter wit. Finally, things happen to him which (though in a less coloured manner) happened to Bulwer also; and the novel is in consequence of direct autobiographical significance, alike spiritually and as a record of incident.

There is little purpose in tracing in detail the similarities between the novel of *Godolphin*, its predecessors and its successors, or the extent to which it may be regarded as a *roman à clé*. These aspects of a book more interesting on other grounds need only summarily be indicated. Among its characters are several which in various forms appear and reappear in many of Bulwer's fictions. "Saville" — the heartless, creedless, cynical man of the world — is as much a relation of "Mauleverer" in *Paul Clifford* as of "Ferrars" in *Maltravers*, or of "Lilburn" in *Night and Morning;* Volkman, the astrologer, is a precursor of Zanoni; his daughter Lucilla stands over against Lady Constance Erpingham very much as Maltravers' Alice is contrasted with Lady Florence. But Lucilla also corresponds to Fanny in *Night and Morning* though with a pathetic difference. Whereas her untutored devotion goes down before the cultured companionship of a lady of education and sensibility, Fanny is her story's unchallenged heroine. And for the reason that by 1840 Bulwer had learnt from experience to value sympathy and devotion in woman above intellect or wit.

Of the extent to which *Godolphin* presents contemporary portraiture so much might be said that it is better to say almost nothing. Lady Jersey and Sheridan were identified by one reviewer; Lord Dudley by several. Miss Martineau's above-quoted reference to the "exposure of poor Lord Dudley" has in this last connection a certain interest, because all mention of "Lord Saltream" was expunged from the later editions published over the author's name. The eccentricities of this unfortunate peer, who had been one of the bitterest opponents of the Reform Bill and died in a private asylum early in 1833, were recent and notorious in the public mind. His appearance [1] in *Godolphin* was unmistakable. Alike his parentage, early circumstances, political opinions and extraordinary behaviour at dinner parties were described so faithfully that one cannot but share Miss Martineau's

[1] See Vol. 3 of the first edition. Chapter VIII and thereafter.

regret at the rather tasteless use of unhappiness so recent and so recognisable, nor wonder at its later deletion. Other attempted identifications can be ignored. It is safe to say that Lady Constance, though the mouthpiece of many of Lady Blessington's theories, was not a portrait of Lady Blessington, nor was Godolphin himself D'Orsay.

Fortunately the drawing of analogies between the characters of various books nor identification of actual persons are really pertinent to the true appreciation of Bulwer's fiction. Its essential quality lies in its blend of powerful descriptive writing with continual and acute comments on social manners as he observed them, and on human nature as, with uncanny shrewdness, he appraised it. *Maltravers* and *Alice*, being works more perfect of their kind, are richer in these incidental observations than the somewhat tentative *Godolphin*. But even this book is far better furnished with worldly wisdom and often disconcerting clear-sightedness than other more famous novels of its day. That Bulwer should nowadays receive so little credit for his wisdom in gauging humanity and for his importance as a witness to the mentality of his time, is probably due to his habit of scattering the fruits of that wisdom and observation over the pages of novels which, superficially, give an impression of stilted melodrama. Many shrewdnesses lurk in the fantastic crevices of the façade of *Godolphin;* and a realisation of the fact, combined with the discussion yet to come of the abiding perceptiveness of *England and the English*, may persuade modern readers to regard Bulwer as something more than a mere story-teller. Let them look for evidence of his knowledge of human nature and of the social attributes of his circle rather in his incidental comments, than in the high-flown conversations of characters on their best behaviour; they will not look in vain.

III

England and the English first appeared in September, 1833; was reprinted almost at once; and a third edition, with an important new preface, was issued a twelvemonth later. When the book was included in the uniform edition of 1840, several passages of ephemeral or controversial interest were removed, and all subsequent editions present the abridged text. This, to the majority of twentieth-century readers, will be adequate enough; only specialists will want to refer back to the two-volume editions for political topicalities which time has made mere matter of past history. But the existence of the fuller text must be recorded, for the sake of the bitter attack on an unsavoury contemporary, which appeared in the first three editions, called forth an infuriated rejoinder from the victim, set Bulwer's old enemies once again yelping at his heels, and was from 1840 onward suppressed altogether.[1]

England and the English is divided into five books. The first, dedicated to Talleyrand, gives a "View of the English Character"; the second deals with Society and Manners; the third, dedicated to Doctor Chalmers, surveys Education and the influences of Morality and Religion; the fourth, dedicated to Isaac Disraeli, gives a View of the Intellectual Spirit of the Times, including Literature, Drama, Art and Science; the fifth is entitled: "A View of our Political State." In Appendices are given a dissertation on Bentham's philosophy (specially written for the occasion by John Stuart Mill) and a brief study of the personality and writings of James Mill.

The outstanding quality of *England and the English* is the sustained applicability of its author's judgments of national character, national burdens and national aspiration, and the "Europeanism" of his general point of view. With an acuteness so inescapable as even nowadays to make uneasy reading for British complacency, Bulwer appraised the foibles of his countrymen and the imperfections of their social structure. His criticisms and, even more directly, the conclusions he draws from a comparison between English civilisation and

[1] This attack and its consequences are dealt with on pp. 306–307.

that of the peoples of Europe, gave much offence to contemporary readers. H. F. Chorley, in a friendly notice of Bulwer and his work, published in 1838, spoke of

England and the English, that too clever and caustic anatomy of our national character which John Bull will not soon forget and forgive, and which may in some wise reasonably excite his ill-humour inasmuch as it dwells too largely upon the foibles and short-comings without sufficiently indicating the charities and the virtues which grow up side by side with them. But it is a book which must do good . . . which must dispose us to look abroad and see what there may be good and great and worthy of imitation in the institutions of our neighbours.

Almost on the first page the author shows that the book has been written with a definite sense of period. "The English of the present day," he says, "are not the English of twenty years ago"; and, as his argument develops, it becomes clear that the incidental reference in Godolphin to a change of social emphasis between 1815 and 1832 was not lightly made, but was the outcome of reasoned conviction. Then (for he is half-addressing his dedicatee Prince Talleyrand, half justifying that dedication to his readers) he passes to a quick characterisation of the English as they must appear to a trained French observer:

The vanity of the Frenchman consists (as I have somewhere read) in belonging to so great a country; but the vanity of the Englishman exults in the thought that so great a country belongs to himself. The root of all our notions, as of all our laws, is to be found in the sentiment of property. It is *my* wife whom you shall not insult; it is *my* house that you shall not enter; it is *my* country that you shall not traduce; and, by a species of ultra mundane appropriation, it is *my* God whom you shall not blaspheme.

A strong sense of property produces at once a determination to increase it and, in its enjoyment, an individualism none the less obstinate for being disguised as social cordiality.

Our crowded parties are not society; we assemble all our acquaintance for the pleasure of saying nothing to them. Our main element is home, and if you believe our sentimentalists we consider it a wonderful virtue to be unhappy and disagreeable everywhere else. . . . But a spirit of general unsociability is not incompatible with the love of festivals, splendid entertainments and luxurious hospitality. Ostentation and unsociability are often effects of the same cause, for the spirit of commerce disdaining to indulge amusement is proud of displaying wealth and is more favourable to the luxuries than the Arts.

The second chapter sums up the special qualities of the English aristocracy, their influence — both administrative and social — on the community as a whole, and the change wrought in their position by the developments of the foregoing twenty years, which had so recently culminated in the great Reform Bill. Bulwer argues irrefutably that the social demeanour of the English aristocracy during the preceding half century had been of a character to strengthen their legislative power but to compromise their dignity. In so far as they have mixed more largely and intermarried more frequently with other classes than the aristocracy of any other country, they have added to the weight of property and rank a weight of caste popularity almost unknown on the continent. But by their non-exclusiveness they have forfeited both the power and the inclination to maintain that disinterested loftiness of mind which is the supreme expression of the true patrician. Just because they are accessible in a social sense, they are also accessible to the rivalry of wealth and shameless ambition. Hence the money-baron, a commodity in whose mass production England was the pioneer. Hence also that peculiarly English form of snobbery which drives men and women (particularly the latter) to assert themselves by stressing their fine connections and, in default of these, to imitate the way of life of persons grander or more exalted than themselves.

The long established custom of purchasing titles has tended to mix aristocratic feelings with the views of the trader. . . . Rank gained

by intellect is open but to few; rank to be obtained by fashion seems
delusively to be open to all. Hence that eternal vying with each
other — that spirit of show — that lust of imitation which characterise our countrymen. As wealth produces the alliance and respect
of nobles, wealth is affected even where not possessed; and as fashion, which is the creature of the aristocracy, can only be obtained by
resembling the fashionable, each person imitates his fellow and
hopes to purchase the respectful opinion of others by renouncing
the independence of opinion for himself.

From this pronouncement there develops naturally one of
Bulwer's favourite arguments (he returns to the plea continually both in essays and novels) — namely, that much of
the social malaise of the England of the day could be cured
by the substitution of intellect for wealth as the test of eminence.

The respect we pay to wealth absorbs the respect we should pay
to genius. We may say truly, with a certain political economist,
that we pay best 1st those who destroy us — generals; 2d, those
who cheat us — politicians; 3d, those who amuse us — singers
and musicians; and least of all those who instruct us. Literary
men [with whom are to be understood scientists, philosophers,
artists etc.] have not with us any settled position. "I am nothing
here" said one of the most eminent men of science this country ever
produced. "I am forced to go abroad to preserve my self-esteem."
. . . A literary man is forced to be proud of something else than
talent — proud of fortune, of connexion, of birth . . . and everyone knows the anecdote of the professor of chemistry who, eulogis-
ing Boyle, said: "He was a great man; he was father of chemistry
and brother to the Earl of Cork."

Not surprisingly, inasmuch as familiarity with rank and
wealth and the power to reproduce the manners of a monied
aristocracy had become the ideal of the majority of the English middle class, the conditions of the poor were hardly
studied at all. In this respect matters have changed with a

vengeance; and to the efforts of Bulwer among other radical propagandists must the change be in part attributed.[1] It would no longer be true to say, as in 1832 Bulwer said, that laws are uniformly unfavourable to the poor; or that the criminal code remains a mere barbarity. But in those more general aspects of social life, where national character and not legislation is the dominant power, matters are still very much as they were a century ago. The English working folk have neither aptitude nor opportunity for simple and natural self-entertainment as have their counterparts in France and Germany. To quote from Bulwer once again:

Their attempts at social intercourse and jollification are discouraged as indolence and disorder. Snobbery takes a share in this irrational state of affairs. . . . In France shopkeepers mix in festivity with the peasantry; the "aristocratic" spirit would forbid this condescension in England.

Inevitably, he goes on to say, the poorer classes — shut out from easy intercourse with other classes by the dread of their immediate superiors of being seen in lowly company — tend to be sullen, to shirk work where possible, to extract from their fellow-countrymen in hush money what they are denied in ordinary fellowship. Their superiors cannot let them starve, but will not help them to that sense of being members of a single community which would stimulate them to work and help to make self-improvement worth while. Also there comes into play a fallacy powerful in English political philosophy that Poverty is the parent of Crime. Let poverty, it is argued, be alleviated at State expense, and in return for the expense the State will be spared the violent attention of criminals. Wherefore the poor are kept at once submissive

---

[1] His attack on the aristocratic bias of the English constitution was an application of the ideas of James Mill, especially those expressed in a long essay entitled *Men and Things in 1823* in the first number of the *Westminster Review* (January, 1824); and there is no doubt that when James Mill's son wrote in his *Autobiography* that *England and the English* was "a work at that time greatly in advance of the public mind", he was thinking principally of Bulwer's plea for a more democratic State.

and alive by doles, and Bulwer has things to say on the effects of a dole system which have an unwelcome familiarity to the reader of today.

These are by no means the only points at which Bulwer's survey of the condition and spirit of the English working class has an uneasy relevance to present discontents. But because many of his other arguments arise from more general considerations of social and moral philosophy, they may be left to the curiosity of individual readers to discover or to deduce for itself, and our present survey may pass on to his exposure of the arrogance, hypocrisy and stupidity which, combined with much kindness of heart and practical good sense, were and still are characteristics of the British race.

These qualities show themselves most frequently among persons of die-hard conviction; and Bulwer, as befitted an enthusiast for the Reform Bill, was intensely aware of them among many of the leading hostile opponents of that measure. He describes the mixture of bravado, obstinacy and eleventh-hour cowardice which characterised their policy, which has ever since distinguished the most blusterous opponents of political or economic change. It might have been written of any one of the most-advertised resistances to inevitable reform, of any one of the chief industrial disputes within living memory. English reaction is always blind to portents until it is too late; always loses the chance of yielding gracefully; always ends by making the concession and getting no credit for doing so.

If we look to the progress of the Reform Bill through the Lords, we shall see the most lamentable want of discretion, the most singular absence of common sense. The peers did not think the Reform Bill necessary; accordingly, they rejected it. Sensible men never do a bold thing without being prepared for its consequences. Were the peers prepared? No! — they expressed the greatest astonishment at Lord Grey's going out of office, after his declaring repeatedly that he would do so if they rejected his proposition: and the greatest consternation at the resolution of the people to get the Bill, after their expressing that resolution uninterruptedly for nearly two years. Taken by surprise, they therefore received the Bill again, and, after refusing to conciliate the people, voluntarily placed themselves in the condition of being beat by the people. Sensible men make a virtue of necessity. The peers put themselves in the condition of granting the necessity, and losing all the virtue in the grant. They paraded their weakness up and down — placed it in the most ostentatious situation, and, with all the evils of concession, insisted on uniting all the odium of resistance. This might be very fine, but your Excellency [*i.e.* Talleyrand, to whom the argument is still addressed] need not think twice to allow that it was not very sensible.

The penultimate section of *England and the English* — that dealing with the Intellectual Spirit of the Age — has the interest peculiar to its theme, and a significance which, in view of its author's future non-political activities, is somewhat more personal than that of the rest of the book. This personal element is of course not explicit. Bulwer's intention was to maintain the discussion on grounds as general as before; and on the whole he succeeds in doing so, merely allowing his own idiosyncrasies to colour, a little more definitely then elsewhere, the texture of his objectivity. Incidentally he provides one or two further passages of social definition, which help us to realise how little is new under the sun, even in post-war psychology. He devotes a page to the transition pains of England in the eighteen thirties which might have been written today; he describes, not only the effect on the quality of literature of a greatly extended reading public, but also the influence of successive preoccupations on the themes of contemporary fiction, in such a way as to show that, although we have travelled further during the last hundred years, we are still on the same road.

The bulk of his argument deals with the politics and economics of literature, the power and pretensions of the press, the state of the contemporary theatre, the ethics of contemporary criticism; and his personal fancy in books and pictures.

His discussion of literature and drama as a mirror of period taste has, to anyone interested in this recurrent problem, a peculiar appeal. His knowledge of the history of literary and dramatic popularity, combined with an unusually keen sense of the changing preoccupations of the intellectually modish during the decade of his own adult consciousness, equipped him for the task of estimating the successive interactions of one on the other. In his treatment of painting, he gives more weight to his personal likes and dislikes, with the result that the chapter on "The State of the Arts", while of only superficial importance to the student of the mentality of the twenties and thirties, is more revealing of the mind of the man who wrote it even than those devoted to literature or the theatre.

The survey of literature, at once a mouthpiece and an echo of the moods and passions of the time, begins with a skilful presentation of Byron as a man whose personality and genius showed themselves at precisely the right moment, blended in precisely the right way, to make the maximum impression on their age:

Sir Philip Sidney represented the popular sentiment in Elizabeth's day; Byron that in our own. He became the Type, the Ideal of the state of mind he represented, and the world willingly associated his person with his works, because they thus seemed actually to incorporate — and in no undignified or ungraceful shape — the principle of their own sentiments and emotions.

We attributed truth and depth to Lord Byron's poetry in proportion as it expressed our own thoughts, and in tracing the career of this remarkable poet, we may find that he became less and less popular, not as his genius waned, but as he addressed more feebly the prevalent sentiment of his times.

That sentiment, shocked more violently than it realised by the dramatic death of its poet-hero, reacted suddenly from

poetry to a taste for prose; but the desire for romantic narrative persisted, and requiring satisfaction even when verse had
lost its lure, settled on fiction as its new favourite. Novels
of every kind were eagerly read; and most popular of all —
because most closely in tune with the social preoccupations
of the moment — were novels of fashionable life.

The paragraphs in which Bulwer describes the general
causes of the appeal of "silver-fork fiction" to the mentality
of the twenties have already been quoted.[1] He has also,
however, a good deal to say of the specific qualities of fashionable fiction; and an example of his acuteness in analysing
the conventional hypocrisy of polite society and its power to
stimulate novelists of manners to some of their happiest
efforts is provided by yet another reference to the work of
Mrs. Gore. This lady is here introduced as the prose-laureate
of British match-making; and very astringent are the comments on a woman-ridden society which, while boasting of
the freedom in choice of mate enjoyed by English girls, contrives nevertheless a greater materialism and cynicism in
man-hunting than exists in any of the European countries.
Bulwer declares that the universal marketing of unmarried
English women — "a marketing peculiar to ourselves in
Europe and only rivalled by the slave merchants of the east"
— not only renders both sellers and sold hard and selfish,
but is also mainly responsible for the tedium of English social
life because by putting a premium on money and titles, it
subjects society to the arrogant stupidity of the owners (or
likely inheritors) of these mind-destroying splendours.

Over Bulwer's discussion of the contemporary theatre and
its personalities we need not linger. He shows his usual dis-
crimination in judging the work of unknown writers, by
praising Browning for *Strafford* and George Darley and Landor
for their literary dramas, at a time when appreciation of these
authors was none too common. His ideas on the drama

[1] See p. 112.

generally are those which continued to possess him; those according to which he was (for the sake of his ultimate fame) only too scrupulously to fashion his own plays. They are, however, sound ideas — logical and essentially practical; and it may here be noted (in anticipation of the time when his theatrical activities come to be considered) that as early as 1832 — that is to say four years before he saw any play of his own upon the stage and five years before he achieved any theatrical success — he had decided in his own mind the exact balance which an ambitious playwright ought to strike between originality and obedience to popular demand.

Painting, as an element in the intellectual Spirit of the Time, is introduced by two pages of criticism of the Royal Academy. Bulwer's objections both to the Academy principle and to its practice, anticipate to a remarkable degree modern criticisms of that institution. After attacking the very idea of instituting Academies for things of the mind ("formidable coteries of exclusives; Almacks for artistic fashion"), he declares that "the Academy of Arts in England has been less injurious than the Academy of Letters in France, only because it has been less powerful. . . . Since the Academy has been instituted, it has not fulfilled either of its avowed objects — it has not educated the masses of our artists nor expounded with diligent science the principles of art." So far so good. The argument is a practical one and suited to Bulwer's practical mentality. But as soon as he proceeds to pass under review the leading artists of the day, he not only betrays the limitations of his taste but also helps us to realise the inability to grasp certain fundamentals of English character which marked nearly everyone of his intellectual activities and served to cheat them of the full reward. He has a civil word to say of Turner, Girtin, De Wint, Copley, Fielding and Varley; but it is clear that the peculiar genius of English landscape painting has no real appeal to him, and of Constable or Cozens (to expect a salute for Richard Wilson were perhaps to expect too much) he makes no mention whatsoever. On the other hand, his essentially dramatic and rather sentencious taste leads him to exaggerated praise of Wilkie and Maclise, and to a shocked denigration of Hogarth which reads comically enough.

Bulwer as a critic of the English painting of his time was, in fact, blind to the essential qualities of his subject. But with failure to share the vision of the artist went a rejection of the moral standards by which too many students of painting pretended to judge an artist's work. Unable to appreciate the English feeling for nature, preferring his art "artistic" if it is to be considered as art at all, he nevertheless shows clearly that over-consciousness or prudish dislike of a painter's theme has no place in his appraisement of talent. His approval of "the vigorous and fluent drawing and bursts of brilliancy and light" of William Etty is peculiarly significant. The angle of approach is European rather than British; and that Bulwer's approach to Etty should be thus cosmopolitan helps to explain the instinctive antagonism between him and Thackeray, who in his time wrote a deal of current art criticism and of a very insular kind. Etty to Thackeray was a painter of nudes; and, because Thackeray's attitude to art was that of a semi-emancipated English puritan, Etty's painting was never appraised without a self-conscious giggle.[1] But by Bulwer, Etty's subjects are forgotten in approval of his colour and the rhythm of his design. For in art criticism, as in everything else, Bulwer was so far above the provincialism of British æsthetic judgments, that he could not conceive either their limitations or their obstinate resistance to criticism of other kinds.

But perhaps more interesting still is the whole-hearted praise which follows for the strange apocalyptic genius of John Martin. Between the pictorial art of Martin and the

[1] Several examples could be given; but Thackeray's articles in *Fraser's Magazine* for June, 1838; June, 1839; June, 1844; and June, 1845, may be specially referred to. His attitude was conventional enough, for Etty was bitterly attacked in other quarters also. (*Cf.* Whitley: *Art in England*, 1800–1837).

literary art of Bulwer, the spiritual likeness is very close. Thackeray, writing more than twelve years later, had achieved consciousness of this likeness, and included both artist and writer in one sarcastic condemnation:

Martin I would venture to place in the theatrical heroic class of artists. One looks at those strange pieces and wonders how people can be found to admire, and yet they do. Grave old people, with chains and seals, look dumbfoundered into those vast perspectives and think that the apex of the sublime is reached there. In one of Sir Bulwer Lytton's novels there is a passage to that effect. I forget where but I am positive you will find the sentiment somewhere. They come up to his conceptions of the sublime, they answer to his ideas of beauty, or the Beautiful as he writes it with a large B. He is himself an artist and a man of genius. What right have we poor devils to question such an authority? Do you recollect how we used to laugh in the Capitol at the Domenichino Sybil, which this same author praises so enthusiastically — a wooden, pink-faced, goggle-eyed, ogling creature with no more beauty or sentiment than a wax doll? But that was our conceit.[1]

It was; — and a conceit to which time has been unkind. It is no longer a cultural chic to laugh at Domenichino; and who shall say but that Martin and Bulwer himself are not once more to have their day? Nevertheless Thackeray was right to declare that Bulwer admired Martin, and to realise the affinity between the writer and the painter. Read what the former has to say of the latter in *England and the English*, and then consider whether the words, with very slight adaptation, could not have been written in admiring defence of Bulwer himself.

Martin, if not the best painter, is, perhaps, on the whole, the most original genius of his age. Vastness is his sphere, yet he has not lost or circumfused his genius in its space; he has chained, and wielded, and measured it at his will; he has transfused its character into narrow limits; he has compassed the Infinite itself with mathematical precision.

[1] "Picture Gossip." *Fraser's*, June, 1845.

Look at his "Deluge" — it is the most simple of his works —
it is, perhaps, also the most awful. Poussin had represented before
him the dreary waste of inundation; but not the inundation of a
world. With an imagination that pierces from effects to the ghastly
and sublime agency, Martin gives, in the same picture, a possible
solution to the phenomenon he records, and in the gloomy and per-
turbed heaven you see the conjunction of the sun, the moon, and a
comet! Look, again, at the "Fall of Nineveh"; observe how the
pencil seems dipped in the various foundations of life itself: here
the moon, there the electric flash; here torch upon torch, and there
"the smouldering dreariment" of the advancing conflagration: the
crashing wall, the rushing foe; the dismay of some, the resignation
of others; in front, the pomp, the life, the brilliant assemblage, the
doomed and devoted beauty gathered round the monarch, in the
proud exultation of his immortalising death! I stop not to touch
upon the possible faults, upon the disproportionate height of these
figures, or upon the theatrical effect of those; upon the want of some
point of contrasting repose to augment the general animation, yet
to blend with it a softer sympathy; or upon occasional errors in the
drawing, so fiercely denounced by rival jealousies; — I speak of the
effect which the picture produces on all, — an effect derived from
the sublimest causes, the most august and authentic inspiration.[1]

Whether or not one is disposed to agree with this eloquent
tribute to the talents of a little remembered artist, the suita-
bility of such a tribute having been paid by Bulwer to Martin
cannot be denied. Both had the same excited love of huge
perspectives, of towering and mysterious heights, of torn
and tragic skies; both revelled in the rendering of immense
disasters; neither scrupled to set off a melodrama with light-

[1] Bulwer's admiration for Martin persisted and was reciprocated. Many years
later the painter was inspired by a passage in King Arthur to paint a picture of Agle and
Arthur, which was publicly exhibited in London. On May 22, 1849, Bulwer wrote
enquiring the price. Martin replied that the painting was priced £300 in the exhibi-
tion, but he would be glad to let the poet of King Arthur have it much cheaper. He
added:
"In endeavouring to illustrate the poetry I have represented a lovely night I saw
some 20 years ago, which was so remarkable for the splendour of the heavenly bodies
that if I fail in doing justice to the poet I trust that I shall please the astronomers as I
have taken every pains to make my picture astronomically correct.'

effects so sulphurous and sudden, with draughtsmanship so peccable as to provoke naturalism to its angriest contempt. A modern critic has already been quoted as describing Bulwer's crime-fiction as of good-bad quality; probably his pictorial magniloquence also — and Martin's too — are by Thackerayan standards bad as bad can be. But of their bad kind they are superb.

IV

One more glimpse at *England and the English*, and we are done, both with consideration of the book itself, and with the survey of Bulwer's literary life up to the date of his return from Italy early in 1834.

Supplementary to the intrinsic features of this notable work is one which, if not actually extraneous to the author's main theme, is inessential to it, which could have been omitted, not only without damage to his argument, but also with great advantage to his peace of mind. It was characteristic of Bulwer that he should have permitted any superfluity at all in a publication so reasoned and so carefully designed; he was always indulgent when self-criticism involved a restraining of his own exuberance. But it was even more characteristic that he should have been reckless enough to embellish a serious piece of argument with satirical personalities, and so have got himself into trouble over a passage of provocative writing, which he could easily have left out altogether. And yet the particular piece of invective which was now to recoil upon his head was the most creditable of all his excursions into personal abuse, because he wrote it partly from a sense of public duty, partly at the bidding of private friendship and only very little from a sense of personal spleen.

Here and there in *England and the English* occur what the author, tacitly avowing them to be inessential, calls "Supplementary Illustrations of Character." These pen portraits claim to present types of contemporary personality, whose nature and activities illustrate the mentality and manners of the English under the various influences of their existing civilisation. One such group of portraits exemplifies English character generally; another depicts men of letters; another the prevalent type of moralist. It was, however, while writing Book IV which deals with literary men and journalists, that Bulwer yielded most considerably to his love of satirical fault-finding; and in the course of so doing he stirred his old enemies, and new ones also, to bitter retaliation.

Among the "Supplementary" Characterisations illustrating the evils of anonymous writing in the press, occurred (in the first three editions of the book) the following: —

From this gentle supporter of the anonymous press [a type previously described], turn for one moment to gaze on the most dirty of its disgraces. Sneak "keeps a Sunday newspaper" as a reservoir for the filth of the week; he lets out a *cabinet d'aisance* for any man who wishes to be delivered of a lie. No trader of the kind can be more obliging or more ill-savoured: his soul stinks of his profession, and you spit when you hear his name. Sneak has run through all the circle of scoundrelism: whatever is most base, dastardly, and contemptible, Sneak has committed. Is a lie to be told of any man? Sneak tells it. Is a Countess to be slandered? Sneak slanders her. Is theft to be committed? Sneak writes to you — "Sir, I have received some anecdotes about you, which I would not publish for the world if you will give me ten pounds for them." Sneak would declare his own mother a drab, and his father a hangman, for sixpence-halfpenny.

Sneak sets up for a sort of Beau Sneak — crawls behind the scenes, and chats with the candle-snuffer: when he gets drunk, Sneak forgets himself, and speaks to a gentleman; the gentleman knocks him down. No man has been so often kicked as Sneak — no man so often horsewhipped; his whole carcase is branded with the contumely of castigation. Methinks there is, nevertheless, another chastisement in reserve for him at the first convenient opportunity. It is a pity to beat one so often beaten — to break bones that have been so often broken; but why deny oneself a luxury at so trifling an expense? — it will be some honour to beat him worse than he has been beaten yet! Sneak is at heart the most miserable of men;

he is poisoned by the stench of his own disgrace: he knows that every man loathes him; he strives to buoy himself from "the graveolent abyss" of his infamy by grasping at some scamp of a lord. One lord, with one shred of a character left to his back, promised to dine with him, and has been stark naked of character ever since.

Sneak has stuck up a wooden box in a nursery garden between Richmond and London, exactly of that description of architecture you would suppose him to favour: it is for all the world like a temple which a Cit erects to the Roman Goddess of Sewers; here "his soul sits at squat." The little house stares you in the face, and reminds you at once of the nightman its owner. In vain would ingenuity dissociate the name of Sneak from the thought of the scavenger. This beautiful effect of the anonymous system I have thus honoured with mention, in order that posterity may learn to what degree of rottenness rascality can be corrupted.

Now the identity of "Sneak" was immediately and generally obvious. His journalistic activity, his way of life, his obstinate survival of much personal misadventure were unmistakably those of Charles Molloy Westmacott, already referred to as a friend of Maginn and as editor of *The Age*. This individual was the son of Susannah Molloy, landlady of the King's Arms Tavern in Kensington, and was born in 1787 or 1788. Whether the father was indeed, as Maginn declared in his Fraserian portrait of the editor of *The Age*, the first of the sculptors named Richard Westmacott, or whether the honour belonged to a chimney sweep of Drury Lane, will never be known. But the use of the famous surname survived challenge [1]

---

[1] Westmacott's enemies — and particularly the editor of *The Satirist*, a paper which ran *The Age* a close second as a scandal sheet — regularly referred to him as "Molloy", and dwelt on his chimney-sweep ancestry. *The Satirist's* persistent attacks on him are as revealing as most charges brought by one crook against another in the same line of business. They also bear out some of the things said by Bulwer about "Sneak." Thus, in *The Satirist* for January 19, 1831, we read: "We are informed that Mr. Charles Molloy has vowed that he will never engage in a duel. The motives, he says, of this *sweeping* resolution are purely conscientious." Again on July 3 the paper publishes a denial of the statement that Lord Harrington is a friend of Molloy's. "My strict orders," says his lordship in his letter, "have been that if he presumes to cross my threshold, he is to be immediately kicked out" (*cf.* this with Bulwer's character sketch). Finally, in October, is printed a paragraph about "Molloy's twenty horse-whippings."

and certainly Charles Molloy's interest in and knowledge of art — particularly that of sculpture — were so considerable as to suggest that at some time he had enjoyed more opportunities of learning the subject than would be normal in a chimney sweep's household.

After a vagrant existence as small actor, tavern-adventurer and hack-journalist generally, Westmacott began the career of blackmail which was to become both his speciality and his livelihood. A complete lack of shame or scruple made him a useful hireling in the campaign against Queen Caroline, and the King's party paid him heavily for his versatility in muck-raking. He assumed in consequence an attitude of the most fervent loyalty, and his various publications during the eighteen-twenties contrive ingeniously to combine slavish adulation of a very fallible sovereign with disagreeable insinuations against nearly everyone else.

After editing for a while a paper called *The Gazette of Fashion* he published in 1823 over his own name the first (and only) instalment of a satirical miscellany called *Points of Misery*, following it immediately under the pseudonym of "Bernard Blackmantle", with the well-known *English Spy or Characteristic Sketches and Scenes of the Present Age*.[1] Both these publications were illustrated by Robert Cruikshank, and the fact that the latter had its engravings coloured and included also two by Rowlandson has secured for it an immortality which the text alone would certainly not have merited.[2] Also in 1823 Westmacott published a coarse satire on "Cockney Critics", with particular reference to Jerdan, whose *Literary Gazette* had offended him by harsh criticism of *Points of Misery*.

Almost simultaneously he made a more pretentious literary appearance with an *Annual Critical Catalogue of the Royal Academy*. This he followed in 1824 with an equally dignified work on the principal *British Galleries of Painting and Sculp-*

[1] *The English Spy* was in some degree continued in the form of a short-lived magazine called the *St. James's Royal Magazine*.
[2] *Literary Gazette*. November 15, 1823.

ture, at the same time launching a new series of an old established annual anthology called *The Spirit of the Public Journals*. Under Westmacott's control this anthology brought together from the more outspoken papers of the previous year (particularly *John Bull*, *Life in London*, *The Literary Chronicle*, *The Morning Chronicle* and *The Morning Herald*) *jeux d'esprits*, reports of scandalous cases, verses, anecdotes and so forth, which, ingeniously arranged and enlivened with a few original contributions from Westmacott and his friends, composed an entertaining and rather scurrilous miscellany. The series ran successfully for three years, and covered the contents of the press for 1823, 1824 and 1825.

In 1825 appeared *Fitzalleyne of Berkeley: a Romance of the Present Times* by Bernard Blackmantle. This work presented under a very thin disguise several of the more notorious of the scandals concerning the family of Berkeley, and introduced many prominent fashionables of the day in so far as they were compromised with ladies of the stage and bagnio or with other people's wives.[1] In 1826 was published a further "Blackmantle" work entitled *The Punster's Pocket Book*, with engravings by Robert Cruikshank. This tedious piece of fooling ended the career of Westmacott's pseudonym. Thereafter he was himself, or "The Editor of *The Age*."

The facts as to Westmacott's connection with *The Age* newspaper are a little obscure. The paper had, after a false start in 1819, been formally revived in 1825. For two years it was a bad-mannered but inconspicuous journal of moderate Tory colouring, and although Westmacott may have had some share in its production, he was not as yet its despot. In July, 1827, however, the character of the paper changed. Its Toryism became more violent, its scurrilities at once more vivid and more obviously designed; and it developed mannerisms suggestive of a conscious imitation of *Blackwood's Magazine*.

---

[1] "Fitzalleyne" is Colonel Berkeley (who combined to such disastrous effect a violent and profligate character with technical illegitimacy); "Maria" is Miss Foote; "Joseph" (as already stated) is "Golden Ball" Hughes.

The alteration marked the accession of Westmacott to power and to proprietorship; but one may suspect (as has already been indicated) that, while he directed the policy, another and a more talented mind carried it out.

Early in 1829 was published a little book called *The Spirit of the Age Newspaper for 1828* — a book unmistakably according to Westmacott's design, alike from its titling, style of editing and ultra-loyal frontispiece and dedication. A selection of extracts from the issues of the previous year (exactly on the lines of *The Spirit of the Public Journals*) was prefaced by an essay, in which "the Editors" make clear that the paper has only recently come into its present hands, and write of their own virtues and the vices of their predecessors with an amusing bravado of the kind already familiar to readers of *Blackwood's*, and destined to be still more familiar to readers of *Fraser's Magazine*. It is a fair guess that the "Editors" were two in number, and that if Westmacott was one, the other was Maginn. In short, from July, 1824, until 1830, when his energies were absorbed by the editing of *Fraser's*, it is almost certain that Maginn was the chief controversialist of *The Age;* an assumption which would not only explain the peculiar pungency of the paper's vulgarisms during those three years but would also help to account for the later entente between Westmacott and his paper and the Fraserian coterie.[1]

---

[1] The mannerisms of *The Age* peculiarly reminiscent of *Blackwood's* and prophetic of *Fraser's* were several. The editor was spoken of as "The Great Captain", and assumed an august and dominating style of speech halfway between the masterful good-fellowship of "Christopher North" and the pseudo-royal despotism of "Oliver Yorke"; the paper ran a series of satirical symposia under the title "Noctes Londonienses"; Lockhart and the *Quarterly* became quite suddenly objects of fervent praise; conversely the principal victims of attack were now precisely the people later to be most cruelly pilloried in *Fraser's*. Indeed the hand of Maginn is everywhere unmistakable. Finally significant is the solemn notice, published on May 9, 1830, of the death of "Sir Morgan O'Doherty" (Maginn's best known pseudonym). Fraser's had recently started, and absorbed the editor to such an extent that he gave up his work even on *Blackwood's*. Such a way of celebrating the transfer of Maginn's whole activity to his new magazine is very characteristic of his style of journalism which, by then, had infected Westmacott also. The "obituary notice" remarks that "the glory of Maga is now defunct"; and it is notable that henceforward compliments to *Blackwood's* are replaced in the columns of *The Age* by compliments to *Fraser's*.

The Age was in appearance another *John Bull* and it resembled its elder competitor in policy and partly in content. But the editor of *The Age* had other sources of livelihood besides his party wages, because beneath the surface of his regular newspaper activity, he carried on blackmail since his paper had a purposeful ingenuity in its criticisms on individuals, which the editor of *John Bull* would have had neither the meanness nor the patience to contrive. Thus, Westmacott used his power and his knowledge of the theatrical world to extort money from Madame Vestris, when in 1833 she was in management at the Olympic Theatre; and against such naturally pregnable persons he did not scruple to move publicly in the columns of his paper. But, as a rule, he was careful to keep from actual weekly print references of an offensive kind to individuals likely to defend themselves. Now and again he made a mistake. In the course of anti-Radical pamphleteering he insulted Thomas Duncombe, and the member for Finsbury flogged him heartily at their next public encounter. On another occasion *The Age* published an ambiguously phrased poem about Fanny Kemble;[1] and shortly afterwards the girl's father, seeing Westmacott in a box during a performance of *The Duenna* at Covent Garden, lay in wait for him in the corridor and knocked him senseless with a property club. It is interesting to note that, according to contemporary newspaper accounts of this incident, the sympathies of the crowd were so fiercely with Kemble that authority contented itself with rescuing Westmacott from a public lynching and did not press a case against his assailant.[2]

[1] *The Age*, October 17, 1830.
Twiss is presented as singing the following verse:
"My feelings I cannot dissemble
A shame to turn off such a man!
For I am the nephew of Kemble
The father of 'my daughter Fan'"

[2] *The Age* published its own indignant account of the outrage on October 24, 1830. Other papers — notably *The Times*, *The Post*, *The Courier* and *The Literary Gazette* (which Westmacott called "The Pawnbroker's Gazette") — almost applauded Kemble for his action.

It was probably after this misadventure that Westmacott
made a habit of carrying a loaded crop wherever he went.[1]
Fear of the loathing in which he was generally held could
not overcome his passion for gain nor his perverse delight in
torturing the victims of his plots.   He pursued his evil way
(with perhaps a little extra caution) and continued to enjoy
his pretentious little villa, between Barnes and Richmond,
where he had a crowd of statues in his garden and a strong
box of marketable secrets in his private room.

The particular action of this social pest which impelled
Bulwer to provoke a public quarrel pre-dated that quarrel by
some three years.   In August, September and October, 1829,
and again in March, 1830, *The Age* published despatches from
its Paris correspondent, in the course of which the recently
widowed Countess of Blessington and her late husband's
son-in-law, Count d'Orsay, were, almost in so many words,
described as lovers.   A year later Lady Blessington left Paris
for London, and quickly realised that the scandal had spread
so widely in English society that the more correct hostesses
regarded her and her household as taboo.   This of itself
would not very seriously have distressed her, for she preferred
intelligence to social cachet, and the company of the virtuous
great was considerably dull.   But it is a fair presumption that
Westmacott, seeing this brilliant and spendthrift victim
apparently within his reach, tried to apply the screw in the
usual way.   Lady Blessington would naturally consult her
nearest friends, one of whom was Edward Bulwer; and he,
already the victim, as has been seen, of insulting references
in Westmacott's paper and therefore inclined in advance to
strike a blow simultaneously for his friend and for himself,
determined to give the creature a chance of honourable com-
bat by kicking him publicly in the pages of *England and the
English*.

---

[1] This crop is shown in the portrait drawn by Maclise for Number 48 of *Fraser's*
"Gallery of Literary Characters", published in May, 1834, and is referred to by Maginn
in his accompanying character-sketch.

But Westmacott was no readier for an actual fight than Lockhart; and for the second time an obvious challenge from Bulwer was cautiously evaded. Like Lockhart, the editor of *The Age* conspired with his more disreputable friends to slander the man he dared not meet; unlike Lockhart, he himself prepared over his own name a pamphlet into which he put all he knew of vulgar insolence.

This pamphlet was published in August, 1833, under the title: *A Letter from C. M. Westmacott to E. L. Bulwer*. To analyse it in detail is unnecessary. Its controversial strong suit is that known to the schoolboy as the *tu-quoque*. Westmacott surveys the various charges Bulwer had made against him, interpolates a few offensive clichés from the Fraserian armoury, and crushingly concludes: "None of these things can be alleged against *me*. There is not a degree of meanness, personal, literary or political, which is not to be attributed to *you*." Bulwer's mockery of the "wooden box in the nursery garden between Richmond and London" went deeply home. The editor of *The Age* splutters with fury at the insult to "the snug, quiet and delightful retreat" which ingenious commerce in other folks' misery had so tastefully adorned.

In literary criticism Westmacott tends to become confused. "Each of *your* productions," he first observes, "has proved a robbery upon some more talented author. *Falkland* is a close imitation of Barry St. Leger's clever autobiographical novels; [1] *Pelham* of *Vivian Grey; Devereux* is a wire-drawn edition of Plumer Ward; *Paul Clifford* (a wishy-washy *Beggar's Opera*) was founded on *George Godfrey*; [2] and in *Eugene Aram* the whole character of the Corporal is transplanted verbatim

---

[1] Barry St. Leger wrote only one "autobiographical novel" — *Some Account of the Life of the late Gilbert Earle* (1824) — and the similarity between it and *Falkland* is one shared by a hundred other "first novels" written during the teens and twenties under the joint influence of *Werther's Leiden* and Byronic *Schwärmerei*.

[2] That the *Beggar's Opera* was to some extent the starting point of *Paul Clifford* had never been denied, even by Bulwer himself; but the introduction as a fellow-inspiration of Gaspey's *The History of George Godfrey* (3 vols., 1828) was an original (if somewhat nebulous) idea of *The Age's* editor.

from Paul de Kock's novel, *Le Cocu; The Siamese Twins* is a decoction of ten drops of Croly's *May Fair* to a hogshead of pump water."

But this one paragraph in demolition of Bulwer's literary reputation did not satisfy Westmacott. His pamphlet only runs to sixteen pages; but it contrives — four pages later on — to return to the subject and to pass another and a completely contradictory judgment on the very books already scornfully dismissed. The pamphleteer is praising *Fraser's* attacks on Bulwer and in particular the way in which "an able writer soon exposed with crushing hand the impudent absurdity of your letter to Lockhart." [1] He goes on: "Base and ingrateful you are in your attack on Lockhart, for the main ideas, brutally perverted, of your novels are stolen from his *Adam Blair* or *Reginald Dalton* or the imitators of these works." With which crowning triumph in literary affiliation Westmacott the critic passed from view.

It was perhaps natural that long-standing fellowship in low-class journalism should have made allies of Westmacott and Maginn. The latter, having earlier stooped to actual collaboration with the blackmailer, did not scruple now to take his side in controversy. Reviewing Westmacott's pamphlet in October, 1833, he (or one of his minions) spoke of "our friend of *The Age*"; praised the letter as "spicy", "graphic" and "splendid"; and allowed himself to invent a few new personal insults to Bulwer, which rivalled in grossness and obvious malevolence anything hitherto produced.

The pen portrait of "Sneak" was indeed a stone thrown into stagnant sewage, and one which churned with significant speed much odorous filth from below the surface. But though Bulwer suffered considerably from his enemies' retaliation, he was less thoroughly tortured than these enemies had hoped. Before *Fraser's* review appeared he had left England for his European tour; and the much-advertised "proceedings"

[1] The reference is of course to the passage discussed on p. 259 and almost certainly written by Lockhart himself.

which Westmacott (according to that review) had already taken against Bulwer's publisher were never heard of more.

But one move was indeed made by "Sneak", and a significant one. Late in 1833 (that is to say immediately after the quarrel with Bulwer) he sold a half-interest in *The Age* for five thousand pounds to Captain Polhill, a wealthy theatrical speculator who had taken over Drury Lane two years before and appointed the preposterous Bunn as his stage manager. *The Age* had always given prominence to theatrical criticism, and Polhill presumably thought that part control over the paper would be good for his publicity. Westmacott's motive may be surmised, and one cannot help wondering whether this sale of half the profits and responsibilities of *The Age* was not a substitute for litigation. A blackmailer can throw *tu-quoques* at his enemies and buy support from other scribblers by standing them free drinks; but when he seeks for monetary compensation through the law he finds the quest has inconveniences. Polhill's five thousand pounds were at least certain, and therefore better balm for wounded *amour propre* than a hazardous libel action against a firm of publishers.

Westmacott's subsequent history may be told in a paragraph. From 1834 to 1838 he and Bunn were in close alliance, the former in and out of the theatre and (in Macready's view at least) responsible for half the managerial shiftinesses and troubles which hindered the actors in their work. Early in 1838 he relinquished *The Age* altogether, but remained for a while longer in England, until early in the forties the country became at last too hot for him. He removed to Paris and there pursued his trade through a lingering old age, dying in 1868 in his eighty-first year. Some of his notebooks appeared in the second-hand book market shortly after his death. They were crowded with compromising facts and usefully lurid particulars of the private lives of eminent persons, among them that very George IV whom, while he was alive, Westmacott had studiously beslavered with obsequious compliment.

The End of a Marriage

Chapter One

The Bulwers return from Italy — Loneliness of Bulwer— Reasons for his friendlessness — Contemporary comments on his personality — Bulwer the dandy— His great popularity as a writer — His conspiracy-mania— Letters to Macvey Napier— His review of Egerton Brydges' Autobiography — The Last Days of Pompeii — *Its immediate success* — Rienzi

I

It was in February or early March, 1834, when Edward and Rosina arrived once more in Hertford Street. Their foreign tour had ended in a misery of rage and cruelty which even today it is intolerable to contemplate. What actually happened, whose was the greater fault — these things can not only never be established, but by the very bitterness of their aftermath have lost significance. Bulwer himself stated no case in his defence; Rosina, writing long after the event, proclaimed her wrongs with a tortuous savagery no less pathetic than unconvincing; Rosina's maid swore a deposition in 1867 which recalled the Italian journey of more than thirty years ago and accused Bulwer of "brutal personal violence toward his wife." Mary Greene, who was not in Italy and whose reminiscences, like those of Rosina, were written long afterward, set down the story as it was told her at the time by both parties, and wisely refrained from taking sides in a dispute which mutual hatred had made insoluble. So let it remain. What mattered to the persons most concerned was that their love was dead.

For indeed by the time they returned to London, the last chance of mutual understanding had been lost. Henceforward these one-time lovers were enemies, and to the already considerable hostility which Bulwer's qualities and defects had alike provoked against him was added the enmity of one who could the more cruelly torture him for being ostensibly his dearest consolation.

The household's road to dissolution was a switchback of anger and remorse. Its ups and downs of hope and despair, of conciliation and revulsion, so increased the strain on the two persons most concerned that their hearts were turned to gall, and when the end seemed to have come, it was not an end at all but the beginning of a greater bitterness. The tale shall be told in the final pages of this volume. But it will be more dramatic, the nervous fret of it will be more vividly understood if, beforehand, we gather up the threads of the preceding chapters; weave in with them the literary and political achievements of Bulwer's last two years of domestic life; and seek to re-create that tapestry of outward personality and public reputation, which he displayed so gallantly before the world at the actual moment when his home was falling into ruin and his very soul was being stripped of its last shreds of privacy and peace. Never before or afterward did the proud façade of Bulwer's existence more fantastically belie its inward degradation than during these years of 1835 and 1836; and no man — whatever his sympathies in the quarrel between husband and wife, whatever his opinion of Bulwer's literary, political or social capacity — can withhold admiration from the sheer intellectual doggedness which toiled for livelihood and kept the world at bay, while behind the fighting front all was chaos and misery.

II

I have spoken of the various hostilities which Bulwer's qualities, no less than his defects, had already provoked against him; and preceding chapters have described so many attacks on his work, personality and manners, but so few

gestures of friendly admiration other than those made in
sycophantic flattery that the reader may be forgiven if he
regard the Bulwer of the early thirties as an almost friendless
man. Indeed, to a point, that is what he was. And his
personal loneliness was the more emphatic because as a novelist he was so widely read. His name on a title page drew
thousands; but his presence in a crowded room laid a restraint on others or even set them whispering. Quite apart
from the enmity and jealousy which his success provoked,
he was the kind of man and lived the kind of life which made
for spiritual solitude. Friendship, particularly for shy people, takes time; and Bulwer was too busy, too desperately
engaged in earning money and keeping abreast of the manifold
duties which in his versatility and energy he had undertaken,
to have the leisure for making friends and keeping them. At
first encounter he would seem hurried, preoccupied and rather
egotistical; and persons of less active mind, or those less bur-
dened by work and engagements, could not understand how
impossible it was to a man of his temperament to clear the
brain of current absorptions and to cultivate a new acquaintance with the unhurried self-forgetfulness which is essential,
if casual association is to become good fellowship. Naturally
self-conscious to an unusual degree, he allowed his overwhelming work to grow, from necessity, into a protective habit.
He never gave himself time to stay long enough in a stranger's
company to throw off his shyness and behave with the ease
and good-nature which underlay his stilted nervousness.
Also, because his days were filled to the last minute and his
crowded programme planned for some while ahead, he tended
to regard every encounter as a sort of business occasion, when
something had to be arranged. Once the point at issue was
clear, he would break off and rush away to his next urgent
duty, leaving his late companion with a faint sense of having
been used and thrown aside. It is easy to see how from many
such momentary irritations developed a general readiness to
criticise Bulwer, and how easy it was for persons seriously

concerned to damage him to exploit that readiness and use
it in his despite.

Hence there arose the legend of Bulwer as an affected,
heartless egotist — a legend which, if it ever died, died hard,
and was destined to haunt his reputation to the day of his
death and even beyond. Fragments of contemporary comment show the evidence accumulating. In February, 1833,
Cam Hobhouse sat next him at a Literary Fund dinner, and
wrote: "He is not an agreeable man, but seems to have some
sense, though with a dash of affectation." In August of the
same year Haydon records that the Duke of Sussex remarked,
a little clumsily, that "Bulwer is one of those who doesn't
think small beer of himself."

And there was a further reason, besides absorption in one
or another of his overwhelming occupations, for Bulwer's
isolation. He lived at a time when literature, although it
might be a gentleman's hobby, was not regarded as a gentleman's livelihood. In consequence the known fact that he
made his living by writing exposed him to the sneers of those
who had not to make their living at all. One of *Fraser's*
favourite insults was to call him "shabby-genteel", and to
deride his threadbare pretence of gilded elegance. This
reflected the contempt of wealthy Toryism. Similarly when
Bunn asked Lord Castlereagh to oppose Bulwer's bill for the
suppression of the monopoly theatres, Castlereagh replied:
"Bulwer? Oh, he's a *low* fellow, is he not?" And all the
while that the great were thus despising him, the humbler
writing folk were equally his enemies. Simultaneously his
own insistence on breeding (and his undeniable tendency to
airs and graces) alienated the working *litterateurs* who might
otherwise have been his friends. He fell therefore, in this
respect as in his political opinions, between two stools and
landed lonely on the ground. They resented his lofty manner, and, assuming him a frivolous trespasser on their ground,
were the more jealous of his success for regarding it as wantonly stolen from themselves.

Wherefore, for a man leading so active and varied a life, Bulwer was an exceptionally solitary figure; and because he had perforce a thousand acquaintances but neither time nor talent for turning even a proportion of them into sympathetic friends, his solitude was that most disconcerting of all isolations — a sort of generalised unpopularity. Men did not like him; and for the reason that neither he nor his circumstances gave them an opportunity of doing so. Naturally he became conscious of his inability to get on with all and sundry, and the sense of being unpopular increased his shyness, which in its turn increased his unpopularity.[1]

And yet he was capable of making himself liked. On the rare occasions when he unbent, he provoked admiration and at times real affection. His intimacy with Lady Blessington and Orsay was both genuine and fond. When the time comes to picture Bulwer as the most trusted and loyal friend of the mistress of Gore House, it will be seen how unaffected and serene he could be, provided he were sure of himself and of the friendly confidence of others; how thoroughly Lady Blessington came to rely both on his friendship and his judgment; how well and faithfully they served her. Equally firmly founded, though of different pattern, was his long friendship with John Forster, also to be chronicled in due course, and presenting one of the strangest psychological duels of the nineteenth century.

Then there was Disraeli, who, largely with Lady Blessington's help, became sufficiently at ease with Bulwer for the pair of them to forget their posing. Under the influence of Mrs. Wyndham Lewis the two drifted later into a more formal relationship, but during the early thirties they were intimate enough. An interesting passage from Disraeli's "Mutilated Diary" of 1833 is quoted in the first volume of Monypenny's biography, and shows the genuine im-

[1] A close parallel could be drawn between the solitariness of Bulwer and that of his friend Macready. Both longed to be on easy terms with their kind; both tried to conquer their self-consciousness; both merely achieved a greater isolation by their too obvious striving after cordiality.

pression made on a clever contemporary by Bulwer's mental distinction:

Alas! I struggle from Pride. Yes! It is Pride that now prompts me, not Ambition. They shall not say I have failed. I remember expressing this feeling to Bulwer as we were returning from Bath together, a man who was at that moment an M. P., and an active one, editing a political journal and writing at the same time a novel and a profound and admirable philosophical work. He turned round and pressed my arm and said in a tone the sincerity of which could not be doubted: "It is true, my dear fellow, it is true. We are sacrificing our youth, the time of pleasure, the bright season of enjoyment — but we are bound to go on, we are *bound*. How our enemies would triumph were we to retire from the stage! And yet," he continued in a solemn voice, "I have more than once been tempted to throw it all up, and quit even my country, for ever."

I have not gained much in conversation with men. Bulwer is one of the few with whom my intellect comes into collision with benefit. He is full of thought, and views at once original and just. The material of his conversation and many a hint from our colloquies he has poured into his *England and the English*, a fine series of philosophic dissertations.[1]

Rather critical, but maybe the more perceptive for its detachment, was H. F. Chorley's impression of Bulwer after their first protracted conversation. In his diary for October 31, 1830, Chorley wrote:

We walked home together from Lady Blessington's, and in his cloak and in the dusk he unfolded more of himself to me than I had yet seen. I had guessed pretty much of what I did see — an egotism, a vanity — all thrown up to the surface. He is a thoroughly satin character, but then it is the richest satin. There was something inconceivably strange to me in his dwelling, with a sort of hankering tone, on D'Orsay's physical advantages; something beneath the dignity of author, in the manner in which he spoke of his own works, saying the new ones never interested him in so far as they were experiments. It is a fine, energetic, inquisitive, romantic mind

[1] Monypenny's *Life of Disraeli*. (*Original edition.*) I, 235.

which if I mistake not has been blighted and opened too soon. There wants the repose — the peace that passeth all understanding.

A year or so later, after dinner at the Reform Club, Chorley writes:

I have found all my judgments confirmed by further experience of Bulwer, both as to cleverness and self-conceit. I am not quite sure about the heart or its opposite but it is amusing to discover that he makes personal appearance his idol and values Voltaire as much for being a tall man as for the sake of his satires or essays.

Macaulay, as befitted an egotist more thorough even than Bulwer himself, wrote tiresomely but amusingly to his sister:

(Undated — 1831 or 1832)

After the debate I walked about the streets with Bulwer till about 3 o'c. I spoke to him about his novels with perfect sincerity, praising warmly and criticising freely. He took the praise as a greedy boy takes an apple-pie and the criticism as a good dutiful boy takes senna tea. He has one eminent merit, that of being a most enthusiastic admirer of mine, so that I may be the hero of a novel yet, under the name of Delamare or Mortimer. Only think what an honour!

Later, reporting to the same correspondent Bulwer's resignation from the *New Monthly's* editorial chair, Macaulay wrote:

I suppose Bulwer is making money in some other way, for his dress must cost as much as that of any five other members of parliament.

It is noticeable that these two otherwise friendly observers felt an amused contempt for Bulwer's personal vanity. There can be no doubt that at this time, and for several years to come, he affected an exaggerated dandyism of dress and manner which, although designed to buttress his rather frightened self against storms of anticipated criticisms, merely had the effect of increasing that criticism and of exposing him to dislike and mockery which he could easily have avoided.

To what extent impertinent comment on his clothes and whiskers caused Bulwer embarrassment is immaterial. Pos-

sibly he found his affectations to be good publicity among the
uncritical public of novel-readers; possibly he was glad to
concentrate the malice of enemies on foppery and thus escape
more painful persecution; in any event he pursued his exquisite way, and references to his scented elegance persist throughout the forties.

As an individual, therefore, the Bulwer who returned from
Italy early in 1834 was a dandified being of few intimate
friends, an object of rather uneasy dislike to a large circle of
acquaintances; and a downright offence to the small but
vociferous group of persons who, for one reason or another,
hated him.

And side by side with this poverty of individual companionship went a wealth of public reputation which few
writers have achieved at so early an age.   The contrast strikes
posterity as ironical; but at the time it served rather to mis-
lead Bulwer than to set him wondering how to put matters
right.   His success as a novelist not only dulled his consciousness of his failure as a man, but led him to misinterpret
alike its cause and its effect.   If he had been able to realise
how much comfort he would have gained from a more cordial relationship with his fellows, he might have gauged
the causes of his isolation and done something to remove
them.   But just because his renown and the sale of his books
were now so great, he tended to throw the blame for his
personal unpopularity on to others, and to believe that the
hostility and indifference with which he was in many quarters received were due wholly to jealousy of his European
reputation.   This was part of the truth, but not all of it;
and from a partial misapprehension of the reasons why many
of his fellows looked askance at him or treated him with nervous constraint, sprang that conspiracy-mania which was to
become almost an obsession with him, and not only to render
his own life miserable but to lay a heavy burden on those of
his friends in whom he sought to confide.

Let one or two contemporary documents bear testimony to the international extent of Bulwer's literary fame at the beginning of 1834, and to the nervous pertinacity with which, in his desire to hear the critical sing his praises in unison with the uncritical, he was already beginning to torment himself and others.

First as to his popularity as a writer. He was himself accustomed, in prefaces and elsewhere, to refer with a deprecating nonchalance to "whatever success I may have gained" or to "novels praised above their merits." Once he broke out into a frank statement of his works' wide dissemination; [1] and, though this piece of self-assertion provoked his critics to angry charges of vainglory, it was really more to his credit than mock modesty, because at least it was true. Abroad, and particularly in Germany, his reputation was by 1834 far greater than that of any other living English novelist. Foreign libraries of English fiction, translators and commentators, vied with one another in preparing and issuing editions of his works. Anyone with the curiosity to hunt nowadays the bookshops of Germany and Scandinavia for English novels of the last century, will find more of Bulwer's books published between 1830 and 1870, both in English and in translation, than those of any of his contemporaries. At the time there seemed no limit to the demand for his works. George Darley, writing from Munich in 1834, described books in general as "scarce, dear and bad." He goes on:

Bulwer's are Tully and Plato beside most of them. They beset all the windows, title-page after title-page, like ballads at a sale. What a deal, to be sure, he contrives to litter in a year! The man must be a codfish. The Germans worship Bulwer — call his productions Shakespearean — a good proof by the bye how exquisitely they must appreciate the latter.

H. F. Chorley, in *The Authors of England* (1838) refers to Bulwer's books as "works which are read wherever the English

[1] In the Preface to the Second edition of *The Last Days of Pompeii*. 1835.

language penetrates, which wall booksellers' shops in Germany and America."

And not only the books, but the ideas and abstractions behind them, tempted serious critics to reasoned debate. Laube, a well-known member of the Saint Simonian group, planned in 1834 to write an article on "Bulwer u. das Saint-Simonismus" for an important review, and by the middle forties there had already begun the stream of theses on this aspect or that of Bulwer's philosophy or literary art which has flowed more or less continuously ever since.

France, though less solemnly bemused than Germany by his lofty idealism and impressive use of capital letters, was hardly less eager to make his stories available for French enjoyment. Keen competition for early sheets of *Pompeii* developed as a result of the great success of pirated editions of several of his earlier books; while the rapidity with which his English texts were reprinted without permission or payment in one or other of the Paris-published series of English novels was before very long to provoke his indignation and set him agitating for some form of legal redress.

In America the piracies began even earlier than in Europe and continued briskly throughout the heyday of his writing life.

Secure in the knowledge of the mounting tide of his international popularity, with, into the bargain, a huge sale in England and flattering reviews in many widely read papers, Bulwer might have been expected to bear with equanimity the embittered, but definitely localised, attacks of the more "difficult" English critics. Of this, however, he was incapable. The more loudly he was cheered by the many, the more intolerable became the sardonic silence or the insolent heckling of the few, until at last he was frankly unable to endure either hostile comment or absence of comment, because in both he thought to detect the deliberate malice of enemies.

His early correspondence with Macvey Napier, of the

Edinburgh Review, shows the beginnings of this conspiracy-mania. Its later stages belong to the distraught history of his friendship with John Forster; but the hysterical demands for consolation and advice, which after each new book had been published and badly reviewed, were to reach Forster daily, in fact represented developed versions of Bulwer's first nervous approach to Napier, which was made as early as 1830 and read as follows:

Bulwer to Napier.

Sept. 8, 1830.

They tell me by the way in more places than one that the *Edinburgh Review* is not friendly to me and point out sundry hints and allusions in the article on "The Manners of the Day"[1] which, they will have it, are meant for me. These said allusions, they also contend, are more bitter and effectual enemies to me than open abuse, if coupled with that marked silence as to my name and works which exists in the article. They affect to consider that they indicate, though unworthy of the honour of abuse I am yet deserving the execution of a sneer.

The singleness with which as a novelist I have contended against all prejudice, all hypocrisy, has of course gained me many enemies too happy to support the wrath of the ultras by any seeming contempt from the liberals, and all envy and all scorn are vented more successfully on works like mine than those of a graver nature. . . . If you had not announced to me an intention to review my novels I should not have said this much, and this much only do I say — not soliciting publicity, not deprecating censure, not expecting praise but will you allow me to say it — asking what appears to me justice. I think I have no pretensions to be praised by the *Edinburgh*, but I think I have some to be reviewed.

My novels have had a certain sale in this country, they have been translated — God knows how! — into most European languages. They have been reviewed (one or other of them at least) in most European Reviews. In America they have been collected and sell in sets to an extent which I hesitate to believe; so that if they now stand at the door of the *Edinburgh Review* it is not cap in hand as a

[1] The reference is to a review of Mrs. Gore's novel *Women as They Are or The Manners of the Day*, published in the *Edinburgh* for July, 1830.

humble mendicant, but rather like a bluff creditor, who answers your accusation of his impertinence by begging you to settle his bill at the first convenient opportunity.

Receiving a reply from Napier, Bulwer writes again. He is laboured and diffuse, begs Napier to understand that he does not want praise, does not deprecate blame, but cannot bear to be sneered at. He is greatly indebted to Napier for his courtesy and is willing to wait any length of time for a review. The letter with its fervent ending "God bless you, my dear sir" — is pathetic but rather ridiculous.

Nor are matters improved when in April, 1831, he reads an advance proof of the *Edinburgh* review of *The Siamese Twins*. It is critical certainly; but kind. Instantly Bulwer is in arms that a book everywhere greeted as a failure should have been chosen by Napier for his opening review. The kindness is forgotten; only the imagined slight remains and rankles. Nevertheless his letter, punctilious and stilted, is written in solemn sorrow rather than in anger.

From this point the Napier letters shade off into elaborate discussions of Bulwer's contributions, current and future, to the *Edinburgh*. Here and there, however, his dread of critical neglect or injustice still finds brief expression; and his perpetual inability to judge himself as he contrives to judge his fellows, or to apply to his own egotism the tests which he could sanely and justly apply to that of another, betrays itself almost with absurdity in the review of Sir Egerton Brydges' *Autobiography*, written at Napier's request and printed in the *Edinburgh* for July, 1834:

This work presents to us an elaborate picture of a species of literary character that may be expected to appear, at times, in that heated and high wrought civilisation to which the world has attained: — a character that has all the acute sensibilities of poetical genius without its energy and its power — its irritable temper — its wayward self-engrossment. . . .

The author before us is as intimately persuaded of the reality of his powers as if the loud huzzas of the literary world were borne to his retreat. All that criticism could prove, all that neglect — severest of critics — could teach, fall vain and unheeded on sons of a nature of this mould. . . .

There is this consequence of a moody and absorbed concentration in self; it vitiates the whole character. Learn to consider yourself alone, make yourself a god; and you deem all who dispute your pretensions little better than blasphemous. . . .

The complaints of Sir Egerton Brydges are impossible to sympathise with because they are wholly selfish. . . . The lamentations are solely for self and for selfish objects — a poem neglected, or a peerage refused. Nor does he ever seek to connect sympathy with himself by sympathy with others. We know nothing of the family — the wife — the children — of Sir Egerton Brydges. He does not burst forth with apostrophes which every lover, every husband, every father can feel in his heart of hearts. . . . We would warn by this example of a man of elegant tastes and doubtless of original and early kindness of disposition — the younger race from self-indulgence and self-absorption, which make martyrs of the intellect as well as of the heart.[1]

It is, from one point of view, barely credible that the man who wrote these words should, at the moment of their writing, have been engaged in anguished warfare with his own wife; should hardly have been conscious of the existence of his own children; and should himself have been in the early stages of that very intellectual and emotional self-martyrdom, as a horrid symbol of which he solemnly adduces the plaintive personality of the ancient Brydges. Thus it was, however; and one cannot be surprised that a man so incapable of including himself in his own judgments on human nature should have struck others as inhuman, nor that, blind as he was to his own share in the nervous shortcomings of the literary character, he should have been unable in more general respects also to see himself as others saw him.

[1] It may be noted that Brydges replied to this review in an article published in *Fraser's* in December, 1834. Clearly neither he nor the Fraserians knew that Bulwer was the *Edinburgh* reviewer.

III

Bulwer brought back with him from Italy half the manuscript of *Rienzi*, begun at Rome and then abandoned, and three quarters of that of *The Last Days of Pompeii*.

The first months of 1834 were passed, partly in domestic wrangling, partly in political activity, and the rest in bringing *Pompeii* to completion.   In July the book was published and won forthwith the most spectacular success of any novel issued since *Waverley*.

The literary quality, historical importance and technical construction of this still famous story have been so often and so fully discussed, that its merits or demerits need not here be canvassed.[1]   Contemporary reviews ranged from the ecstatic to the respectful, and hardly a critic but spoke with admiration of some one element in the tale.   Eminent individuals were equally generous with their praise.   Lord Lytton has printed in his biography contemporary letters of commendation, written to the author by Isaac Disraeli, by Mrs. Hemans, and by Lady Blessington, of which the first has real significance and the last a certain unconscious humour. It is impressive to read that, in the opinion of the elder Disraeli, *The Last Days of Pompeii* "is the finest and the most interesting fiction we have had for many years"; it is agreeable, with Lady Blessington's help, to conjure the scene in a country house in Suffolk, where her ladyship "lent my copy of *Pompeii* to an ultra-Tory, a most accomplished man who

---

[1] The extent to which *The Last Days of Pompeii* and its successors marked a development of the historical novel as created by Sir Walter Scott;   their comparative standing vis-à-vis the costume romances of Ainsworth and G. P. R. James;   their correctness of detail;   their proximity to, but actual falling short of, the "consummate" in romantic reconstruction of the past; — these and other aspects of Bulwer's achievement as a historical novelist are examined in every current history of nineteenth-century literature, have occupied the attention of Professor George Saintsbury and Professor Oliver Elton, and have lately been summarised by Mr. Alfred Tressider Sheppard in his interesting and combative defence of *The Art and Practice of Historical Fiction*.   For detailed examination of Bulwer as a costume-novelist the curious may be referred to E. G. Bell's painstaking *Introductions to the Prose Romances, Plays and Comedies of Edward Bulwer* (Chicago, 1914).

occupied the chamber next to mine, and the partition was so slight that I could hear his frequent exclamations."

Of distinguished opinions not addressed personally to Bulwer the most interesting recorded is that of William Beckford:

I was pleased with *Pompeii* (he said to Cyrus Redding) but there was a fault in it, that its author might easily have rectified if his attention had been drawn to the advantage he would have gained in throwing more sturdiness and energy into his characters, for he is dealing with Romans. He has the power to delineate well when he pleases.[1]

Bulwer's own attitude to the book, both before its completion and after its appearance, can very briefly be summarised. The first idea is said to have come from seeing a picture in Milan. On his way abroad in the autumn of 1833, he went to the Brera and saw a large painting of the destruction of Pompeii, in the foregound of which a child, watching a gaily plumaged bird struggling in death, stretched out its arms in delighted and uncomprehending wonder. When he reached Naples, he made the acquaintance of Sir William Gell (who became the novel's dedicatee) and under his guidance plunged into historical and topographical study relevant to the subject of his book. The inevitable preface, published in the first edition and retained in subsequent editions also, laid down the principles upon which he had constructed his story, and described the efforts he had made to unite correctness of detail in costume, architecture and way of life with natural ease of conversation and liveliness of character. "If I have succeeded," he said, "in giving some interest and vitality to a description of classic manners and to a tale of classic age, I have succeeded where all hitherto have failed."

When in March, 1835, a revised and corrected edition was published, he added yet a further "Advertisement" in which

[1] Redding: *Fifty Years' Recollections*. III, 107.

he defended himself over-emphatically against charges of inaccuracy brought against him by various critics; and also, with a characteristic lack of judgment, expanded one of the footnotes to the original preface so as to introduce a little sneer at Lockhart's classical novel *Valerius*.[1]

The tremendous popularity of *Pompeii* delighted its author; and, as was his way when pleased and excited, he adopted a manner of careful reserve in mentioning the success to others.

On October 12, 1834, he wrote to Disraeli from Ireland:

Tell me if you have read *Pompeii* and what you think of it. I hear from England that it is thought my best work. I am no judge, but fear it won't please the women. They don't appreciate elaborate plots and artful management. They want sentiment or wit and *Pompeii* has neither.

And in November to his mother:

Pompeii seems to have generally met with an applause I never expected. I was far from thinking highly of it myself. In fact I have scarcely thought about it at all, so painfully was my mind occupied during the time I wrote it.

And a letter of a few days earlier has a pathos and sounds a note of generalised self-pity which (in view of what was happening domestically) are very characteristic:

Rosina has expressed herself pleased with *Pompeii*, but that is nothing. She always did justice to whatever talent I may possess, nor is she the only one to estimate justly the author but to wrong the man.

Oct. 23, 1834

---

[1] "They who think the *Valerius* of Mr. Lockhart an exception" [*i.e.* to a statement just made that *Pompeii* is the first tale of a classic age to contain the interest and vitality of an actual romance] "are of course at liberty to do so. Many reasons concur to prevent *my* pointing out what appear to me the errors and failings of that work. But to my (probably incompetent) judgment, it wants the vitality and interest to which I have referred."

This paragraph had a short life. When *Pompeii* appeared as one of Bentley's Standard Novels in 1839, it had vanished.

It was natural that the triumph of *Pompeii* should have
decided Bulwer to finish without unnecessary delay the interrupted story of *Rienzi*. But political engagements and the
increasing trouble of his private life delayed the work beyond
his expectation, so that it was not completed till the late
autumn of 1835. On October 27, as he neared the end, he
wrote to Forster:

I write this ere I sit down to what I hope will be my last chapter of
Rienzi whom I have made into three volumes, poor fellow. I have
got a capital fine scene in the plague at Florence, and have made
two indifferently good characters of Rienzi's wife and a Provençal
bandit, but otherwise I fear there are too many historical scenes and
declamatory speeches.

In order, perhaps, to make a virtue of a regretted necessity,
he affixed a preface to the novel, in which he explained that
the book had been visualised as a biography and, although
now transformed into a romance, still adhered with unusual
care to historical chronology and fact. The preface concluded with an elaborate reference to Mary Russell Mitford,
whose successful tragedy *Rienzi* had been produced and published seven years earlier.

After suitable compliments, he declared that the lady's
rendering of character was probably more just than that of
Gibbon, from whose history she had first taken her idea.
But he went on to assert that his own was truer than either;
and certainly events have proved him right. The considerable research into the period and personality of Rienzi, which
has taken place since this novel was written, has in no material particular challenged the admiring estimate of the tribune's character which Bulwer, by sheer intuition and by a
sort of instinctive feeling for the nobility of mystical fanaticism, evolved for himself and propounded in the teeth of the
contrary view at that time generally held.

Rienzi was published in December, 1835. Albany Fonblanque, editor of *The Examiner*, wrote to the author within a

few days of the book's appearance one of his rare letters of personal commendation:

I have thought you inferior to Scott in the management of incident and dramatic situations, as much as you have been superior to him in fine reflection and a pervading loftiness of sentiment and moral aims. In *Rienzi* you seem to have equalled or surpassed Scott in the essence of romance and to have transcended yourself in thought, spirit and moral. . . . Since I read *Guy Mannering* I never felt such an interest in a story. After this I cannot wish you to write another novel; hitherto alp has risen above alp, but I doubt another ascent beyond *Rienzi*.

(Dec. 19, 1835)

This was high praise, and, one hopes, compensated Bulwer for two or three definitely unfavourable comments. Of these the oddest accused the novel of being disguised Radical propaganda. Rienzi was declared an impersonation of the author, and his career a forecast of the part which Bulwer himself meant to play in English politics.[1]

---

[1] *The Conservative.* December 19, 1835.

Chapter Two

Bulwer the politician—His special interests — A Letter to a Late
Cabinet Minister on the Present Crisis — *Lord Durham* — *His
character and melancholy life* — *His betrayal by Brougham* — *His
influence over Bulwer* — *Bulwer's tribute in* King Arthur — *Rumor
of Bulwer's death* — *A chance of minor office* — *Why he refused*

I

That a newspaper should late in 1835 have thought it worth
while to suspect Bulwer of serious political ambition and to
suggest that he saw himself as potentially a "tribune of the
people", is evidence of the position in which his four and
a half years of parliamentary life had placed him. He had
entered the House in April, 1831, as out-and-out Reform member for the borough of St. Ives. He made his maiden speech
on July 5, on the second night of the second reading of Lord
John Russell's second Reform Bill. The Bill was read again
in September and passed by the House of Commons on September 22. On October 7 it was rejected by the House of
Lords and Parliament was prorogued. On December 12 Lord
John Russell introduced his third Reform Bill in a reassembled
House of Commons. The House of Lords put up a last fight;
but the violent agitation in the country and the strong Reform
colouring of the Commons overbore their opposition. The
Bill became law in June, 1832; and one of its immediate effects
was to unseat Edward Bulwer, whose constituency of St. Ives
was swept away under the provisions of the new Act.

The first Reformed Parliament was elected in November,
1832, Bulwer reappearing at St. Stephens as member for Lincoln. He sat for Lincoln until in 1841 he began his ten years'

retirement from parliamentary life; and the most agreeable and valuable result of his long association with that city was the friendship which sprang up between him and Charles Tennyson d'Eyncourt of Bayens Manor, a friendship cordially reflected in the long correspondence and frequent visits exchanged between the two men.

The incidents of Bulwer's parliamentary work are so fully described in his grandson's biography, that the task of the present chronicler has been rather to select those most relevant to an appreciation of his character, writings and social reputation, than to repeat a tale already told. Throughout 1832 and 1833 he devoted his time to various measures connected with the organisation of intellectual life. Attempts to compass the suppression of the two Patent Theatres, the securing of Dramatic Copyrights, and the reduction of the Tax Upon Newspapers occupied his continuous attention. But in so far as his unchallengeable arguments assumed a respect for things of the mind and a genuine desire to stimulate national intelligence without restricting individual liberty, they met with a rather hesitating response, neither of these impulses being part of the traditional equipment of British politicians or British officialdom.

In the spring of 1834 he interested himself in a scheme for raising money for the support and development of *The Examiner*. His friendship with Forster, many meetings at Seamore Place with Albany Fonblanque, and a general sympathy with the liberal ideas behind the paper's policy encouraged him to invest some money of his own and to persuade his friends to do the same. His letter to Disraeli on this subject is printed in Lord Lytton's book, as well as a characteristically business-like reply sent by Lord Melbourne to the same or a similar appeal.[1]

In November he wrote in two days, and immediately published, a pamphlet entitled *A Letter to a Late Cabinet Minister on the Present Crisis*. This letter was addressed ostensibly to Lord

[1] Lytton, I, 487-488.

EDWARD BULWER
About 1838
From a model by E. W. Wyon

Normanby and was issued as a preliminary to the general election caused by the King's dismissal of the Melbourne government and summons to the Duke of Wellington. It made a passionate plea to the electorate to insist again, as they had insisted three years before, on a parliament pledged to the principle of Reform. Bulwer wrote high praise of Melbourne; defended the King against the murmurs of the extreme radicals, who spoke of petticoat influence and sought simultaneously to discredit royalty and Toryism; drew several effective historical analogies between the present crisis and earlier political events; and took occasion to criticise, courteously but directly, the attack made by Lord Brougham in an already notorious speech at Edinburgh on certain ardent supporters of Reform and in particular on a late colleague of his own in the Grey administration.

Twenty-one editions of this pamphlet were sold in six weeks (to the tenth edition was added a letter from Brougham replying, a little vaguely, to Bulwer's comments on the Edinburgh speech) and its influence on the elections was everywhere admitted to have been very great. Indeed the retention of the Whig majority in the Commons was in many quarters attributed directly to its cogency and opportune appearance.

But more relevant to its author's personal career than even his pamphlet's success was the fact that it allied him, openly and intimately, with a man whom he had in so many words saluted as the hope of progress and prosperity, a man who, had he lived, might have changed the whole course of Bulwer's life. This man was John George Lambton, first Earl of Durham.

II

Lord Durham, a tragic example of a fine mind destroyed by the selfish timidity of party politics and the jealousy of an embittered rival, was the only being who might have inspired Bulwer to endure, and finally to overcome, the ob-

stacles which commonplace men set between idealists and
political power.

The friendship of Bulwer and Durham began in Lady
Blessington's drawing-room. The latter was the senior by
nearly ten years. Son-in-law to Lord Grey, the Reform
Prime Minister, he had been one of the leaders of the pro-
Reform minority in the House of Lords, and was a person
of enormous influence with the north country mob in Scotland and the north of England where he was known as
"Radical Jack." A brief period in 1832–1833 as Ambassador
to St. Petersburg, then to Berlin and Vienna, was followed
by resentful protests against the shuffling timidity of his
father-in-law's cabinet, by angry resignation, and by the
conferring of an earldom. Durham's impatience with the
sacred policy of compromise had been so clearly shown as
to give serious offence to his more wily and opportunist
colleagues. Among these was Brougham; and to the persistent hostility of Brougham, was chiefly due the obstinate
thwarting of all Durham's subsequent efforts on his country's
behalf, as well as the gradual attrition and final treacherous
destruction of his aspiring, reckless and brilliant spirit.

From the time of his resignation to his death as a prema-
turely broken man in 1840, the history of Durham is the history of a genius outlawed for his genius' sake. He was too
quick-minded, too eager a visionary, too forgetful both of his
own material interests and those of others, to be a welcome
colleague of men whose love of intrigue, personal ambition
and blend of ruthlessness and pliability had brought them to
the forefront of British public life. It became the custom to
speak of Durham with fair words but a regretful shrug. He
was of course a wonderful creature; but he was unfortunately
an impossible man to work with; he had no sense of humour;
he was an admirable theoretician but unpractical, tactless and
arrogant. All of which, from the point of view of those who
said it, was perfectly true. But there was also the point of
view of the nation whom these people claimed to represent;

and the nation, had they known how, would have chosen Durham for their Prime Minister in 1834, so huge was his personal following, so great the reliance placed on his honesty and on his determination to carry out any promise made in letter or in public speech.[1] But the king hated him, and his colleagues were either resentful of his zeal or jealous of his public reputation. The professional Whig politicians wished to go thus far on the road to Reform but no further. They knew that Durham's influence alone had saved the north of England from barricades and bloodshed in 1831 and 1832; they realised his continued hold upon the populace; but they were too indolent or too nervous to like the idea of so powerful and explosive a radical in their midst, and Brougham, at any rate, was determined to keep him from office. Wherefore every ingenuity of flattering evasion and suave chicane was used to keep him away from home — a policy helped by his own rigid sense of duty and by his persistent bad health. No task was refused if it seemed for the country's good; no work, as Durham understood work, but undermined a little further his frail constitution. He was invited to preside over committees of enquiry into Belgian and Russian affairs; he was given diplomatic appointments abroad. He did what was asked of him; and each effort left him weaker and more pain-ridden than before.

In 1837 Melbourne made a passionate appeal to his patriotism to accept the Governor Generalship of a rebellious Canada. The latter mastered his by then alarming sickness and went — after a few months' hesitation and on receipt of Melbourne's pledge that from himself and his colleagues Durham's policy had received "the firmest and most unselfish support." At the crisis of his work there, when loyalty from the ministry which had sent him was essential to the successful fulfilment of his task, his old enemy Brougham launched a

[1] *Cf.* Lytton, I, 464, for a letter from Bulwer to Lady Blessington in which Durham's premiership is mentioned as almost a certainty : "Durham has written his horoscope on the people's heart," the letter concludes, "and they only want the occasion to tell him of his destiny."

savage attack on his dictatorial policy, and on his choice of colleagues, chief among whom were Sir Charles Buller and Edward Gibbon Wakefield. Melbourne, rather than risk the defeat of the government, went back on his own solemn promise and threw Durham over. The dying man resigned and came home; spent some months in arranging and coördinating the materials prepared by Buller and Wakefield in the pages of his great report; refused all the offers of the radicals who clamoured for him to lead them against Whigs and Tories alike; for his Report's sake spoke no word of reproach against the jealous lawyer who had stabbed him in the back or the Prime Minister who had betrayed him; and, in the summer of 1840, died.[1]

That this enlightened, gifted, but rather isolated man should have been welcome and at ease in Lady Blessington's house was natural and inevitable. He found there precisely the freedom from prejudice, the interest in advanced ideas, and the complete absence of calculating hypocrisy which he sought in vain among the members of regular political society. And because Bulwer shared many of his enthusiasms and even some of his experiences, Durham came to a rapid intimacy with the young member for Lincoln, which endured until the departure for Canada, and would likely have developed into a lasting alliance. For in character, as well as in opinion, the two men had much in common. Both possessed a certain cosmopolitan quality of mind, with its inevitable corollary, an undisguised impatience of insularity; both were ahead of their time in their ideas for social reform and educational improvement; both were outspokenly opposed to religious intolerance, to rigid sabbatarianism and to undue censorship. And with similarity of ideals went similarity of conviction as to the best way of obtaining them. Durham, in several of his speeches, insisted that intelligence

---

[1] In addition to Stuart J. Reid's *Life and Letters of Lord Durham* (2 vols. 1906), students may be particularly referred to an admirable article on Durham published in the *Times Literary Supplement* for January 9, 1930.

rather than property should be the test of a man's fitness for government. An identical plea is made by Bulwer in the pages of *England and the English*. But (and this is where their policy failed to reckon with English character and the peculiar nature of English democratic conviction) both men were too quick-minded for slow-moving public opinion and, in their impatience to get something done, looked for government by a few enlightened and well-born individuals in the interest of the common people. They hated reaction; but they also hated the timid bargainings of party politics and shrank fastidiously from the extremism of radical agitators who combined social subversiveness with demands for political reform. They did not realise that the tide of democracy was already flowing too strongly to be controlled by an accomplished autocracy, however liberal in its benevolence. Politics were already too complex a matter of give and take, of compromise, of mass-bribery and of indirect corruption, to make the prospect of government by a high-minded oligarchy tolerable to any party. Durham (and Bulwer in his train) offended existing politicians and on principle refused to play for mob-support. They went too far to conciliate official Whiggism, not far enough to satisfy the more ardent Radicals, not slow enough to take the public with them, and therefore, having only the suffrage of the small group of liberal intellectuals who were sensitive enough to recognise their practical idealism behind the screen of their exclusiveness, they paid the penalty of their own too great intelligence. The leader died; the disciple faded from the political consciousness of his contemporaries.

Bulwer's withdrawal from politics occurred the year after Durham's death; and it is hard not to regard the two events as cause and effect. Without any powerful and sympathetic friend to dispel his self-consciousness, and give popular expression to the enlightened theories and idealised common sense for which he was unable to find simple and telling words, he was a politician doomed to failure. Half realising the fact, he turned in upon himself and tried to forget public ambition in the making of books.

It was fitting that the long epic poem into which Bulwer threw all that he possessed of poetical enthusiasm should contain his tribute to the only statesman of the time whom he wholeheartedly admired and would unquestioningly have followed. Four verses from *King Arthur* are Bulwer's salute to Durham; and incidentally, his verdict on Brougham's treachery:

But who, with eastern hues and haughty brow,
    Stern with dark beauty, sits apart from all?
Ah, couldst thou shun thy friends, Elidir! — thou
    Scorning all foes, before no foe shalt fall!
On thy wronged grave one hand appeasing lays
The humble flower — Oh, could it yield the bays!

Courts may have known than thou a readier tool,
    States may have found than thine a subtler brain,
But States shall honour many a formal fool,
    And many a tawdry fawner courts may gain,
Ere King or People in their need shall see
A soul so grand as that which fled with thee!

For thou wert more than true; thou wert a Truth!
    Open as Truth, and yet as Truth profound;
Thy fault was genius — that eternal youth
    Whose weeds but prove the richness of the ground.
And dull man envied thee, and false men feared,
And where soared genius there convention sneered.

Ah, happy hadst thou fallen, foe to foe,
    That bright race run — the laurel o'er thy grave!
But hands perfidious strung the ambush bow,
    And the friend's shaft the rankling torture gave —
The last proud wish its agony to hide,
    The stricken deer to covert crept and died.

            "King Arthur." (Book V, stanzas VIII–XI.)

III

It has been necessary, in order to round off an account of the part played by Lord Durham in Bulwer's life, to outstrip our own chronology. There now remain to be recorded one or two incidents in the public career of the member for Lincoln, which took place between the sensational publication in November, 1834, of the *Letter to a Late Cabinet Minister* and the date of Bulwer's separation from his wife.

His pamphlet was, as stated, issued on the eve of a general election. Its beneficial effect on Whig fortunes was shared by its author, who was returned once more for Lincoln and by a large majority. Almost immediately afterward, in January, 1835, a strangely circumstantial rumour went about London that Bulwer was dead. Lady Blessington sent an urgent messenger to discover the truth; Lady Charlotte Bury demanded details; a Lincoln paper announced the tragic news with sad solemnity. To Lady Blessington the *cadavre imaginaire* wrote:

The reports concerning me appear to progress in a regular climax. First I had not a shilling and an execution was in my house; then I was bought by the Tories; and now I am dead. . . . I consider that I have paid the debt of nature, that I am born again with a new lease and that the years I have hitherto lived are to be struck off the score of the fresh life I have this morning awakened to.

I believe, my dearest friend, that you were shocked with the report, and would in your kind heart have grieved for its truth. So would four or five others. The rest would have been pleased with the excitement.

To Forster he was more frivolous:

I consider that my death having taken place I have a new life to begin. I leave town tomorrow and on my return we must meet. I shall then be six weeks old and luckily they bring me up by hand.

Nevertheless it is likely that the queer rumour startled him more than he cared to admit. He was always susceptible to premonitions, and a superstitious habit accorded with his inherently brooding and self-centred nature. It is significant that at this moment he first began that study of occultism which became so absorbing an interest and later expressed itself in *Zanoni* and *A Strange Story*. Also he must have been aware that circumstances generally had an air of pending crisis. Matters between himself and Rosina were heading for catastrophe. An interesting correspondence with Durham [1] shows that at precisely this date he was becoming consciously unhappy about his own position in the Whig party and looking for a lead. When, shortly afterward, his only trusted guide and leader was for the second time appointed Ambassador to St. Petersburg and left England, Bulwer was abandoned to his own hesitating conscience. Should he smother his personal dislike of the new men who were agitating for a more enterprising liberalism and join them in their attempt to jar the Whig party from its vacillations and its compromises? Or should he step aside altogether from the turmoil of politics and wait on circumstance?

In this mood of indecision there came to him from Lord Melbourne, the offer of a small post in the new Whig administration. Peel's Minority Government had held on until April, then resigned. "The Melbourne Ministry", in the words of Mrs. Gore, "ready to swallow camels without straining at gnats, shuffled back in its nightgown and slippers into Downing Street." [2] Bulwer recognized that the first of the threatened crises was upon him. If he accepted Melbourne's offer, he was launched on an official political career. Half his writing work would have to be given up; the reputation he had made as an author and a good part of the income upon which he still greatly depended would be jeopardised. This risk he might well have taken, had Durham been destined to act as member of the new ministry. But Durham had gone away; there was to be no one in the Cabinet who really believed in Bulwer or in whom Bulwer

---

[1] *Cf.* Lytton. I, 496 *et seq.*   [2] Cecil: a Peer, vol. III, p. 113.

really believed. Wherefore, after rapid but careful thought, he refused Lord Melbourne's offer.

Almost immediately afterward a second and far bitterer crisis was upon him. His domestic dissolution had entered on its final agonising stage.

Chapter Three

Domestic strife — Testimony of Mary Greene — Rosina at Glouces-
ter — The condition of the children — Extravagance and brandy
— Irresponsibility of Rosina — First thoughts of separation —
Another quarrel — Reconciliation — Bulwer at Gloucester — Berry-
mead Priory, Acton — Rosina writes a terrible letter — "Another
woman" — Quality of Rosina's jealousy — Bulwer decides on
separation — Rosina raids his rooms in Albany — Incautious
scandalmongering of Mrs. Wyndham Lewis — She never forgives
Bulwer for her own fault — Deed of Separation signed — The end of
Bulwer's marriage

It will be remembered that when the Bulwers left England
in the autumn of 1833 they were only too willing to leave
their daughter Emily in the care of Miss Greene who, for her
part, was glad to be able to keep the little girl a while longer
under her undisputed charge and in the cheerful household
of her friends at Hounslow.

The two of them were still in that pleasant suburb when,
early in 1834, the child's now embittered parents returned to
London.   Mary Greene has set down her recollections of that
miserable homecoming:

The first account I learnt of their arrival [she says in her reminis-
cences] was one evening, when I received a note from Rosina begging
that immediately upon the receipt of it I would hasten to Town, as
she had the most pressing business with me.   It was too late that
night for me to go, but I determined to go in the morning, which
morning brought me also a note from him, urging me in the same
manner to come quickly to Town as he had "business of consequence
to consult me upon."

From the tone of both these notes, I feared all was not right, and
lost no time in hastening to hear what it was, and upon my arrival

in Hertford Street, asked to see Mr. B. first as his Library was at the
bottom of the House and I did not wish to appear to take either side
(if anything was wrong) which I might have appeared to do, had I
walked straight upstairs to Rosina's dressing room to her. I was
accordingly shown into him. Directly I saw him he struck me as
looking very fierce and odd. His hair and whiskers had grown to
a most ridiculous length, and there was a fiery expression fixed in
his eye, which I had never before seen, except in a flash. I told him
that I had received his note, and one from Rosina the post before
making the same request that I would come immediately to Hertford Street, and that I had come to him first before I went upstairs.
He cried out, "Did she desire to speak with you? Well, then go to
her first, and I beg to speak with you afterwards."

I consequently went up to her, and found her in bed, grown very
thin, very quiet, but frightened and subdued. She opened the business by saying — "Mary you have often heard me say, ' thank God
he never takes it into his head to be jealous of me.' He did so at
Naples. Made us fly from it at a moment's warning; and how I
have travelled home with him and escaped with my life is next to
miraculous, as he has certainly been mad with rage the whole journey, as Byrne can testify. Now he demands an immediate separation, and will not allow me to remain in this house more than two
days while it is arranging where I am to go." She then told me
a long story of all that had passed. . . .

After a long conversation with her, I went down to him and he
said circumstances had occurred which made it absolutely necessary
that they should separate. He begged that I would remain in Town
for a day or two till it was arranged. He then went out of the house
and I went upstairs to Rosina, whom I found dressing and talking
over with her maid all the horrors they had endured on their journey, and which the maid had been an eye and ear witness to. When
she was dressed, she and I sat down in her dressing room to talk all
over and she said she was surprised at his allowing her to remain so
long as he did in his house after all that he had said. And I kept
saying, "Oh, you will see it will pass away." But she insisted
that it would not.

Whilst we were speaking, a message came up, saying, that he was
coming up. I shall never forget the scene of violence I witnessed
between them. For the first time I saw her turn upon him with

violence and throw back whatever he said. And at last he rushed out of the room saying, "We never then meet again except upon our mutual death-beds." They both seemed much exhausted with rage, but he so much the most that she was able to say to me when he tore out of the room, "Mary, Mary, follow him", which I did to his Library, and after a short time he became more calm and reasonable, and I began to congratulate him that all was as well as it was, and that he had brought his wife and himself safe back to England. Upon which he said, "If I had not brought her safe back I would have torn her heart out." Those were his very words.

All I could gain in this interview was permission for her to remain another day under his roof, and my negotiation finished at the end of a few days by her coming with Teddy and his nurse down to Hounslow to remain, whilst he looked out for some place where she and her children could go and reside. By this move one thing at least was gained, time to let all the bad passions which had been aroused subside, and give time for the consideration of duty and prudence.

The extraordinary fluctuations of temper which marked the relationship of Edward and Rosina during the next two years can only be understood if one appreciates the part played by Miss Greene in the whole sorry drama, and realises that her desperate struggles to save a hopeless situation were made solely in the interests of the children. In so far as her efforts failed, she did in fact prolong an agony which might have ended sooner. But she believed that the children would best be served by a working arrangement, however artificial, between their parents; and that belief she regarded as justification for anything.

Read as a mere narrative of events, the story of this couple's continual reconciliations, outbreaks of temper, submissions, renewed insults, partings, meetings and final embittered sundering is so fantastic as to be hardly credible. But there were not only two parties to the quarrel; there was a third — the children — and their cause was championed by a woman who knew quite clearly what she wanted and why she wanted it; who dared to say anything at any time to a furious man or

to a hysterical woman if, by saying it, she thought herself
better able to fulfil the duty of a self-appointed guardian.
For that in effect was now Miss Greene's position. Very
shortly after the passionate scene just described, she, who had
hitherto concentrated her care on Emily, took the small
Robert (or "Teddy" as he was at this time always called)
under her protection also. Why she did this, and the toil
and difficulties implicit in doing it, are best told in her own
words, which also describe with a singular impressiveness
the beginnings of poor Rosina's slide into bad company and
squalid intemperance:

Rosina had gone to Mrs. Bulwer-Lytton to make a complaint of
Mr. B's usage [*i.e.* on the journey home from Italy], in which quarrel
his mother took a most kind part, and brought about a reconciliation and invited him and her on a visit to Knebworth. Whether
Emily was invited I do not know; but I do know that when it was
settled that they were to go with Teddy and his nurse, I got Emily
to myself to take to Cheltenham, where I was going on a visit to
some old friends. . . .

Alas, we were not allowed to go on long in this promising way
for poor Emily — for the visit to Knebworth brought forth fresh
jealousies and quarrels, which I never heard all the particulars of,
and what I did hear from Rosina I could not depend upon. The
first news I heard that we were to be again disturbed was in a letter
from her, saying Mr. B. was going to pay a visit to Ireland, and
that she and Teddy would come down to join us, and begged I would
take some pretty cottage in the vale of Gloucestershire, which would
suit us all for some months. . . .

I went to Gloucester, where I also had some pleasant acquaintance, and took a good furnished lodging there by the week where
Rosina, Teddy and his nurse and a cook-maid soon joined Emily
and myself. She was not frank upon the reason of her coming to
me to Gloucester, but I found out soon after from the length of time
she remained (9 months) and the little correspondence which passed
between them for much of that time, that this was another attempt
at a "temporary separation." From her account the visit to Knebworth had done harm rather than good; and though the old lady

was both kind and attentive to her, she did not seem very grateful
to her for it, but railed at her and said it was all hypocrisy, and that
all the unhappiness between her and her husband was brought on
by her and his two brothers.

Poor thing! she was much to be pitied, thrown upon me, and her
children whom she did not love, in a dull country town; and to
amuse herself she seemed as if she would try what lavishing money
away would do. Instead of remaining in the comfortable apartments which I had taken for her, where she would have been well
attended by the landlady and her own two servants, she took a furnished house at a high rent and with Teddy's nurse and a kitchen
maid, whom she brought from London, expected to have everything
in the same style as she had had things in Hertford Street, where
she had servants in every station. Teddy's good fortune again
followed him, as in the fortnight which we stayed at the lodgings,
our landlady and her daughter, very kind and respectable people,
took such a fancy to him, that when we went to our house, he used
to spend all day with them. . . . I felt myself pulled two different ways, and felt I could do little for poor Emily, and her mother
could not bear to have her in her company, and was jealous of me
when I sometimes stole away to her. . . . The poor child passed
much of her time alone, except in the morning for about an hour
when I stole out of her mother's bed (where I slept) to see her get
her breakfast and read a little to her and try to keep up what she had
learnt with me within the last year. She slept in a room behind
ours, and although we used to dine at two o'clock and only her
mother and myself, I found, after attempting to have her with us
three or four times, that I must give it up. Rosina kept making
faces, as if disgusted with her company. . . . Even when she went
out to walk, I found Emily was in the way, and I at last began to
see perhaps it was better she should not be too much at the dinner
parties Rosina gave to Miss Frazer, a Scotch lady, whom she took a
great fancy to, and was come to live at our lodgings where we had
been, and also took a great fancy to Teddy.

This lady was well connected, but appeared to be cut off in an
extraordinary manner by her relations. We soon found out there
was a cause, when we saw her unprincipled extravagance and love
of brandy, the two worst temptations which could have fallen in the
way of my poor friend in her present situation.

Whilst we were thus getting over our time at Gloucester, both from Ireland and afterwards from London Rosina was receiving from her husband the most clever and bitter answers to her letters of the same kind, in which she taunted him in the most violent manner with everything terrible she had ever said or thought of him. However, he kept supplying her with money in the most surprising manner, and which she spent in a most wasteful and unprofitable manner for clothes, etc., etc. I used to warn her that he could be but trying her how much she could spend, and she never had one penny for necessaries, but was always borrowing from me.

And now indeed wretched did I feel, seeing Rosina going on in a manner which I thought would ruin her, heartless about her children, unsettled in every way, continuing the warfare, and railing, even to strangers, against her husband, children and family. I did not see how it was to end; besides, her jealousy of my love for Emily made her not always as kind to me as she had been.

Now my niece, Mrs. Wilkinson, had come expressly to Gloucester that I might be with her when she was confined. The day before Xmas Day Mrs. B. came to me to beg I would on Xmas Day go up to London to Sir John Doyle, to consult with him upon her separation from Mr. B., and that if she did not go that day it would injure her cause much. She seemed to put herself as a rival to Mrs. W. in my affections and to want to put me to this painful test, and much against my inclination I consented. . . . Rosina and I set off for London in the Mail Xmas night and travelled all night, and in the morning went to Haydon's Hotel in Oxford Street, when we sent for Sir J. Doyle. He came, and she related her story. I think she somewhat exaggerated it; however, I was silent, as I was too happy to find she had so influential and high-minded a relative, in case matters should come to the sad alternative which she said she wished for. He was most kind, but said he highly disapproved of this coming to London without Mr. B.'s knowledge. He assured her she might depend on his steady friendship, and upon her letting him understand how badly she was off for money, he presented her with £20.

After this interview with Sir J. Doyle, we were like the King of France and forty thousand men, for the next night we travelled back to Gloucester, and found that Mrs. Wilkinson had been confined of a daughter the night we left her, and was, thank God, going on well.

In the midst of all this, we used to dine with large companies at the Bishop of Gloucester; and the Frazer Soirées increased so much in number and impropriety, that writing violent letters to her husband and buying dresses against the coming season in London was all her employment.   Now Emily seemed the best off for a time, as poor Teddy's nurse (a widow) began to court, and the little she had to do for poor Teddy was neglected.   When sitting in the drawing-room with his mother in the evening after he had been tumbled into bed, I used to hear him screaming and used to run up and find him tossing about with terror, and swimming in wet, and saying there was a "bogie" coming to take him.   Sometimes his nurse had run up (if in the house) and I found her scolding and frightening the child.   I told all this to his mother, but to no purpose. . . .   I now began to take my first great interest in the boy, and as I had never lost sight of my wish to have him baptized, I proposed to his mother that it should be done now at Gloucester, as we knew the Clergyman and the Church was close to where we lived and Mrs. Wilkinson's baby was also to be baptized.   She consented, and I sent the Clergyman to her.   It was settled that it was to be done; and I asked two gentlemen of my acquaintance — both Post Captains in the Navy — to stand as his Godfathers, whilst I was to be his Godmother, adding that I wished it to be as private as possible. . . .   He was baptized by the name of Edward Robert Lytton, the name his mother had chosen. . . .   I did all I could to prevail upon his mother to go to the Church with him, but "Gallio cared for none of these things."   I had the boy's baptism registered at the Spa Church, Gloucester, by Mr. Holmes, and there it now is.

Such is Miss Greene's account of the events of 1834, events which could hardly be more vividly pictured than in this artless narrative.   But although the story as told by Mary Greene needs neither paraphrase nor confirmation, its moral may be pointed and its sequence a little amplified.

It is obvious that the angry incidents of the foreign tour had definitely unbalanced Rosina's mind.   She had never found it easy to control either her temper or her self-indulgence; but hitherto she had sufficiently loved her husband and believed in the possibility of achieving with his help the social position she craved, to submit herself at moments of crisis to his nervous exigence, and in a rather fitful way to try and strengthen the household at its weakest points. From the beginning of 1834, however, her sense of realism seemed to have vanished. She could still have moments of self-debasement when she wrote him long and often moving letters, begging for forgiveness, promising amendment, and taking on herself all the blame for the disasters of the past. But she was capable the very next day of writing a letter as bitter and as insulting as its predecessor had been pathetic; so that one cannot but regard her as henceforward the helpless victim of recurrent moods, a being without continuity of memory or intention, and as little to be blamed for fury or insolence as to be praised or believed in moments of seemingly dignified sincerity.

It is this hopeless irresponsibility of Rosina during the final stages of her married life which renders the story of her separation from Edward Bulwer well-nigh impossible to tell. Her apologists can without difficulty so select documents from the tragic mass of evidence which has survived, as to present her in the light of a persecuted, if wayward, victim of a man's selfishness and arrogant injustice. Similarly anyone concerned to exonerate Bulwer from all but a small share of the blame for his marriage failure can condemn poor Rosina a hundred times over in words taken from her own reckless mouth. Even an attempt to marshal the evidence on both sides fairly and dispassionately and to leave the verdict to posterity (such an attempt as that made by Lord Lytton in his two-volume work) cannot conjure coherence from a story irrevocably incoherent. Let us, therefore, be content to pity these two unhappy souls, whose errors were many and frailties indefensible, but who were doomed to expiate their faults by life-long torment.

The salient incidents of their last two years together can be briefly summarised. From the very moment of their return to London the possibility of a separation became the dominating element in the situation. First he wanted it; but was dissuaded by Mary Greene. Then she wanted it; but partly because of Sir John Doyle's influence, mainly because a sudden revulsion of her own incalculable temper turned anger into fear and self-assertion into self-pity, she changed her mind and begged her by now distracted husband to give their joint existence one more chance.

A few extracts from letters will help to make clear how intermittent and how tragically maladjusted were the angers and propitiations of both parties. Although each was capable of writing and acting with forbearance and even generosity, their moments of restraint seldom tallied; and because neither was able to sustain a conciliatory mood for long enough to bridge the gulf between them, the good impulses were wasted and, in reaction, helped to embitter matters worse than ever.

Early in May, 1834, Bulwer wrote from his mother's house the long letter to his wife which letter is printed at the beginning of Chapter VII of the second book of his grandson's biography.[1] This dignified and touching appeal moved Rosina sufficiently to make her letter of May 28, addressed to her mother-in-law, at least restrained in its melancholy. She shows a realisation of the drudgery which Edward had for so long endured and concludes:

Teddy and I a e sitting for our pictures, a very old friend of mine having been silly enough to waste her money in getting it done. As you may suppose it is not an easy matter to keep Teddy quiet. His is very like, so I shal keep it to show you, but mine is flattered out of all likeness. The artist who is doing it paints most exquisitely. I wish you could persuade Edward to sit to him. I feel not a little hurt at never having been able to get him to give me his picture, and somewhat offended at his never even wishing to have one of me, even before he had time to tire of the original.

But Rosina's fatal inability to connect sentiment and action allowed her, as Miss Greene's narrative shows, to continue

[1] Lytton. I, 281–283.

her extravagant expenditure and thus to render meaningless her sympathy with her husband's overwork. Possibly the hopelessness of making her realise that he worked for money rather than for pleasure, that if less money were needed, less work would be required, helped to weaken his self-control. When they next met, which was very shortly before the publication of *Pompeii*, he so maltreated her in the course of a violent quarrel, as to plunge himself into an agony of humiliation and to put her into possession of a story whose damaging potentialities she ruthlessly exploited over a period of many years.[1] From the memory of this scene Bulwer fled to Ireland. But he was in England again by the autumn, writing his pamphlet for the election and fighting for his own seat. Suddenly, during the week after Christmas and without any previous warning of his wife's change of heart, he received a silly little picture, cut from a child's story and showing a dog begging pardon with one paw. Under the picture was scrawled: "Poodle wishes Pups a Happy New Year."

This message was of course the direct result of Rosina's Christmas visit to London to see her uncle and the advice which Miss Greene records his having given her; and the message itself was even more significant than its impulse. There is something at once poignant and distasteful in this cheap but pathetic gesture from such a woman as Rosina to such a man as Edward Bulwer. But the incident was very characteristic of her, and helps us understand how hopeless was any prospect of permanent cordiality between them. Under the stress of her sorrow, she had rapidly developed

---

[1] *Cf*. Lytton. I, 284, *et seq*. and Devey 83-84. The only mention in Miss Greene's recollections of this meeting and its consequences occurs in the second paragraph of the passage quoted above (p. 351). The scene occurred in London after the return from the unlucky visit to Knebworth, so that Miss Greene was admittedly not present. But it is curious that so sensational an episode should be passed over, not only because Rosina would certainly have spoken of her husband's violence when complaining at random of his treatment of her, but also because it is probable (as Lord Lytton suggests) that the fear and fury produced by the episode finally destroyed her mental control and left her unable to resist the temptation of drink.

dog-mania to a degree little short of fantastic. It was not thwarted maternal instinct, because her children were with her and, as we know, she had regularly treated them with indifference, neglect and at times unkindness. Rather was it a queer expression of immature egotism, a blend of silly senti- ment and pathetic longing for uncritical devotion. Foolish references to her dogs appear continually in letters to her friends; she had visiting cards printed with their names and would leave these when herself paying calls. Of the indul- gence with which they were fed and treated, and the nuisance they were permitted to be to everyone else, Miss Greene's recollections offer continual evidence. And now, at an acute crisis of her relations with her husband, she could think of no better formula for conciliation than a little wood engrav- ing of a dog begging!

To Bulwer's credit, he responded readily and eagerly even to so trivial an overture. Perhaps the recollection of the days when he still loved her and the two of them exchanged letters full of baby talk and dog nonsense, rose and softened him. There followed an exchange of letters of which his, written in a moment of forbearing calm, succeeded very fairly in presenting the assessable causes of their mutual trouble, but could not of course affect or touch upon the profound spiritual disjunction which foredoomed them to enmity. Of the four long letters which Bulwer wrote in January, 1835, those of January 16 and 22 are printed in full by his grandson and interpolated with Rosina's answers, and the others men- tioned.[1] Perhaps a very brief summary of the central argu- ment as it emerges from the two later letters may, if read in conjunction with those already printed, serve to present Bulwer's case, which, if she had only been able to realise it, was Rosina's case also:

1. I prayed you to strive with me to avoid as much as possible all petty disputes, and when they had occurred to avoid all recurrence to the past.

[1] Lytton. I, 292, *et seq.*

2. I entreated you to take as kind an interpretation of my character and conduct as affection would take and reason would allow.

3. I implored you to enter as much as you could into my political objects, or at least not to sneer at or attack, to me or to others, the principles I profess.

4. I besought, as a great personal favour which I could thoroughly appreciate, that you would not speak slightingly of my relations.

This is the substance of what I ask you. Think only on the substance; put it into the kindest words you can imagine and those words will translate my heart.

My dear Rosina, when we were first married, you say that every time I found fault with you I said "Don't do this because my brother [William] dislikes it." I was very young and not perhaps very judicious, but my motive was clear. Proud and fond as I was of you, I wished everyone to see you with my eyes. As my family stood aloof I was morbidly anxious that you should please the only one who offered to assist me. I may have shown this injudiciously, but the very error arose from my anxiety that you should be valued as I valued you.

The final letter concludes:

As to what you say of yourself, I have nothing to reply to wound your self-esteem. I allow that your beauty and merit would make any man proud of you and I have been so. But just as you have said to me "So and So are coming, now don't be cold and stiff"; just as Lady Blessington once said to me "You are going to meet Durham and he is prepared to admire and like you pray don't be supercilious to him as you are to most people" — so I might, and may, often have asked you to avoid little peculiarities, not in the least detracting from my pride in your qualities, but which with certain persons might mar their effect.

In late February or early March, in order to give practical effect to their greater mutual kindliness, he came to Gloucester to visit her. But once again the momentary brightness was blotted out by Rosina's erratic and ungovernable temper:

The act of his coming [says Mary Greene] she thought gave her the best of it, and to my utter astonishment, when he did come at the end of nine months, she received him with coldness and hauteur, and was very angry with me for making Emily run down to the door to meet her father.

Three most miserable days did I spend with this poor self-willed woman who thought, as she had so often conquered by holding out, she could gain a still greater victory over him. . . .

One morning when I came down to breakfast with him and had left her in bed, he said to me "There is no use in my staying here. I shall return to London today. You see how Rosina behaves and how I have been with her." He seemed much affected whilst saying this, and so was I, and I begged him not to leave at least for a day or two longer and said I would again go up to Rosina and speak with her. . . . I persuaded him to come upstairs to her and directly I had got him into the room, I stole away to my friends at the hotel. I had been there about half an hour when Teddy and his nurse came flying after me, for Mrs. B. wanted me in all haste. Mr. B. had rushed downstairs in violent anger, drunk two glasses of brandy, sent for a post-chaise and drove towards London. I found Rosina half distracted and crying most bitterly. "Oh, Mary," she said "he is gone. Follow him in our carriage and bring him back."

I did follow him and found him, as I often had done before, very ready to receive any advance toward reconciliation. I had the pleasure of bringing him back to her. She met us on the stairs, and this time received him as she ought to have done the first night he came down.

For the moment prospects seemed brighter than for a long while. "I think things are now so smooth as to promise more favourably than I had ever anticipated," wrote Bulwer to his mother. "They showed themselves most conjugally in Gloucester," says Miss Greene, "walking about the small town several times together and also appearing at a ball, where we all went."

In this mood of optimism he returned to town to make arrangements for setting up his household again, but elsewhere than in Mayfair. He had doubtless summed up Miss Frazer while at Gloucester, and could sufficiently foresee what she and Rosina would make of fashionable life, if they were allowed to go into society from Hertford Street. Wherefore, while once again prepared for a joint establishment, he determined that it should be on the outskirts of the city.

But no sooner was his back turned than the devil in Rosina rose once more to undo the good which had been done. With her friend Miss Frazer she launched into expensive dress-buying, making all manner of plans for the London season and, worst of all, speaking ill of her husband and his family to everyone she met. The temporary improvement in her treatment of the children, which their father's presence had produced, came to a sudden end. She turned to her old policy of (in Miss Greene's words) "dividing in order to rule." With Miss Frazer she conspired against Miss Greene; to Miss Greene she complained that Miss Frazer tried to borrow money; to Miss Greene's niece, Mrs. Wilkinson, she appealed for sympathy, because she was convinced that both the other ladies were intriguing against her. In short she showed herself already infected with that unmanageable wrongheadedness which was to grow worse and worse as time went by; to lose her one friend after another; and finally to bring her to a permanent state of passionate irrationality, which was just not madness but something more mischievous because uncontrollable.

In May having let Hertford Street, Bulwer rented a house at Acton called Berrymead Priory for Rosina and the children, and rooms for himself in Albany. The moment the news reached Gloucester Rosina became a different being. All smiles and benevolence, and full of the cleverness and kindness of her husband, she, Teddy and her servants removed joyfully to Acton, leaving Emily to go to Cheltenham with Mary Greene. The first few weeks in the new home were calm and happy. Rosina wrote to Miss Greene that she liked the house and garden, that Teddy was well; that Bulwer was affectionate and attentive. But in July, without a word of warning, she shattered her own serenity and his by a letter charging him with infidelity, a letter so strident and so vulgar that one would wish to regard it as written in temporary insanity.

If Bulwer's brutality on the way home from Italy had killed Rosina's love for him, and for the first time led her to envisage as a remote possibility the end of their marriage, this letter of hers, written from Berrymead, made possibility a certainty and turned remoteness into an immediate menace. It would have been an unforgivable letter, if only because of the outrageous words in which it was written; it was doubly unforgivable to Bulwer, because the charge which it made was perfectly true and because it insulted a woman who was now dear to him.

II

It will seem strange to anyone looking back on this protracted tragedy of married unhappiness that neither party had earlier found consolation in some other, more sympathetic quarter. Bulwer's Mrs. Stanhope, like Rosina's Neapolitan, had been a mere distraction; and it is evidence of the length of time that at the bottom of his heart the old love still lingered, that not until the beginning of 1835 did he look to some other woman for the support and comfort which his official home no longer gave.

Rosina's continence is perhaps less remarkable. She had from the first regarded her sexual attraction as a means to extort pleasure and luxury from foolish men, and to secure for herself a position in the world. She was by nature hard and frivolous and curiously lacking in physical vanity. Material things appealed to her more than emotional experience, and even flattery she was willing to forego in order to save herself the trouble of being agreeable. Once married, she considered that she had done enough in the way of charming those whom she met; and the impression made on visitors by her indolent, uninterested manner at dinner parties in her own home during the first years of her married life has already been described. Wherefore, so long as she could compel her husband to provide her with money, she was not likely to entangle herself in any emotional complication, which could only make unwelcome demands on her time and energy and might endanger her regular livelihood.

To equally material causes must be attributed her furious indignation when she realised that her husband now really had a mistress. She might play the injured wife and invoke the sanctity of the British home; but the real motive of her anger was fear for her own pin-money. She had had no scruples in forcing Bulwer to work himself to nervous exhaustion in order to earn cash for her to spend; but once she realised the possibility that another pair of hands might also have access to the treasury, she awoke, not to a sense of wifely duty, but to one of wifely privilege.

The secret of Bulwer's extra-marital love affairs has been well kept. The liaison which provoked Rosina's letter was the first of a considerable series and one of the longest-lived. The woman with whom he formed a connection in 1835 was still with him in the early forties, and it is to her that reference is made in a private diary quoted by Lord Lytton and written about 1840. As the years passed, other mistresses came and went. Without the sympathy and companionship of someone who would cheer him in times of depression, allow him to forget the world in enjoyment of her uncritical affection, Bulwer could never have survived the years of drudgery and loneliness which were the four remaining decades of his life. Such private relaxation was necessary to him, and that he procured it was no concern of anyone but himself. It is even comprehensible that he should more than once have deliberately denied the existence of his left-handed amours. One may regret the falsehood, while appreciating its impulse. Bulwer was never a person of great moral courage, and the society in which he lived was based on the assumption that, even if irregularities existed, they must never be admitted.

Wherefore, Rosina's letter from Berrymead offended in every possible respect. Its language was gross and insulting, its accusation was unanswerable, and it pierced that one of his disguises which he desired most anxiously to keep intact. Small wonder that it drove him into a final hostility toward its writer from which he was never to relent.

But even now the end did not come all in a minute. There were attempts at apology, even suggestions of forgiveness. Yet, after every truce, the fight broke out afresh and more bitterly.

At last he made up his mind to the formal separation he had so often postponed, to the preventing of which Mary Greene had worked so doggedly. "You must be no less convinced than myself," he wrote to Rosina from Paris on December 21, 1835, "that all hope of constituting the happiness or even the comfort of each other is over. . . . After a letter which it was impossible to receive and to forgive, you wrote to me again. You apologised as I thought sincerely. In a few days you drove me again from my house. I shall submit no longer. . . . My mind is made up finally and irrevocably. We must part. Take your own residence where you will. I grudge not your happiness or liberty. I demand only no more to sacrifice my own. . . . After this letter I need scarcely again tell you not to attempt to shake a resolution taken calmly, deliberately and irrevocably, and by which I can alone secure to the rest of my life something of tranquillity and peace."

Her reply to this, submissive and touching, and the simultaneous entry in her diary, coldly furious, are given in Lord Lytton's book.[1] They are typical in their contradictoriness, but unusual in that on this occasion both sides of the contradiction can be seen at once.

Early in 1836, soon after making his decision, Bulwer wrote his mother a letter which fairly expresses the despair to which he had been reduced. It will also be noticed that he had already so far visualised a possible obsession of Rosina by

[1] Lytton. I, 318-319.

hatred for him and by pity for herself, as to conceive her publishing his letters:

Bulwer to his mother.

Jan. 11, 1836. Paris.

I am just where I was. I comprehend your delicacy in not wishing to interfere, nor should I have applied to you if I thought that we two could have settled it alone. But Rosina has no commonsense and will come to nothing definite — flies off at every letter and runs on so much about her health and dying and so forth that it puts me in a most harsh and brutal point of view to insist while she affects to be so ill and miserable — especially as my letters are all likely I think to be published. So I am quite at a nonplus. As to Rosina's talking as if she were an injured angel, it is a singular mania of hers. For two years I have borne every species of irritation and even insult. I have done nothing hostilely; I have forgiven again and again. I have now acted deliberately, calmly and with full consideration. My career is blighted; my temper soured; my nerves shattered; and if I am to go on for ever in this way because she insists on continuing to force herself upon me, God knows what I shall do at last. She has gone on in a series of petty wounds to my pride, self-esteem and heart, till she has rooted out of my very nature all sentiments but those of dread at her presence and relief at her parting.

If the separation cannot be effected before I return I must be again the victim. For what can I do if she comes to the Albany, throws herself on the ground and declares she won't leave till it is made up? I cannot have scenes in a place like that. I despair of my release.

The last paragraph of this letter was prophetic, and of immediate happenings. In February Rosina made a raid on her husband's room in Albany, which has become almost famous as the origin of one of the angry witticisms for which she had a real talent. "I went," she said, "to visit my husband in his rooms, which he kept in order to have undisturbed communion with the Muse. I found the Muse in white muslin seated on his knee."

The statement was in fact wholly untrue. But it made a good story, and for a while at least was accepted by several of Rosina's temporary sympathisers. Few people troubled to enquire what really happened, preferring an agreeable bit of gossip to a probably uninteresting truth. Actually Rosina saw through the opened door of her husband's apartment two teacups on a tray. They had been prepared for Bulwer and Frederick Villiers, but the latter had failed to keep his appointment. The unexpected caller, conscious of Bulwer's annoyance at her intrusion, leapt jealously to a false conclusion, broke into screaming fury and had to be removed, still raving, from the outraged precincts of Albany.

After this disagreeable scene matters moved quickly to an end. As on an earlier occasion, both parties, exhausted by their rage, wrote independently and summoned Mary Greene to their help. Miss Greene, who had left Emily in charge of some friends in Manchester, and gone to Ireland to attend to private business of her own had just got back to England when the appeals reached her. She hastened to London, heard the story of the latest outbreak, and prepared once more to take up the burden of other folks' unhappiness. Her recollections show that at first she did not despair even now of salving a semblance of marriage from the wreck. But as soon as she realised the end had really come, she placed herself resolutely by Rosina's side and sought so to control events as to save the now fatherless children from being abandoned to the influence of their mother:

Emily and I arrived at Acton late in the evening, and after receiving a kiss from her mother, she was soon dismissed to the Nursery to Teddy. Mrs. B. was indeed in a most pitiable state of mind, and very sad, though she had been, I soon saw, keeping herself up with cold Punch, which she told me Mrs. Fonblanque had sent her, and she produced an immense stone jar full of it. She told me this was by much the most serious quarrel there had ever been and that Mr. B. was dreadfully determined, that Sir J. Doyle had been formally applied to, and that a form of separation was now being drawn out. All this Mr. B. had written to me in a letter which I received at Manchester, urging me to come speedily to Acton, and which I answered, telling him frankly that on my arrival in Town, I should

leave no effort untried to reconcile him and Rosina, which had, as
I found afterwards, the bad effect of making him keep out of my
sight, till all was settled.

Rosina's account of all that had occurred during my short absence,
shocked me much, and if it was only from the shocking letters she
had written to him, which she showed me the copies of, I feared
indeed there was no chance of a reconciliation. . . . She however
said she would get me to see him and say to him things she would
not trust other persons with. And when he declined seeing me, I
wrote to him whatever she chose to dictate, till Sir J. Doyle begged
me not to quarrel with Mr. B. as I had more power of serving the
children, (in case matters came to a separation, which he much
feared) than any other person in the world. . . .

I really think from one thing and another poor Mrs. B. was at this
time distracted and used to say the most shocking things of Sir J.
Doyle, and his Lawyer, for being imposed upon by the "plausible hypocrisy" as she used to call it, of Mr. Bulwer. In vain was she told
that he had all the power and that she could not resist, as the Trus-
tees, that she at last appointed, said his offers of money were sufficient, considering his property. She, then, hoping he could not and
would not give it, demanded more money, and when Sir J. Doyle and
Sir T. Cullum said she ought to be much pleased that the payment
of this money was secured by Mrs. Bulwer-Lytton off the Knebworth
estate, she was angry with them instead of obliged. . . . At last
the dreaded day arrived, when the lawyers, Mr. B. and Sir J. D.
were to meet at Sir J. D.'s house, to have the last arrangements
made about the separation. Rosina went into London some days
after, and signed the sad papers at Mr. Wyndham Lewis', who as
well as Mrs. W. Lewis had been, since ever I had known them, very
steady friends to her. . . .

All this business was now concluded on the 19th of April, 1836,
and as all the plea for the separation had been incompatibility of
temper, it was arranged that she was to remain at Acton, for a couple
of months whilst arranging where she would go to, and also that she
might go into society, as usual, in London, to prove that there was
nothing against her character.

Mrs. Wyndham Lewis, mentioned in the course of the
foregoing, was the lady who, three and a half years later,

was to marry Benjamin Disraeli; and because the subsequent cooling off of friendship between Disraeli and Bulwer must to a great extent be attributed to her influence, the part she played in the events of the first months of 1836 may perhaps be noted.

Mrs. Wyndham Lewis was one of the most active champions of Rosina after the raid on Albany. She went about London repeating the story of a scandalous discovery in Bulwer's rooms, until at last incaution brought retribution on her head. She received the following letter:

Bulwer to Mrs. Wyndham Lewis.

April 20, 1836. Albany.

My dear Madam, You must permit me to place strongly before you what I venture to consider grounds for a certain caution on your part relative to the situation of Mrs. Bulwer and myself. Paragraphs have appeared in more than one newspaper containing a very grave calumny upon me, namely that Mrs. Bulwer found some person in my rooms and that our separation is in consequence of that discovery. Similar rumours have been industriously propagated. On tracing the origin of them, I think it right frankly to say that many of those who spread them sheltered themselves under your authority — in fact they assert that you told them such was the fact.

You are perfectly aware that this is not the truth. You yourself told me, that Mrs. Bulwer was convinced of the injustice of her suspicions. The real grounds of my separation are these: violent provocation on her part, over a series of years, frequently forgiven by me; the last act of coming to my rooms and without the smallest excuse making a scene, going then to your house and writing me from thence a letter which if I published it would justify fifty separations. Fully persuaded that you would not do me the wrong, Mrs. Bulwer the injury, or bring on yourself the consequences of accusations against me which you know to be false, you will be cautious in the statements you make of my affairs.

A high-spirited and rather self-satisfied woman does not easily forget either a letter of this kind or its writer. Mrs.

Wyndham Lewis beat a hasty retreat from the advanced positions of her partisanship. She remained accessible to Rosina, but was henceforward very wary in listening to stories and in repeating them. At the same time, although she showed a new discretion toward the wife, she never forgave the husband. After her marriage with Disraeli, when she came to possess great political and social influence, she saw her chance of revenge and quietly took it. Wherefore, among the various causes which were to cheat Bulwer in middle life of the material and social rewards to which his intellect and political assiduity would normally have entitled him, must be numbered this hostility of a woman who having long before been detected in spiteful gossip, and called to account for it, was thereafter full of resentment against the man she had herself sought to injure.

On the day before the letter to Mrs. Wyndham Lewis was written, there had been signed in London the deed of separation between Edward and Rosina.

They had been married not quite nine years; were the parents of two children; and bore a name already universally known both in politics and literature. Edward was almost exactly thirty-three years old; Rosina some six months older. Looking back on the almost fabulous history of passion, disillusionment, quarrelling, hatred, ostentation, toil and achievement, which these two still young people had crowded into the brief period of their married life, one is tempted to wonder why the tale of their sorrows and their struggles has not yet found a place among the classic calamities of human frailty. The reason may be that nine years of drama were followed by nearly forty years of racking and remorseless misery, so that the grim tragedy of the play itself has been forgotten in the weary squalor of its epilogue. The tale deserves a nobler fate than to be shrugged into perfunctory sympathy; and for this reason the opening phase of it has here been isolated from what came after, so that, when the narrative begins again, a new perspective can be given to it. Perhaps by this means the weariness of the onlooker will be alleviated and, instead of suffering impatiently a persistent recital of the woes and cruelties of two embittered souls, he will follow with the pity it deserves the tragic story of a love soured into relentless hate.

Finale

Rosina and Edward signed their names; then went their ostensibly independent ways.

Of plans for her immediate future the former seems to have had neither thought nor power to think. As Lord Lytton says: "The past could not be recalled, nor its mistakes unmade, but the future was still to a certain extent in her hands. It was for her to determine how best to dispose of her life apart from him. This she appears to have been incapable of doing. . . . The very qualities which made it impossible for her to live amicably with her husband made it equally difficult for her to live alone."

As usual, Mary Greene stepped into the breach, and made one more sacrifice of her own prospect of a peaceful life. Acting as always for the children's sake, she conquered her dread of introducing Rosina to the quiet households of her friends and relatives. An arrangement was agreed, by which the separated Mrs. Bulwer, her two children, her two servants and Mary Greene herself should occupy part of a large house five miles from Dublin, in which lived Miss Greene's widowed sister Mrs. Shaw. Thither they removed at the end of April, 1836.

Of Bulwer's feelings as he signed the document which put an official end to his disastrous marriage no evidence survives. Did he remember that almost exactly ten years earlier he had written to Rosina:

If, says La Bruyère, we cannot make all the happiness, we would make all the unhappiness of the woman we love. This is so far

true that I do not see any one has a right to make you unhappy except
me. I wish I alone could do so, because then you should never *be*
unhappy.

A thousand memories must have thronged his tired, tormented brain; why not this one also? Of all ironies the bitterest are love letters to which life has given the lie; few
aphorisms could so tellingly have risen from the past as this
from La Bruyère, once quoted with such gallant nonchalance,
now proved so tragically true.

Poor Bulwer! One can picture him, hurrying homeward
from Sir John Doyle's house, his long melancholy face — the
face of a man of thirty-three — already wrinkled with care
and nervous strain, his frightened eyes flickering miserably
from side to side. Did he — even for a little while — believe
that the unhappy woman who had been his wife had really
vanished from his life for ever? "I despair of my release",
he had written to his mother a few weeks earlier.

Was this release?

Or did he still despair?

THE END

Calendar of Events in the Lives of Edward
and Rosina up to April, 1836

1773.	Birth of Elizabeth Barbara (daughter of Richard Warburton) Lytton
1789.	Elizabeth and her father at Knebworth
1790.	She joins her mother in London
1797 (winter).	She meets Colonel (afterwards General) William Bulwer of Heydon Hall, Norfolk
1798, June 1.	She becomes Mrs. William Bulwer
1799, April.	Birth of William Bulwer at Heydon
1801.	Birth of Henry Bulwer at Heydon
1802, November 3.	Birth of Rosina, second daughter of Francis Wheeler of Ballywire, near Limerick, Ireland
1803, May 25.	Birth of Edward Bulwer in London
1807.	Death of General Bulwer. His widow leaves Heydon Hall and buys a house at Nottingham Place
	Richard Warburton Lytton takes a part in Edward's education
1810, December.	Death of Richard Warburton Lytton
1811 (late).	Mrs. Bulwer (now Bulwer-Lytton) settles with Edward at Knebworth
1812.	Edward sent to his first school at Fulham
	Sent to his second school at Sunbury
August.	Break-up of Wheeler household at Ballywire
	Mrs. Wheeler leaves her husband and goes with her two daughters to her uncle, Sir John Doyle, Governor of Guernsey
1813.	Edward sent to a third school at Brighton

1814.	Sent to Doctor Hooker's school at Rottingdean
1816.	Sir John Doyle resigns his office and leaves Guernsey for London
	Mrs. Wheeler and her daughters go to Caen
1818.	Edward refuses to go to Eton
	His first meeting with Lady Caroline Lamb
1819 (early).	Sent as private pupil to Rev. Charles Wallington at Ealing
	Rosina quarrels with her mother and returns to Ireland; she stays with her uncle at Kilsallaghan
	Her first meeting with Mary Greene
	Edward's first love affair (Ealing)
1820, April 3.	*Ismael* published.
1821.	Rosina meets her father after nearly ten years
1822, January.	Edward goes to Cambridge
1823.	Death of Francis Wheeler. His widow returns to Ireland and stays with her brother at Kilsallaghan
April 1.	First number of *Knight's Quarterly Magazine;* Bulwer contributes
	Falkland sketched out
1824, July.	Long vacation in the Lakes
	A History of the British Public planned (later transformed into *England and the English*)
	Mortimer begun (later transformed into *Pelham*)
	Walking tour over the Border
	Visits Robert Owen
	Becomes a temporary gipsy
September.	Joins his mother at Broadstairs
	Lady Caroline Lamb invites him to Brocket Park
October.	Returns to Cambridge and corresponds with Lady Caroline

1825 (summer).   *Sculpture* awarded Chancellor's Medal. He reads it in public

Rosina quarrels with her mother and comes to Sir John Doyle in London

Bulwer leaves Cambridge and goes to Paris and Versailles

(late).   Rosina is taken up by Lady Caroline Lamb

Weeds and Wildflowers privately printed at Versailles

1826, April.   Bulwer returns to England

O'Neill in the press

Falkland completed and awaiting a publisher

April 25.   Meeting of Edward Bulwer and Rosina Wheeler at Miss Benger's party

August.   Lady Caroline invites them both to Brocket

Unofficially engaged

Mrs. Bulwer-Lytton disapproves

October.   Engagement broken

Rosina stays at Brocket

Bulwer returns to Knebworth

November.   Engagement renewed

1827, March.   *Falkland* published

June.   *O'Neill* published

August 29.   Rosina becomes Mrs. Edward Bulwer

Definite break with Mrs. Bulwer-Lytton

Edward's allowance stopped

The Bulwers settle at Woodcot, Nettlebed, Oxon

1828, May 10.   *Pelham* published

Mary Greene's first visit to the Bulwers at Woodcot

June 27.   Birth of Emily Bulwer

Mrs. Wheeler visits Woodcot

September.   Rosina goes to Weymouth

Woodcot sublet to the William Bulwers

October (late).   *The Disowned* published

Greville begun (never finished)

December.	*Devereux* begun
1829, January.	Bulwer meets his mother for the first time since his marriage
	Contributes to *The New Monthly Magazine*
	Paul Clifford preliminaries begun
May.	Mrs. Bulwer-Lytton renews her son's allowance
	Bulwer buys Number 36 Hertford Street for 2,400 guineas
	Woodcot given up
July 29.	*Devereux* published
September.	Temporary home at Fulham
1830, January.	Edward and Rosina open house at Number 36 Hertford Street
February.	First number of *Fraser's Magazine* published
	Paul Clifford published
June–July.	Bulwer invited to stand for Parliament. Considers Penryn and Southwark
1831, January.	*Siamese Twins* published
	Eugene Aram in course of writing
April–June.	General Election
	Bulwer rejects an offer to contest St. Albans, stands for St. Ives (Hunts) and enters Parliament as a Reform member
November 1.	Becomes editor of *New Monthly*
November 8.	Birth of Edward Robert Bulwer
1832, June.	Reform Bill passed. The constituency of St. Ives swept away
December.	General Election
	Bulwer elected as a radical for Lincoln
1833, late April.	*Godolphin* published
August.	Resigns editorship of *New Monthly*
	Pilgrims of the Rhine written
September.	*England and the English* published
	Bulwer and Rosina leave England for Rome, Naples, etc.
	Rienzi begun
	The Last Days of Pompeii three parts written
	First serious quarrel of Bulwer and Rosina

1834, February–March.	They return to London
	Another quarrel
July.	*The Last Days of Pompeii* published
September.	Rosina goes to Gloucester
October.	Dismissal of Melbourne Ministry
November.	*A Letter to a Late Cabinet Minister on the Present Crisis* published, in anticipation of General Election
	Pilgrims of the Rhine published
December.	General Election. Bulwer re-elected for Lincoln
1835, January.	Rumour of Bulwer's death
	Temporary reconciliation with Rosina
February–March.	Bulwer visits Rosina at Gloucester
April.	Peel ministry resigns. Second Whig administration under Melbourne
	Bulwer refuses minor office, offered by Melbourne as reward for his pro-Whig pamphlet of the preceding autumn
May.	Hertford Street disposed of
	Bulwer rents Berrymead Priory, Acton, for Rosina and the children
	Takes rooms for himself at Albany
October.	Finishing *Rienzi*
December.	*Rienzi* published
1836.	Rosina's raid on Albany
April 19.	Deed of Separation signed

Appendices

Appendix I

KNIGHT'S QUARTERLY MAGAZINE: BULWER'S CONTRIBUTIONS

Bulwer contributed to *Knight's Quarterly* under the pseudonym of "Edmund Bruce."

His contributions were as follows:

No. I.   *June, 1823.* Poems to Zoë

II. *October, 1823.* The first Songstresses in Town

III. *January, 1824.* Stanzas (quoted in the course of the Editorial)

      Madame Catalani

      Sonnet written on the first leaf of Keats' Poems

      Despair

      Song

      To M—— [1]

      To M——

IV. *April, 1824.* Narenor; a Tale (I) [2]

      Sonnet to A. T. on her birthday

V. *August, 1824.* Narenor (II).

Appendix II

L. E. L. AND BULWER: EXTRACT FROM *ROMANCE AND REALITY*, AND A POEM FROM *THE AGE*.

The passage in L. E. L.'s novel *Romance and Reality* which presents Edward and Rosina Bulwer is as follows:

[1] *Cf.* this poem with "To M——" in *Weeds and Wildflowers* verses dated from "E(aling), 1820."

[2] *Cf.* with *Arismanes* and *Cheirolas* in *The Student*.

[Emily and her friends have come on a ladies' afternoon to view the lions at the Athenaeum Club:

"Do you see," asks Lorraine, "that gentleman seated by the fire-place? He is one who has excited your most enthusiastic admiration."]

"Emily turned, and saw a face that riveted her whole attention: melancholy and intellectual, it was of the noblest order, and the expression seemed to impart something of its own thoughtfulness to the beholder. The shape of the head, the outline of the face, had more the power and the decision of the Roman, then the flowing softness of the Greek; in a bust it would have been almost stern, but for the benevolence of the mouth. It was as if two natures contended together, — the one, proud, spiritual, severe, the expression of the head, — the other, sad, tender, and sensitive, the expression of the heart. There was melancholy, as if the imagination dwelt upon the feelings, deepening their tenderness, and refining their sorrow, and yet intellectual withal, as if the thought and the feeling sprang up together: perhaps the most striking effect was the change from their natural look of abstraction to that of observation, — the one was the glance of the poet, the other of the falcon. He is one of our most distinguished authors, in whose novels it is difficult to say whether philosophy, wit, or poetry, most abound — the appreciation of whose excellence has been as prompt as it has been just; yet never was one less likely to find enjoyment in the course of literary success, — a course in which the meanness of the obstacles, the baseness of the opponents, the petty means of even the most entire triumph, must revolt the conqueror at his own victory; truly do they say fame is for the dead.

. . . .

"Emily gazed on the individual before her with that intense exaltation and enthusiasm which is literature's best triumph. But her attention was now attracted to the lady who took his arm. Ah! poets and painters have truth for the foundation of their dreams, — she, at least, looked the incarnation of her husband's genius. . . . Her mouth, which was like chiseled coral, had many smiles, and most of scorn; and its speech had as much of sarcasm as of sweetness. Her step, her height — the proud sweep of a neck which was like the swan's for snow and grace — were such as make the

artificial distinctions of society seem the inherent aristocracy of
nature. . . . Her exquisite laugh, like the sound of a shell which,
instead of the night wind, is filled with the morning sunshine and
bursts into music — the fascination of such feminine kindliness —
wit so airy, yet so keen, whose acid was not that of vinegar, dis-
solving all the pearls of gentler feelings, but the acid of champagne,
whose pearls dance on the surface and melt into blending sweetness
— Ah! one moment's pause — I have renounced poetry, of which,
sweet lady, you were to me the embodied spirit. I know flattery is
impertinent, and praise is vain — yet I cannot pass the shrine of
my early faith, and not at least fling a flower on it in passing: I
never yet beheld being so lovely — and I never shall again. . . ."

The portraits here so flatteringly drawn were everywhere recognised, and among hostile critics Bulwer and L. E. L. became for a
while objects of joint derision. Soon after the publication of
Romance and Reality an amusing poem appeared in *The Age* (December
25, 1831):

LITERARY DIALOGUES No. I
NEDDY BULWER AND LETTY LANDON

N. Child of Love and Muse of Passion
Pretty Letty — that is you.

L. E. L. Ned, in all *you* lead the fashion
Neddy mine, indeed you do.

N. Letty, sweet is thy *Romancing*
Charming thy *Reality*

L. E. L. But appear! what eyes are glancing
Ladies eyes — dear Ned, at thee

N. Beauteous *Improvisatrice!*
Violet of *Golden* hue.

L. E. L. Spare my blushes, I beseech thee —
Falkland, Pelham, Devereux

N. Poesy's enraptured dwelling!
Song-born Sappho of our Age.

L. E. L. Cease, O poet, all excelling
Senator and peerless sage!

[*Neddy bows, brays and exits*]

Appendix III

THE *WESTMINSTER REVIEW* ON *PELHAM* AND *THE DISOWNED*

The passage in the essay on "Fashionable Society", published in this magazine in January, 1829, dealing with Bulwer's two novels, reads as follows:

"Though belonging to the class of Fashionable Novel, the novels which are the immediate object of present attention are almost wholly free from the narrow, exclusive, and clannish bigotry which disgraces the majority. *Pelham*, indeed, is in many respects, a satire on the world of fashion which it assumes to pourtray, as well as upon the dandyism which is to be apparently exalted. There is, however, a keen although playful earnestness in much of the observation, that proves the anxiety of the author to mix up a portion of Epicurean dignity, in his abstract notions of the finished gentleman of the day. . . . Neither as to story or full length portraiture, does *Pelham* advance any very extraordinary claim to attention; and yet it is by far the most amusing book we have lately read, for wit, irony, good-humoured satire, and playful vivacity. It is obvious, too, that the author has mingled in the society which he has undertaken to describe; has been attentive to its spirit; and caught a due impression of its real caprice and waywardness. . . . He also occasionally displays still higher qualities — his wit not unfrequently deepens into wisdom; and remarks from time to time escape him, exhibiting solidity approaching to the profound. . . .

"The second production of the same author, *The Disowned*, to a certain degree partakes both of the merits and defects of its predecessor; but as to unity of design, and felicity of execution, it is doubtless inferior. . . . *Pelham*, upon the whole, is too episodical; but the story of *The Disowned* absolutely proceeds in parallel lines in the most respectful, mathematical disconnection. In a very ingenious preface to the second edition, the author endeavours "to defend this defect as altogether unimportant, if not an advantage, being more natural and analogous to real life. Would it not have been more candid to admit that he wrote in haste, under the forcible stimulus of a previous flattering reception, and of a bustling bookseller's recommendation? . . . One parting remark is, however, indispensable. Novels are not only improved by an attention to form, connection, and development, but are usually written better in six months than in three. It may also be added, that men of wit and brilliancy are more celebrated for quick observance than fertile invention, and that they can seldom manage very broad humour at all; the point of all which, simply speaking, is that it is always better to do that which can be well done, and to avoid modes of handling, which are obviously uncongenial with the powers to be exerted in their display. . . . *The Disowned* is a magnificent failure."

Appendix IV

WILLIAM MAGINN 1794–1842: BIBLIOGRAPHY AND EPITAPH

Book issues of the work of Dr. Maginn were as follows:
Whitehall: or the Days of George IV. (Anon) 1 vol. William Marsh. (1827)
Magazine Miscellanies by Dr. Maginn. 1 vol. No imprint or date (1841)
John Manesty, the Liverpool Merchant. By the late William Maginn, LL.D. With illustrations by George Cruikshank. 2 vols. John Mortimer. 1844.
Maxims of Sir Morgan O'Doherty, Bart. 1 vol. Blackwood. 1849.
Homeric Ballads, with Translations and Notes. By the late William Maginn, LL.D. 1 vol. John W. Parker. 1850.
Shakespeare Papers: Pictures Grave and Gay. By William Maginn, LL.D. 1 vol. Bentley. 1859.
A Gallery of Illustrious Literary Characters 1830–1838 drawn by Daniel Maclise R. A. and accompanied by notices chiefly by the late William Maginn LL.D. Edited by William Bates, B.A. Chatto & Windus [1873].
This is the first book edition, with text, of the pen portraits of prominent personalities published in *Fraser's Magazine* between the dates mentioned. Of the eighty-three "notices", seventy-eight were written by Maginn, the others being as to three by Francis Mahony, as to one each by Carlyle and Lockhart. Mr. Bates' "Notes" are often valuable and, so far as I have tested them, always accurate. His

introduction is somewhat coloured by a fear of offending certain
still living individuals. The book itself is clumsy and ugly, but of
great utility to any student of the period.

A *Story without a Tail* (first published in *Blackwood's Magazine*,
April, 1836, reissued in) "Tales from Blackwood", Vol. II, and in
Montague's *Miscellanies* was separately printed with an introduction
by George Saintsbury as No. 4 in the "Baskerville Series" (Mathews
and Marrot. London. 1928).

Collected editions of Maginn's periodical contributions appeared
as follows:

Miscellaneous Writings of the late Dr. Maginn.   Edited by R. Shelton
Mackenzie, D. C. L. — 5 vols. Vols. 1&2 The Odoherty Papers,
1855; Vol. 3 Shakespeare Papers, 1856; Vol. 4 Homeric Ballads,
1856; Vol. 5 Fraserian Papers, with a Memoir of Maginn, 1857.
All published by Redfield, New York.

Noctes Ambrosianæ. By the late John Wilson, Wm. Maginn,
LL.D., J. G. Lockhart, James Hogg and Others. Revised Edition
with Memoirs and Notes by R. Shelton Mackenzie, D. C. L.   5 vols.
New York. W. J. Middleton. 1863.

Miscellanies: Prose and Verse. By William Maginn. Edited by
R. W. Montague. In 2 vols. London: Sampson Low, Marston,
Searle and Rivington. 1885.

In addition to Dr. Mackenzie's essays affixed to the foregoing,
attention may be drawn to two memorial tributes to Maginn by his
friend Edward Kenealy.

(I) in *The Dublin University Magazine*, (January, 1844). "Our
Portrait Gallery No. XXXIV. William Maginn, LL.D." By Edward Kenealy.

(II) *Brallaghan* or the *Deipnosophists*. By Edward Kenealy, Esq.
Dublin & London. 1845. Contains several references to Maginn in
the account of the Club's debates, and also a brief memoir based on
Kenealy's longer essay in the *Dublin University Magazine*.

LOCKHART'S EPITAPH FOR WILLIAM MAGINN
"Walton-on-Thames, Aug. 1842."

"Here, early to bed, lies kind William Maginn,
Who, with genius, wit, learning, Life's trophies to win,
Had neither great Lord nor rich cit of his kin,
Nor discretion to set himself up as to tin;

So, his portion soon spent (like the poor heir of Lynn),
He turned author, ere yet there was beard on his chin —
And, whoever was out, or whoever was in,
For your Tories his fine Irish brains he would spin,
Who received prose and rhyme with a promising grin —
'Go ahead, you queer fish, and more power to your fin!'
But to save from starvation turned never a pin.
Light for long was his heart, though his breeches were thin,
Else his acting, for certain, was equal to Quinn;
But at last he was beat, and sought help of the bin
(All the same to the Doctor, from claret to gin),
Which led swiftly to jail, with consumption therein.
It was much, when the bones rattled loose in the skin,
He got leave to die here, out of Babylon's din.
Barring drink and the girls, I ne'er heard of a sin —
Many worse, better few, than bright, broken Maginn."

Appendix V

THE *AFFAIRE* BULWER — LANDON — MAGINN

It is essential to remember, when considering the facts of Letitia
Landon's life, that her appearance in literary and semi-Bohemian
London, as a very young woman with no protective background to
speak of and a living to earn, was in 1820 a most unusual appearance.
In consequence comments on her behaviour and gossip as to her
indiscretions must be very considerably discounted in advance.
She was in herself a phenomenon so startling as almost by her very
existence to be a scandal; only those aspersions on her character
can therefore even be examined which are supported by some degree
of actual evidence.

Within these limits let us consider the facts as to her associations,
on the one hand with Bulwer, on the other with Maginn.

L. E. L. visited Bulwer at Woodcot in 1827 and Miss Greene considered that the two were needlessly flirtatious. L. E. L. and
Bulwer exchanged flowery compliments in novels and in criticism
during the early thirties, and for a while became comically notorious for mutual back-scratching. Bulwer and Lady Blessington
remained uniformly kind to L. E. L. during the final unhappy years
of her life in England; consoled her after the breaking of her engage-

ment with John Forster; stood by her to the moment of her sailing on her ill-fated voyage to the west coast of Africa.[1]

Yet it is very noticeable that, despite this protracted intimacy between a solitary young woman and a much-talked-of novelist, the only suggestions that the relationship was an amorous one were made, one at the time by Miss Greene (very tentatively), a second in 1832 by Maginn, and a third over twenty years later by an embittered Rosina.

In his pen portrait of Bulwer (published in *Fraser's*, August, 1832) Maginn used a phrase already quoted[2] which implied some element of dalliance in the friendship of Bulwer and L. E. L. Such a comment from such a source must be considerably discounted.

The statements subsequently made by Rosina have a reckless scurrility even more unconvincing. By the time she (in February, 1855) wrote to the painter A. E. Chalon her reminiscences of the days when gossip had played mischief with Miss Landon's name, she was so far gone in hysterical loathing of Bulwer and everything connected with him, that to throw filth at his friends had become a form of indulgence of her hatred of himself. Wherefore, she said all the evil she could imagine of Miss Landon, not only (as one would expect) accusing her of having intrigued with Bulwer, but charging her also with liaisons both with Maginn and Jerdan, and with the writing of obscene letters.[3]

The only credible witness to a philandering between Bulwer and L. E. L. remains Miss Greene. Therefore it is not difficult to believe that she, fresh from her quiet Irish home and on her very first visit to a household where the lax manners of smart English bohemianism were in vogue, should have mistaken a casual familiarity for something more significant; thus we may surely dismiss as idle the suggestion that any love-making took place between Bulwer and Miss Landon. The theory of an intimacy between her and Maginn is, however, more strongly supported; and there can be no doubt whatsoever that the early thirties saw a fairly widespread scandal coupling their names together.

[1] The main events of Miss Landon's life may conveniently be learnt from Mrs. Enfield's charming, if rather modish and inconclusive, biography, *L. E. L.: A Mystery of the 'Thirties*, London. 1928.

[2] *Cf*. p. 257.

[3] This letter is printed in *Unpublished Letters of Lady Bulwer-Lytton* to A. E. Chalon, edited by *S. M. Ellis*. Nash. 1914.

L. E. L.'s acquaintance with Maginn was of earlier origin than that with the Bulwers. In the early twenties the two were thrown frequently together. The young woman was an honoured contributor to Jerdan's *Literary Gazette* as early as 1821, and so often at his house as to start malicious (but in this case frankly foolish) tongues wagging eagerly; Maginn, whose first English-printed work had appeared in the same paper during the teens, used Jerdan's house as cover-address on first arriving in London in 1823 or 1824, was continually there during the years which followed, and is known to have become intimate with the editor's protegée.[1]

It was surely at this period, and not in or after 1830, that thoughts of a liaison would have been provoked in the mind of so ready a love-maker as Maginn. And if it be assumed that he did indeed lay siege to Miss Landon during the twenties but, having failed in his object, thereafter ostensibly behaved to her as an ordinary literary acquaintance, certain otherwise puzzling elements in the situation as it later developed become comparatively clear.

In the first place it is known that Maginn continued to be on terms with L. E. L. during the early thirties. He helped her with her *Drawing Room Scrap Book*[2] and, according to Kenealy, actually wrote many of the poems therein published.

In the second place, the scandal started in 1830, took the form of anonymous letters[3] written to Miss Landon's friends, accusing her of being the mistress of a married man. These letters damaged poor Miss Landon very seriously. They gave to Grantley Berkeley,[4]

---

[1] *Cf.* Jerdan's *Autobiography*. III, 86 and 168 *et seq.*

[2] An Annual, containing poems and engravings which started publication in 1832 and was edited by L. E. L. until 1837.

[3] What was the source of these letters?
One story declared that about 1830 Mrs. Maginn found compromising letters from L. E. L. in her husband's pocket, and circulated the horrid news among her shocked but gloating friends. But Maginn's intimates all agree that, during the thirties, he lived on good terms with his wife and children — a state of affairs hard to credit, if Mrs. Maginn had indeed been responsible for discovering and making public his incontinence.

[4] The Hon. Grantley F. Berkeley (1800–1881), one of the several tempestuous sons of the 5th Earl of Berkeley, was the author of two or three novels, some sporting books and a four-volume autobiography *My Life and Recollections* (1865-1866). He fought a duel with Maginn (after thrashing the publisher of *Fraser's Magazine* in the latter's shop in Regent Street), because of a bitterly destructive review of his first novel *Berkeley Castle*. His rather offensive interference in the affairs of Miss Landon is described in his *Recollections*.

crudest of Victorian bullies, an excuse to force his insolent Bayardism
on a helpless young woman; they caused her jilting in 1834 by a
shocked John Forster, who was only twenty-two at the time and as
serious as he was inexperienced in the evil wiles of jealousy; they
drove her, three years later, into a forlorn and unconvincing marriage
with the saturnine Maclean.

Is it likely that in fact these letters had any connection whatsoever with Mrs. Maginn? Is it even certain that Maginn was the
married man with whom L. E. L. was said to have been involved?

One inclines to answer the first question in the negative. The
second can never be resolved. Here, however, is an attempt to
reconstruct the whole affair on lines different from those hitherto
followed:

In the middle twenties the doctor had made overtures — maybe
applied indirect pressure — to Miss Landon and had been repulsed.
A definite part in his discomfiture had been played, not only by Bulwer, but by Rosina also, whose friendship with L. E. L. had pre-
dated her marriage and had developed as early as 1827 into a joint
intimacy between the poet, young Mrs. Bulwer and young Mrs.
Bulwer's husband. The Bulwers were told by their friend of the
persecution to which she was being subjected, and deliberately took
a hand in thwarting the unwelcome lover. Maginn relinquished
an intrigue which threatened to cause more trouble than it was
worth, but did not forget Bulwer's interference or the lady's evasion
of capture. He determined on a double revenge — a public one on
Bulwer, a private one on L. E. L. The very purposeful belabouring
of Bulwer at the hands of *Fraser's* was the former; the anonymous
letters were the latter. These letters were written by Maginn (even
more probably at Maginn's instigation by Westmacott, who was an
adept at this sort of meanness and whose intimacy with the doctor
was at its height about 1830) and the identity of the married man
was probably left purposely and conveniently vague.

In support of this theory, two arguments may be urged.

It may claim to cover all the known facts which no alternative
theory has yet contrived to do. Further, it helps to account for
the following important, but hitherto unknown letter written by
L. E. L. to Bulwer some time in 1834 after the severance of the
Forster engagement.

L. E. L. to Bulwer. n.d. [1834]

I prefer writing to speaking. When I speak I become ashamed and confused and never say precisely what I mean. Misunderstanding there certainly is, if you suppose that I wish all connection between myself and Mr. Forster at an end on account merely of the steps he has taken in the late most miserable business. . . .

From all I can learn, the cruel slander was old; was well known to have originated in the very lowest portion of the press; was put down by the kindly countenance of friends — and, I may add, by the whole tenor of my life. It was forgotten by most and scorned by all. . . . I will not admit that Mr. Forster *vindicated* my conduct, inasmuch as there was nothing to vindicate. Still holding as I do this opinion, I should not consider it a sufficient justification of my resolve that the gentleman can never be to me more than a friend. Mr. Forster states that he will not consider me as bound to him if I can prove that he mentioned the report to any to whom it was previously unknown ! Yet there was one person it was utterly unknown to — one person to whom, if he had common feeling or delicacy he could not have named it — and that is myself. If his future protection is to harass and humiliate me as much as the present — God keep me from it. . . . I cannot get over the entire want of delicacy to me which could repeat such a slander to myself. The whole of his late conduct to me personally has left behind almost dislike — certainly fear of his imperious and overbearing temper. I am sure we never could be happy together. He is clever, honourable, kind; but he is quite deficient in the sensitiveness to the feelings of another which is to me an indispensable requisite. I bitterly regret what has passed and any pain my determination may inflict upon him; but we are quite unsuited to each other and the proof is the very first question of opinion — feeling — that arises between us. How differently do we view it!

I must repeat my thanks for your kindness. I cannot say what I owe to your friendship on this occasion — its delicacy, its generosity, and its patience can never be forgotten. I am grateful, most earnestly, deeply grateful.

Now this letter is only explicable on some such assumption of what had previously occurred as that outlined above. The contents of the anonymous libels were evidently a complete surprise to

L. E. L., and revived old gossip long ago lived down and forgotten. The only justification for her asking Bulwer's advice would have been that he had earlier helped her in a similar predicament and knew the facts to which the letters referred. What other status could he have had in the matter? He was not at this early date more than a mere acquaintance of Forster's, and it seems therefore inevitable to conclude that the young woman turned instinctively to him, because he alone understood the significance of the scandal-mongering and had a shrewd suspicion of its origin.

Appendix VI

NEW MONTHLY MAGAZINE

(This list makes no reference to such regular features as the "Monthly Commentary" and the "Lion's Mouth", although Bulwer certainly contributed to both. Items were *unsigned* save where otherwise stated.)

1831, November.   Address to the Public.

How Will The Peers be Gained. Signed: "A Reforming Member of Parliament."

Conversations With an Ambitious Student No. VI. (Parts I–V were published as follows: I. December, 1830; II. January, 1831; III. March, 1831; IV. April, 1831; V. May, 1831.)

The World as it is. Signed: "Mitio."

Society. Signed: "H."

Ourselves, Our Correspondents And The Public. Unsigned, but by E. B. L. and S. C. Hall.

Living Literary Characters, No. XI. Samuel Rogers. Signed: "B. L." (o. e.)

December.   The Times. Signed: "A Reforming Member Of Parliament."

A Foreigner In England. Signed: "B. E."

A Knowledge Of The World In Men And Books. "By the Author of Conversations With An Ambitious Student" and signed "A." (o. e.)

Review of L. E. L.'s *Romance And Reality*.

1832, January.   The New Year.

On English Notions Of Morality. Signed: "A." (o. e.)

Asmodeus at Large. Unnumbered, but announced as "To be continued."

The Universal Education of the People essential to the Public Happiness. (reprinted in revised form in Appendix B. to *England And The English*.)

Conversations with an Ambitious Student. No. VII.

February.   *The Quarterly Review.*

Asmodeus at large. No. II.

The State of the Drama.

The Society for the Diffusion of Useful Knowledge.

March.   On the State Of the Rural Population.

The Influence and Education Of Women. Signed: "A." (o. e.)

Conversations with an Ambitious Student. No. VIII. and last. (These "Conversations" were republished in *The Student* in abbreviated form, under the title of *The New Phaedo*, with an extra conversation on Plato's *Phaedo*.)

The Law of Arrest. Signed: "Mitio."

?   Political Conveniences: or the Results of the Reform Bill. A Dialogue.

April.   A Few Plain Words on a Great Question.

Asmodeus at large. No. III.

Upon the spirit of true Criticism. Signed: "A." (o. e.)

The Wilful Misstatements of *The Quarterly Review*.

May.   The Recess.

Review of "*The Contrast*", by Lord Normanby.

The Utilitarians.

Asmodeus at large. No. IV.

Hereditary Honours. A Tale of Love and Mystery. Signed "Mitio."

Retrospective Criticism. (A Review of
Laman Blanchard's early poems.) Signed:
"A." (o. e.)

June. Our Present State.

Death of Goethe.

Recent Dramas.

Review of *Fiesco*. *A Tragedy*. (Translated from
Schiller by Col. d'Aguilar.)

? Review of M'Culloch's Commercial Dictionary.

July. The Politician.

Asmodeus at large. No. V.

Character of the Unreformed House Of Commons. Signed "A." (o. e.)

Note to the "Illustrious Dead: Sir James Mack-
intosh, Jeremy Bentham." (Of these tributes, the first was likely written by Henry
Bulwer. The summary note at the end signed
"H" was Edward's.)

Review (with long extracts) of "Another Epic,
by The Author of Corn Law Rhymes."
(Elliot)

August. The Politician.

Asmodeus at large. No. VI.

On the True Spirit of Religious Poetry. Montgomery's "Messiah."

Aristocracy.

October. The Politician. No. IV.

Death of Sir Walter Scott. "By the Author of
Eugene Aram."

November. On Preserving the Anonymous in Periodicals.
(Some of the material of this leading article
was used in *England And The English*.)

? The Politician. No. V.

The "True Sun." Another Argument Against
The Taxes On Knowledge.

The Difference between Authors and the
Impression Conveyed of them by their
Works. (Republished in *The Student*) signed
"A." (o. e.)

	Asmodeus at large. No. VII.
	Proposals for a Literary Union. Signed "A." (o. e.)
	The Nymph of the Lurlei Berg. A Tale. Signed "Mitio."
December.	The Politician. No. VI.
	Asmodeus at large. No. VIII.
	The English Abroad: or, The Prince of Seidlitz Powders.
1833, January.	The Politician. No. VII.
	Count Pecchio's Notions of England.
	The Modern Platonist. I. "By the Author Of *Devereux* and *Eugene Aram.*"
	Asmodeus At Large. No. IX.
	The Faults of Recent Poets. Poems By Alfred Tennyson.
	Letter to the Editor of the *Quarterly Review.*
February.	The Politician. No. X.
?	The Politician. No. XI.
	On Moral Fictions: Miss Martineau's Illustrious Political Economy.
	Asmodeus at large. No. X.
March.	The Politician. No. XII. The Last Petition of the Irish People. Position Of Independent Labourers Under The Operation Of The Poor Laws In England. (Republished in part in *England And The English*.)
	Paul Louis Courier. Signed "A." (o. e.)
	Review of Leigh Hunt's Poetical Works.
May.	The Politician. No. XIV.
June.	The Politician. No. XV.
	Modern Novelists and Recent Novels.
July	View of the Character of Goethe. (Falk's *Goethe*, translated by Mrs. Austin.) Signed "A." (o. e.)
August.	The Editor's Farewell.
	The Politician. No. XVIII. and last.
	On the State of Eloquence In England. Signed "A." (o. e.)

Elegy to the Memory of H. W. Signed "E. L. B." (H. W. is probably Henrietta Wheeler, the sister of Rosina, who died in Paris in 1828.)

Eugene Aram, A Tragedy.

The Consolations of Sleep. Signed "B." (o. e.)

Fi-Ho-Ti, Or the Pleasures of Reputation. Signed "Mitio." (Republished in *The Student*.)

An Essay On Breakfasts. Signed "A." (o. e.)

A Few Specimens of an Unpublished Translation of Horace.

Watering Places.

Appendix VII

BOOKS ABOUT EDWARD AND ROSINA

Here follow the titles of only those books exclusively devoted to Bulwer and his wife. To attempt to catalogue all the memoirs, novels and periodicals which have been consulted in writing this present work and have direct or indirect bearing on its theme, would at this stage be labour largely wasted; but a briefly characterised list of the volumes actually devoted to its central figure may prove helpful to other students.

The Life of Edward Bulwer, First Lord Lytton. By his grandson, the Earl of Lytton. 2 vols. Macmillan. 1913.

This work (referred to in the present text as "Lytton") must remain the starting point of any examination of Bulwer's life story. Indeed, only the fact that it was based on the Knebworth papers solely, while I wished to extend the scope of my survey to include many of Bulwer's literary contemporaries, to estimate the influence of society on his mind and work, and to bring together the more important of the manifold references to him from the books and periodicals of the time, could have justified my risking a repetition of a story already admirably told.

I hope, however, that repetition is more apparent than real. Because it is hardly possible to deal more objectively or comprehensively with the actual story of Bulwer's life than is done by Lord Lytton, I have purposely referred readers to his pages again and again, omitting nearly all documents there printed in full and seeking to supplement his narrative rather than to condense or rewrite it.

A complete hand-list of Bulwer's works appears at the end of his second volume, and may be recommended to anyone desiring facts as to publications post-dating those mentioned in the present work.

The Life, Letters and Literary Remains of Edward Bulwer Lord Lytton. By his Son. 2 vols. Kegan Paul, Trench, & Co. 1883.

This work (referred to in the text as "Owen Meredith") is incomplete and in places inaccurate. It takes the story of Bulwer's life no further than his election for St. Ives in May, 1831.

It is, however, indispensable to the student as offering the only printed texts of several unfinished manuscripts, most of which are of autobiographical importance. Thus here alone can be read *Lionel Hastings; de Lindsay; Glenallan* and *Greville*, as well as certain essays written at Cambridge and the draft *History of the British Public* which, designed in 1824, developed by 1832 into *England and the English*.

Edward Bulwer First Baron Lytton of Knebworth. By T. H. S. Escott. Routledge, 1910.

A confused and rather careless piece of bookmaking, which nevertheless contains certain details and observations worthy of notice.

Andrè Maurois. Les Derniers Jours de Pompei. "Collections; Les Images du Temps." Aux Editions Lapina V. Paris. 1928.

A pretentious little work, recorded for the benefit of those who for the sake of its author's style are willing to reread what has already been written elsewhere.

A Blighted Life by the Right Hon. Lady Lytton. London Publishing Office. 1880.

Refutation of an Audacious Forgery of the Dowager Lady Lytton's name to a book of the Publication of which she was Totally Ignorant. 1880. A pamphlet printed privately.

The former of these two publications contains a long statement of Rosina's wrongs at the hands of her husband, her son and their friends, written in the form of a letter signed " Rosina Bulwer Lytton " and dated " Feb. 10, 1864." As appendices are printed newspaper comments on her case, and brief character sketches of persons concerned, by the anonymous editor of the work. These latter are written with great scurrility and the statement printed over Rosina's signature is violent, reckless and vulgar. It libels numerous people by name and could not conceivably have been composed with an idea of verbatim publication.

The pamphlet " *Refutation* " declares on Rosina's behalf that a document of the kind printed in *A Blighted Life* was indeed written by her many years earlier and forwarded privately to a man of letters who was investigating the scandal of private madhouses (probably Charles Reade): that he returned it; that it was next sent (for no very obvious reason) to a lawyer, who also returned it after a short delay. Rosina's apologist can only presume that it was copied while in the lawyer's possession and that the copy had somehow come into the possession of "The London Publishing Office" who have now printed it without authority and issued their book as a piece of catchpenny sensationalism. Miss Devey's *Life of Lady Lytton* (see below) re-states the pamphlet's argument.

Students will note that the main portion of *A Blighted Life* is a genuine production of Rosina's unbalanced hatred of her husband, although not written for publication, and, when it was published, issued without her authority or foreknowledge. This latter fact may destroy the standing of *A Blighted Life* as a piece of genuine publishing, but it does not affect the authenticity of the actual text. The painful farrago of crude insult, hysterical inconsequences and a spiritual anguish, none the less terrible for being largely self-inflicted, is a true expression of the state of mind in which the unhappy woman spent the last forty years of her life. It will be observed that the *Refutation* does not challenge the genuineness of the document or even seek to extenuate its grossness; it is merely concerned to show that Rosina had not inspired its publication and that, consequently, the extra two hundred pounds per annum, granted to his mother by Robert Lytton on Bulwer's death in 1873 but instantly withdrawn on the appearance of *A Blighted Life*, should once again be paid to her.

Letters of the late Edward Bulwer, Lord Lytton to his Wife. "Published in Vindication of her Memory." Edited by Louisa Devey. Sonnenschein. 1884.

An injunction brought against this book, on copyright grounds, by the family of Lytton prevented more than a few copies getting into circulation. In so far as a majority of the letters are of the most intimate kind imaginable, one cannot but condemn Rosina's executrix for the mistaken zeal with which she sought to vindicate her dead friend's memory. Nevertheless, decency apart, the publication of this very voluminous correspondence cannot honestly be regretted by students of the present day. Many of the letters provide valuable facts and evidence from the days of Bulwer's courtship and early married life, and during the writing of the present volume have been considerably consulted.

Life of Rosina Lady Lytton. By Louisa Devey. Sonnenschein, Lowrey & Co. 1887.

Miss Devey's second book, like her first, bears on the spine the words "A Vindication." It is written in that spirit. Rosina's manuscript autobiography *Nemesis* is here printed, for the advantage of anyone able to read it.

Unpublished Letters of Lady Bulwer Lytton to A. E. Chalon, R. A. Edited by S. M. Ellis. Eveleigh Nash. 1914.

These letters all date from the fifties: and though they deal at length with the incidents of Rosina's early married life, she had become, by the time she wrote them, so obsessed with loathing for her husband and a sense of her own wrongs that actuality and propaganda had become inextricably confused in her mind. Wherefore, while the documents are of interest as revealing the loneliness of their writer and as an example of her power to bore everyone who ventured to be kind to her by a dreary and often vulgar recital of her own sufferings, they are worthless as historical evidence. The editor's notes are valuable, and among the illustrations is a fine picture of Berrymead Priory.

Bulwer Lytton. An exposure of the Errors of his Biographers. By Alfred William Frost. London. Lynwood & Co. Ltd. 1913.

Designed to correct some of the errors made by "Owen Meredith" in his biography of his father, by Miss Devey, by T. H. S. Escott and by the writer of the memoir of Bulwer in the D. N. B., Mr. Frost's little work fulfilled a real want at the time of its publication. But with the appearance, also in 1913, of Lord Lytton's official biography (to the accuracy of which Mr. Frost made a direct contribution) this once valuable corrective was no longer needed.

Introductions to the Prose Romances, Plays and Comedies of Edward Bulwer Lord Lytton. By E. G. Bell. Chicago. Walter M. Hill. 1914.

Summaries of the plots and main characteristics of all Bulwer's published works. Useful for reference, but of little critical pretension.

INDEX

Tunbridge Wells, 132
Turner, Joseph M. W., 301

ULLESWATER, 38, 43
Utilitarian philosophy, 166

VARLEY, JOHN, painter, 301
Vestris, Madame Lucia E., 311
Villiers, Charles, 130
Villiers, Frederick, 189, 366

WAKEFIELD, EDWARD GIBBON, 173, 342
Walker, William Sidney, 40
Wallington, Rev. Charles, 28, 34
Ward, Robert Plumer, his career, 108; quoted, 108; his *Tremaine*, 108, 109, 193; other novels of, 109 *n.*; his influence on Disraeli and Bulwer, 109, 110; *De Vere* and *De Clifford*, 193; on *Eugene Aram*, 248; and *Devereux*, 313
Watts, Alaric A., 224, 235, 242; on *Falkland*, 170; his *The Conversazione*, 236, 237
Weeds and Wildflowers, 37 *n.*, 60, 189 *n.*, 379 *n.*
Wellington, Duke of, 225
Westmacott, Charles Molloy, 144; his novel *Fitzalleyne of Berkeley*, 104 *n.*; Bulwer's attack on, 184 *n.*; buys *The Age*, 224, 309, 310; and Maginn, 224, 227, 229, 310, 314; withdraws to France, 226, 315; as "Sneak", 307; his career and character, 307-309, 311; replies to Bulwer, 313, 314; sells half-interest in *The Age*, 315; relinquishes *The Age*, 315; notebooks of, 315
Westmacott, Richard, 307
Westminster Review, 166, 181, 266, 268; on *Pelham* and *The Disowned*, 198, 382, 383; disapproves of *Devereux*, 202
Weymouth, 129, 132
What Will He Do With It? 280
Wheeler, Francis, of Ballywire, his household, 67-69; sees Rosina again, 75; death, 75, 76; his property, 77

Wheeler, Mrs. Francis, 85; her home at Ballywire, 67-69; joins Sir John Doyle in Guernsey, 69-72; goes to France, 72; at Caen, 72, 73, 75, 76; as "Goddess of Reason", 72, 76; relations with daughter, 75, 76, 77; re-enters her daughter's life and becomes almost an habituée of the Bulwers' home, 128; described by Disraeli, 140
Wheeler, Henrietta, 68, 69, 71, 76, 77
Wheeler, Rosina, at Miss Benger's party, 64; meets Bulwer, 63, 82; her home life at Ballywire, 67-69; in Guernsey, 70-72; at Caen, 72, 73; returns to Ireland, 73; meets Mary Greene, 73; her intimacy with Mary Greene, 74, 75; finds father vulgar, 75; relations with mother, 75, 76, 77; with Sir John Doyle in London, 77; her life and friendships in London, 78-82; her intimacy with Lady Caroline Lamb, 79-81; and Bulwer, course of their love before marriage, 83-94; marriage, 94. *See also* Bulwer, Mrs. Edward Lytton
White, Charles, author of *Herbert Milton* (*Almacks Revisited*), 122, 173
Wilde, Oscar, 199
Wilkie, Sir David, 302
Wilkinson, Mrs., Miss Greene's niece, 353, 361
Willmott, Robert Aris, 42 *n.*
Wilson, Harriette, her *Memoirs*, 53, 213; and Bulwer, 212-220; and the Duke of Wellington, 225
Wilson, John ("Christopher North"), 114, 310 *n.*; of *Blackwood's*, 180, 181, 221-223
Wilson, Richard, painter, 301
Woodcot, home of the Bulwers, 121-133

YATES, EDMUND, 230

Zanoni, 195, 290, 346

IN PREPARATION

GORE HOUSE

or

The Life of Lady Blessington
with portraits of
Count d'Orsay, Sir Edward Bulwer-Lytton
and other fashionables of the
thirties and forties

being

PART TWO

OF

BULWER: A PANORAMA